GREAT
RIVALS
IN HISTORY

GREAT RIVALS IN HISTORY

WHEN POLITICS GETS PERSONAL

JOSEPH CUMMINS

METRO BOOKS
NEW YORK

© 2008 by Murdoch Books Pty Limited

This 2008 edition published by Metro Books,
by arrangement with Murdoch Books Pty Limited.

Chief Executive: Juliet Rogers
Publisher: Kay Scarlett
Project Manager: Emma Hutchinson
Editor: Christine Eslick
Design concept: Peter Long
Design layout: Jacqueline Richards
Photo researcher: Amanda McKittrick
Production: Monique Layt

Metro Books
122 Fifth Avenue
New York, NY 10011

ISBN-13: 978-1-4351-0385-6
ISBN-10: 1-4351-0385-8

Printed and bound in China

1 3 5 7 9 10 8 6 4 2

ON REFLECTION, WHO IS AS GOOD AS I AM? I KNOW OF NO ONE.

GENERAL GEORGE S. PATTON, JR.

CONTENTS

INTRODUCTION

In the future, let any communication you wish to make with me be addressed to the King of all Asia. Do not write to me as an equal. Everything you possess is now mine; so, if you should want anything, let me know in the proper terms or I shall take steps to deal with you as a criminal. If, on the other hand, you wish to dispute the throne, stand and fight for it and do not run away. Wherever you may hide yourself, be sure I shall seek you out.

The above note, sent by the upstart Alexander the Great to his great rival Darius, King of the Persians, may strike us as a little harsh—does he really need to humiliate the man in this way? But, in truth, who has not written a similar letter, if only in our heads? Most of us have sent such bitter (if telepathic) messages to rivals in all walks of life—colleagues, siblings, rivals in love, or even that obnoxious person who just stole our parking spot.

This competitive streak may seem a trifle shocking, but rivalry is, quite literally, only natural. "If evolution and the survival of the fittest be true at all," wrote William James in 1890, "the destruction ... of human rivals must have been among the most important of man's primitive functions." Humans are born adversarial—signs of rivalry have been observed in infants as young as six months, especially among siblings.

Most of our rivalries affect only our lives and those of a few around us, but there are times when rivalries change the course of human events, and it is these fascinating personal battles that make up *Great Rivals in History: When Politics Gets Personal*. Moving from the above-mentioned Alexander and Darius all the way to a couple of competitive Cold War spymasters, the book shows what happens when people with personal enmity have huge resources at their disposal and few compunctions about doing whatever may be necessary to destroy their rivals.

The single-mindedness with which some of the characters in these stories attempt to do away with their opponents is breathtaking. Thus Darius and Alexander fought through hordes of men locked in hand-to-hand combat in an attempt to personally slay each other, Alexander Hamilton and Aaron Burr ended up dueling on a cliff in New Jersey, and Adolf Hitler had Ernst Röhm blasted to bits in a jail cell.

But other rivalries can be more complex. Most definitions of rivalry center on the fact that opposing parties are competing for something of mutual interest. It follows that when two people badly desire the same thing, they may discover that they are quite similar. Thus Elizabeth I and Mary Queen of Scots had much in common and both expressed a heartbreakingly fond wish not to be queens of their realms, but carefree friends. Thomas Becket and King Henry II loved each other—of this there can be no doubt—but each desired to have the upper hand, and there was no reconciling this need.

Whatever the nature of the rivalry, in each of the twenty-four stories collected here personal rivalry changed the contours of a society, a battle, a country, or even the world at large. Although history is shaped by many complex causes, the competitions between Julius Caesar and Gnaeus Pompey, between William the Conqueror and King Harold, between Benedict Arnold and Horatio Gates, just to name a few, changed the lives of millions. The rivalry between Charles XII and Peter the Great took Sweden off, and put Russia on, the world map. The fierce competition between King Philip IV and Pope Boniface VIII established important principles of church–state separation. Chiang Kai-shek and Mao Zedong fought for and decided the future of the most populous nation on earth.

In a very real sense, these rivals made us who we are today.

ALEXANDER THE GREAT

ALEXANDER THE GREAT AND KING DARIUS III: A GREAT CLASH OF KINGS

THE ERA OF ALEXANDER THE GREAT OF MACEDONIA and King Darius III of Persia was an age of epic heroes, a time when warrior-kings personally fought in the front lines, surrounded by throngs of fanatical bodyguards. Alexander was known for wading into battle, sword flailing, no matter what the odds. Darius, over twenty years older, was less reckless but, fighting from his royal chariot, also threw himself into the bloody melee of ancient combat.

These two rulers, both raised in treacherous royal courts, shared many characteristics, including the ability to react quickly in dire situations—Darius turned the tables on a would-be poisoner and forced the assassin to drink his own deadly potion, while Alexander's cool thinking in the face of great danger is like that of no other general, unless we count Napoleon. The two men also shared a sense of noblesse oblige and an ability to admire each other's stratagems. Ultimately, however, in the power politics of the fourth century BC, theirs was a rivalry that had to be fought out to the death. Alexander and Darius engaged in three momentous battles within the space of four years; in two of these they personally sought to kill each other.

Only one would survive, and history would be decided by the outcome.

THE WORLD OF ALEXANDER AND DARIUS For 150 years before the time of Alexander and Darius, the controlling force in the known world was the mighty Persian Empire. Founded in 559 BC by Cyrus the Great, conqueror of the great city of Babylon, the empire eventually extended from Pakistan in the east, westward through Central Asia, to Egypt in the south. The

Persians divided their conquered world into provinces run by Persian imperial governors, or satraps, whose main job was to collect tribute, which flowed back to the Persian treasury and made those in power extraordinarily rich.

The Persians were not interested in controlling their conquered people's religions or even their way of government, up to a point, as long as they paid their taxes, but they did insist that people make obeisance to the august figure of the Great King, or One King, the man-god the Persians considered to be the most blindingly glorious ruler on the face of the earth.

Paying this kind of tribute was something a pesky race called the Greeks refused to do. In the Greco-Persian Wars of 500–448 BC the might of King Xerxes and his massive Persian army was held back by the forces of the united Greek city-states at famous battles such as Marathon, Thermopylae, and Salamis, under leaders including the Spartan King Leonidas and the Athenian Themistocles. With Persia kept at bay, the Greek Golden Age ensued, but unity did not last long—it never did with the fractious ancient Greeks. The Peloponnesian War tore apart the country in the later fifth century, after which King Philip II of Macedonia—that wild and mountainous region to the north of Greece—conquered all of Greece except for Sparta and set his covetous eyes on the Persian satrapies in Asia Minor, across the Hellespont.

In 356 BC, Philip had a son named Alexander. He grew to be a glorious youth—handsome, ruddy-cheeked, and red-haired, although possessing, as more than one ancient chronicler noted, unusually small, sharp, pointy teeth. His tutor was Aristotle—not a bad mentor for a future conqueror—but it was not all book-learning for Alexander, as he fought alongside his father during Philip's conquests and distinguished himself by his almost reckless bravery.

PHILIP IS DEAD—LONG LIVE ALEXANDER Then, one summer night in 337, Philip—vulgar, hard-drinking, and tough as nails—was run through with a sword on his way to a wedding banquet. The assassin, who was immediately killed by Philip's bodyguard, was a young man named Pausanias, with whom Philip had had an affair (homosexuality, as well as polygamy, were commonplace in Macedonian royal society), so it may have been a killing of passion. However, the intrigues in the Macedonian royal court were as entangled as Medusa's hair. Philip had also been feuding with his third wife, the formidable Olympias, who happened to be the mother of his now twenty-year-old son, Alexander. Some ancient sources have placed Philip's murder at the door of this mother and son duo: Olympias, who was fiery, beautiful and a member of a snake-worshipping cult, and Alexander, who was brilliant but essentially unstable, and who was convinced that his real father was Zeus, who had impregnated Olympias with a thunderbolt to her womb.

However it happened, Alexander assumed the kingship in 336 and, with it, command of the veteran Macedonian army, which had been hardened in Philip's wars against the Greeks and was now being prepared for an invasion of the Persian lands in Asia Minor, in what is now western Turkey. These lands belonged to the One King, Darius.

DARIUS, THE GREAT KING

Darius had assumed power under circumstances equally as violent as those of Alexander. Born in about 380 BC, Darius was not descended in a direct line from the great Persian rulers Darius I and Xerxes, who had fought the Greeks of old. Instead, our Darius, whose birth name was Codommanus, was probably a distant cousin. Still, the royal blood of Persian kings did run through his veins and he was raised in luxury in the rich Mesopotamian lands between the Tigris and the Euphrates, spending a great deal of time in the sumptuous royal palaces in Babylon.

Darius, as a young man, was a fierce warrior. In those days, it was often the practice before two enemy forces collided in battle to have champions engage in individual, gladiatorial combat, while both armies looked on. Sometime around 360 or so, Darius challenged the leader of a rebellious Persian tribe to just such a duel, and ended up decapitating his foe after only minutes of dusty combat.

Despite his bravery, Darius, who was a royal courtier in Babylon, was not a cruel man and he watched in dismay as the Persian King Ataxerxes Ochus III and his son, the unfortunately named King Arses, treated their subjects harshly, taxing them mercilessly and savagely putting down any resistance. Because of their unpopularity, Ataxerxes and Arses were vulnerable. A scheming vizier, court eunuch Bagoas had both of them murdered and then cast about for someone to place on the Persian throne, someone he could easily control.

He came up with Darius, who took the throne the same year as Alexander—336—and assumed the dynastic name Darius III. However, Bagoas decided Darius was not quite malleable enough; one summer day, as the songbirds fluttered in the green gardens of the Persian court, he handed Darius a bejeweled cup of poison. Darius smiled at him, raised the cup, and then, taking the eunuch by the hair, poured the liquid down his throat. Bagoas died at his feet, gasping and choking, and Darius was now the true ruler of Persia—and most of the known world.

ALEXANDER'S INVASION

The new Great King hardly had time to enjoy his untrammeled power and glory, for, in the spring of 334, Alexander put his fine Macedonian army into 150 triremes and crossed the fabled Hellespont (now the Dardanelles) into Asia Minor. Why? A good question, with various answers. He was a young man in love with the supposed noble past of the Greeks (he carried a copy of Homer's *Iliad* with him on his journey of conquest and even crossed the Hellespont at the exact spot used by the early Greeks on their way to Troy). Alexander also wanted to free the Greek cities in Turkey that were under Persian control—it was important for him, as for so many conquerors, to be seen as a liberator. Too, his ego, his overwhelming sense of self, was so big that he sought to impose it on the world. And there was also a more mundane reason—he was severely in debt. Philip had left Macedonia practically bankrupt and the best way Alexander could think of to fill empty coffers was with Persian gold.

So Alexander came, his army probably forty thousand strong: five thousand cavalry on swift Macedonian ponies (no more than two-thirds the size of the horses used by knights in medieval times) and the rest of the force composed of the feared phalanxes, each a unit of sixteen soldiers armed with an eighteen-foot long hardwood spear known as a *sarisssa*. These phalanxes—the individual soldiers were known as *phalangites*—had been trained to move in unison, to wheel left, right, and center on command. They were a fearsome sight in the ancient world, so impenetrable as to almost be a tiny, portable armored fortress.

THE BATTLE OF GRANICUS While Darius took the threat of Alexander's invasion seriously, he did not at first understand just how extraordinary a problem the young Macedonian was. After all, the Persian king could summon forth on short notice an army of 150,000 infantry and cavalry, more lightly armed than the Macedonians, but swift, brave, and highly maneuverable, with archers who could rain down showers of deadly arrows. Cloaked in a feeling of invincibility every bit as impenetrable as Alexander's, Darius summoned his ablest general, Memnon of Rhodes (yes, a Greek—there were many who served in the Persian army), and asked his advice about how to handle the upstart Macedonian. A scorched earth policy, answered Memnon—burn everything, retreat before Alexander, and leave nothing for him or his army to subsist on. Alexander's straitened financial situation was well known; unable to feed or pay his army, he would soon be forced to give up and return home.

But Darius and his lords, with great estates in Asia Minor that would be destroyed by such a policy, would not allow this. Nor would Darius's pride. Instead, Darius sent Memnon with an army of seventy-five thousand—more than enough, it was assumed, to deal with forty thousand Macedonians—to guard the banks of the Granicus River (now known as the Kocabas River) in western Turkey. Surely the Macedonian would not be crazy enough to charge directly across a river, under a storm of Persian spears and arrows, and up a steep embankment?

Yet that was exactly what Alexander did on a June day of 334 BC. As the Roman writer Plutarch wrote:

> *Alexander plunged into the river with thirteen cavalry squadrons. He was now driving into enemy projectiles and heading towards an area that was sheer and protected by armed men and cavalry, and negotiating a current that swept his men off their feet and pulled them under.*

Plutarch calls this behavior "reckless and senseless, rather than prudent." Exactly. Alexander lost his horse, his helmet, and was dealt a severe saber wound to the head by a Persian nobleman (his life was saved only at the last moment by his Companion, Cleitus the Black) and yet the shock of his surprise attack finally sent the Persians fleeing, leaving behind 2,500 dead. Alexander had won the day.

DARIUS GOES TO BATTLE

Buoyed up by his victory, Alexander proceeded through Asia Minor, liberating Greek cities as he went. This was a lengthy process, so it was not until August of 333 that he arrived in an area of Turkey near what is now Ankara. In the meantime, Memnon had died, of causes lost to history, and Darius's advisors were frantically telling the Great King that he could delay no longer, that he must now *personally* lead an army against this Macedonian. It was the only way to rally the Empire. Any more losses to this Alexander and they would everywhere have rebellion on their hands.

Darius agreed, although we have the sense that it was reluctantly. He had been trying for a year now to send assassins to kill Alexander—had, in fact, put a price of 1,000 silver talents on his rival's head—and he apparently hoped one of them might do the job for him. When this did not happen, Darius rallied his forces—some 100,000 troops—and marched against Alexander. The first part of his campaign was sheer brilliance and shows Darius's abilities in their best light. Within three months, he had brought this huge army from Babylon to eastern Turkey, circled behind an unsuspecting Alexander as the Macedonian moved south and cut his supply lines. Alexander was trapped with the Mediterranean behind him.

When Alexander realized he was being hunted, however, he wheeled around northward and in a lightning-quick overnight march confronted the Great King near the shores of the Gulf of Issus. The two armies arrayed themselves, anchoring one part of their lines on the sandy beach, the other near a line of low hills—the battlefield was no more than three miles wide. Each of the commanders was surrounded by his chosen bodyguard—Alexander by his Companions and Darius by his Immortals. As the two armies closed in on each other, Alexander rode his horse the length of the Greek lines, calling to his lieutenants by name, rallying them to him. Then he moved out in front of the army and straight towards the Persian lines, cantering slowly so that his phalanxes did not lose formation as they followed.

In the meantime, Darius, conspicuous in his high chariot—it was embossed with gold and silver images of the gods, with precious gems embedded in its yoke—drove towards the Greek lines. When the armies got to within a javelin's throw of each other, thousands of men gave voice to their full-throated battle cries and the two forces charged at each other, hitting with a mighty clash. The carnage of the battle of Issus was extreme; descriptions we have speak of hacked limbs flying everywhere, the ground red with blood, the very air misty with sprays of body fluids, the shouting and screaming so loud that it could be heard for miles around.

Alexander took the battle to Darius in a way that was both brilliant and bold. Noticing that the infantry stationed on the inland side of the Persian lines had archers supporting them—a sign that these infantry were inexperienced—Alexander led the charge there first, broke through these green soldiers, then turned and raced with his cavalry directly towards the center of the line, where Darius was visible in his chariot. Alexander and his bodyguards knew that if they could kill or capture Darius, not only the battle but the entire war would be over. As the two kings closed the gap between each other, Immortals and Companions clashed in brutal combat and the bodies of horses and men piled up—noble Macedonians fighting noble Persians, each to protect his king. Alexander and Darius were so close to each other that Darius was able to stab Alexander in the thigh with his dagger—or so chroniclers later claimed, although Alexander would refer to the wound after the battle as a mere trifle, without mentioning Darius as its perpetrator. But the two men seem to have been at least within shouting distance of one another, fighting desperately. Then the panicked horses of the Great King's chariot began to bolt, heading straight into the Macedonian lines. At this moment, Darius's courage failed him: the king leaped onto another chariot and bolted from the battlefield, as the Persian forces began to scatter.

Alexander and his bodyguard chased Darius for twenty-five miles, as dusk fell on this November evening, but the Persian eluded them.

"THE KING OF ALL ASIA" Now, as Alexander turned back to the bloody battlefield, he perhaps understood for the first time the immense wealth of the Persian Empire. Supposedly, it was at this moment that he turned to a Companion and said, "So this, it would seem, is to be a king."

The biggest prizes of all were Darius's mother, wife, two daughters and six-year-old heir, Ochus. As was the Persian custom, the One King had brought them with him to witness his great victory but had now abandoned them in his headlong flight. These captives could hear the sounds of raping and pillaging coming as Macedonians rampaged through other parts of the captured Persian camp, but Alexander ordered that they should be well-guarded and treated with civility. They were far too valuable to harm.

Dawn of the next day saw Darius fleeing eastward towards Babylon with a force of some four thousand Greek mercenaries who had been in Persian employ. He did not stop until he had reached the gates of his capital city, at which point he was finally able to take stock of his situation. Alexander had beaten him soundly, driven him from the battlefield, and now held his mother, wife and children hostage. Not to mention the fact that all of Asia Minor was now gone and that Darius's spies reported to him that Alexander was moving south, apparently intending to conquer the Mediterranean coast and rob the Persians of their naval bases there.

Yet Darius, or so he felt, was still in a position of strength, still with superior forces and riches, still with over half an empire. So Darius did the only thing he

FOLLOWING PAGES
The family of Darius III kneels before Alexander the Great after their capture following the battle of Issus (as shown in a painting by Paolo Veronese in 1566).

17

GAIUS JULIUS CAESAR VERSUS

felt he could do—he decided to negotiate. While many have seen this as a sign of weakness in the man's character, it was in fact a not unreasonable idea and the offer he made to Alexander—which reached the Macedonian on his way south—was quite generous. Protesting that Alexander had been the aggressor in all this (true) and that the battle of Issus has gone "as some god had willed it" (meaning some non-Persian god, of course), he offered a huge ransom if Alexander would send back his mother, wife and children. Not only that, but Darius would cede Alexander "all the territories and cities of Asia west of the Halys River" in Turkey—the territory, in other words, that Alexander had already conquered.

After pondering this message for a very short time, Alexander gave the Persian courtier who had brought the Great King's offer the following reply:

> *King Alexander to Darius,*
> *In the future, let any communication you wish to make with me be addressed to the King of all Asia. Do not write to me as an equal. Everything you possess is now mine; so, if you should want anything, let me know in the proper terms or I shall take steps to deal with you as a criminal. If, on the other hand, you wish to dispute the throne, stand and fight for it and do not run away. Wherever you may hide yourself, be sure I shall seek you out.*

If Darius had had any doubt as to who he was dealing with before this, he certainly had none now. The duel between the two men would be a battle to the death.

ONE MORE BATTLE Of course, Alexander's reply to Darius had been, in the main, a bluff. After all, the Great King—now at the rear of Alexander as he headed south, capturing the coastal cities, including Tyre, and even Egypt—was still rich and powerful. But even if it were a bluff, the note was an inspired one, for Alexander knew his rival well enough to understand that Darius had been humiliated and could not take being humiliated again. Now, more than ever, Darius's honor was at stake. Alexander hoped that the Great King would raise another massive army to fight him. For Alexander, never one to be cowed by overwhelming odds, any confrontation with Darius would be his chance to win the world, once and for all.

Darius reacted as Alexander expected. His honor and the honor of the empire (inseparable, of course) were stung to the quick. He now levied the largest army ever put together during the course of his reign, the largest army the world had seen since the mighty Xerxes had invaded Greece a century and a half earlier. And this time he was smarter. Instead of deciding to do battle with Alexander on narrow fronts—as at Granicus and Issus—he would fight Alexander on the plains of his homeland, in the broad lands between the Tigris and the Euphrates.

As Darius put together this force—which threatened Alexander's newly conquered settlements in Asia Minor—the Macedonian leader turned his army and, in the spring of 331, began marching towards the Persian heartland. The army pushed through Syria, during heat that reached 110 degrees, and horses and men began to drop. Alexander's forces crossed the Euphrates and then reached the Tigris in mid-September as autumnal flash floods roared through the river, and hundreds of men and horses were swept away to their deaths. Yet still the Macedonians, Alexander at their head, kept on coming. The young general knew that he was facing the pivotal battle of his life.

As did Darius. While his scouts watched Alexander's progress, he debated where to do battle. He had expected the Macedonian to head for Babylon, but Alexander surprised him, as usual, and bypassed the great city. Racing ahead of him, Darius took the field on a broad plain called Gaugamela, in northern Iraq. Here, at last, he had ideal conditions for fighting Alexander, with no hills or rivers to impede the progress of his chariots or stop him from using his overwhelming superiority in numbers. While Alexander approached, Darius had his men smooth out chariot runs along the plains, so that these scythed vehicles (powerful but prone to breakdowns) would have an easy dash at Alexander's flanks. He also prepared pits full of stakes, to trap Alexander's unwary cavalry. Then he waited.

GAUGAMELA On September 29, 331, surrounded by a small group of his ever-present bodyguards, Alexander topped a ridge overlooking the plain of Gaugamela—and then stopped, open-mouthed. Although he had heard of the size of Darius's forces, the shock of seeing 250,000 Persian troops spread out before him—galloping squadrons of cavalry raising tornadoes of dust, sunlight flashing from thousands of spears and swords—must have been intense.

Alexander, with perhaps forty thousand men, was outnumbered five to one. Darius had forty thousand heavily armored cavalry alone. However, Alexander seems to have fairly quickly recovered from the surprise. He spent the next day surveying the battlefield; Persian deserters informed him of the hidden pits full of stakes, of the broad chariot runs. Still, he was in a tough position—outflanked by the enemy even before he began. Alexander's ablest general, Parmenio, advised a night attack, but Alexander rejected this scornfully, speaking of himself in the third person: "Alexander must defeat his enemies openly and without subterfuge," he told his general.

This was not just pride, however. Night attacks were risky in the extreme, and he was right—the world had to *see* him beat his rival Darius and *see* him destroy Persian power. However, feigning a night attack would not be a bad idea, and so he sent spies into the Persian camp to spread rumors of just such a Macedonian threat, thus keeping a good part of the Persian army up the whole night. In the meantime, he retired alone to his tent, thinking long and hard about how to place his troops the next day. Having apparently come to a decision, he fell asleep and slept so hard that he had to be awakened the next day by Parmenio himself, who was astonished at the young king's *sangfroid*.

DARIUS'S WOMEN

Although Darius was prepared to fight to the death as the battle of Gaugamela approached, it is touching to realize how much he loved the women who were held captive by Alexander. Even as Alexander's forces approached Darius's army before that last pitched battle, word came to Darius that his wife, for two years now a captive of Alexander, had died, either in childbirth or during a miscarriage. Just who had made her pregnant was an open question, but conceivably it was Alexander himself.

Now Darius made Alexander another, more secret offer. If Alexander would return his mother and daughters, he could have the hand of one of the girls in marriage, thirty thousand talents, his young son Ochus as a permanent hostage *and* all the land in Asia west of the Euphrates.

Alexander's general Parmenio told him: "If I were Alexander, I should accept this offer."

"So should I," Alexander replied, "if I were Parmenio."

Alexander rejected Darius's offer out of hand. He had not yet seen the Persian forces at Gaugamela. Perhaps, high on that ridge, when he first laid eyes on them he had a twinge of regret—but by then it was too late.

RIGHT Alexander, at the
head of his cavalry, smashes
into the Persian lines at the
Battle of Gaugamela in
331 BC to finally defeat
his rival Darius.

On the bright sunlit morning of October 1, 331, Alexander lined his men up to face the might of the Persian army. Darius, watching again from his high chariot, was heartened by the puny numbers of the Macedonians, as compared to his own force, but, like his generals, he was puzzled—for Alexander had lined his men up facing the Persian left flank, instead of directly in front of the Persian center, facing the Great King, which would be the normal formation. This was odd; odder still was the way the Macedonians began to approach: in a kind of diamond formation, phalanxes of infantry pointing their deadly sarissas outward, the whole Macedonian army advancing obliquely towards the Persian left (Alexander's right), offering up their left flank as an inviting target to the cavalry massed on the Persian right.

This strange formation was the fruit of Alexander's hard thought during the night, and it paid off. Finally, Darius could restrain himself no longer and sent the cavalry on his right wing charging at the Macedonian left. However, Alexander had advanced so far to his right flank that the Persian horse took too long to reach him— they were intercepted by the Macedonian cavalry Alexander had reserved for this purpose and were fought off in a pitched affray. Then Darius ordered his chariots, scythes hissing, to charge straight at the Macedonian center, but Alexander had prepared for this as well. Knowing where the chariot runs were, he had prepared his lines to open up as the chariots reached them. The chariots continued into the Macedonian ranks and the drivers and their horses were then easily speared.

Finally, now, both armies clashed in a roar of hand-to-hand combat. Despite Alexander's stratagems, he was still completely surrounded, and Darius's superior numbers began to tell. Much of ancient combat had to do, quite literally, with physical strength—one force simply pushing another backwards—and this is what began to happen to the Macedonian troops. Darius, from his chariot, could at last smell a victory over the rival who had humiliated him in such a profoundly personal way.

Then Alexander, once again thinking quickly in a desperate situation, saw an opening in the Persian lines. It was probably merely a gap where a company of men had momentarily fallen back to regroup, but it was all he needed. Gathering his cavalry in a wedge around him, he drove straight at the gap and smashed through. In the space of perhaps ten minutes, the battle, and history, changed forever. Wheeling, Alexander now drove straight at the Great King's bodyguards. The Macedonians got so close to Darius that the Persian ruler's chariot-driver was killed by a spear—and then Darius, as he had at Issus, fled, just as the ring of Macedonians was closing.

Alexander chased his rival once again—this time until midnight—but without success. However, when he returned to the battlefield—where some fifty thousand Persians lay dead—he found waiting for him the Great King's gold chariot and bow, left behind in Darius's panic. It was understood: Alexander was now king of all he surveyed.

THE FINAL CHAPTER In the next months, Alexander entered the great Persian cities of Babylon, Susa and Persepolis. He was truly a conqueror, the man who had brought to an end the two-hundred-year-old Persian Empire.

Darius fled to the mountains in the north. It was his avowed intention to carry on a guerilla war against Alexander but, with his nerve broken, he was never able to mount any real challenge to his former nemesis.

Darius's end is a sad one. As Alexander's men hunted him in the year following the battle, he was put in chains by his traitorous cousin and former general, Bessus, and stabbed numerous times with javelins. Left in a wagon on the side of a road in the province of Bactria, near present-day Afghanistan, he was discovered by a Macedonian soldier. The Great King was bleeding to death and begged for water, which the soldier gave him. Thanking him politely, Darius said: "Now, at least, I don't have to die alone."

A few hours later when Alexander was taken to the body of his rival, he knelt down and threw his own purple cloak over Darius. He then ordered the former One King taken back to Persepolis, where he was given a state funeral. Then, and with a vengeance, Alexander tracked down Bessus. When he caught up with him, in 329, he had his nose and ears cut off—a traditional punishment for regicides in Persia. Bessus was then publicly decapitated.

Darius might have been his rival and enemy, was Alexander's point, but only a king had the right to kill another king.

THE FATE OF ALEXANDER

By 324, Alexander had conquered much of Central Asia and part of modern-day Afghanistan, and had invaded the fabled lands of India, fighting pitched battles there. However, his loyal Macedonian army had at last grown tired of him, especially after their arduous trek back from India. For Alexander—who appears to have begun drinking heavily—had begun to adopt Persian customs, including the Persian obeisance of hand kissing (*proskynesis*), at his court.

In the summer of 324, Alexander's close friend and possibly lover, Hephaestion, died of a fever after a drinking bout. Alexander had his physician killed and was practically prostrate with grief. It was a prefiguring of his own end, a year later. After a year of alcohol abuse and violent outbursts, Alexander died in June of 323—some ancient sources say that he was poisoned, although modern historians believe his symptoms were those of malaria aggravated by copious amounts of alcohol.

The last words from Alexander were: "I foresee a great funeral contest over me." With no children left behind to assume his throne, the empire he had conquered fell apart in bloody division after his death.

HANNIBAL BARCA VERSUS

SCIPIO AFRICANUS

HANNIBAL BARCA AND SCIPIO AFRICANUS: LEGENDS AND GENTLEMEN

THE SEPTEMBER SUN SHONE RELENTLESSLY DOWN on the seemingly endless North African plain as the two men rode slowly out to greet each other—although perhaps greet is the wrong word. Scrutinize? Appraise? Evaluate.

They had long been rivals but they had never before met. The older of the two, his skin deeply bronzed, wore a long white cape with a silver shoulder clasp, had an eye-patch over his left eye and sat astride his horse with a kind of weary dignity. The younger man, shorter and more compact, wore the armor and vermilion cape of a high-ranking Roman officer. Despite the fact that he was not yet in his middle thirties, he had an air of keen intelligence about him; in fact, it was rumored among his troops that he possessed the gift of second sight, a supernatural ability to see into the future.

It was 202 BC. Thousands of armed men belonging to the armies of these two generals, the Carthaginian Hannibal Barca and the Roman Publius Cornelius Scipio—soon to be known as Scipio Africanus because of what would happen that very day—watched with apprehension as the rivals stopped a few feet from one another, holding their horses steady.

It is not known how long these two men appraised each other, but finally, according to Polybius, a reliable ancient source, it was Hannibal, the weathered man with the eye-patch, who spoke first.

"It is fate that has bought us here," he told Scipio.

And the younger man looked at him steadily and said: "Not fate, sir, but Carthaginian treachery."

CARTHAGE AND ROME

Carthaginian treachery. Roman perfidy. It is truly hard, looking through history, to find two nations who loathed and despised each other more than the Romans and the Carthaginians. The result of their enmity was a series of three wars, which lasted from 264 to 146 BC and were the longest and most destructive in ancient history—the world wars of their time.

The city of Carthage was founded in the eighth century BC on the shores of North Africa, in what is presently Tunisia, by the adventurous Phoenicians, antiquity's great traders and seafarers. As the third century BC began, the Carthaginians—whose mercantile ability exceeded even that of their Phoenician forefathers—had become the greatest power in the Mediterranean world. The influence of Carthage spread through trading settlements in North Africa, Spain, Sardinia, Cyprus, Malta, and on the west coast of Sicily.

At home, Carthage stood on rich agricultural land and the city itself, with its marvelous circular harbor and many-storied temples and buildings, was the greatest in Africa. In a way, however, Carthage lacked a soul. Corruption was a way of life and any high political office could be obtained by bribery. While individual, aristocratic Carthaginians were patriotic, most sought mercenaries to do their fighting for them. Among the gods worshipped by the Carthaginians were Baal Hammon and his consort Tanit, who desired the flesh of human children. And so the Carthaginians practiced infant sacrifice—at the cult site where this ritual occurred, archaeologists have found the bones of hundreds of infants. The spirit of the Carthaginians, as one historian has put it, was one of "commercial adventure, and a love of gold, blood, and pleasure."

Rome was a different story, although gold, blood and pleasure certainly figure prominently there too. Founded in about 750 BC on Italy's Tiber River, at the confluence of several important trade routes, the city was first controlled by kings but later became a republic. By the mid fourth century BC, through aggression and trade, it had annexed most of the territories of Italy. Romans were family-centered, proud of their freedom, religious, and not without arrogance.

By the beginning of the third century BC, Rome had conquered the ancient Greek settlements in the south of Italy and was in the process of conquering the Greek city-states still remaining in Sicily—a fact that put them in direct competition with the Carthaginians for control of the trade in this rich island.

THE FIRST PUNIC WAR

The First Punic War, beginning in 264 BC and lasting until 241, ended up as a resounding defeat for the Carthaginians. (The name Punic derives from the Latin *punicus*, which comes from the Greek *phoinix*, meaning "Phoenician," a reference to the Carthaginians' origin.) Their powerful navy was broken by the Romans in a series of important battles that gave Rome control of the Mediterranean. Although the Romans tried and failed to invade North Africa, they forced the Carthaginians to sue for peace. The ensuing treaty

THE HORRID RITUAL

The Carthaginians were by almost any standard, ancient or modern, a civilized people. And yet ... they practiced infant sacrifice.

The ancient Phoenicians themselves killed infants on the altar of the god Moloch, but they had abandoned the practice well before the start of the Punic Wars. The Carthaginians, however, continued to sacrifice babies—by hurling them alive into a fire—in front of their god Baal Hammon and his mistress Tanit.

The site where this cult ritual occurred in Carthage has been found by archeologists and excavated, and it shows that infants were killed there right up until 146 BC, when the city was destroyed by Rome. In fact, it appears that as the Punic Wars wore on, more and more infants were sacrificed to appease the gods.

Carthaginian infant sacrifice is controversial. Many historians postulate that the children were already dead from disease and were merely being cremated. They point out that much of the history we have on the Carthaginians comes from the Romans, their conquerors, who hated them. The latest forensic anthropological evidence, however, does seem to indicate that infant sacrifice was practiced by the Carthaginians.

gave Rome complete control of Sicily and forced the humiliated Carthaginians to pay hefty reparations. Yet, because of its size and distance from Rome, Carthage could not be absorbed and co-opted into a subordinate position, ruled by Roman puppets, in the way Rome had handled most of its previous foes.

Carthage, seeking to restore its fortunes, expanded to the west, to Spain. There, Carthaginian commander Hamilcar Barca, of the soon-to-be-quite-famous Barcid family, conquered the Celtiberian tribes in much of the southern half of the Iberian peninsula, setting up Carthaginian outposts so that revenue flowed back to Carthage from the Spanish silver mines. As Carthage gradually grew stronger, Rome became more and more worried—a Carthaginian power base in Spain directly threatened Roman interests. In 229, it was arranged that Hamilcar should be assassinated—by Celtiberian tribes, to be sure, so that it looked like a mere rebellious attack.

But if Rome thought it could breathe easier, it was sorely mistaken. For now Hamilcar's son, Hannibal, would take his place on the stage of the Punic Wars.

HANNIBAL BARCA For centuries after Hannibal Barca—*barca* means "lightning" in Punic—had turned to dust Roman mothers would scare their unruly children by whispering that Hannibal was at the gates of the city. Born in 247 BC and so just a small child when the First Punic War ended, Hannibal grew up steeped in hatred of Rome, a hatred engendered mainly by his father, whose fine fleet of Carthaginian warships had been utterly destroyed by Rome. Hannibal himself would later tell the story that, all of nine years old, he had to swear an oath to his father that "as soon as [my] age will permit ... I will use fire and steel to resolve the destiny of Rome."

Whether the story is true or not, he certainly sought to destroy Rome. At the age of twenty-six, in 221, he took control of the Carthaginian forces in Spain and defeated several Celtiberian tribes allied with the Romans. Finally, when he besieged the Roman city of Saguntum (now Sagunto) the Romans could endure no more: they demanded that this upstart young Carthaginian be brought before them in chains. This Carthage refused and, in 218, with much bloodshed, Hannibal captured Saguntum. The Second Punic War had begun.

Hannibal wasted no time—a hallmark of his actions as a commander. Knowing the Romans would never expect an attack from the north, he decided to cross the Pyrenees, move through southern Gaul, and then descend into the Italian Peninsula through the Alps. This was an extraordinarily bold strategic move, something that had never before been done. The young Carthaginian brought with him forty thousand men (as well as, famously, forty war elephants). While commanded by aristocratic Carthaginian officers, Hannibal's army was made up of mercenaries—Celtiberians in furs, deadly stone slingers from the Balearic Islands (who demanded to be paid in women rather than gold), and Nubian horsemen who, for ferocity and swiftness of movement, were unequaled anywhere in the world.

After extraordinary hardship, using a route most historians now think was one of the most treacherous high passes of the Alps, Hannibal descended into the alpine foothills of Italy in the late fall of 218. Half his men were dead, as well as all but two of his war elephants. Yet the fertile checkerboard fields of Italy spread out before him and—not seen but certainly envisioned—the glorious city of Rome shone in the distance, ready for the taking.

SCIPIO AFRICANUS Rome, given scant warning that Hannibal was on his way, scrambled to stop him, and now the men of another distinguished and warlike family came into play. The Scipio branch of the Cornelius family had long been considered one of Rome's most distinguished, with several of its members having been consuls. At the time of Hannibal's invasion of Italy, Publius Cornelius Scipio, the Elder, was the Roman consul and had been preparing to invade Spain to stop the Carthaginian forces. Discovering Hannibal was in his rear, he moved his army north while Hannibal was still trying to recruit new men from the local Gallic tribes, playing on their hatred of Rome. As soon as Hannibal heard that the elder Scipio was on his way, he moved quickly to meet him. The two forces closed on each other near the Ticino River, a tributary of the Po River, in northern Italy.

The elder Scipio was accompanied by his son and namesake, Publius Cornelius Scipio, whom we will call Scipio Africanus, for clarity's sake, although he was years away from earning that honorific. Scipio Africanus was born into this distinguished family in 236 BC and raised as befitted a young man of such high estate in Rome. He was handsome, athletic, and excelled at the warlike arts learned by any young Roman patrician. Yet there was something a little different about this young aristocrat, for he was also scholarly (he could read and write fluently in Greek) and serious about religion, worshipping often at the Temple of Jupiter. (He would later become a high priest of Mars.) Scipio Africanus also believed in dreams and omens—and not just the way most Romans did, casually, the way we might glance at an astrology reading: Scipio apparently thought he could foretell the future. And, one other thing: legend has it that, like his rival Hannibal, the young Scipio was forced by his warlike father to swear an oath to destroy Rome's vicious enemy, Carthage.

THE BATTLES IN ITALY At the Ticino River, Scipio Africanus and Hannibal became opponents for the first time, although it is doubtful that the latter was more than casually aware of the existence of the former. He was mainly concerned with vanquishing Scipio's father. In the cool, dry November weather, Carthaginians and Romans were alerted to each other's movements by clouds of dust. Ticino was mainly a battle of cavalry. Scipio the Elder set up his *velites* (his light infantry, armed with javelins) in front of his Roman horse, but they barely got a chance to enter the fray because the cavalry of both sides surged forward in close formation, each confident that they would destroy the enemy.

The battle surged back and forth until Hannibal's swift Numidians rode around the Roman flanks, causing the *velites* to panic and retreat, and then setting on the Roman cavalry from the rear.

In the chaos, the Roman horse began to retreat and here, for the first time, Scipio Africanus literally charges into history. Stationed at the rear by his doting father, in command of a reserve troop of cavalry, Scipio apparently saw or sensed that his father was in danger, for he rode—some say alone—into the wheeling, slashing fray of horsemen and rescued his father, who had been badly wounded by a Carthaginian spear thrust. Gathering a small force around him, Scipio Africanus forged through the chaos and carried his father to safety.

Ticino, a small battle in itself, is important because it showed Hannibal's army—and various Celtic tribes who were watchfully waiting—that they could beat the Romans on their own soil. Now a string of glorious Carthaginian victories—and dreadful Roman defeats—ensued. Moving steadily southward down the Italian peninsula, Hannibal beat the Romans at the battles of Trebia, Lake Trasimene, and, most extraordinary of all, Cannae in August 216. It was the glorious year of Hannibal's victories, his *annus mirabilis*. His fast-moving forces and fluid campaign strategies—Hannibal fought with a large army yet thought like a guerilla fighter—overwhelmed the powerful, yet inflexible Roman legions.

Already, however, the seeds of Hannibal's undoing were being sown. For one thing, after Cannae the Carthaginian commander decided not to march on Rome. Perhaps this was a wise decision. With ever longer supply lines, he could not afford a pitched, endgame battle (although the Romans had lost fifty thousand men at Cannae, Hannibal had also lost a significant portion of his much smaller force). Yet this decision allowed the Romans to rally, to learn how to fight him. For another, Scipio Africanus was still alive. While his father recuperated from his wounds, Africanus had fought Hannibal at Trebia and, most notably, at Cannae, where he rallied a force around him to escape the massive carnage that saw his father-in-law, Consul Lucius Aemilius Paullus, killed, as well as hundreds of other elite Romans.

Back in Rome, panicked politicians met and decided to surrender to Hannibal. At which point Scipio, all of eighteen, stormed the meeting with like-minded officers and forced the politicians, at sword point, to swear they would never surrender to the Carthaginians. It would be a fight to the death.

THE TIDE TURNS Hannibal continued to fight the Romans in southern Italy, but with far less success, as they had finally learned not to allow themselves to be drawn into pitched battle with the military genius of his age. And now another military genius was rising—young Scipio Africanus. In 212, he became a Roman senator, despite the fact that he was not yet thirty, the legal age to hold such a position. The following year, his father and uncle were killed fighting Carthaginian forces under Hannibal's brother Hasdrubal in Spain, and so in 210 he asked for and received the position of proconsul and general of the Roman forces (apparently, no other Roman was brave enough to want the job). Scipio then went to Spain and began to turn the Second Punic War around. Spurred on by the death of so many of his family at the hands of the Carthaginians, he won a string of victories and wrested Spain from Carthaginian control.

By 205, Scipio had conquered Spain and returned to Rome, where, at the age of thirty-one, he was named consul. Hannibal was still operating in the southwest of Italy, and by now was definitely aware of Scipio's existence. This man, eleven years his junior, had defeated his brother and destroyed the Carthaginian forces in Spain, and now, rumor had it, he was aiming right for the heart of the Carthaginian empire: the city of Carthage itself.

THE RIVALS CLOSE IN
On a late spring day in 204, Scipio stood on a Sicilian beach in front of his army of some thirty thousand Roman infantry and cavalry. Offshore, riding the choppy waves of the Mediterranean, were some four hundred transports and forty quinquireme warships, a huge invasion fleet. But because Scipio believed so firmly in fortune and the gods, he refused to allow his men to embark on their planned invasion of North Africa until sacrifices were made to Mars, the Roman god of war, and Victoria, the goddess of Victory. A sheep was brought to the beach, and Scipio Africanus himself slit its throat and reached inside its still twitching body to grasp its entrails and throw them into the azure waters that lapped the shore.

A cheer went up from his men and the invasion was on. After three days' sail, Scipio's force made landfall in what we now call Tunisia, at modern-day Cape Farina, which was not far from the Carthaginian city of Utica. His invasion came as a complete surprise. He defeated a small Carthaginian force of cavalry and took some eight thousand civilian captives, whom he shipped back to Rome as slaves. Then he ravaged much of the fertile Bagradas valley and, in the late summer of 204, laid siege to Utica, which he took after defeating a large Carthaginian force. Scipio was aided in this by his alliance with a former ally of the Carthaginians, a Numidian leader named Masinissa who brought with him his renowned cavalry.

In Italy, Hannibal heard of these victories and, even more to his astonishment, heard that the Carthaginians had approached Scipio to sue for peace. Not only that, but they were blaming the entire war on Hannibal and his family. Scipio, given the power to negotiate by Rome, proposed generous terms, which included the recall of Hannibal's army from Italy and a yearly tribute to be paid by Carthage to Rome. This was agreed to, and Hannibal's army began its return. Hannibal, now in his middle forties, appeared much older than his age, beaten down by years of campaigning in a foreign country, and by the betrayal of his countrymen, who had attempted to place all the blame for the war, once quite popular, on the shoulders of himself and his family.

A PERFECT SLAUGHTER: THE BATTLE OF CANNAE

The Roman dead at the battle of Cannae amounted to fifty thousand, the largest single-day slaughter in the history of warfare right up until the first day of the battle of the Somme in 1916.

The death toll at Cannae was simply incredible, but the reason generals throughout history have studied Cannae was because of Hannibal's tactics. He was outnumbered by the Roman forces, perhaps two to one, and yet when he faced his enemy he deliberately created a weak center, putting his most unreliable troops right at the spot where the Roman legions would strike the hardest. Predictably, the Romans pushed them back farther and farther, without realizing, however, that the Carthaginian wings—where Hannibal had stationed his strongest troops—were stretching out and surrounding them in what became the most famous double-envelopment in history. The more the Romans struck at Hannibal's center, the more they were surrounded.

And so, in the course of a hot August afternoon in 216 BC, they were slaughtered. Perhaps ten thousand fought their way out of the trap—with Scipio, of course—but it was the worst day in the history of Rome.

ABOVE This reconstruction of the battle of Zama shows the fearsome charge by Hannibal's eighty elephants against the Romans, who retaliated with spears and arrows as the elephants passed through their ranks.

Still, Hannibal was ready for peace. His father and brother Hasdrubal had died at the hands of the Romans. Scipio's peace was the best they were likely to get. It was time to end the war. Then, in the spring of 203, a Roman supply fleet ran aground during a storm, just off the shores of the city of Carthage itself. The Carthaginians, who may have been starving, looted the ships. Scipio sent a delegation insisting on the return of the ships, and the Carthaginians finally agreed, but not before treating the Roman delegates harshly—it is a sign of how much the Carthaginians hated Rome that they would do something that would so adversely affect their chances of survival.

When Scipio heard the news, he was enraged. It was one more sign of "Carthaginian treachery." In the fall of 202, he went to war, rampaging through the North African countryside outside Carthage. This time he refused to offer mercy or quarter, destroying the great estates of Carthaginian landowners and cutting off supplies to the capital city itself, which began to swell with refugees.

Predictably, the Carthaginians who ran the city—the same Council of Elders who had cravenly blamed the war on Hannibal—now begged their commander to go to war again to save their country.

Which is how, on that September day in 202, Hannibal found himself face to face with the only man on earth who could rival him as general: Scipio.

ZAMA The two men probably spoke for no longer than a few minutes. After Scipio had mentioned "Carthaginian treachery" there was probably little else to say. Staring at each other, he and Hannibal may have sensed that the coming battle would decide both their fates.

In any event, both men returned to their lines as great shouts arose from the armies. For the battle was now on. The thirty-five thousand Romans were lined up in classic fashion, divided into maniples (meaning "handfuls"), each maniple a company-strength unit of some 120 men. These, in turn, were divided into three groups: the *hastati*, the young men who formed the front line; the *princeps*, slightly older men, who formed the middle line; and the *triari*, the veterans in the rear. These men wore body armor and each carried a *gladius*, a short sword used for stabbing, and a *pilum*, a heavy throwing spear. On the wings were Masinissa's fleet Numidian cavalry.

The Carthaginians outnumbered the Romans by perhaps ten thousand men, but these men of Scipio's were veterans of Spain and the previous year's campaigning in North Africa. Hannibal had a nucleus of Carthaginian veterans, but his army also had a number of raw recruits with little experience, mainly Celts or Ligurians who, while brave, did not necessarily fare well in army-to-army combat. This may be one reason why Hannibal launched his elephant charge first—sending eighty of the thundering beasts directly at the Roman lines. This was a frightful experience in ancient times, but Scipio had prepared for such an eventuality. He ordered his legions to open up lanes, down which they drove the elephants, which were shot with arrows and speared as they went by.

Maddened, many of the creatures raced back and wreaked havoc among the Carthaginian lines. At this moment, Masinissa's Numidians charged and chased away the Carthaginian's own small force of mercenary Numidians, and the battle became a hard, slogging infantry match. Hannibal had kept his veteran troops in reserve for the moment and the Roman maniples now slammed into the more inexperienced Carthaginian troops. Hannibal had been hoping that these Romans would be disorganized and scattered by the elephant attack, but this had not happened and now the Romans, according to the ancient historian Livy, pushed their opponents back "with their elbows and the bosses of their shields ... they advanced at a considerable pace, as if there had been no one there to resist them."

However, when the Romans had pushed these troops away, they came upon the third line, consisting of Hannibal's veterans, and a ferocious battle ensued. Now veteran met veteran in a fight to the death, in the true fashion of the Punic Wars. Scipio and Hannibal, surrounded by their staffs and generals, watched the fight anxiously and for a while it seemed as if Scipio's dreams were false, as if Hannibal might pull out another miracle and prevail. Then Masinissa's Numidians returned from chasing off the Carthaginian horse and fell upon the rear of the Carthaginian infantry, much as Hannibal's cavalry had done to the Romans at Cannae. Hard-pressed on both sides, the Carthaginian army caved in and scattered in defeat.

By nightfall, Hannibal had made it back to the city with a small group of his staff, but the Second Punic War was now all but over.

WHO WAS THE GREATEST? The fall of the Carthaginians was harsh. Scipio's terms were not as brutal as they could have been—the city of Carthage was not razed, for instance, nor were its leaders crucified—but Carthage was stripped of all its foreign holdings and forced to pay a fifty-year indemnity to Rome. Even so, this resilient people began to rise from the ashes, and by 151 BC, having paid their debt to Rome, they began to prosper again. Their prosperity haunted the dreams of the Romans so much that, in a war entirely instigated by Rome, they finally destroyed Carthage in 146 BC. Literally destroyed it—the city was left in ashes and the remaining population driven into slavery. The man who presided over this final slaughter was Scipio Aemilianus, adopted grandson of Scipio Africanus. Now, with Carthage gone, Rome began its legendary rise to glory.

What of Hannibal and Scipio Africanus? After his defeat, Hannibal spent his last days in exile, wandering the Mediterranean and fighting for various enemies of Rome, but he was a hunted man. With the Romans closing in on his refuge in the kingdom of Bithynia, near the Black Sea, he committed suicide by taking poison,

RIGHT The triumph of Scipio Africanus in 201 BC celebrated his victory over Hannibal and the Carthaginians in the Second Punic War. A triumph was a signal honor in Rome (see page 40).

in 183. He was sixty-four years old and, as the Greek historian Plutarch put it, had become "a bird that has grown too old to fly."

Interestingly, Scipio died that same year, at his country home in Campania, perhaps by committing suicide as well. While he had returned to Rome in triumph, officially celebrated as Scipio Africanus, he had not fared well in the hornet's nest of Roman politics. There were many who thought his terms to the Carthaginians had been too generous; others resented what they thought were his high-handed ways. In the end, he was wrongly accused of taking bribes, and this may have pushed him to end his life.

Legend has it that these two men, Hannibal and Scipio, had one more meeting. According to the Greek historian Appian of Alexandria, it took place years after Zama, when Hannibal was in the employ of King Antiochus of the Syrians. Scipio was an ambassador sent by the Romans to parlay with Antiochus and met Hannibal at the king's court. Supposedly, Scipio asked Hannibal who he felt was the greatest general of all time, to which Hannibal answered, "Alexander of Macedonia."

Scipio replied: "And where would you place yourself, Hannibal, if you had not been defeated by me?" Politely, Hannibal responded that normally he might place himself even before Alexander—but, having lost to Scipio, he had to relinquish that position to the Roman commander.

Neither was fooled by the other's politeness, of course. The two men were rivals to the end.

P. DUJARDIN. ENG.

GNAEUS POMPEIUS MAGNUS

GAIUS JULIUS CAESAR AND GNAEUS POMPEIUS MAGNUS:
A BATTLE FOR THE SOUL OF ROME

I T IS IRONIC NOT THAT THESE TWO MEN EACH DIED violently—a violent death was almost to be expected in the bloody and chaotic decade of Republican Rome's undoing—but that each of their deaths began with a supposed ally stretching out the hand of friendship. Then came the sharp knife of the assassin.

Gnaeus Pompeius Magnus, better known as Pompey, bled out on the shores of Egypt, the waters of the *Mare Nostrum* ("Our Sea"), the Roman name for the Mediterranean, lapping around his body. His rival, Julius Caesar, perished in the very heart of Rome, on the floor of the Senate, attempting to fight off his attackers with the stylus he used to sign documents. While the two of them lived, however, theirs was a rivalry that signified all that was both glorious and self-destructive about Rome as it entered the death throes of the Republic.

A REPUBLIC GROWN TOO LARGE Rome had been a republic ever since the sixth century BC and a relatively stable one at that, without civil wars or other domestic upheavals. After the Punic Wars (see pages 26–35) in which it utterly crushed its Carthaginian opponent, the republic went through a century-long period of unparalleled advancement, controlling the entire Mediterranean world and moving on to fight wars in Asia Minor, Spain, and Gaul. The proud Roman legions literally never lost a war.

The Roman Republic was set up under a very simple guiding principle: no one man should be able to seize and permanently hold power. In order to ensure this, two prominent men were appointed as co-consuls to lead the country for a year's term, after which they returned to civilian life and two more were chosen. While possible, it was extremely rare for consuls to hold office more than once. In the meantime, Rome's most prominent (and wealthiest) citizens formed the Senate—sometimes as many as six hundred men strong—which advised the consuls and basically formed the bureaucratic machinery that operated the country. There were no political parties. Wealthy people gained votes by trumpeting their individual deeds of military valor, promising civic improvements, and even directly paying off the citizenry, via bribes and huge festival parties.

But by the mid second century BC, the republic was starting to show cracks at its foundation. The booty from Rome's conquests was only reaching the hands of a very small group of prominent families, who got richer and richer, while other noble families became impoverished. Control of the Senate and the consulships passed to a tiny cabal of the super-rich, and this led to great resentment among the men who could no longer afford a political career. These men, borrowing large sums of money to fund their campaigns, began to seek support among the common people, stirring them up with promises of free land, lower taxes and, basically, a larger slice of the ever-growing Roman pie. Naturally, the rich Roman elite who controlled the Senate—they were called *optimates*, which literally means "the best men"—saw this as potentially dangerous, bringing up the specter of mob rule, mob violence.

The politicians who sought to appeal to the throngs of ordinary citizens were known, sometimes scornfully, as *populares*. One such *popularis* was a highly charismatic fellow named Julius Caesar.

THE GREAT CAESAR Julius Caesar was born in 100 BC in the month of Quintilis—later to be named July in his honor. He was a member of that group of people who were rapidly losing power because of the inequities in the Roman system. His family, the Julii, was one of the original first families of Rome, the *nobilitas*. Caesar's father had been a praetor, the second highest rank of magistrate, and had governed a province in Asia, but the family was far from wealthy and had gradually lost influence over the years.

The time of Caesar's early childhood was a time of extraordinary upheaval. Throughout the 90s, the Social War was fought between Rome and its allies on the Italian peninsula as they demanded the rights of citizenry. After bloody battles, Roman citizenship was finally extended to all, but then the republic faced a new threat. Lucius Cornelius Sulla, a Roman commander and one of the *optimates*, took six Roman legions and marched into Rome in 81—violating the ancient constitutional tenet that no armed soldiers should appear in the city. There he seized power as dictator, holding it for two years. His death squads roamed at will through the city, sinking their knives into leaders of the *populares* and all those who disagreed with Sulla.

One of those who opposed the dictator was the young Caesar, who was allied by marriage to one of Sulla's chief opponents. At one point, Sulla ordered

**MARCHING
IN TRIUMPH**

In republican Rome, one of
the highest honors a military
commander could wish for
was to be accorded a triumph
(*triumpus*), a public festival
in honor of a great military
deed. There were strict
rules governing triumphs.
A commander had to have
engaged in a major military
action that killed at least
six thousand of the enemy
and he needed to bring his
army home intact, signifying
that the victory had been
complete and the army could
now be disbanded.

The triumph would begin
with a procession through
Rome headed by the Senate,
prominent prisoners, the army
(disarmed and in togas, since
they were now within Rome
itself) and the triumphant
general—or *imperator*, as he
was called—who was painted
red and accompanied by a
slave who whispered in his ear
"Memento mori" ("Remember
that you are mortal").

Caesar was awarded a grand
triumph after his glorious
victory in Gaul. Pompey had won
one a few years earlier, after
his victories in Africa, although
he had to threaten the dictator
Sulla before he gave it to him.
In revenge, Sulla made sure
that he and another general
had their triumphs first, thus
detracting from Pompey's.

Caesar's arrest (and almost certain execution) but he fled into rural Italy and went into hiding. Thinking it expedient to remove him from the country, the Julii had Caesar sent to Asia Minor as a soldier. This was invaluable training for Caesar, who spent two years campaigning there, gaining a reputation as a tough and resourceful captain. When he returned to Rome after Sulla's death in 78, he became a sort of legal advocate for the masses: a young man, already balding, known for the high-pitched voice in which he delivered nonetheless passionate and inspiring speeches. He was extraordinarily confident. Traveling to Rhodes in 75 BC to study philosophy, he was captured by pirates who set his ransom at twenty talents. Caesar insisted they ask for fifty. Then, while still imprisoned, he told them he would return, find them, and have them crucified. And he did.

GNAEUS POMPEIUS MAGNUS
While Caesar was beginning his rise to prominence, his rival Pompey was already well established on the path to fame. Born in 106 BC, he was the son of Pompeius Strabo (*strabo* means "squinty"), the scion of a wealthy provincial family who had overcome his lack of ties to Rome's aristocracy to rise to the position of consul in 89 BC. Six years later, Pompey, at the age of only twenty-three, came to Sulla's aid, raising three legions of veterans who had served under his late father. He fought against Sulla's *populares* enemies in Italy, Sicily and North Africa, distinguishing himself to such an extent that Sulla dubbed him "Pompey the Great," although there may have been more than a dollop of sarcasm in this title, since the relationship of the two men was marred by mutual suspicion and jealousy. The two were, nonetheless, close and Sulla had persuaded Pompey to divorce his wife and marry Sulla's stepdaughter.

After Sulla's death, Pompey continued to wage war against the late tyrant's *populares* enemies, showing no mercy to those who opposed him—one of the young general's other nicknames was "The Butcher Boy." After fighting successfully against a *populares* army in Spain and offering belated help to Marcus Licinius Crassus as he put down the slave revolt of 73, Pompey, still only thirty-six, gathered his legions outside Rome, in contravention of Roman law, and thus forced the Senate to make him consul in the year 70. Crassus became his co-consul. However, Pompey surprised the Senate. After his year as consul, he took his place in the Senate and seemed to change his political orientation, lending his power to certain *popularis*-style reforms. These sought to undo some of the damage done by Sulla's dictatorship and provide land for the legionary soldiers who were clamoring for reward after their years of service.

THE FIRST TRIUMVIRATE
At this point, the paths of Caesar and Pompey crossed, initially in a way that might serve as model for any working relationship between two powerful men. Caesar, having returned from years as a successful military governor in Spain, was named consul in 59 BC. His co-consul was the weak and easily influenced Marcus Bibulus (the joke in Rome that year

was that there were indeed two consuls—one named *Julius*, the other *Caesar*). As he began his year in power, Caesar approached both Pompey and Marcus Licinius Crassus, the two most influential men in Rome, and formed a secret alliance that historians refer to as the First Triumvirate. Crassus, in return for Caesar's political support as consul, paid off Caesar's debts, while Caesar was only too happy to support Pompey's desire for land reform for his legionaries. Not only that, but Pompey married Caesar's daughter Julia, an arranged marriage that turned into a genuine love match.

While there was friction between Pompey and Crassus, and between Caesar and Crassus, the relationship between Caesar and Pompey was extraordinarily close. Caesar, with Pompey's patronage, secured the governorship of the important provinces of Cisalpine Gaul and Transalpine Gaul (essentially southern France) and in 58 went there to begin fighting his famous wars of conquest against the Gauls, wars that were to keep him out of Italy for eight years. These were Caesar's glory years. He conquered an area of western Europe about 300,000 square miles in size—the area of modern-day France, Belgium, Luxembourg, and Germany west of the Rhine—and twice invaded the (to the Romans) myth-enshrouded island of Great Britain. Vast wealth poured into the coffers of Rome—and into Caesar's personal accounts. Each winter, in northern Italy, Caesar would pen a volume of his famous *Commentarii de Bello Gallico* (*Commentaries on the Gallic War*) and send it to Rome to be published, thus increasing his reputation.

While this sort of glory enhanced Caesar's standing with the common people (and certainly among the soldiers he led) it made him powerful enemies among certain senators—Cato the Younger and the famous orator Cicero among them—who feared and envied him. In 57, Caesar made the mistake of backing a *popularis* demagogue named Publius Clodius, whose street mobs turned on Pompey. He, in turn, was forced to send out thugs to battle those of Clodius. (There was at this time no police force in Rome, so street battles between rival factions often resembled small but extremely bloody military engagements.) It is doubtful Caesar sanctioned this attack on his one-time friend, but Pompey was quite naturally offended. While Pompey and Caesar were temporarily reconciled and Caesar backed the consulship of Crassus and Pompey in 55, things went downhill. In 54, Caesar's daughter Julia died in childbirth, thus destroying another bond between the two men; two years later, Pompey married the daughter of one of Caesar's aristocratic opponents. The stage was now set for armed confrontation.

CROSSING THE RUBICON After the Gallic War ended in 50 BC, Caesar was faced with a hard decision. Once his governorship of Gaul came to an end and he crossed into Italy he would be forced by law to give up his army, but his success had gained him many enemies who might attempt to imprison or even assassinate him. Only Pompey might protect him—but Pompey was sending increasingly mixed signals. He was refusing to support Caesar against the Senate, which was trying to pass measures to strip Caesar of his power or prosecute him for certain irregularities that had occurred during his governorship. The measures did not pass, but Pompey—his brief flirtation with the *populares* over—sided with the *optimates* on political issues. Caesar now had the Sisyphean choice of either giving up his legions and returning to Rome, where he must depend on Pompey's patronage to protect him, or taking his army into Italy and starting a civil war.

On January 11, 49, Julius Caesar chose war. He crossed the Rubicon, a river that then marked Italy's northern boundary, and uttered the famous line *alea iacta est*—"the die is cast." Moving quickly with just one legion, he seized several towns in northern Italy. He was completely unopposed; in fact, the swiftness of his move had created panic in Rome, where it was felt that Caesar would become a dictator, like Sulla before him, and send out executioners to deal with his enemies. Pompey himself continued in indecision, for several possible reasons. He was fifty-seven years old, with many of his great military victories behind him, while Caesar, six years younger, was coming fresh, with battle-hardened legions, from a great victory. One senses that Pompey's heart was not quite in the conflict—that his former close relationship with a man who was once his father-in-law kept him from acting as decisively as he might otherwise have done. He even offered to leave for Spain with his legions if Caesar gave up his command, but by now Caesar did not trust him enough to agree to this.

By the end of January, Pompey had fled Rome, heading south, followed by most of the Senate. Pompey's plan was to cross the Adriatic to Greece, where he had numerous allies who could provide him with soldiers. This made good military sense, but politically it was an unwise move, as it appeared to most ordinary Romans that Pompey was simply abandoning them to their fate. Caesar, for his part, chased Pompey down the Italian peninsula, and very nearly stopped him at the southeastern town of Brundisium before Pompey slipped away with ships carrying thousands of soldiers and many of Rome's most prominent senators.

Without a fleet, Caesar could not follow, but in the space of two months he had conquered the entire country. Wisely, he chose to act humanely, offering clemency to those who had opposed him, even the senators who had so vilified him.

Then it was time to set about the business of destroying Pompey.

THE BLOODY CONFLICT In a surprise move typical of him, Caesar did not immediately pursue Pompey, but instead, in an amazing twenty-seven day march, brought his legions to Spain, where there were significant forces loyal to Pompey. He declared that he was going first to fight an army without a leader, and then to defeat a leader without an army. From April to August 49, he campaigned through Spain and, despite setbacks, defeated all Pompey's forces there, once again offering clemency to those who sought his forgiveness. His legions swollen with soldiers once loyal to Pompey, Caesar then turned east. He stopped in Rome

SPARTACUS THE SLAVE

In 73 BC—during the century of Rome's discontent—there occurred one of the most devastating episodes in Roman history. A slave rebellion, led by a former gladiator, seriously destabilized Rome and devastated much of Italy.

As the richer got richer in Italy at this time, they began to buy up much of the land that for generations had been farmed by families, families who were now often forced to sell their land-holdings because their menfolk were away fighting in foreign wars. When these men returned to find their land gone, they could not even get a job laboring for the new owners, because most of these wealthy people were now using slave labor.

The slaves were prisoners of war or men and women simply bought from the pirates and slave-traders who plied the coastline of Italy. Historians estimate that by 80 BC there were two million slaves in Italy (out of a total population of six million people).

One of these slaves was a gladiator named Spartacus. He was probably born about 120 BC in Thrace, northern Greece, and at some point was taken captive and forced to fight as an auxiliary in the Roman army. He then became a gladiator, one of the men who were forced to fight each other to the death in order to provide entertainment for the Roman masses.

In 73, armed with kitchen knives, Spartacus and about seventy gladiators escaped from gladiator school and fled to the heavily wooded slopes of Mount Vesuvius (then dormant). Slaves from all over the countryside flocked to join them and, trained by the gladiators, they fought several successful battles against the increasingly large Roman forces sent against them.

Spartacus's goal was to head north, out of Italy and into Gaul, and he nearly made it. In 72 he destroyed two Roman legions in northern Italy and sent perhaps ten thousand of his women and children successfully across the Alps. But then he turned back to fight the Romans, destroying another army under future consul Licinius Crassus and fighting all the way back down to the toe of Italy, where he may have made a deal with pirates to transport him and his followers across the Strait of Messina. The pirates never materialized, and finally both Crassus and Pompey arrived with numerous legions and defeated Spartacus in an epic pitched battle near the Silarus River. Spartacus was killed, though his body was never found. Thousands of slaves were crucified on the Via Appia, the main Roman road from the south to the capital city. Their bodies hung there for years, a macabre warning to any other slave who might try the might of Rome.

RIGHT The story of Spartacus and his doomed rebellion has resonated through the centuries. This idealized image of the former gladiator is by Dennis Foyatier (1793–1863).

ET TU, BRUTUS?

This famous phrase, directed by a dying Caesar at the man who had just stabbed him, was not said in real life. It was invented by Shakespeare for his play *Julius Caesar*, but its message of stunned betrayal has resonated down through the ages.

Marcus Junius Brutus, forty-three at the time of Caesar's assassination, was the son of Sevilia, Caesar's longtime and much-favored mistress. Caesar treated the young nobleman with great favor. Even though Brutus had sided with Pompey in the civil war, Caesar had forgiven him, even going so far as to make Brutus governor of Gaul and, in 45 BC, nominating him to be a praetor, a kind of magistrate.

Brutus, who considered himself a patriot of the republic and a student of philosophy, felt that Caesar was trying to establish a dictatorship in Rome and that he, Brutus, was engaging in justifiable tyrannicide. But Caesar's popularity was so great that the aristocratic assassin and his friends became hunted criminals. Eventually, Brutus was defeated by Mark Antony at the second battle of Philippi in 42 BC. Hiding in the hills immediately after the battle, he committed suicide, his dream of a preserved Roman republic forever shattered.

in late 49 and had himself appointed dictator, although he held the post for only eleven days before resigning, having engineered it so that he would be elected consul. Assembling his legions at Brundisium in January of 48, he made a surprise winter crossing and was able to get much of his fleet across to Greece, although Pompey's far larger navy (commanded by Caesar's old co-consul Bibulus) was able to stop the transports on their return voyage to pick up Mark Antony, Caesar's chief lieutenant, and his troops.

Caesar now faced a rival who had had nine months to prepare for this moment and who had amassed nine legions (a legion had a paper strength of five thousand men), as well as five thousand light infantry and seven thousand cavalry. Caesar had perhaps half this number of men and was short of supplies, while Pompey, ever the organizer, had amply supplied his men. But Caesar had one great advantage: he knew Pompey's mind. Pompey, Caesar realized from all their political and personal dealings, was intelligent but cautious, and would move slowly against him. Thus Caesar spent much of his time maneuvering to avoid Pompey's men, although his legionaries slowly starved, eating bread made from a local root called *charax*. When Pompey's men captured some of this fare, they brought it to their leader who exclaimed, in typical aristocratic fashion, that Caesar's men must be more beasts than soldiers.

Still, these beasts managed to survive until April when Mark Antony made it across with the rest of the legions. In July, at the battle of Dyrrhachium, the forces of the two leaders lined up at last. It was Roman legion against Roman legion, both sides commanded by officers who had formerly fought together and were now bitter enemies. The legionaries on both sides were armed with their famous *gladius*, or short sword, and their *pilum*, a wooden javelin with a two-foot-long iron tip that was usually thrown from a distance of only fifteen yards and could pierce any shield and hole a man.

Then two of Caesar's Gallic chieftains, in charge of auxiliary forces, defected to Pompey, giving him essential information about Caesar's positions. Pompey launched an attack against Caesar's fortified works. Caesar and Mark Antony repulsed it and even launched a counterattack, but this was defeated by Pompey's men, whose fierce opposition engendered a rare sight: Caesar's troops fleeing in panic.

Caesar personally tried to stop the rout, attempting to rally the standard-bearers whose job it was to rally the men to them, but it was useless. Pompey had won a great victory, killing a thousand of Caesar's men. Only ... it was as if he could not believe his eyes. He did not follow up his victory with an assault on Caesar's camp, thus allowing the Roman commander to live to fight another day. As Caesar later said, all would certainly have been lost, that day at Dyrrhachium, had Pompey only known how to win.

PHARSALUS Given the chance to regroup, Caesar withdrew into the province of Thessaly, his men finally able to feed themselves properly on the ripening harvest. Pompey followed them, preferring, in typical fashion, to follow a Roman strategy generally called "kicking the enemy in the belly"—avoiding battle while attempting to cut the opposing army's supply lines. This might eventually have been successful—or Pompey could have simply turned and headed back to Italy, since he was now between Caesar and home—but many of the *optimates* senators with him urged him to make a fight of it *now*, to end this war and destroy Caesar.

And so, on the morning of August 9, 48, he brought his army out onto a plain near the River Enipus, not far from the town of Pharsalus. Both sides knew that this would be the ultimate battle to decide the fate of the republic. Caesar gave his men the password "Venus, Bringer of Victory," while Pompey's men used the equally stirring phrase "Hercules, Unconquered."

The battle began when Pompey's cavalry, superior in numbers to Caesar's though less experienced, swept into the side of Caesar's lines. But Caesar, who had kept a line of infantry in reserve for just such an attack, sent these men forward. They charged, using their *pila* as thrusting spears rather than javelins, and routed the cavalry, sending them fleeing to the rear.

Now the main lines of infantry clashed, with Caesar's better-trained men advancing first at a walk and then a dead run, before throwing their *pila*, which they did from the devastating distance of only fifty feet. Pompey's men returned fire, but the fearsome deluge of spears had taken its toll, with the first line of Pompeians now lying groaning on the ground, spears quivering in their bodies. Pompey's second line fought fiercely for a time, until Caesar threw more and more men into the battle, gradually pushing back the enemy until the tipping point was reached and Pompey's legions began to flee, pursued by Caesar's gleeful forces.

Caesar sent word that all of Pompey's men who wished to surrender should be allowed to do so. Among those who threw down their swords was Marcus Junius Brutus—the son of Caesar's mistress Servilia—whom Caesar welcomed with open arms. As for Pompey ... well, he threw off his scarlet general's cloak and headed immediately for the coast with a small bodyguard, to set sail for Egypt. His family was with him. He was tired and worn-down, and had shown little fighting spirit at Pharsalus. As he fled, Caesar celebrated a great victory, having taken twenty-four thousand Pompeian prisoners and with fifteen thousand enemy dead, compared to the loss of perhaps two hundred of his own men.

THE END OF POMPEY In September of 48, Pompey's ship floated at anchor offshore from the city of Alexandria, waiting word from King Ptolemy XIII (who ruled Egypt jointly with his sister Cleopatra). The king and his advisors were frightened to allow Pompey into Egypt, fearful that the pursuing Caesar would wreak his vengeance on anyone who dared help the fallen Roman commander. And so the Egyptians decided on another tack. Why not murder Pompey, and thus curry favor with Caesar?

On September 28—as it happened, Pompey's fifty-eight birthday—Pompey was asked to come ashore in a small boat for an audience with the king. When he landed, he recognized two former Roman soldiers who had been comrades of his, Achillas and Lucius Septimius. He greeted them cordially and went on studying the speech he was to give to the Egyptian king. The two men closed on him with smiles and then thrust their swords into his back. Pushing his body out of the boat, they decapitated him and left his body to float in the shallow water, until his servant arranged for him to be burned on the beach.

When Pompey's family, on board ship, saw what had happened, they set sail and fled. Caesar arrived a short time later and was given Pompey's head and signet ring in an ornate basket—a gift the Egyptians thought would be quite welcome to the great commander. Instead, he turned away and burst into tears. This was not the end he had imagined for his rival. In revenge, he deposed the young king

BELOW Caesar defeated his rival Pompey only to be murdered because he had too much power. Here his body is displayed outside the Senate in Rome (painting by Guillaume Lethière, c. 1780–1832).

Ptolemy, executed his advisors, and installed Cleopatra—who eventually became Caesar's lover—as queen.

CAESAR—DICTATOR OR LIBERATOR? Caesar and Rome were stained with blood, but by 46 BC—after fighting Pompeian forces in Egypt, Africa, and Asia Minor—Caesar returned in triumph to Rome. The long civil war was over, it seemed. Caesar was made dictator, but an enormously popular one among the rank and file of Rome. He distributed land to some eighty thousand Roman civilians, making a point of giving farmland to those citizens who had three or more children. He also energetically set about doing public works—building aqueducts, draining swamps—that improved the lives of thousands.

For this he was loved by the common people but hated by the *optimates*. These men, many from the most ancient families of Rome, saw Caesar's reforms as cynical ploys to win over the masses so that he could gain more power for himself. Some of them, led by Marcus Brutus and Gaius Cassius Longinus, formed a secret group called "the Liberators." The more Caesar was awarded public honors—on February 15, 44 BC, his dictatorship was extended for life—the more they seethed, until they decided that the only course open to them was killing him. (Under Roman law, the assassination of a tyrant was not a crime.)

On March 15—the Ides of March, as it was called—the plotters anxiously awaited Caesar in the Roman Senate. In a few days, he was to leave the city to put down a rebellion in Asia Minor, and he might be gone for some time. The dictator entered the Senate quickly, in the mood to take care of details before his departure, a stylus in his hand. The Senate stood as one when he crossed the floor and sat down on his chair, the purple robe of the dictator around his shoulders.

The conspirators clustered around him, distracting him with talk of clemency for a former Pompeian still on the run. They gave Caesar a petition to read, but he waved it away—he had more important matters to discuss. Then, suddenly, a conspirator named Tillius Cimber tore the purple robes from Caesar's shoulder while another nervously attempted to stab him from behind, but only grazed him. Caesar reacted by jabbing at the man with his stylus, but then the conspirators were on him, knives lashing out, stabbing and slashing. The trapped Caesar could only twist in fear and rage until finally, wrapping his toga around his head, he sank to the ground unconscious. His body, ravaged by twenty-three stab wounds, lay directly at the foot of a statue of Pompey.

Ironic, but not the final irony. For, in assassinating this man they thought was a dictator, Brutus and his fellow conspirators had in fact sounded the death knell of the Roman Republic they so revered. As a direct result of Caesar's death, Imperial Rome—with Caesar's adopted nephew Octavian as emperor—would begin its five-hundred-year existence.

UBI HAROLD : SACRA

VVILLEL

WILLIAM THE CONQUEROR

ENTVM:FECIT:⁊ HICh

DVCI:⁊

WILLIAM THE CONQUEROR AND KING HAROLD GODWINESON: ONLY ONE KING SHALL RULE

I N MARCH OF 1066, MEN AND WOMEN ALL OVER ENGLAND ran from their homes, eyes turned to the night sky. There, above them, was a speeding comet, its long, blazing tail shooting behind it, so close that it shone as large as the moon. A beautiful sight—in fact, it was the comet we now know as Halley's Comet—yet the Anglo-Saxon population of England looked on it with horror, as a dreadful portent. A Benedictine monk named Eilmer of Malmesbury sat down to his quill and parchment and scribbled furiously, seemingly unable to contain himself:

> You've come, have you? You've come, you source of tears to many mothers. It is long since I saw you, but as I see you now you are much more terrible, for I see you brandishing the downfall of my country.

Eilmer was seventy-six years old, which means he must have been only five the last time Halley had passed by, in AD 990. Now he feared that the terrible power of the comet signaled the end of Saxon England at the hands of one man: William of Normandy, sometimes known as William the Bastard.

Another Anglo-Saxon watching the comet was the new king of England, Harold Godwineson, who had been crowned on January 6, the same day his predecessor, King Edward the Confessor, was interred in Westminster Abbey. Harold—tall, handsome, a fierce warrior, but as pious and superstitious as any English peasant—may have cringed inwardly when he saw the comet speeding through the heavens as if hurled by a vengeful god. He knew William the Bastard considered the throne that he, Harold, sat on to be his own—in fact, Harold himself may have promised him that throne. And Harold knew that soon, quite soon, William would be coming to lay claim to it. Now was no time to worry about portents—now was the time to raise an army and defend England.

BEFORE 1066 The appearance of Halley's Comet in 1066 signaled a year of extraordinary change in the history of England, a time when two cultures would collide, eventually to form one society that would contain the seeds of present-day Great Britain and, in fact, the laws and language of the entire English-speaking world. Yet the situation in England before the arrival of the comet in the night sky was already a chaotic one.

Centuries after the Roman occupation of Britain, the Celtic population had faced an influx of invading Germanic tribes—the Angles, Saxons, and Jutes—who occupied much of the southeastern part of the country. Then, in the late 700s, the Vikings began raiding the British Isles, and within two hundred years or so had destroyed a good deal of the old culture of Ireland and Scotland and settled in large areas of England.

In 1012, the ferocious Danish King Sven I, nicknamed Forkbeard, enraged by the massacre of Danish inhabitants of England by the Anglo-Saxon King Ethelred the Unready, invaded the country and forced Ethelred to flee to Normandy. Sven died in 1014; his son, Cnut, established a northern empire that included Denmark, Norway, and England.

Had Cnut and his successors been able to hold onto this empire, English (and European) history might have been very different indeed. However, internal tensions, as well as the opposition of certain English Anglo-Saxon barons, caused it to fall apart, and in 1042 England reverted to Anglo-Saxon rule under Edward the Confessor, son of Ethelred the Unready and his wife, the Norman-born Emma.

THE NORMAN CONNECTION There was a major problem with Edward as far as many Anglo-Saxon lords were concerned: he had grown up in exile, away from the Danes, in Normandy, and thus had Norman habits and Norman advisors, as well as a Norman mother. The Anglo-Saxon lords—chief among them Godwine, Earl of Essex, and his twenty-year-old son Harold Godwineson—did not want any more foreign influence on the throne of England. They had endured decades of suffering under Danish rule, and now resented the influential Normans.

Fierce warriors descended from the Vikings, the Normanni, or Northmen, had been granted the land that would become Normandy in 911 by the French King Charles the Simple, who hoped this would keep these aggressive people away from the heartland of France. In Normandy they thrived, developing a warrior society and roaming the world over—at one point, Norman adventurers took control of Sicily.

Ethelred's wife, Emma, was one of these Normans and, it just so happened, the great-aunt of one William of Normandy, born in 1028 and just a teenager when Edward the Confessor took the throne.

WILLIAM THE BASTARD

He may be known to all of us as William the Conqueror, but until 1066 William of Normandy was known by the far humbler name of William the Bastard. He was the son of a capricious but brave Norman knight known variously as Robert the Magnificent and Robert the Cruel (he displayed both traits), who inherited the dukedom of Normandy after having his brother Richard killed. When Robert died of natural causes on a pilgrimage to Jerusalem to atone for his sins, he left young William, whose mother was probably a tanner's daughter, as his sole heir, to be raised by regents.

Duke William's childhood and young adulthood were tumultuous as he fought off pretenders to the throne and honed his skills as a knight. He was, one historian has written, "an admirable and soldierly figure on horseback, skilled in the use of lance and sword." At one point, a plot to kill William was foiled at the last minute by his "fool," or court jester, who snuck into the duke's room and woke him, enabling him to flee on horseback through the countryside.

By 1050, having survived numerous bloody battles with rival barons and their knights (all in chain mail, carrying swords and lances, and mounted on horseback), William was undisputed Duke of Normandy. He had married and was gloriously happy with Mathilda, the woman by whom he would have four sons and four (perhaps five) daughters.

He was a pious man who kept good relations with the Catholic Church—something that would stand him in good stead in the future—and loved to entertain in his castle at Rouen, holding court in the rectangular, colonnaded Great Hall, hosting hordes of nobles, knights and their ladies, priests, jesters, and musicians.

Then, in 1052, something momentous happened. William visited England to pay his respects to King Edward the Confessor. A contemporary English chronicler wrote: "William Earl came from beyond the sea with [a] company of Frenchmen and the King received him, and as many of his comrades as to him seemed good, and let him go again." During this visit, according to William, the childless Edward promised him—the grandnephew of Edward's mother, Emma—the crown of England.

At least, this is what William and the Normans said.

In 1064, the tables were turned and William had a visitor from England, one who was literally storm-tossed onto his shores. It was a strange stroke of fate that brought Harold Godwineson to William's land—but what happened (or did not happen) in Normandy that autumn of 1064 precipitated a great change in the world as it then was.

HAROLD GODWINESON In 1064, Harold Godwineson, Earl of Essex, a good-looking man with a prominent blond moustache and shaggy, shoulder-length hair, was thirty-two years old and a veteran of much internecine fighting in England. In the early 1050s his father, Godwine, had led a band of barons against King Edward the Confessor in a civil war in which he killed Edward's brother Alfred. Exiled for a time (including the period when William visited England), Godwine and his son Harold returned and were able to force Edward to oust his Norman advisors and cede a good deal of power to Godwine. When Godwine died in 1053, his estates and title went to his son Harold, with Harold's brother Tostig becoming Earl of Northumbria, in the north. Somewhat surprisingly, Harold was able to forge a good relationship with King Edward. He mainly accomplished this by a brilliant campaign against the rebellious Welsh in 1063, a campaign that ended with his sending the head of the Welsh leader, as well as the figurehead of the man's ship, to King Edward.

Edward by this time was falling into decline both mentally and physically, spending much of this time obsessed with religious matters and building a huge abbey in honor of St. Peter. According to Harold Godwineson, King Edward became so reconciled to him that he promised him the English throne upon his death.

HAROLD SHIPWRECKED IN NORMANDY In the September of 1064, Harold boarded a ship with numerous thegns, or royal retainers, and set sail on the English Channel. Why he did this is still being argued by historians. Some say he was on a diplomatic mission of some sort to the Continent—although he did not bring with him the usual large retinue of followers that such a mission usually called for. Other historians point out that contemporary chroniclers have Harold boarding ship in a gay mood, carrying a hunting falcon attached to his wrist and followed by friends with hunting dogs. It is possible they were headed for Flanders, to a friendly court ruled by a brother-in-law of Harold's brother Tostig.

In any event, his retinue sailed in two ships—Viking longships, with a single, multicolored sail, narrow in the stern and prow. A ferocious storm blew up and tossed Harold's ship off course, to run aground on the French coast near Abbeville, in the territory owned by the French Count Guy de Ponthieu. Under Guy's rather draconian law, any shipwrecked traveler was his to hold and ransom, and thus he seized Harold and his friends, took away their swords and, according to at least one account, placed the future king of England in manacles in his dungeon.

When Duke William heard of this, he sent two of his men to Guy's castle to demand Harold's freedom—and Guy, fearing William's power, was forced to acquiesce. With a large retinue of French knights, he personally escorted Harold and his friends to William, who himself had set out with members of his court to meet the English Earl.

This momentous meeting occurred in open countryside, as the two companies of men came upon each other on the main road leading to Normandy. Guy rode forward, turning in his saddle to point out Harold to William. The two rivals and pretenders to the English throne then met for the first time—the tall, slender, mustachioed Harold and the even taller, but solid and square, dark-haired William, who was clean-shaven in the Norman style. Taking Harold to his palace in Rouen, William showered him with kindness and courtesy, in what one historian has aptly called "a political seduction."

William entertained Harold with tourneys and exhibitions of arms, and, despite Harold's impatience to return to England, even convinced him to go on campaign with him, against the rebellious province of Brittany. There, Harold acquitted himself admirably on the field of battle, but no doubt must have had mixed emotions—risking his life for the man who was a rival to the same throne that he claimed.

What followed was even more extraordinary. According to Norman sources, including the Bayeux Tapestry (see pages 50–51), after the hostilities were over Harold swore fealty to William in a ceremony attended by Norman noblemen. Not only that, but—once again, according to Norman sources—he had already in private accepted the superiority of William's claim to the English throne and agreed to give his sister to one of William's barons in marriage. In return, Harold would marry William's daughter Adelisa.

Although no one will ever know for sure, it seems likely that Harold, finding himself a hostage in a strange land—for no matter how kindly he was treated, that is indeed what he was—had decided to go along with this ceremony to secure his release. A few days later he was sailing back to England, but onlookers could see that he was deeply troubled. Even though he may have been forced to give his oath, he had indeed given it—and in medieval times one's word was one's bond. As one French chronicler wrote of Harold:

The Englishman was very tall and handsome, remarkable for his physical strength, his courage and eloquence, his ready jest and acts of valor. But what were these gifts to him without honor, which is the root of all good?

1066 And so we return to the fateful year of 1066. On his deathbed, despite whatever promises he may have made to William, Edward did give his kingdom to Harold, who was anointed king on January 6th. William's spies in England were watching, of course, and William heard about the coronation only three days later, the news traveling across the Channel on a fast ship and then by horseback to Rouen. In accounts written later, William, on hearing the news, paced a park near his castle, his features contorted by anger. His first response was to send Harold a series of communications—the first one arriving perhaps ten days after the English king's coronation—accusing him of perjury in going back on his oath and demanding that he give up the crown.

HARALD HARDRAADE: THE LAST VIKING

One of the most fascinating characters in the whole drama of the year 1066 was Harald Hardraade—the name means "Hard-Ruler"—King of the Norwegians. He was convinced by Harold Godwineson's brother Tostig to join him in a bid to oust Harold from the throne of England.

Hardraade was born in 1015, third in line to the Norwegian throne then held by King Olaf. When Olaf was killed by King Cnut of Denmark during his invasion of Norway, fifteen-year-old Harald, already a seasoned warrior, fled with a band of Vikings. He made his way to the land of the Rus (the Russians), where he and his men fought in the service of the Russian king. After several years of this, Harald—always restless— took his men and headed for Constantinople, capital of the Byzantine Empire, where he joined an elite mercenary unit in the employ of the Byzantine emperor. There he enriched himself, and his reputation as a warrior grew—supposedly, he single-handedly killed one hundred men. He and his small army even invaded Palestine and conquered the city of Jerusalem, which Harald, a devout Christian, wished to open to Christian pilgrims. Hardraade was physically prepossessing. One historian has described him as "a gigantic and glittering figure" (he may have been six and a half feet tall) with long, flowing blond locks, who wielded a great sword that it took two ordinary men to lift. Wherever he fought, he unfurled a huge banner with a picture of a raven on it. Known as the Land-Waster, it was a feared sign of the presence of this man, who was a throwback to the Vikings of the old swashbuckling days.

By 1045, at the age of thirty, he had made his way back to Norway and seized the throne, killing Magnus I, his nephew, who was then ruler of both Denmark and Norway. For twenty years, Hardraade ruled these countries, claiming, however, that the throne of England should also be his, because the Danish King Cnut had once conquered England and ruled jointly over England, Denmark and Norway. When Tostig approached him, Hardraade, citing this extremely tenuous connection, agreed to throw in his lot with the Anglo-Saxon and invade England.

Now aged fifty-one, Hardraade was so sure of victory in England that he even took his wife and daughters with him, but he was killed underneath the Land-Waster by an arrow in the throat, before the fighting at Stamford Bridge had even fairly begun. Still, Harald Hardraade's efforts to take the throne of England had a serious effect on Harold Godwineson's ability to defend himself against William the Conqueror.

BELOW Less than three weeks before the battle of Hastings, Harold Godwineson quelled an uprising in the north of England at the battle of Stamford Bridge. Here he finds the bodies of his rebellious brother Tostig and Harald Hardraade.

Harold's replies to these missives were unsatisfactory from William's point of view, but he did not really expect Harold to hand over the throne. He was, if you will, setting up a paper trail, so that he would appear to be an aggrieved party doing everything possible before resorting to force of arms. This was especially important because William's next appeal was to Pope Alexander II, and here William's generosity to the church in the past played a large part in the pope's decision to side with him. Also, the English church had been notoriously independent of Rome and slow in paying its tithes, and the main reason the pope authorized William to invade England was to bring these fractious Anglo-Saxon clergymen back into line. William immediately set about gathering an army and building a massive fleet.

In the meantime, Harold did the same, even as Halley's Comet hurled itself across the sky. But he had other troubles besides William. His brother Tostig had rebelled against him and was joining forces with Harald Hardraade, King of Norway, an epic figure of the era who had a very tenuous claim to the English throne. Throughout that spring and summer of 1066, messengers from the English king rode throughout the countryside, gathering support from his thegns, the landed gentry who had sworn loyalty to him, and housecarls, his large personal retinue of nobility who would form the heart of his army. Each of the thegns brought with them peasant retainers known as liens, more lightly armed than the rest of the army and perhaps less reliable in battle.

William's Norman force was somewhat different, featuring cavalry—the Anglo-Saxon army was mainly foot soldiers—who had a fearsome reputation throughout Europe. These armed nobles, wearing knee-length chain mail shirts, or hauberks, as well as metal leggings, inspired fear in any army they faced. Accompanying them were infantrymen armed with spears and the archers who would play such a pivotal role in the battle of Hastings. (The English army, not yet known for its longbowmen, had few, if any, archers.)

William's massive preparations took a long time, and he did not set sail across the English Channel until September 27, on a brilliantly sunlit morning. His ships filled the waters off Normandy. William did not know that two days before, King Harold had won an extraordinary victory at the battle of Stamford Bridge in York. There, he faced an army led by Harald Hardraade and his own brother Tostig and, in a ferocious clash, killed both men, as well as thousands of their army.

It was a great feat of arms, but King Harold lost many of his finest men and barely had time to enjoy his victory. For, while still in York, he heard the news— probably around October 1—that William and his force had landed on the south coast of England, at Pevensey Bay, near Hastings. Harold immediately retraced his steps from the north, reaching London—a distance of some hundred and ninety miles—in only four or five days. There, he gathered his exhausted force about him, attempted to levy new men, and then marched south to the coast through the then thick Forest of Weald, which covered that area of England.

His army emerged from the woods on October 13 and took positions along the hill of Senlac, astride the road leading from Hastings to London. This was the route William must take to the English capital, and here Harold intended to stop his rival, once and for all.

THE GREAT BATTLE Harold, intimately familiar with the land, had chosen his position well. Arriving from Hastings in the misty early morning of October 14, William looked up at the hill to see the fearsome shield wall of the English army awaiting him. Harold's housecarls, as well as those of his loyal brothers Gyrth and Leofwine, stood behind their shields, forming a barrier as impenetrable as an ancient Greek phalanx. Each of them carried a fearsome two-bladed fighting ax. Used in the old Danish style of fighting, these swinging axes (the Bayeux Tapestry depicts this) could easily decapitate a horse, let alone a man. Standing firmly planted on the ground, the Anglo-Saxon fighters could not be easily overcome. This was their land. William was the invader. Let him come, and see what he might get.

Surrounded by his housecarls, Harold raised his standard, the Fighting Man, a warrior depicted on a large cloth of gold embroidered with precious stones. His forces numbered perhaps seven thousand men altogether. As the Normans appeared, Harold's men began banging their fists on their shields and crying *Ut! Ut!* (meaning, "Out, get out, you foreigners").

William's force, numbering roughly the same as Harold's, stared up the hill at the formidable shield wall. There was little option but to attack. William was on foreign ground, far from supplies, and time was not on his side. But there is the sense that he and his warriors thought that God was, indeed, on their side, that, since they were fighting a man who they considered had broken a great and holy oath, they would certainly prevail.

One man who was imbued with this spirit was an extraordinary poet of the Norman court, a man named Ivon Taillefer (Cleave-Iron). Seeking and receiving permission from William to strike the first blow against the English, he rode up the hill towards their lines, tossing his sword in the air and singing a song about the exploits of Roland and Charlemagne, which was then popular in France but had not yet been exported to England. It is hard to imagine what the hardened English warriors must have thought of this strange apparition—until he charged straight into their lines and killed an Englishman with one thrust from his sword. He was immediately struck down, hacked to death with axes, but the Normans had indeed struck the first blow.

The hillside then exploded with the cries of men on both sides and the sound of warlike trumpets. William ordered his archers to unleash a hail of arrows, which they did, but the English protected themselves with their huge, kite-shaped leather shields. The Norman duke then sent his heavy infantry up the hill and a fierce clash ensued, with the English housecarls swinging their axes to deadly effect,

THE BAYEUX TAPESTRY

Much of what we know about the year 1066 and the rivalry between William the Conqueror and King Harold Godwineson we know from an extraordinary tapestry that now resides in Bayeux, France, in the William the Conqueror Center, a repository of artifacts and information on Norman life.

The tapestry, some 230 feet long by 20 inches high, was commissioned by William the Conqueror's half-brother Odo, Bishop of Bayeux, in the 1070s and is essentially the entire story of the rivalry between William and Harold told in a series of embroidered linen panels, which were then stitched together. The tapestry begins all the way back with Edward the Confessor still king, moves on to capture Harold's fateful voyage to France, where he is captured, fights for William, and swears an oath (in the tapestry, the nature of this oath is not clear, but it is almost certainly the pledge William claimed Harold made to give him the throne of England).

The tapestry then moves on to show the coronation of Harold, the dread appearance of Halley's Comet, William's preparations for invasion, and the battle of Hastings itself—ending with Harold receiving an arrow in the eye and the Anglo-Saxons fleeing. There may have been a further panel, now lost, which showed William the Conqueror's coronation as King of England.

This is history as told from the victor's point of view, and so cannot be trusted to be a completely unbiased portrait of the tumultuous year of 1066, but historians love the tapestry for its peek into everyday life at the time. For instance, it shows in great detail how, after William landed in England, a meal was prepared by his men, supervised by a knight named Wadard. A calf is killed and a large joint of meat is placed on a roasting spit, which is in turn lowered onto two forked sticks and turned slowly over a fire. The meat is then served to William and his general staff, who can be identified by their physical features. All in all, the Bayeux Tapestry is a work of art, as well as narrative history.

while the more lightly armed thegns and liens hurled spears and even stones from slings. The Normans were driven back. William then poured in his cavalry, who urged their horses up the hill crying *Diex aie!* ("God aid!") the Norman war cry. But the English hurled them back too, shrieking shouts of victory.

With seemingly the whole left flank of the Norman army in retreat, some of the English fighters joyously broke their shield wall and chased after them down the slopes of the hill. It was around this time that Duke William was reported killed, further panicking the retreating Normans. But now, in a pivotal point of the battle, William himself rode to the forefront of the Norman lines, wrenched off his helmet, and yelled: "Look at me, all of you. I still live and with God's help I will conquer. What folly has driven you to flight?"

He led the Norman horse back up the hill. The English infantry who had chased the Normans down the hill were now easy prey for the cavalry—away from the protection of their shield wall, they were cut down and trampled. Perhaps a thousand Anglo-Saxons died here, but when the Normans, led by William, again attacked the English shield wall rallying around Harold at the top of the hill, they were again driven back in fierce fighting. While Harold and William did not meet in combat, Harold's brother Gyrth fought hand-to-hand with William, even killing the duke's horse (William had three steeds die under him that day) before being killed by one of William's retainers. (Leofwine, Harold's other brother, was also killed that day.)

The day wore on with repeated Norman charges. Having seen how staging a retreat could draw the English infantry to give chase, William ordered his men to retreat on two occasions. Each time, when the battle-maddened English pursued the "fleeing" men, the Norman cavalry turned and cut them to pieces, and then renewed their attacks on the English shield wall.

Monks who were watching the battle from a nearby hill (although not all Anglo-Saxon monks watched—some donned armor over their cassocks and rode to aid Harold) later reported that the English shield wall was growing ever smaller around the pennant of the Fighting Man; indeed, it appeared to be packed so tight that the dead had no place to fall and so stood, crushed in among the living, fighting warriors.

A FINAL SHOWER OF ARROWS
As day faded to early evening, the embattled and exhausted English circle grew ever smaller, but still the shield wall stood, blocking the Norman way. William then ordered his archers to aim a shower of arrows high into the air, so that they dropped down upon the heads of the Anglo-Saxon fighters. The arrows must have looked like so many birds winging across the faint light of the autumn sky, but they reached their mark and more Englishmen fell, at last opening up gaps in the shield wall.

Chief among the English fighters to be hit by the arrows was King Harold, who is famously depicted in the Bayeux Tapestry as being struck in the eye. Even then he continued to fight, blood spurting from his face, surrounded by his housecarls, until four Norman knights broke through and killed him with their swords. One of them cut off his leg—an unchivalrous act that William punished by expelling the man from his army.

With their king dead, the rest of the English army fell apart. Fleeing down the opposite side of the hill, they lost themselves in the forests, pursued through the darkness by the Norman cavalry—who, however, became prey themselves in this unfamiliar territory and were often jumped and stabbed to death by vengeful English peasants. Still, the field belonged to William, and as night fell he was the master of England. The English had lost their king and almost all their leading warriors. Harold's body lay unrecognized among the hundreds of English dead, until his mother, Princess Gytha, and his mistress, Edith Swan-neck, she of fabled beauty, came to the battlefield in search of it. Edith finally recognized Harold's body by secret marks only she knew, but William refused to allow them to take the corpse and bury it—for he claimed that Harold, as a perjurer, did not merit a Christian burial. Perhaps he believed this, or perhaps he wanted to make sure that Harold, now the last Anglo-Saxon king of Britain, would not be honored in a grand burial ceremony that might stir up the English masses. Instead, he had Harold's body buried under a cairn of rocks at Hastings. Later, when he felt more secure in his kingship, William would move the king's corpse to another, grander resting place.

Now, though, his rival vanquished, William stood in sole possession of England: he would be crowned king on Christmas Day, 1066.

On the crest of the hill where Harold fell, William erected Battle Abbey, to thank God for vanquishing the man who had failed to keep his oath.

KING HENRY I

KING HENRY II AND THOMAS BECKET: "WILL NO ONE RID ME OF THIS TURBULENT PRIEST?"

I T WAS DECEMBER 29, 1170, WITH ENGLAND'S EARLY winter dusk setting in. Canterbury Cathedral was cold and dark, lit only by a few flickering candles. In ones and twos, townspeople entered the church for vespers, but thoughts of God or the Christmas season were quickly driven away by the clamor of a crowd of monks gathered around a figure girded in white vestments in the central area of the cathedral. The monks were speaking urgently to the man, and seemed to be dragging him along towards the altar. Then there came the unmistakable clatter of armored men running on a stone floor. Those arriving for vespers, squinting from the rear of the cathedral, could barely make out the knights as they entered a side door of the cathedral, but they could hear the ringing shout:

"Where is Thomas Becket, traitor to the king and realm?"

There was silence in response to this, and then another knight cried out:

"Where is the archbishop?"

And to this there was a reply:

"A priest as well as archbishop. If you seek me, you will find me here."

Having spoken these words, Thomas Becket began to walk through the darkness to his fate. In a few seconds he would become England's most famous martyr, his very blood worshipped for the miracles it could bring. And on the other side of the English Channel, a king waited anxiously to discover the fate of the man whom he loved—and hated—above all.

BECKET Thomas Becket was born in London on December 21, 1118, the feast date of the apostle for whom he was named. Despite attempts by nineteenth century historians to paint Becket as being from a downtrodden Saxon family (hence his eventual rebellion against the Norman rulers of the land), his father, Gilbert, was a well-to-do Norman merchant who had served as sheriff of London. His mother—variously known as Roesa (Rose) or Matilda—was also Norman, from Caen originally, despite a legend that arose after Becket's death that she was a Saracen maiden who had met Gilbert while he was on Crusade and later converted to Christianity and married him.

Becket grew up in a lively upper-class London household with three sisters. He was sent at a young age to a preparatory school in Surrey, where he learned Latin and Greek, studying classic writers such as Cicero, Ovid, Virgil, and Plato. At the age of thirteen—when, according to an admiring early biographer, "the sweetness of God's grace was clearly seen in him"—he was sent to St. Paul's School in London, where he met a young nobleman, perhaps a few years older, named Richer de L'Aigle, who later became a member of King Henry II's court. Richer taught Thomas how to hunt with hawks and hounds, a skill of the aristocracy at which Thomas later excelled.

Already, Becket's life was marked by the dichotomy that would later become so notable: he was a fine scholar with a religious turn of mind who, nonetheless, possessed an almost fatal attraction to the finer things of medieval life.

HENRY Henry II—the man who would, for a time, fulfill both aspects of Thomas Becket's personality—was born in France on March 5, 1133, the son of Geoffrey Plantagenet, heir to the Norman provinces of Anjou and Maine, and Empress Matilda, daughter of King Henry I of England and widow of the Holy Roman Emperor. Henry I was the third son of William the Conqueror. He became king of England in 1100 and reigned until the year of Henry FitzEmpress's birth. Henry I had brought order to the land of England, troubled since the Norman invasion, but on his death there were stirrings of discontent. A prolonged war was fought for the English throne between Count Stephen of Blois, a nephew of Henry I—who, despite an oath sworn to the king, refused to acknowledge Matilda as heir to the throne—and the forces loyal to Matilda.

The seesaw battle ended in 1153. By then, Henry—a precocious and turbulent twenty-year-old—had won the hand of Eleanor of Aquitaine in marriage, thus joining her lands to his. With both his mother's and Eleanor's domains, Henry was in control of almost the entire western half of France. In January of 1153, he invaded England with a sizeable force and by November of that year—aided by Theobold, Archbishop of Canterbury—was able to work out a truce with Stephen. This named him as Stephen's heir, on the condition that Stephen hold the English throne for the rest of his life.

Henry FitzEmpress did not have long to wait, for Stephen was to die six months later and Henry was crowned Henry II, King of England, at Westminster on December 19, 1154.

THOMAS AT COURT At the age of twenty-one Henry had become one of the most powerful monarchs in Europe: King of England, Duke of Normandy and Aquitaine, Count of Anjou. He was less a breath of fresh air in the English court than a gale-force wind. Henry was notorious for never staying in one place for very long, rushing off at a moment's notice to visit all corners of his kingdom, something that drove his courtiers crazy but struck fear into the hearts of dishonest officials, who never knew when the king himself might show up on their doorsteps. Physically, he was short of stature and barrel-chested, with red hair that he kept close-cropped (not the style at the time), probably because he was going bald. His clothes were generally caked with dust from the endless riding and hunting he did.

Henry could be extremely affable and approachable and was charitable towards common people, but he could become ferociously angry and, in such moods, could lash out physically at anyone who approached him. Part of his temper was inherited, but part of it may have been overwork and frustration. For Henry was trying to put back together a court and country that had fallen apart under the chaos of civil war and the rule of Stephen of Blois. The king had to dismiss and prosecute corrupt officials, levy new taxes, issue a new silver coinage (under Stephen it had become debased) and, in general, restore public confidence in the monarchy.

To do this he needed help, and he turned to Theobold, Archbishop of Canterbury, who had long supported Henry and his family's battle against Stephen and, in fact, had been interregnum ruler of England after Stephen died and before Henry assumed the throne. Theobold knew that Henry needed an organizer, a man who would function as the country's secretary, keeping track of the flow of money in and out of the treasury, making sure records were kept and the proper appointments made, both secular and clerical ones. And so, in late 1154, he brought Thomas Becket to meet Henry.

Becket—after leaving St. Paul's and receiving further education in law in Paris and Bologna—had returned to London, where he learned accountancy and business skills. In 1143, Archbishop Theobold had made the twenty-five-year-old his household clerk, but before long promoted him to the position of Archdeacon of Canterbury (Becket was not ordained a priest at this stage, but did take the minor order of deacon). Becket was sent by Theobold on numerous diplomatic missions to Rome, where he made a good impression. He was very tall and slender, dark-haired, and a good conversationalist; his slight stammer was charming rather than obtrusive.

When Henry and Becket met for the first time, the thirty-six-year-old man of the world and the young, rough-and-ready king hit it off immediately. Without so much as a moment's hesitation, Henry made Becket Chancellor of England.

THE FRIENDSHIP The office of chancellor was the third highest in the land, behind that of treasurer and justiciar (roughly equivalent to today's prime minister), but within the space of no more than three months, Becket seems to have vaulted over these in his importance to the king. "Nothing of great moment is done, or ought to be done, without [Becket's] consent or advice," a contemporary wrote. Becket had fifty-two secretaries reporting to him; they kept all the king's household records and the records of his kingdom as well. Becket was in charge of payments made for royal charters, filling vacancies in bishoprics and archbishoprics, sifting through pleas, land grants, and much more. Although he was a deacon, he was first and foremost the king's man, even when dealing with such matters as naming prelates to important positions. He "put off the deacon and put on the chancellor," as one of his contemporaries put it.

Although Thomas was fifteen years older than the king, they "played together like little boys of the same age, at the court, in church, in assemblies, in riding." Becket had taken a personal vow of chastity, unlike the king, so the chancellor did not share Henry's libidinous pursuits—despite being married to the beautiful Eleanor, Henry had mistresses all over the country—but did enjoy riding, hunting, and matching wits with him. In one famous story, they were riding through London on a cold winter's day when the king saw a beggar on the street, shivering in the freezing wind.

"Would it not be a meritorious act to give that poor old man a warm cloak?" Henry asked Becket.

Becket agreed that it would.

"Then let it be your merit!" shouted the king and, grabbing Becket's cloak, tossed it to the beggar and rode off, with Becket chasing him with curses and laughter.

THE OPULENCE OF THOMAS BECKET
Not that Becket could not afford a spare cloak. The king had richly rewarded him for his labors on behalf of England, and Becket himself may not have been above skimming from the revenues flowing through his hands. Becket set up a household in London that was far more ostentatious than any the king maintained. He gave frequent dinner parties, serving his guests all manner of savory dishes. Fresh rushes were strewn on the floor of his dining room daily—a huge extravagance.

His plates were made of gold and silver and the meals they held were served by pages who were the sons of the greatest nobles in the land, sent to learn at the feet of the great man, Becket. Henry and Eleanor did the same. In 1161, they sent their six-year-old son and heir, Lord Henry—commonly known as the Young King—to live with Becket, who became so close to the boy that he began referring to him as his adopted son.

ARCHBISHOP OF CANTERBURY
Theobold, Archbishop of Canterbury and faithful friend to Henry II, died on April 18, 1161, and Henry sought about him for a replacement who would be just as loyal, but who would also

help him secure the agenda he had in mind for the church in England. Henry had long felt that the church needed radical reform—for instance, he wanted the ability to try corrupt clerics in civil courts, rather than the religious ones where they were currently judged.

Rumors swirled that Henry would seek to name Becket for the position, although many felt that this would be a bad idea—Becket, after all, was far too worldly, and he was not even a priest, for that matter. Becket, who knew everything that happened in Henry's realm, knew that he was being considered, yet he seems to have done little to dissuade the king from making him archbishop. It is possible that he felt he had done all he could as the king's chancellor; it is also possible that he felt the life he was leading was a wasted one. This chaste, erudite, wealthy and powerful man was neither quite priest, nor quite nobleman: Becket may have longed for a closer union to God.

It is tempting to psychoanalyze Becket and wonder if he did not welcome some position that would put him in conflict with the king and give him a chance to test their wills, to see if he, Becket, could for once come out on top. But speculation is useless at a distance of nine hundred years. We do know that in May 1160, King Henry II ordered Becket to leave France with the Young King and return to England, where Henry's barons would swear fealty to the boy in a ceremony recognizing him as Henry's heir. When Becket stopped by the king's castle in Normandy, Henry took him aside and said: "You do not yet know fully the reason for your mission. It is my will that you shall be Archbishop of Canterbury."

There are numerous contemporary accounts of Becket's reply; all agree that Becket begged Henry to reconsider. Becket looked down at the colorful robes he was wearing and said wryly: "How religious, how holy a man you wish to appoint to that holy see." Then he went on, in a more serious vein: "I know for sure that if God should permit it, you would swiftly turn against me, and the affection which is so great between the two of us would soon be changed to violent hatred."

But it was no use. Henry insisted and Becket had no choice. That month in London he was formally nominated archbishop. On June 2 he was ordained a priest, and the next day he was consecrated Archbishop of Canterbury.

"THE KING HAS WORKED A MIRACLE" When Becket knelt and received the sacraments in Canterbury Cathedral that day, those in attendance were astonished to see tears pouring down his face. Many of these powerful nobles and prelates had little use for Becket—as the king's man he had alienated them with his access to power, his arrogance, even his shady business dealings. They may have assumed that his tears were mere show from a man who had a reputation for great theatricality. Gilbert Foliot, Bishop of Hereford, who envied and hated Becket, announced sarcastically after the ceremony, "The king has worked a miracle. Out of a secular man and a soldier he has made an archbishop."

OPPOSITE Canterbury Cathedral was the scene of Thomas Becket's consecration as Archbishop of Canterbury and his martyrdom, when he was killed on a winter evening in 1170, at the behest of his king.

Yet in the months that followed everyone, even Becket's enemies, agreed that he had undergone a profound change. Throwing away his colorful robes, he wore the garb of a simple monk and, underneath it, a knee-length hair shirt swarming with vermin. He had himself flagellated frequently by monks, ate the most rudimentary diet, and drank only "water used for the cooking of hay." He was doing penance for what he called his "sinful past," for life as "a patron of actors and a follower of hounds." Early every morning he arose to wash the feet of thirteen beggars and to give them alms; late each night, he kept vigils.

Henry had confidently expected that Becket would continue to serve him as Chancellor of England, but Becket refused to do so and sent a messenger to France—where Henry still resided—with the Great Seal of the chancellor's office. Henry looked at it in astonishment. "Doesn't he want to keep it anymore?" he asked.

The messenger replied tactfully: "He feels that the burden of two offices are too much for him."

"He no longer cares to be in my service," Henry snapped. "I can feel it."

In revenge, Henry took away Thomas's title of Archdeacon of Canterbury and the huge amounts of revenue that came with it. While Becket had personally changed, he still entertained on a lavish scale, and the lack of revenue began to pinch.

It was only the beginning of the disagreements between the archbishop and the king. Henry returned to England in January 1163—the first time he had set foot in the country in five years. Becket met him on the coast and gave him the kiss of peace, but their relationship was beginning to fracture.

"YOU OPPOSE ME IN EVERYTHING" The king spent the next three years in England putting his kingdom in order—or attempting to. Years before, William the Conqueror had separated the English judicial system into secular and ecclesiastical courts; men who were clergy—deacons, monks, priests—could not be tried in a secular court, but only by the church, which was notorious for giving miscreants light sentences (by law, ecclesiastical courts were not allowed to shed blood). This, literally, gave some clergy license to kill— Henry discovered that more than one hundred murders had been committed by clergy during his relatively short reign. (It also created a special class of robbers who, disguised as clergy, robbed and plundered at will, and then claimed ecclesiastical immunity.)

Henry insisted on having clergy tried in secular courts. The suggestion was a sensible one and he expected Thomas Becket to go along with it. There is no doubt Becket was aware of the failure of the religious courts to deal with criminal acts but, knowing the king as he did, he felt that any infringement on the rights of the church would soon see it completely under Henry's sway. In October of 1163, Henry demanded that Thomas and his bishops swear fealty to him in all matters;

Becket infuriated him by insisting that he and his bishops would do so with the qualifier "saving our order."

The feud began to spiral out of control. Henry confiscated two of Becket's finest estates; Thomas retaliated by refusing, on a religious technicality, to allow Henry's brother William to marry. He also seemed to go out of his way to protect highwaymen and murderers who were clergy or pretended to be. Finally, in January 1164, at a council held in Clarendon, Henry ordered the drawing up of sixteen points, which became known as the Constitutions of Clarendon. Article number three included civil trial for clerics.

Here, knowing how serious the king was, Becket began to vacillate. At first he opposed the constitutions and directed his bishops to do so. When the king began howling "like a roaring lion" and even threatened to put some bishops to the sword, Becket relented. He would not sign the constitutions, but he would give his private oath that he would obey the new laws. Then Pope Alexander saw a copy of the constitutions and supported Becket, causing him to regret that he had capitulated.

Becket then changed his mind once again, but by this time Henry had had enough. He decided to remove Becket from his archbishopric and in this he was supported by a good many of Becket's bishops, who felt that his stubbornness and instability were destroying the dignity of the position he held.

In November 1164, the king had Becket arraigned in his council on charges of contempt of the king, and also accused him of stealing money while acting as chancellor. Becket arrived at court carrying his own episcopal cross to show that he was claiming the protection of the church. The king ignored it and called for this, his secular court, to pass sentence on Becket. Refusing to wait for the inevitable, Becket simply left the court, to cries of "Traitor!"

That night, disguised as a monk, he fled across the English Channel to Flanders, and finally to the court of King Louis VII of France. He would not see England again for five years.

EXILE AND RETURN
A sympathetic King Louis arranged for Becket to stay at a Cistercian abbey in Burgundy, protected from the angry Henry. From there, Becket wrote letters to the pope and prominent clergymen all over Europe, claiming that Henry was persecuting the church. It appears to have been his goal to have Henry excommunicated. While he garnered much support over the years of his exile, Becket's plight also caused the pope to step in and try to reconcile Henry and his archbishop—having the King of England and his archbishop estranged was simply not good for the church. Finally, Henry and Becket met in France in July of 1170, with Henry, in a typically emotional moment, throwing his arms around Becket and crying out: "My lord Archbishop, let us go back to our old love for each other."

Henry asked Becket to come back to England in peace to oversee the coronation of the Young King (he was practicing the French custom of crowning his heir while

THE MIRACLES OF THOMAS BECKET

In 1170, December 29, the night of Thomas Becket's death, was a Tuesday. By Thursday, New Year's Eve, the wife of an English knight who had prayed to "St. Thomas, martyr precious to Christ," was cured of blindness. It was then as if a spigot had been turned on and miracles gushed out. Tiny drops of blood scraped from the floor of Canterbury Cathedral cured the deaf, exorcised devils, and made the paralyzed walk again. By Easter of 1171, miracles were being reported by people who made pilgrimages to Becket's tomb. Even King Henry had his miracle at Becket's grave. In the summer of 1174, facing a war in Scotland, he spent the night in Becket's crypt praying and fasting. Shortly thereafter, he learned that on the very night he had been praying to his former chancellor, William the Lion, King of the Scots, had been taken prisoner.

Becket's tomb remained a popular place of pilgrimage for centuries, as evidenced by Chaucer's *Canterbury Tales*; in fact, the word "canter" entered the English language as a description of the unhurried pace pilgrims adopted on their long journeys to pray at the grave of Thomas the Martyr.

he himself was still alive). Becket agreed, but the rift was smoothed over, not healed. There was no mention of Becket's condemnation in the king's court, no discussion of the Constitutions of Clarendon. There was still so much antipathy to Becket in England—both from Henry's barons and from Becket's own bishops— that in October of that year, in France, Henry issued Becket a formal safe conduct pass, allowing him to return to England "in accordance with my wishes."

Then, as the two met in Normandy to bid farewell, Thomas blurted out: "My lord, my mind tells me that I will never again see you in this life."

Henry began angrily: "Do you think I am a traitor?"

"God forbid, my lord," Becket replied.

DEATH OF THE ARCHBISHOP Back in England, it was
apparent that Becket was not in a conciliatory mood. Arriving in the country in early December, he was warmly greeted by the lesser clergy and the public, with whom he had been a favorite because of his modest habits and charitable works. But the Young King—whom Becket had essentially raised from childhood—refused even to see him, as did many of Henry's officials. In response, speaking from the pulpit in Canterbury Cathedral, Becket railed against those bishops who had supported Henry in his absence. He then publicly excommunicated them.

This was a slap in the face to the King of England with whom he had just been reconciled, but the hostility Becket had met with since his arrival in England may have precipitated it. The repercussions of his actions were almost immediate. Three of the bishops who had been excommunicated immediately went to the king's court in Normandy, arriving there on Christmas Day. Henry and his barons listened in anger as the clerics described Becket's behavior. One of the bishops said: "I assure you, my lord, while Thomas lives you will have no good days, nor quiet times, nor a tranquil kingdom."

And Henry—given to fury at far lesser provocations than this—shouted: "Who will rid me of this turbulent priest? A curse! A curse on all the false varlets I have nursed and promoted ... who let their lord be mocked with such shameful contempt by a low-born priest."

It was one of Henry's usual, dramatic rages, but there were men in the room who took him literally. Four of them—the barons Reginald FitzUrse, William de Tracy, Hugh de Morville, and Richard de Brito—stole away into the night, heading for England. When Henry discovered they were gone, he sent messengers after them, guessing at their intentions, but by that time they had set sail. There has been some dispute over whether Henry really tried to stop them, but the fact that the barons left secretly, even going to the precaution of sailing from separate ports, shows that they expected the king to try to stop them—once he had calmed down.

The four knights made their way to Canterbury, arriving on the afternoon of December 29th. They burst into the archbishop's study as he was conducting business with his clerks. Interestingly enough, it appears that Becket was warned

OPPOSITE A panel from the St. Thomas Altar in St. John's Church, Hamburg, shows the murder of Thomas Becket by the four barons who had been impelled into action by Henry II's rash words.

THE FATE OF THE BARONS

A tradition has come down in history that the barons who killed Thomas Becket were rough, dimwitted thugs. In fact, Reginald FitzUrse, William de Tracy, Hugh de Morville, and Richard de Brito were high officials; the first three men had sworn fealty to Becket when he was archbishop.

On the Easter Sunday following Becket's death, the pope excommunicated the four knights—"satellites of Satan" he called them. They themselves, now fully aware of the furor they had caused, remained hidden in Knaresborough Castle in Yorkshire for an entire year, awaiting punishment from Henry that never came. (Henry had finally decided that punishing the barons would make him look even guiltier, as if he were seeking scapegoats.) Hugh de Morville made a pilgrimage to the Holy Land to seek absolution, which was given to him; William de Tracy died on a like pilgrimage, having first donated his manor to Canterbury Cathedral in atonement. All four barons performed acts of expiation and were eventually taken back into the king's good graces.

Hugh Mauclerc, the "evil cleric" who jabbed Becket's brains out on the floor of the cathedral, horrifying all of Christendom, disappeared from history without a trace.

at least a day ahead of time that the men were coming, but he refused to hide. Pretending that King Henry had sent them to arrest him, the barons accused Becket of plotting against the Young King (by excommunicating some of the bishops who had helped crown him). This was a wild accusation and was followed by threats that the archbishop must absolve the bishops he had dismissed or face the consequences. FitzUrse made these clear when he took a step closer to Becket and said: "I warn you, you speak in peril of your head."

When Becket refused to go back on his excommunications, the men left Becket's study and raced out into the courtyard, shouting: "To arms! To arms!" They then forced one of Becket's servants to help them don their armor, a time-consuming procedure that involved putting on steel shinguards, breastplates, and helmets. They then raced up the stairs to the archbishop's residence, but his alarmed monks had already led him from his study and into the cathedral, never dreaming the barons would follow—for spilling blood on consecrated ground was a mortal sin. The monks attempted to close the doors to the cathedral, but Becket called out: "Christ Church is not a fortress. Open the door!"

By now citizens coming for vespers or attracted by the tumult were pouring in the front door of the cathedral as the four knights came crashing in from the side. Becket's monks became frightened and raced away to hide in the dark corners of the cathedral, except for a visiting monk, Edward Grim, who courageously remained by the archbishop's side. After Becket identified himself in the dark, he approached the barons, who were accompanied by a subdeacon named Hugh Mauclerc, a clergyman who hated Becket.

"Absolve the bishops you have excommunicated," shouted Mauclerc.

"I have already said what I will and will not do," said Becket.

The barons then laid hands on Becket and tried to carry him bodily from the church. It may be that they had not yet quite resolved to kill him, or it may be that they were planning on slaughtering him outside the door, on unconsecrated ground. But Becket, showing great physical strength, grabbed FitzUrse by his armor and threw him to the floor.

"Let go of me, Reginald. You are my vassal, you owe me fealty. Let go of me, you pander!"

Pander meant "pimp," and the use of the word enraged FitzUrse. He brought his sword down in a flashing circle, slicing off the skin on the top of Becket's head, as Becket, joining his hands, called out: "I commend myself and my church to God and the Blessed Mary and to St. Denis and St. Alphege." Now de Tracy leaped forward and brought his sword down. The monk Grim, with amazing courage, threw his arm out to shield Becket and the blade nearly severed it, in the meantime dealing a blow to Becket's head that drove him to his hands and knees, still praying: "Into Thy Hands, O Lord, I commend my spirit."

Grim, writhing in pain in the darkness nearby, then heard Becket say: "For the name of Jesus and the defense of the Church, I embrace death." Then de Brito brought his sword down so hard on Becket's head that his skull was split open and the blade shattered on the paving stones. At this, the cleric Hugh Mauclerc walked up, placed his foot on Becket's neck, and, with the tip of his sword, scattered his brains over the floor. "Let us away, knights," he sneered. "This fellow will rise no more."

BECKET RISING
After Becket's murderers had left, there was an awesome natural occurrence—a rare winter thunderstorm burst over the town of Canterbury. In flashes of lightning and peals of thunder, Becket's monks carried him to lie on the altar of the cathedral, while other monks and townspeople collected the blood and brains and the shards of de Brito's sword, which immediately became relics. People fell to their knees, cut pieces from Becket's garments, and kissed and caressed his corpse, marveling at the hair shirt he wore under his robes. The next morning, the monks buried him in the crypt below the cathedral.

In death, Becket did in fact rise, to become far more powerful than the king he had served so long. Miracles attributed to the archbishop began in England within a few days of his death and then occurred all over Europe. In the meantime, Henry was reviled in England and on the Continent, since all assumed that he had ordered Becket's death.

In fact, when King Henry heard that Becket had died he was stricken with horrible grief. Putting on sackcloth and ashes, he "burst into loud lamentations," wrote one cleric who was present, and seemed to fall at times into a stupor. He remained this way for six weeks and then, recovering somewhat, addressed his court, swearing that he had nothing to do with Becket's death. There were only a few who believed him. Pope Alexander excommunicated Becket's killers but delayed a decision on Henry for two years. Finally, Henry was forced to publicly swear on a Bible that he had not ordered Becket's death; furthermore, he was made to furnish two hundred knights to fight in the Holy Land (a highly expensive proposition for the cost-conscious king). Most significantly of all, Henry was forced to revoke what the pope called "the wicked Statutes of Clarendon."

This was Thomas Becket's final victory over the king—restoration of the separation of church and state in England. It would not last forever, but while it did Henry was laid low. Strangely enough, Henry did not chafe at this, as he might have. Instead, he told others that he had "not grieved so much over the death of his father or mother" as he had over Becket's demise. Henry never got over Thomas Becket's death and history has forever linked the two—the turbulent king and his turbulent priest.

BECKET'S BONES

By the mid-sixteenth century, Becket's grave had become a source of great revenue to the city of Canterbury. Pilgrims visited continuously, and kings and high nobles made it their practice to donate lavishly to the cathedral, in particular bestowing precious gold and silver plates and jewels upon Becket's tomb, until it was nearly hidden from sight.

This all came to an end in 1538 with Henry VIII who—quite rightly from his point of view—identified Becket as the culprit who, some 360 years earlier, had won a victory for the supremacy of the church over the crown. He therefore ordered the shrine broken to pieces and Becket's bones scattered, in the meantime confiscating all the treasure for himself. A long train of wagons apparently left Canterbury, guarded by the king's men; Henry VIII later wore the so-called "Regale of France," a ruby said to be as large as a hen's egg, which had been given by King Louis VII of France, in a thumb-ring.

Becket remains to this day an important saint of the Catholic Church, but the Church of England does not recognize him.

VERSUS   KING JOHN

KING RICHARD I AND KING JOHN:
BROTHERS AND RIVALS

EVERY NEIGHBORHOOD HAS ONE—THAT CRAZY, loud and often violent family that lives down the block and makes life miserable for one and all. The police have to be called to quell their noisy parties and to break up family feuds, which often devolve into fisticuffs. They drink like fish and threaten everyone who looks at them cross-eyed, and the men do a lot of mysterious digging in the backyard late at night. Burying treasure or relatives? No one knows.

If you lived in the mid to late twelfth century and your neighborhood was France and England, then your noisome neighbors would have been the Angevin family—in particular, King Henry II and his sons Richard and John, although other sons, wives, mistresses and homosexual lovers also got mixed into this witch's broth. For fifty years, from 1154 to 1216, Henry, Richard and John took turns ruling England.

The family originated in the province of Anjou in France, hence the name Angevin. And what a family they were. Charming, handsome, filled with passion and energy—but also violent and temperamental. Henry II went into a fit of rage one morning when a courtier said a faint word of praise about one of his enemies, and literally ate his mattress. Richard was often likened, in his tempers, to a wounded animal, one that no one would dare come near, and, as one contemporary writer put it, he "cared for no success that was not reached by a path cut by his own sword and stained with the blood of his adversaries."

And John? John, nine years younger than Richard, was given to immature temper tantrums, some of which resulted in the death of those around him. When he was angry, the chronicler Richard of Devizes wrote, "Rage contorted his brow, his burning eyes glittered, bluish spots discolored the pink of his cheeks."

"FROM THE DEVIL THEY CAME" For these unstable individuals to hold absolute power for so long—even in an age where instability seems to have been a prerequisite for noble calling—was extraordinary. Contemporaries marveled at, and muttered about, the Angevins. The House of Anjou was, quite literally, supposed to be descended from Satan, who at some unspecified point in the past had sent his beautiful daughter Melusine to earth, where she married an Angevin prince, gave birth to four sons—and then flew shrieking away into the sky when the Eucharist was shown to her. So when St. Bernard of Clairvaux wrote of the Angevins: "From the Devil they came and to the Devil they will return," he meant it.

The Angevins thought this was quite funny. "Do not deprive us of our heritage," Henry II and Richard used to joke, according to chronicler Gerald of Wales. "We cannot help acting like devils."

Henry II was a man of protean intelligence and endless ambition. He became King of England in 1154 at a time, less than a hundred years after the Norman Conquest, when that meant controlling large swathes of France as well—Normandy, Anjou, Poitou, and other provinces. Henry married into the rich province of Aquitaine by betrothing himself to the extraordinary Eleanor of Aquitaine, eleven years his senior, by whom he had eight children, including five boys: William, Henry, Richard, Geoffrey and John. William died in infancy, but Henry II still had the problem of dividing his lands and possessions between the other sons and he botched this, promising land to young John (whom he had dubbed "Lackland" for his paucity of inheritance) that the Young King, as Henry fils was known, thought to be his. In 1172, the Young King and Richard rebelled against Henry II. The Old King, as Henry II became known, beat them off and forced young Henry to sign over part of his inheritance to John, but the seed was set for further discord. The Young King died of dysentery in 1183 and Richard rapidly established himself as the most powerful Angevin heir, a fierce warrior who—this was commented on time and again by contemporaries—seemed to know absolutely no fear whatsoever.

In more fratricidal combat, Geoffrey and John joined forces to attack Richard (in this they were urged on by the Old King, who thought Richard was getting too big for his breeches) but were defeated. John, still without a patrimony, was sent to Ireland to quell the rebellious natives there but, young and untried, made a mess of it and came home with his tail between his legs. In the meantime, brother Geoffrey was killed accidentally in a tournament; his wife gave birth to a posthumous child, Arthur, who was raised away from the Angevins.

It was now endgame between old and young Angevins. Richard refused to part with the province of Aquitaine (his inheritance from his mother, Eleanor) and so Henry refused to formally recognize him as his heir. And, for good Angevin measure, he began sleeping with Richard's fiancée, Princess Alice, in an affair that became an open secret at the English court. This was embarrassing for Richard, not because he felt any affection for Alice—it was an arranged marriage and, in any

THE MURDER OF ARTHUR

The sorry history of the Angevins became even sorrier after Richard died. Although he had officially bequeathed his kingdom to John, the laws of primogeniture really indicated that the kingship should go to their nephew Arthur, son of their brother Geoffrey. Geoffrey died in a tournament in 1186, and after his death his wife gave birth to a son, Arthur, who was twelve years old when Richard Lion-Heart died. Arthur had been raised in Brittany and had become the duke of that province. Arthur immediately claimed the English throne and took his grandmother Eleanor of Aquitaine hostage. This so enraged John that he invaded France, managed to release Eleanor, and captured Arthur, whom he had imprisoned in Normandy.

Then, in 1203, Arthur disappeared from history. The baron William de Briouze left behind written records in which he claimed that John got drunk one night and, "possessed by the devil," killed Arthur "with his own hand." With the help of Briouze, John then dumped Arthur's body in the Seine.

While this sounds like a television murder mystery, most historians actually accept the story is true. Certainly, such a scenario is possible, given what we know of the Angevin temper.

event, Richard was probably homosexual—but because the Old King was, in a real sense, stealing his property.

In the summer of 1189, Richard allied himself with Philip Augustus, King of France, and attacked Henry, forcing him to surrender and recognize Richard as his official heir. The main reason Henry capitulated was because he found out that his youngest and most beloved son, John, had joined Richard. Ill and weak, Henry II died on July 6, 1189, cursing Richard. When Richard came to the funeral of his father, according to a widely told and believed story, blood spurted from the nose of Henry's corpse—a sign that Richard had murdered him.

Now only two of the male Angevins were left: Richard and John. The fun was just beginning.

KING RICHARD Richard was crowned king on September 3, 1189, in Westminster Abbey. Although it was broad daylight, a bat flew in swooshing circles around the throne Richard sat in during the ceremony, providing more fodder for those who believed that his reign would be bad for the country. Things were not helped by the fact that the misogynistic and anti-Semitic Richard had ordered that no women or Jews were to attend the coronation. Nevertheless, a delegation of London's Jews showed up, determined to bring the new king gifts, and was set upon by Richard's courtiers, touching off anti-Semitic rioting that spread to other English cities. Richard finally quelled it, but things were off to a bad start.

It was not like the new king to worry long about such matters, however. He was thirty-two years old, in his prime, supremely confident, and had finally gotten what he wanted and felt he deserved—the crown of England. The English king cut a glorious figure—tall, with a mane of red-gold hair, broad-shouldered and with extremely long legs and arms, Richard was a movie matinee idol of a king and, despite rumors swirling around his sexuality and the death of his father, the common people thronged the streets to see him wherever he went.

The only problem was, Richard did not want to stay in England. "It's cold and rainy here," he complained on more than one occasion. In fact, during his ten-year reign, he spent a total of six months, divided into two separate visits, in England. Despite the fact that he has been celebrated by such British luminaries as Winston Churchill, he was probably one of the worst rulers England ever had.

THE CRUSADES Richard, essentially, saw England as a cash cow for his pet project: launching a Crusade against the Muslims who were in possession of most of the Holy Land. To this end, he had "taken the Cross"—made a Crusader's vow—two years before he was crowned. His would be the Third Crusade—the first, in 1099, had recaptured Jerusalem and carved out a slice of Christian territory, known as the Outremer States, along the Mediterranean, but the second had been a failure and Muslim forces under their ruler Saladin had retaken Jerusalem and were everywhere threatening the slim Christian hold on the Holy Land.

WAS RICHARD THE LION-HEART GAY?

The answer to this question is probably, although we will never know for sure. Certainly this was the rumor, often whispered in his lifetime, that caused a hermit to shout at him: "Be thou mindful of the destruction of Sodom and abstain from what is unlawful."

Richard, while handsome and virile-seeming, was far from a lady's man. He was married to Berengaria of Navarre in Cyprus, but he spent only a few weeks with her before he went off crusading. They had no contact between 1192 and 1195 and spent little time together thereafter. Even when he knew he was dying, Richard called his mother, Eleanor, to his side, not Berengaria, and it is doubtful the marriage was even consummated. Richard apparently had sexual relations with only one woman, a mistress whose name is not known but by whom he had an illegitimate son, Philip of Cognac.

With the exception of his mother, Richard formed no deep or lasting bonds with women; in fact, his relationships with them were superficial and somewhat cold. It was widely rumored that in his youth Richard had a homosexual affair with King Philip of France, with whom he had allied himself against his father, Henry II. It was said of them that "they ate every day from the same table and from the same dish and at night their beds did not separate them." On his way to the Holy Land, Richard's urges for men apparently became too much for his conscience. In Messina, he called a conference of the leading clergy who accompanied the army and, in an extraordinary moment, appeared before the priests barefoot, kneeling with scourges in his hand, begging to be whipped or otherwise punished for his sins against God. The clergy, knowing which side their bread was buttered on, pronounced him absolved.

What did all of this mean to his subjects? To the ordinary citizen of England, sodomy was a sin, but Richard was out of the country so much, and such an elevated figure, that his sexual preferences probably did not figure too much In their lives. (More important was the fact that, although aged forty-two when he died, Richard had not produced an official heir.) Richard obviously felt some guilt and shame over his desires, as shown by the Messina conference, although there is some evidence that he had affairs with men after the Crusade was over. However, it is true that he was a staunch Catholic who died having forgiven his enemies and taken communion. What did he see fit to confess to the priest as he lay dying of gangrene? We will never know.

RICHARD 1.er
(RICHARD CŒUR DE LION)
ROI D'ANGLETERRE.
✝ 1199.

ABOVE The romantic view of Richard the Lion-Heart as a great and noble warrior and king may not be entirely realistic, but it has continued to grow over the centuries, as this nineteenth century depiction illustrates.

ROBIN HOOD AND KING JOHN

Although we know that John was not all bad, just as Richard was not all good, a set of stories concerning a noble outlaw who lived in central England—in Barnesdale Forest, just south of Sherwood and Nottingham—has been handed down to us as evidence of John's perfidy. Robin Hood is supposed to have stolen from the rich to give to the poor and protected England from nasty Prince John while Richard the Lion-Heart was away fighting the Third Crusade.

First mentioned in William Langland's *Piers Plowman* in the mid-fourteenth century ("I kan [know] not parfitly my Paternoster as the preest it singeth / But I kan rymes of Robyn Hood!"), Robin Hood was almost certainly an invention, but his story, most historians think, stems from tales of actual outlaws, such as Hereward the Wake, who led a rebellion against William the Conqueror after 1066, and Fulk FitzWarin who, interestingly enough, was an English outlaw at around the time of King John. Fulk was a noble who may have quarreled with John, was stripped of his possessions as a result, and went into the deep woods of England to build up a band of outlaws.

So Richard's first acts as king were essentially mercenary ones. He began to raise money. Everything that was not tied down was for sale. High officials and sheriffs who were in office were made to pay money to keep their offices, and castles were sold to the highest bidder, as were lordships, earldoms, and even entire towns. Richard released the Angevins' fierce enemy King William I of Scotland from jail in return for ten thousand silver marks. Monasteries had to chip in to keep their rights and privileges. At one point he declared that he would sell London for the right price. As one chronicler noted dryly, Richard "most obligingly unburdened all those whose money was a burden to them."

Before he set off on his Crusade—which would take years and from which, all were aware, he might never return—Richard knew that he had to name officers to take care of official business and act in his stead. Since he was childless, he also had to name an heir. The former task he assigned—showing he was not much of a politician—to several ambitious men, but in particular to William Longchamp, whom he made Chancellor of England.

In the ticklish matter of his heir, there were two obvious choices. One was his nephew Arthur; the other was his young brother, John. In the Angevin way of thinking, the obvious choice was Arthur, who was only four years old and who would obviously be less likely to seize the kingdom while Richard was away. However, this left the little matter of brother John for Richard to deal with.

JOHN Aged twenty-three when Richard was crowned king, John was considered by his brother and by others who knew him as a scheming ne'er-do-well who had squandered his chance at control of Ireland and had wasted the money showered on him by a doting Henry II. Nevertheless, as a close blood relative of Richard, John had a claim to the throne that was, at the time, probably as legitimate as that of Arthur's, and he had to be dealt with. Interestingly, Richard's solution was to shower gifts upon his brother. Richard made him Count of Mortraine, in Normandy, and married him off to the heiress Isabelle of Gloucester. The church frowned upon the match because the two were second cousins, but Richard pushed it through. As a result, John began to receive the third penny of every fine levied against wrongdoers in Gloucester, quite a lucrative windfall. Richard also granted six counties to John (including Nottingham, home, supposedly, of Robin Hood) and let him know that Ireland, once again, was his for the taking.

At the time there were people who thought Richard had lost his mind, or that he was in ill health and did not expect to return from the Crusade. How in the world could he give what amounted to a huge portion of the British Isles to such a greedy and untrustworthy person? Apparently, in return for this largesse, Richard wanted only one, simple thing: that John take an oath to stay out of England for three years, by which point Richard expected to be back from the Crusade and ready to run things. But even in this he was foiled. John and Richard's mother, Eleanor, stepped in. She considered John, not Arthur, the true heir to the throne and prevailed upon Richard to release John from his oath to stay out of England. With many misgivings, Richard did so—and nearly handed his brother his kingdom.

WHILE THE CAT'S AWAY ... One historian has written that "few monarchs could have created so potentially disastrous a situation as Richard did during the first four months he spent in England." Not only had he taxed his people relentlessly, he had sold most of the offices in the land to the highest bidders and had set up a situation where John could not help but be tempted by the luscious apple hanging before his face. John has been much criticized by historians for his behavior while Richard was out of the country, but he would not have been an Angevin, descended from the Devil, if he had acted otherwise.

Richard, joining forces with King Philip of France, set off on his great Crusade on July 4, 1190. John returned to England from France and set about securing his power base—for, if Richard did not return, John wanted to be sure to have the men and money to immediately seize the throne. The first thing he did was set up a court for himself in London as if he were king—he had his own chancellor, seal-bearer, chief justice, and treasurer. While some of this may have been needed to run his large estates in England, it did give the strong appearance of establishing a competing court. Next, he made sure that he welcomed anyone who had a grudge against William Longchamp, Richard's handpicked chancellor. These men included the vicious Hugh of Nunant, Bishop of Coventry, who was such an evil man, the story goes, that when he confessed his horrible sins on his deathbed, no one could be found to absolve him.

Together with Nunant, John began a power struggle with Longchamp, who was not, in any event, a popular figure. When Longchamp tried to arrest a baron for malfeasance, besieging his castle, John came to the man's aid by taking two castles belonging to Longchamp. However, by this time it was the spring of 1191 and reports had already drifted east to Richard of discord in England. He sent Walter of Coutances, Archbishop of Rouen, to act as a mediator, with orders to take over, if necessary. Coutances had a reputation as a fair and honorable man, and John's hopes of discord were temporarily dashed. To make things worse came the news that Richard had actually married while in Cyprus on his way to the Holy Land—the indomitable Eleanor of Aquitaine had actually crossed the Alps in winter at the age of sixty-nine, dragging the bride Berengaria of Navarre with her. Both Eleanor and John knew of Richard's sexual inclinations—but Eleanor, at least, wanted a grandson. For John, a son for Richard—an indisputable heir—would be the worst news possible.

RICHARD IN CHAINS Finally arriving in the Holy Land in June 1191, Richard won a great victory against the Muslim Sultan Saladin at Acre, but then found himself deserted by his ally and former friend King Philip of France:

in July, Philip declared that he was returning to Europe. The excuse he gave was that his health was poor, but in reality he was not the warrior Richard was, and he also wanted to take advantage of Richard's absence to weaken the English king's holdings in France. Left to his own devices, Richard gamely fought on alone, winning a victory over the Muslims at Arsuf that fall and another at Darum in the spring of 1192. By the fall of that year, however, Richard had been unable to recapture Jerusalem and felt forced to conclude the Treaty of Jaffa with Saladin. This gave Christians safe passage for pilgrimages to the Holy City, but the city itself remained in Muslim hands.

While his was one of the most successful Crusades, Richard was not happy with the outcome. Part of the reason he sought a negotiated end to the war was the stories reaching him of more trouble at home. According to the news that reached Richard, John had made a secret alliance with King Philip of France to rob Richard of his holdings in France. Worse, John was usurping power in England, bankrupting the treasury, imprisoning those loyal to Richard, and forcing other royal officials to take an oath naming him as Richard's official heir. Even their mother could not restrain him.

Richard set sail from Acre in September, intending to head home to resolve the matter, but by Christmas still had not been heard from. John started to tell people that his brother would never return, that he had been killed somewhere on the journey back. In fact, Richard had been captured and taken hostage. Foolishly attempting to travel overland in disguise—this may possibly have been because seasickness made him loath to contemplate a long sea journey through the Straits of Gibraltar and up the English Channel—he was taken hostage by his enemy Leopold V of Austria who, for a fee, sold him to another enemy, the Holy Roman Emperor Henry VI, who was quite delighted by the turn of events. He could sell Richard to the highest bidder for an enormous sum. One person who was quite interested in hearing this news was King Philip of France. What a coup if he could actually purchase Richard and then use him as a bargaining chip to force the English to give up their territory in France!

And John? Upon hearing that his brother was held captive he did something truly treacherous, even for an Angevin. He brokered a deal with Philip, offering to give up his own wife and to marry Philip's sister, if Philip would support John in an invasion of England. Fortunately, Eleanor and those barons loyal to Richard laid siege to John's castle and stopped this from happening. News of this treachery even reached Richard in captivity, but he airily dismissed his youngest brother's attempted coup: "My brother John," he said, "is not a man to win land for himself by force if there is anyone to put up a mere show of resistance."

Yet even when Eleanor finally came up with the king's ransom needed to free Richard from Henry VI, Philip and John continued to plot. They offered the Holy Roman Emperor an equal amount of money if he would keep Richard in captivity indefinitely—or even just a year longer. ("Behold how they love him," wrote one

OPPOSITE Richard's capture of the city of Acre in 1191 was the high point of his Crusade, but only a century later it was recaptured by the Muslims, despite William de Clermont's desperate defense (shown).

chronicler sardonically.) But Henry, while informing Richard of his brother's treachery, stuck to the bargain and Richard was released in February 1194.

When he heard this news, Philip sent John a message: "Look to yourself for the devil is loosed." John at once sought refuge at the French court.

RICHARD'S RETURN Upon arriving in England, Richard immediately set about reclaiming his kingdom. With John gone, those who had supported him capitulated, throwing themselves on Richard's mercy. He held a council in John's county of Nottingham in which he very publicly debated what to do about his brother before decreeing that John needed to show up in England within forty days to stand trial for treason or forfeit all his lands and his right to the throne.

John, who was perfidious but not stupid, did no such thing, and continued to lie low in France. In April, Richard crossed the Channel with an army and a hundred ships, determined to do battle with Philip, who had been spending a good deal of time capturing English lands in France. John was probably secondary on Richard's menu, but Eleanor had been urging that Richard forgive his brother. On his way to do battle with Philip's forces in Normandy, Richard happened to stay the night with an archdeacon who had formerly served in his court. The archdeacon seemed unaccountably nervous, until Richard apparently said to him: "Out with it—I know you have seen my brother John. Tell him to come to me without fear. He is my brother and should not be afraid. I will not hold his folly against him."

The archdeacon was able to produce John, who approached his brother trembling, throwing himself at Richard's feet. Richard, in an extraordinary gesture, raised him to his feet and said: "Think no more of it. You are a child. You have had bad companions and your counselors shall pay." And then he invited his brother to dine with him on some fresh Atlantic salmon.

This astonishing reunion represents a new low in the tale of the family's dysfunction. Here was Richard treating his brother—who essentially tried to steal his throne and keep him in prison—literally as if he were a child who was not responsible for his own decisions, rather than a man of twenty-seven years. This reflects Richard's supreme self-confidence, and possibly recognition of the fact that he had simply tempted John too far. Or perhaps he just knew John better than we do. For Richard did not rescind the decree making John landless; John was forced to prove himself to Richard, which he did over the ensuing years of war against Philip. Because of this, according to chronicler Roger of Howden, Richard "laid aside his ill will" and restored to John some of his territories, as well as an annual allowance. When, in 1199, Philip signed a truce with Richard and then tried to convince him that John had been (recently) a traitor, John was able to prove his innocence. He had, for once, not betrayed his brother.

THE THIRTEENTH CENTURY'S WORST BRITON?

In a sense, these two brothers and rivals died as they had lived. In the early spring of 1199, Richard, during a minor siege of an unimportant castle, exposed himself too recklessly and received a crossbow bolt in the shoulder. The wound was not fatal, but the gangrene that set in afterwards was. Richard died ten days later, on April 6, having bequeathed his kingdom to John.

Despite their rivalry, blood proved to be thicker than water and John had shown himself, at least in the last few years, capable of loyalty. He was crowned king on May 27, 1199 but faced a stormy reign. He was not the warrior Richard had been and he lost Normandy and other French territories to Philip, who had now become his implacable enemy. Also, facing bankruptcy because of his warring in France (and, to be fair, because of the fiscal policies of his dead brother), John levied more and more taxes and fees upon his barons. Not only that, but he so offended Pope Innocent III by his insistence on filling clerical offices himself—and charging fees for them—that for a period the pope held the entire country excommunicate, meaning that no one could get married, go to communion, or even be buried or baptized in the church.

In 1214, John's barons turned against him, eventually forcing him to sign a momentous document in English history: Magna Carta, which limited the power of the monarchy and guaranteed basic rights and liberties. It was a first step on the road to democracy; the fact that it was taken by an Angevin is somehow ironic.

John, harried by rebellious lords, died of dysentery in 1216, leaving behind a reputation as one of England's worst kings—in 2006, he was named by the *BBC History Magazine* as "the 13th century's worst Briton." John's brother Richard—whom the historian W. L. Warren has astutely called "lionhearted but soulless"—was a terrible and absentee king, while John at least stayed in the country and attempted to run it. But if, even in death, these two are rivals, then Richard the Lion-Heart wins out, while his baby brother remains forever the duplicitous wretch.

De Larmessin. Sculp.

BONIFASIVS · VIII · PAPA · ROMANVS ·

POPE BONIFACE VIII

PHILIP IV OF FRANCE AND POPE BONIFACE VIII: THE EPIC BATTLE BETWEEN BODY AND SOUL

I N MEDIEVAL TIMES, IT USED TO BE THAT WHEN THE pope called, kings came running. Pope Gregory VII, who ruled from 1073 to 1085, forced the excommunicated German King Henry IV to kneel abjectly before him to beg forgiveness. Innocent III (1109–1216), the greatest of the medieval popes, not only chose the Holy Roman Emperor, Otto IV, but when Otto did something Innocent did not like, he deposed and excommunicated him and gave the job to someone else. Innocent also excommunicated King John of England and his entire country. Then, when John was back in his good graces, Innocent attempted to declare Magna Carta null and void.

Innocent summed up this philosophy in a nutshell: "Princes have power on earth, priests over the soul," he wrote. "As much as the soul is worthier than the body, so much worthier is the priesthood than the monarchy."

However, starting eighty years after the end of Innocent's reign there came a dispute between soul and body—between pope and king—that was to momentously and forever reshape the relationship between church and state. The dispute was embodied in two decidedly unpleasant rivals, King Philip IV of France and Pope Boniface VIII.

PHILIP THE FAIR *Le Bel*, they called him—handsome or fair—because of his almost supernatural good looks, his truly angelic mien. Philip IV was born in 1268, the son and successor of Philip III of France, and began his reign in 1286, when he was only eighteen years old. Philip was an odd man, an enigmatic presence whose essence few contemporaries or historians have quite been able to tap into. Some thought him vacant; the citizens of the French province of Languedoc called him "King Owl," because, although he looked all-knowing and wise, "he could do nothing but stare fixedly at people without a word." An opponent of his, Bishop Bernard Saisset, wrote of Philip: "He is neither man nor beast. He is a statue." Yet he definitely had his admirers, including one chronicler who called him "pope, emperor, and king all in one."

Part of the problem was that Philip usually spoke through a cadre of advisors, a group of men the historian Brian Tierney has called "a screen of efficient and ruthless royal servants," ministers like Guillaume de Nogaret and Pierre Flotte. The question is, did they serve the ends of a brilliant but cold-hearted Philip, or was he merely a dupe or puppet, a figurehead doing their bidding? The answer will almost certainly never be known for sure, but there is a consensus that Philip, although perhaps no heavyweight intellectually, knew what he wanted and used his men as a means of achieving it during a reign that lasted a quarter of a century.

And what, indeed, did Philip want in these late days of the thirteenth century? His goals were actually forward-looking in an era when countries such as France and England were just beginning to emerge from feudalism and the kernel of the idea of nations was taking hold. The Hundred Years War, beginning in 1337, would eventually end with the formation of European nation-states; for now, Philip (like his contemporary King Edward I of England) wanted to strengthen his monarchy at all costs, bringing the country together under one ruler. To this end, recalcitrant barons were bribed to fall in line with the throne, while others were undermined or slandered by rumors spread by the French court. A continuing war was fought against England, to oust her from French territories. War, bribery, and slander cost money, of course, and the primary task of Philip's well-trained group of royal advisors—who might be called the first modern state bureaucracy—was to fill the coffers of France.

MONEY AT ANY COST It was the way Philip and his men went about making their country (not to mention themselves) rich that made them such controversial figures. Essentially, they used their office as a license to steal. For instance, the Lombards were Italian bankers living in France and doing business there; Philip borrowed heavily from them and then, when he decided he was not going to pay them back, he simply expelled the entire group from France and took possession of their property and money. He did the same thing to the Jewish moneylenders of France, a group that had been operating in the country for perhaps two centuries, subject to periodic pogroms, to be sure, but valued for the services they could provide. Suddenly Philip decided that the Jewish religion "dishonored Christian custom and behavior," and sent them packing. Naturally, all their cash and worldly goods went to Philip.

It was when Philip turned his eyes to the brimming bank accounts of the church that the trouble truly began. According to Innocent III's Fourth Lateran Council of 1215, clergy could not be taxed unless the pope gave his permission first. Still, in practice and with the pope's at least tacit approval, churches and monasteries were taxed when kings wanted to mount a Crusade against the Muslims holding the Holy Lands, something that happened frequently in the thirteenth century. The ostensible reason for allowing such taxation was that a Crusade was a "just war," which would benefit all of Christendom (even though many rulers had less-than-spiritual reasons for undertaking such expeditions).

However, in 1296 England and France were at war with each other, and both Edward I and Philip IV were taxing the churches in their respective countries because each considered his battle a "just war." This did not sit well with a certain irascible pontiff by the name of Boniface.

POPE BONIFACE VIII Boniface was born in 1235, a member of the powerful Caetani family. He lived at a time when most popes functioned as princes, making sure they enriched their families through outrageous acts of nepotism. While by no means the most corrupt period for popes—that would be the ninth and tenth centuries, which saw numerous pontiffs murdered, one dead pope dug up and put on trial by his successor, and another pope succeeded by his own son—it was common to see thirteenth century pontiffs enriching themselves and those close to them with *benefices*, or gifts of property.

Boniface rose to prominence in the church as a priest and canon lawyer and succeeded Celestine V to the papacy in 1295. Celestine, a pious man who lived in a hermit's cell in a monastery, was a compromise candidate who was thoroughly unprepared for the bureaucratic and political demands of the papacy and decided to resign the post. The church lawyer he consulted about this was none other than Boniface, who encouraged him to do so and was then himself elected pope. There were outcries that no pope should ever resign and rumors that Celestine had been pushed into the act by Boniface. Poor Celestine wanted only to return to his hermitage, but, fearing his supporters might use him to create a schism, Boniface had him imprisoned in a remote castle. He was not otherwise mistreated, but he died unhappily a year later, and rumors would soon spread that Boniface had murdered him.

Boniface probably did not have Celestine killed, but he was at least as ruthless as Philip and, like the French king, had a personality that did not endear him to many people. He was already sixty years old when elected to his high office and suffered grievously from "the stone"—kidney stones—which may have contributed to his irascibility, evidenced in the screaming fits he often threw when someone displeased him.

And kings' indiscriminately taxing clergy *really* displeased Boniface.

THE "LAITY HAVE ALWAYS BEEN HOSTILE" On February 26, 1296, Boniface threw down the gauntlet. He issued a papal bull (a proclamation so called because it was stamped by the papal *bulla*, or seal), entitled

RIGHT For Rabban Sauma, one of the most memorable aspects of Paris was the number of students who flocked to its university, the most respected in Europe at the time. Here students at the Sorbonne attend a lesson c. 1300.

RABBAN SAUMA

While Philip IV did not have good relations with the Roman Catholic Church, to say the least, he did have a very interesting meeting with a little-known historical figure, the monk and world traveler Rabban Sauma.

Sauma, born in eastern China in 1225, was a member of the Nestorian Church, which held that there were two separate beings within Christ, one human and one divine, and that the Blessed Virgin Mary was mother only of the human Christ. The Catholic Church considered this heresy, but Nestorians spread the word of their religion to Central Asia and China, where it became for centuries the predominant form of Christianity.

Sauma was well traveled and a revered holy man among the Nestorians when he was approached in 1286 by the patriarch of the church, who had an interesting proposition. The Great il-Khan of Central Asia, Persia and Syria, Argun, wanted an alliance with the Christians in order to help fight off the Mamluk Muslims of Egypt and he needed someone to carry this message to the great Christian kings of France and England. Would Sauma be willing?

Sauma, carrying secret letters for the kings of France and England, became the first Chinese-born person to traverse the then-known world from east to west. In France, he met with Philip IV, who treated him respectfully but could not commit to any crusade, embroiled as he was in a continuing war against King Edward I of England. Edward, with whom Sauma met as well, felt the same way. Although his mission would turn out to be a failure, Sauma was able to return home with fascinating depictions of the great cities of Paris and Rome—Paris, Sauma later wrote, was filled with students learning law, architecture, and theology, bustling everywhere with scrolls and tablets under their arms.

Clericis Laicos, which began with the statement that "the laity have been from the most ancient times hostile to the clergy" and went on to remind temporal authorities that "all power over clergymen and over the bodies and properties of clerical persons is forbidden to them" under pain of excommunication. Essentially, what *Clericis Laicos* did was tell clergy that they could disobey the law of the land in the country they lived in and heed only the pope, not their king.

Naturally, Edward and Philip did not take kindly to such a communication. Edward's response was to issue an English law stating that his own officials were free to do whatever they pleased, without repercussions, simply because they were *his* officials. However, it was Philip who responded most ferociously. In August of 1296, he issued a royal order forbidding the export from France of precious jewels, metals, and any type of negotiable currency. He did this knowing full well that Boniface depended heavily on income from his French church properties to keep the Vatican running. The church would, after a time, cease operating without this money.

This enraged Boniface, but there was little he could do about it. It may have been around this time that he was heard to say that he "would rather be a dog than a Frenchman," an utterance that would come back to haunt him. In September, he wrote a defiant letter to Philip saying that he would suffer anything Philip might choose to hand out before allowing any more liberties to be taken with the church, but by the winter of 1297, as the Vatican treasury became poorer and poorer, he changed his tune. In February, in a major concession, he wrote privately to Philip to say that, in periods of dire emergency, when there was no time to consult the pope, a king might tax his clerical subjects.

PHILIP STRIKES BACK Even this concession was not enough for Philip, which is what made him such a formidable adversary. Once aroused to anger against the pope, he would not stop until Boniface was thoroughly discredited. Despite Boniface's letter, Philip was still not happy and insisted on sending one of his chief ministers, Pierre Flotte, to Italy to meet personally with the pope. This could not have come at a worse time for Boniface, for there were two groups inside Italy who were trying to bring about his downfall. One was the Colonna family, who thought Boniface was passing out too much loot to his Caetani relatives; members of the Colonnas even went so far as to highjack a convoy bearing papal treasure. The other group was the Spiritual Franciscans, members of the ascetic holy order who though that Boniface had ousted and even killed their sainted mentor, Celestine V.

On his way to the Vatican, Pierre Flotte met with both groups and thus, when he finally confronted Boniface, he was able to hint that France might support Boniface's removal if he did not fully rescind *Clericis Laicos*. With little choice in the matter, Boniface issued another bull, *Etsi de Statu*, which clearly conceded a king's right to tax clergy without the pope's permission.

Even more humiliatingly, Boniface was forced to canonize Philip's grandfather, Louis IX.

THE JUBILEE If Philip thought that would be the end of things, he was sorely mistaken. In 1300, at the beginning of a new century, Boniface declared the very first jubilee in Rome, an *anno sancto*, or holy year, to celebrate the church (a jubilee has been declared every hundred years ever since). He was heartened and gratified by the tens of thousands of pilgrims who arrived, drawn to Rome by the promise of plenary indulgences (the remission of all their sins in purgatory). He even began dressing in imperial clothing and declared on at least one occasion that he considered himself as much emperor as pope.

It seems that neither Philip nor Boniface had been satisfied by their previous encounter and were seeking the chance to renew their rivalry. This happened in 1301, when Philip arrested and imprisoned the French bishop Bernard Saisset on what were almost certainly trumped-up charges of treason. With incredible arrogance, Philip then sent a list of his grievances against this bishop to the pope and demanded that Boniface not only agree with the French king's actions, but degrade (defrock) Saisset. To do so would have been to agree to the principle that temporal rulers had authority over clergy, and this Boniface refused to accept.

Seeking to defend the French church against the king of France, he wrote yet another bull, his famous *Unam Sanctam*, which was published on November 18, 1302. In it he claimed: "We declare, proclaim and define that it is altogether necessary to salvation for every human creature to be subject to the Roman pontiff." Along with his bull, Boniface sent a letter to Philip demanding Saisset's release and further stating his position. The salutation of the letter alone would have been enough to set Philip off (it began *Ausculta fili*, or "Listen, son ...") but in the body of the missive Boniface also scolded Philip as if he were a child ("Let no one persuade you that you have no superior or that you are not subject to the head of the ecclesiastical hierarchy").

PROPAGANDA WAR Philip was now determined to destroy Boniface utterly and he began by launching a propaganda campaign worthy of any twenty-first century nation at war. First he called a great council, made up of lay nobility and French clergy, in Paris. A rebuttal to the bull was drafted by Guillaume de Nogaret, one of the king's chief ministers, and presented to the council. It was a work of genius, containing all the old charges against Boniface: that he had forced Celestine V to resign, that he had had him murdered, even that he had claimed to prefer the estate of a canine to that of a Frenchman ("He is not ashamed to declare that he would rather be a dog or an ass or any brute animal rather than a Frenchman, which he would not have said if he believed a Frenchman had an immortal soul"). De Nogaret went further. Boniface was sexually licentious ("he is reported to

say that fornication is not a sin any more than rubbing the hand together is"); idolatrous ("he has caused silver images of himself to be erected in churches"); immoral ("he is guilty of the crime of sodomy"); and he even had his own personal devil ("he has a private demon whose advice he takes in all matters").

Philip and de Nogaret burned the actual papal letter—not the bull, but the private missive sent to Philip—and issued instead a forgery that had Boniface saying quite flatly that he and he alone was Philip's superior and that Philip was "subject" to him.

Philip was calling for the removal of Boniface, but, despite his slanders and threats, the French clergy would not go along with this. So he decided to settle the matter by force.

ATTACK ON BONIFACE

So began one of the most extraordinary episodes in the history of the papacy. Deciding now that Boniface needed to be dealt with as he might deal with any temporal ruler, Philip sent Guillaume de Nogaret to Italy in June 1303. Boniface was not in Rome, having made it his practice since the beginning of his papacy to summer in his papal palace in the hilly and pleasant city of Anagni, southeast of Rome. There, he let it be known that he had decided to publish a bull excommunicating Philip. But a few days before this was to happen, the little town was seized by three hundred mercenaries led by de Nogaret and Sciarra Colonna, a member of the family who were Boniface's fiercest enemies in Italy.

It was their intention to force Boniface to resign. After hours of fighting against his bodyguards, de Nogaret and Colonna and their men broke into the papal chambers, where they found Boniface fully dressed in his finest vestments, holding a crucifix in his hands. One of the assailants slapped the pope across the face.

De Nogaret demanded that Boniface resign, on the spot, but Boniface refused. *E lo col, e le cape*, he said. It means, "Here is my neck, here is my head!"

In other words, they would have to kill him. He would not resign. Colonna had to be restrained from killing him then and there, but de Nogaret wanted to take Boniface back to France and try him on charges of blasphemy and heresy. The two men argued for three days over what to do with the pope, but they had delayed too long. The citizens of Anagni now rose up against the invaders and drove them off, de Nogaret and Colonna being lucky to escape with their lives. His rescuers bore the pope back to Rome, but Boniface never recovered his health after this shocking attack, and he died on October 12, 1303, a broken man.

STATE TRUMPS CHURCH Boniface's final stand had also been his finest moment, but in the end Philip IV won the victory. The next pope, Benedict XI, excommunicated de Nogaret, but absolved Philip and his family from any role in Boniface's death and actually pardoned the gang who had carried out the assault at Anagni. Benedict died less than a year later, however. The new pope, Clement V, was a Frenchman who was completely under Philip's sway. He not only rescinded de Nogaret's excommunication, but completely renounced Boniface's doctrines as represented by *Clericis Laicos* and *Unam Sanctam*.

Never again would popes be able to bring serious challenges against kings, or get them to do their bidding by threat of excommunication. In the centuries ahead, the church would hold a subordinate position to European states. The church would have no political power at all: it could scold and try to persuade, but it could not make kings bow low to kiss the feet of the pontiff.

The amazing thing is that Philip the Fair's brutal attack on Pope Boniface VIII was actually a successful move—Philip even bullied Clement into saying that the Anagni assault was "praiseworthy zeal" on Philip's part. Philip went on to seize the property of the Knights Templars and begin the Avignon papacy, which saw popes ruling from France, not Rome, for the next seventy years. By the time he was done, the church, for the first time in its history, had lost prestige in front of the entire Western world. The countdown to the Protestant Reformation had begun.

THE KNIGHTS TEMPLARS AND THE CURSE OF JACQUES DE MOLAY

The Knights Templars formed an extraordinarily powerful medieval organization that began early in the Crusades, in Jerusalem, as a brotherhood of monks that cared for pilgrims. Since times were so tense in the Holy Land, the Templars were knights as well as religious brothers, and patrolled the roads near Jerusalem to keep Christians arriving from Europe safe. By the 1130s, given the continuing Islamic threat, the Templars had become fighting men first, religious second. They accepted knights who sought salvation from all over Europe, and the order, highly secretive and run by a powerful grand master, grew rich with donations, so that their holdings soon extended across the Holy Land.

After the last Crusader forces surrendered at Acre in 1291, the Templar headquarters moved to Paris. The order by this time had become so large (perhaps fifteen thousand "warrior-monks") and so wealthy that it could function as a kind of bank, with a sophisticated financial network that spread across Europe, loaning money for a percentage. After King Louis IX and his son Philip III nearly bankrupted the country with their wars and Crusades, Philip IV sought to make up the difference, as we have seen, through increased taxation.

But this was not nearly enough and so he decided to wreck the power of the Templars, much as he had destroyed that of Boniface. On Friday, October 13, 1307—some legends have it that the superstition about unlucky Friday the 13th came from this day—Philip ordered the arrest of hundreds of Templars, including the Grand Master Jacques de Molay. These Templars, including de Molay, were mercilessly tortured until they confessed to blasphemy—in the case of de Molay, that the Templars did not believe that Jesus Christ was God.

This was transparently false, but it was enough for Philip. At his behest, Pope Clement—the first of the Avignon popes and Philip's puppet—ordered the Templars disbanded and insisted that all their money and possessions be transferred to another religious order, the Knights Hospitallers (known today as the Knights of Malta). However, in reality, Philip took control of the Templar treasury for his own means.

Jacques de Molay was burned at the stake in Paris, in 1314. The story goes that, as the flames began to consume him, he cursed Philip and Clement V, shouting that within a year he would summon them to appear before God's tribunal to be judged. Within three months, Clement V had died of stomach cancer and Philip had been mortally wounded by a rampaging boar.

RIGHT Jacques de Molay, Grand Master of the Knights Templars when Philip disbanded the order, was tortured and burned at the stake so that Philip could gain control of the order's huge wealth.

FRANCISCO PIZARRO

FRANCISCO PIZARRO AND DIEGO DE ALMAGRO: CONQUISTADOR RIVALS

At the setting of the sun, the same day, on the square of Acla, the head of Vasco Nunez de Balboa rolled in the ocher dust ... Arrested by his dearest friend, condemned by his father-in-law, executed by his own soldiers, this was almost a normal end for a Conquistador.

So writes Jean Descola in his classic work *The Conquistadors*. He is describing the infamous 1519 execution of Balboa, the European who first viewed the Pacific Ocean, at the hands of his enemies. Betrayed by just about everyone he knew—that "dearest friend" mentioned just happens to have been Francisco Pizarro, of whom we will be hearing a great deal more—and executed in the public square of a Panama town whose name meant "the bones of men," this was still just a normal day at the office for a conquistador. These men bred rivalry and treachery the way other people grow tomatoes. Hernán Cortés battled with Pánfilo de Narváez, who tried, quite tiresomely, to arrest him while he was busy conquering Montezuma's great empire in Mexico. Gonzalo Pizarro, Francisco's brother, carried on an epic rivalry with Francisco de Orellana, deep in the wilderness of eastern Peru—it was to get away from Gonzalo that Orellana rowed two thousand miles east down the length of the Amazon River to the Atlantic Ocean, the first European to do so.

Conquistadors. The word is from the Spanish for "conquerors," but it would take a century or more for these men from Spain to be called that. They thought of themselves as adventurers or soldiers of fortune. The conquistadors were mercenaries. They came for the gold and hired themselves out to the captain most likely to get them to it. At the same time, they were fierce, proud, patriotic, prodigiously religious, and took the slightest insults to their person, their faith, or their honor very, very seriously.

Hence, they got into a lot of scrapes—and not just with the indigenous Mexican and Central and South American populations they were bent on destroying, but with each other. One of the fiercest such clashes occurred in the land of the Inca between Francisco Pizarro and Diego de Almagro.

And yet, they used to be such good friends.

FRANCISCO PIZARRO Francisco Pizarro, a man whose unmitigated gall, unapologetic treachery and immense bravery stole the rich kingdom of Peru from its Inca rulers, was born in 1471 in Trujillo, Spain, the illegitimate son of a soldier and a prostitute. He was an illiterate young man—would remain so all his life—who made a living herding pigs. (If you did not like Pizarro—and there were many men who hated his guts—you called him "that swineherd" and spread the rumor that his wetnurse had been a sow.) For a time he fought as a common soldier in campaigns in Italy, but by the age of forty, had returned to Spain. With almost no future ahead of him, he decided to try his hand in the New World, in 1501 shipping off to Hispaniola, where he sought about him for a chance to go adventuring for gold. It helped that Hernán Cortés, who by 1520 would destroy the mighty Aztec empire, was his second cousin. With a recommendation from Cortés, he was taken along on Vasco Núñez de Balboa's arduous journey across the Isthmus of Panama to discover the Pacific Ocean in 1513. Pizarro then threw in his lot with Balboa's father-in-law, Panama Governor Pedrarias Dávila, and helped capture and hand Balboa over for execution.

It was Pizarro's habit at this time, and would be throughout his entire life, to switch friends and mentors whenever expedient. After Balboa's death Pizarro was rewarded by Dávila, becoming a magistrate in Panama City and being given land, natives and cattle. Pizarro at this time was older than most of the conquistadors, a harsh man with a black beard and deeply sunburned face, given to monosyllabic conversation and almost never laughing. The men who served under him feared him but did not love him. He had three brothers (or perhaps half-brothers), Hernando, Juan, and Gonzalo, who would accompany him on his invasion of Peru, but there was only one man who could be described as close to him. That man was Diego de Almagro.

DIEGO DE ALMAGRO Almagro's background was not dissimilar to that of Pizarro. He had been born illegitimately in 1479 in the Spanish city of his last name to impoverished parents. To save his mother's reputation, he was taken away to another city and raised by relatives (this gave rise to the rumor, not true, that he had been left as a foundling on the steps of a church). When he

THE EPIC AMAZON JOURNEY OF FRANCISCO DE ORELLANA

Francisco de Orellana was born in Spain in 1511 and arrived in the New World, probably in the West Indies, at the ripe young age of sixteen. From there he went to Nicaragua where, as one biographer has put it, "he cut his teeth as a conquistador" fighting the indigenous peoples.

Key to both the success and tragedy in Orellana's life was his relationship with the Pizarro family—he was a close friend, quite possibly a cousin. In any event, he was one of the band of 150 hardy conquistadors who fought with Francisco Pizarro and his brothers in the conquest of Peru in 1533. Orellana acquitted himself admirably at battles in Lima, Trujillo, and Cuzco; he also lost an eye to a stone hurled by an Inca slinger.

At the end of 1540, Orellana heard that Gonzalo Pizarro, the youngest of the Pizarro brothers, was organizing an expedition to lands east of Peru, lands where there supposedly lived a king whose skin was coated with gold dust. There were also supposed to be vast forests of cinnamon trees, a spice much valued back in Spain.

Gonzalo welcomed Orellana into the expedition, although the latter was forced to start late while he gathered a team of men together. Pizarro left Quito in February 1541 with perhaps 250 conquistadors and four thousand Inca prisoners who were kept shackled together until the day the expedition marched. Two thousand pigs also went with the men, to be used for food. Naturally, after a few hundred miles many of the Inca had disappeared into the jungles; the rest, since they were mountain people, succumbed to lowland fever and heat prostration.

By the time Orellana and about twenty-five men caught up with Pizarro, the men of the original expedition were beginning to starve and die. They forged ahead together through swamps and marshes until they reached a point about 260 miles from Quito, on the shores of the Napo River, which feeds into the Amazon. They had left Quito ten months before and had nothing to show for their hardship but death, no gold, and no cinnamon. Finally, Orellana approached Pizarro with a suggestion. He would take fifty men, a boat they had built, and a dozen or so stolen Indian canoes, and travel downriver to find food. When he did, he would bring it back for the 140 men waiting with Pizarro.

This agreement was recorded by a Dominican friar who accompanied the expedition, but Pizarro was later to say that Orellana had simply taken off with all the weapons of the party and abandoned them. In fact, Orellana claimed, when the Napo took him into the broad Amazon and its swift-flowing current, there was simply no way the party could go back upriver. The mighty Amazon, two thousand miles long, carried him and his men along. On the way, they found numerous villages full of well-to-do Indians, including some who were white-skinned and quite tall (other explorers in later centuries would also note this, but no one really knows who these "white natives" were). Later on his journey, Orellana's men were attacked by Indians, some of whom were women, leading Orellana to call them "Amazons" and thus giving a name to the river and the region.

In August 1542, Orellana and his men became the first Europeans to travel down the length of the Amazon and reach the Atlantic Ocean. From there, they made their way to the island of Trinidad. Around the same time, Gonzalo Pizarro and eighty emaciated men straggled back to Quito, having finally retraced their steps through the jungle.

Gonzalo Pizarro was executed in 1548 after an attempt to take over Peru following the killing of his brother Francisco. Orellana had died two years previously, during a disastrous expedition in which he sought to take his men *up* the Amazon from the Atlantic.

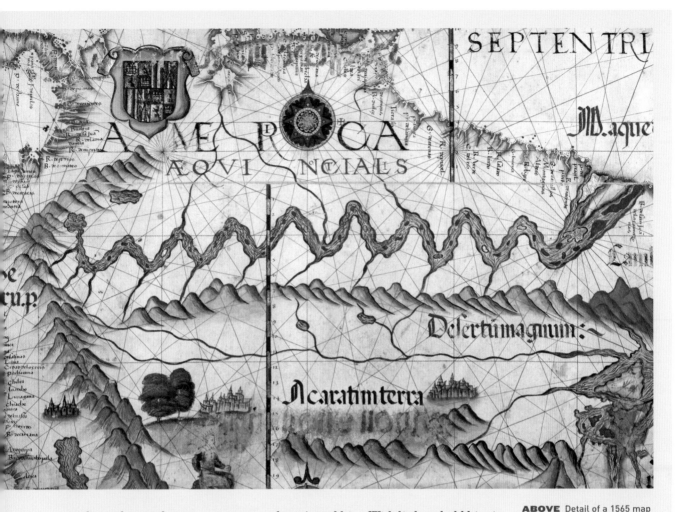

SEPTENTRI

AME_P_OCA
ÆOVI_NCIALS

Defertúmagnum:

Acaratinterra

ABOVE Detail of a 1565 map
of northern South America
showing the Pacific coast and
Peru with the city of Cuzco
and Lake Titicaca. Across the
Andes can be seen the Orinoco
and Amazon rivers.

sought out his mother as a young man, she rejected him. With little to hold him in the countryside, he went to Seville, where he became a servant to the mayor, but stabbed a fellow servant in a fight and fled to avoid going to jail.

And what better place to flee to than the New World? Hiring himself out to Pedrarias Dávila, Almagro arrived in Panama in 1514, and joined forces with Balboa to explore the treacherous jungle and Pacific coastline of Panama, chasing down rumors of gold. After this, Almagro settled down to manage the lands and cattle given to him for his service to Spain.

During this period, Almagro became close friends with Francisco Pizarro. They were alike in a number of ways—both illegitimate, illiterate, and brave, although Almagro could be charming where Pizarro was stiff and severe. And—as he would find out, to his dismay—he was nowhere near as ruthless as Francisco Pizarro.

PIRU! PIRU! In 1522, a conquistador named Pascual de Andagoya sailed south along the western coast of Central America on a voyage of exploration. He returned to Panama City where he reported with great excitement not only the apparent existence of a huge land mass to the south, but the fact that the natives

THE FABULOUS CITY OF CUZCO

It is no wonder Pizarro and Almagro—not to mention the rebellious Inca—fought so hard over the city of Cuzco. Founded in the eleventh or twelfth century, the Inca capital was an extraordinary place. In order to get there, the Spaniards headed south on the great north–south Inca highway, which stretched across the arid Andean plateau. The road in itself was a wonder: straight as an arrow, made of hardened mortar or cobblestones, with steps perfectly carved into the sides of mountains and stone bridges arching over high chasms. The road was formerly used by Inca courtiers who carried messages (either committed to memory or in *khipu*, knots twisted into ropes made of human hair) in relays. If the Inca ruler sent a note from Quito to Cuzco—a distance of 1,200 miles—it could reach there in ten days. A single runner could go 150 miles in a day.

The Spanish were even more amazed when they arrived in Cuzco in November 1533. Situated at 11,000 feet on a barren and rocky plain, mountains ringing the horizon on all sides, Cuzco was shaped like a giant puma. Inside its towering walls were numerous grand edifices, temples and palaces. At the heart of the city was a huge central plaza carpeted in white sand, which was brought in from the Pacific Ocean on a regular basis and raked daily by maintenance men. The plaza was surrounded on three sides by Sun temples plated with gold. When the setting sun hit sand and gold, it was as if the heart of the city were ablaze in the purest white and gold light.

"Every street, every fortress, and every stone [of Cuzco] was regarded as a sacred mystery," wrote one Spanish chronicler, but the Spanish sacked, burnt, and destroyed Cuzco, turning it into a Spanish-style city. Over the next fifty years, they knocked down hundreds of buildings to make wide avenues, destroying four hundred Inca temples in the process.

BELOW An engraving from 1556 shows the city of Cuzco. Its huge palaces and temples covered with gold astonished the Spanish, although they later demolished many of them to make a city in the European style.

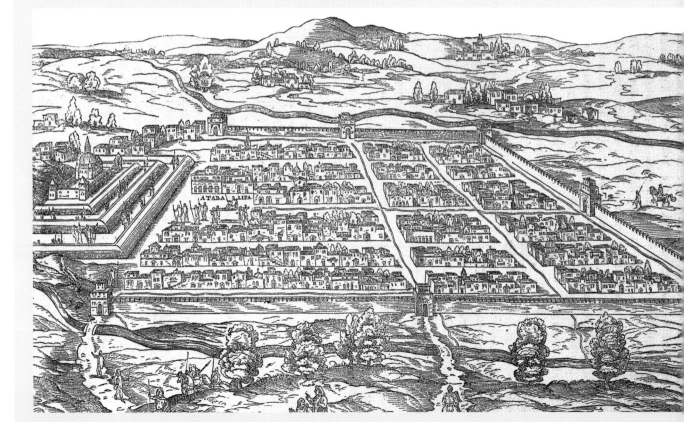

he met on his voyage kept pointing southward and saying *Piru!* According to translators he had brought with him, these peoples claimed that a huge empire ruled by a divine king existed to the south, where gold was used as commonly as stones and mortar.

Naturally, this inflamed the imagination of conquistadors like Pizarro and Almagro. Together with a third friend, a priest and schoolmaster by the name of Hernando de Luque—who had become rich investing in land—the two aging conquistadors (it is important to remember in what follows that both Pizarro and Almagro were now over fifty) formed a company to explore this fabulous Piru. Pizarro would be the military leader, Almagro would provide the supplies, and Luque would be in charge of finances. To ratify the deal (since neither Almagro nor Pizarro could write) all three swore on a Bible to uphold their ends, and then the two conquistadors drew a large sign of the Cross on the frontispiece of the Good Book.

THREE ATTEMPTS Pizarro left Panama on his expedition to Peru in November of 1524, with two vessels and eighty sailors and soldiers. Almagro trailed with a smaller expedition; Luque stayed behind. Things were not to be easy. Pizarro first sought out a great river he had heard about (the San Juan) and after several weeks of hardship found the mouth of the river pouring into a large and empty bay. He sent one of his ships under the command of a lieutenant of his, Montenegro, further south along the coast to explore while he rested his men, but it took weeks for that ship to return and Pizarro and his men began to starve in this desolate bay, which was infested with dangerous caimans and where there was little to eat. By the time the exploring party had returned, Pizarro's conquistadors were eating their belts.

Montenegro reported no golden empire, so Pizarro decided to strike inland. No sooner had his men penetrated a few miles into the jungle than they were ambushed by Indians. Pizarro was almost killed and five of his men died before the attack was beaten off. Almagro, up the coast just north of Pizarro, was also ambushed and lost his left eye fighting off his attackers. Both he and Pizarro fled back to Panama, realizing that finding this fabled empire was not going to be so easy after all.

The two of them made two more attempts, in 1526 and 1528, getting further south each time, fighting off Indians. On the third expedition, Pizarro and Almagro finally reached the northern Peruvian town of Tumbes, and there the Inca empire began to open before their eyes. Tumbes had white-washed, cube-shaped houses, temples and small palaces; the people wore gold, silver and diamond studs in their ears and were far more prosperous than those recently encountered. Pizarro and his fellows saw, for the first time, llamas (which they called "little camels"). The Peruvians were themselves astonished at the Spaniards, their horses and their bright armor, which made the Incas call them "Children of the Sun."

Pizarro and Almagro now knew for certain that a few hundred miles to the south, beyond towering and rugged mountains, was a powerful king who ruled an astonishing empire. The two men shook hands gleefully—for a triumph on the level of that of Hernán Cortés seemed now within their grasp.

They returned to Spain to plan their final expedition.

THE INCA At the height of its short-lived power—for, like the Aztec state, the Inca empire was cut down as it was reaching its prime—the land of the Inca stretched through what is now Peru, Ecuador, and northern Chile. The empire was a hodge-podge of environmental systems: the flatlands of the Pacific coast, the eastern jungles, and, in between, the Andes. On an upland plateau between those huge mountains the Inca had founded their capital city of Cuzco.

The Inca state was established when a band of wanderers from present-day Bolivia migrated south into the Andes; by the mid fourteenth century, this tribe had expanded out of the mountains east, west, north, and south, for two thousand miles. They called their land in their Quechuan language *Tawantinsuyu*, or "The Land of Four Quarters," and it was all ruled by an extraordinarily powerful person, the Inca (meaning "lord"), whose abode was Cuzco. Inca rulers were held to be divine, holding earthly sway even after they were dead.

The empire, connected by an extraordinary highway network, was run along the lines of a Soviet co-operative. As an early conquistador was to write:

> The Incas governed their subjects in such a fashion that among them was neither a thief, nor a depraved man, nor an adulterous woman ... the mountains and the mines, the pastures, the game, the wood ... were controlled and shared so that each knew and possessed his own without anyone else being able to take it ...

A rosy picture, but a little narrow. The Inca people were subjected to forcible relocation, either because they were needed to work on major projects or because the bureaucracy wanted to separate newly conquered tribes from their homeland. And, despite the fact that the trains ran on time, as it were, the country was rife with civil war. A battle for succession had gone on after the death of the Inca Huayna Capac in 1525, pitting his sons Huascar and Atahuallpa against each other. In the summer of 1532, Atahuallpa had just destroyed the forces of his brother in a bloody battle in northern Peru, leaving thousands rotting on the battlefield (the Spanish were later to come across this scene of carnage and be amazed at the number of corpses).

Just after his victory, Atahuallpa heard of the arrival of these white, bearded men riding their strange creatures. Swollen with confidence from his recent victory, he decided to go and see these visitors, and instructed that they meet him at the town of Cajamarca.

THE GLORY DAYS OF PIZARRO AND ALMAGRO

One biographer of Francisco Pizarro has written that one can accuse Pizarro of "every vice but hypocrisy," but that probably provides too favorable an impression of his character. In a move that would mark him in history as one of the cruelest and boldest conquistadors of all time, Pizarro, accompanied by only 168 men, set a trap for Atahuallpa in the plaza of Cajamarca, suddenly attacking the Inca's thousands of retainers (many of whom were unarmed) with terrifying cannon, fire-tempered Seville steel, and rampaging horses.

When the smoke cleared, Pizarro was in charge of Atahuallpa himself—and the fate of Peru. Atahuallpa promised the Spanish a room full of gold and another two rooms of silver if they released him. Pizarro agreed, collected the rich treasure, made a secret agreement to name a half-brother of Atahuallpa as Inca, and then offered Atahuallpa a choice: death by burning if he did not accept baptism; the garrote if he did. Atahuallpa, at last, was no fool—he was choked to death publicly with the new Christian name Juan de Atahuallpa on August 29, 1533. The next day, Pizarro and his men celebrated a solemn mass for the repose of the Inca's soul. A crepe veil covered the hilt of the conquistador's sword.

Their mourning did not stop them from the business at hand: dividing up the spoils of empire. Almagro, as was their practice, had followed Pizarro into Peru and so had not been part of the initial conquest of Atahuallpa and his men, but he soon made his mark. He joined Pizarro and the two headed south along the fine Inca highway, making their way to the astonishingly beautiful highland city of Cuzco. A religious festival was taking place as the conquistador partners and their men entered. At the order of Pizarro and Almagro the Spanish charged with swords and lances into the crowd, dispersing what they considered to be pagan worshippers, and then settled down to the serious business of stripping the city of its riches.

A new threat arose as word came that a Spanish conquistador named Pedro de Alvarado had journeyed with an expedition from Mexico, in order to conquer a part of Peru for himself. Pizarro, intent on founding himself a new capital city (soon to be called Lima) sent Almagro to deal with the man. In true fashion, instead of fighting Alvarado, Almagro bribed him: if he would return north, Almagro told him, Pizarro would pay him a hundred thousand pesos. Alvarado accepted and the matter was closed. Pizarro, now so wealthy a hundred thousand pesos meant nothing to him, congratulated Almagro on a job well done.

"MAY YOU CONFOUND ME" Such peaceful relations could not last long among conquistadors. The trouble began as the spoils were divided up. Pizarro went to Spain to meet with Charles V, Holy Roman Emperor; when he returned it was with royal documents allocating all of northern Peru (it was now to be called New Castile) to himself and all of southern Peru (to be called New

LEFT The funeral mass held on August 30, 1533, for the Inca Atahuallpa, as portrayed in a later painting. Francisco Pizarro had had him executed the previous day after capturing him in the town of Cajamarca.

A LAND RULED BY THE DEAD

When Francisco Pizarro arrived in Cuzco fresh from his conquest of the Inca, he stared around him in wonder, for he was just starting to realize what a strange and fabulous civilization he was encountering. "The greater part of the people, treasure, expenses and vices," he wrote, "were under the control of the dead."

This was no figure of speech or exaggeration. The Inca himself, emperor of all he surveyed, was immortal, naturally, and so when he died, he did not really die. The extremely sophisticated Inca embalmers simply had him mummified (preservation was further aided by the extremely dry air of Cuzco) and he was placed in his own palace, surrounded by his own set of faithful relatives and other retainers. This might have been all right if the dead Inca were merely worshipped as a god, but in fact the corpse—and dozens of other such dead rulers—became involved in temporal politics, intriguing against the living, giving orders to special assistants through whom he "spoke."

An extraordinary way to run a country and it is no wonder the Inca, when Pizarro first arrived, were in the midst of a desperate civil war.

Toledo) to Almagro. But no one had quite figured out where northern Peru left off and southern Peru began. Worse, to whom did the amazing city of Cuzco belong? Almagro claimed it as his own, but so did Pizarro's brothers Juan, Hernando, and Gonzalo. All parties were present when the city was taken; all now inhabited it.

The Pizarro brothers and Almagro were on the point of attacking each other with drawn swords when Francisco Pizarro himself showed up to mediate. The two men appear to have had a genuine reconciliation, even falling into each other's arms. Pizarro told Almagro that neither he nor any member of his family would ever attack him; in return, Almagro pledged that he would not seek any claim within 130 leagues of the city of Cuzco.

To seal their deal, the two men crossed hands over a consecrated Host during a public Mass, and Almagro even went further, exclaiming: "Lord, if I break my oath, may you confound me and punish me in my flesh and in my soul."

Almagro then turned south, on what would be a fruitless expedition (except that he became the European discoverer of Chile) to find gold. He spent a great deal of money wandering through the wilderness, losing dozens of men, finally returning in the spring of 1537.

Then he heard news that lifted his heart: Cuzco, ruled by the three Pizarro brothers, was under siege by rebellious Indians under the leadership of an heir to the Inca throne, Manco Inca, who had managed to raise an army—an estimated two hundred thousand men—and was intent on re-capturing the holy city. Hernando Pizarro held out fiercely, even after his brother Juan was killed by a stone launched by an Indian slinger. The Inca were gradually pushed back and Manco began to retreat with his forces.

But Almagro had seen his opportunity. Marching to Cuzco with a small army, he attacked the Inca as they were retreating, catching them by surprise and slaughtering thousands of them. His oath apparently forgotten, he then entered Cuzco triumphantly and demanded that the two remaining Pizarro brothers hand the city over to him. When Hernando and Gonzalo refused, Almagro had them thrown in jail.

CONQUISTADOR VERSUS CONQUISTADOR

Triumphant, Almagro then decided to march on Francisco Pizarro in Lima. It is hard to understand what, possibly, he might have been thinking—here he was attacking the man favored by the Holy Roman Emperor, the man with whom he had had a twenty-year friendship, the man with whom he had just recently sworn an oath of eternal loyalty. But Almagro was a conquistador, and, therefore, gold and riches came before all else—capturing all of Peru, Holy Roman Emperor be damned, was simply too tempting.

However, before Almagro even got to Lima, a priest arranged a meeting between the two rivals and another deal was made: this time, Almagro would get his beloved Cuzco, while the Pizarro brothers would be released from prison (and

Hernando was to be sent back to Spain). Pizarro then invited Almagro for dinner. It was all a sham; during the night, Almagro was warned that Gonzalo Pizarro had escaped from prison and was coming to kill him. Mounting his horse, he took off, flying down the Inca road, back to Cuzco.

It was now open warfare between the two old friends, although this time Pizarro, sixty-seven years old, and Almagro, sixty-three, let others undertake the actual combat. Hernando and Gonzalo raised an army of eight hundred and brought them to a valley two miles outside Cuzco, where they met Almagro's six hundred conquistadors in April 1538. Francisco Pizarro stayed in Lima; Almagro watched from a promontory overlooking the battlefield. Hundreds of Inca climbed high up in the mountains, jeering, to watch the clash of white man against white man. Rodrigo de Orgonez, a veteran captain, was in charge of Almagro's men and fought fiercely, but Pizarro's army had more guns and gradually drove back Almagro's force until they turned and fled. The combat was bloody, with no quarter given—Orgonez tried to surrender, only to be shot at point blank range.

Resistance collapsed and Almagro was captured and taken back to Cuzco—the city he loved so much—tied over the back of a mule. Hernando Pizarro condemned him to death for high treason and refused to listen to any appeal, even after Almagro had thrown himself at his feet, begging for his life. Hernando said: "You're a gentleman with an illustrious name ... it marvels me that a man of our mood fears death so much."

A "man of our mood." A conquistador. Thus shamed, Diego de Almagro was dragged to a public square in Cuzco and beheaded.

PIZARRO'S LAST DAYS When he heard the news of his old rival's death, Pizarro apparently broke into tears—he had not, he claimed, wanted Hernando to go quite so far. But he never punished his brother and, in fact, seems to have felt real relief that his old companion was no longer around to plague him. Francisco Pizarro went on building his city of Lima and ruling the country of Peru until 1541, when he was seventy years old.

Then Almagro finally got his revenge. For he had a son by a native woman, a young man whose name was also Diego, and Diego had burned with a desire for revenge in the three years since his father had been executed. Secretly gathering a force around him, he attacked Pizarro's palatial headquarters one Sunday afternoon, as Pizarro was dining with friends. Pizarro did not even have time to buckle his armor as Diego and his men burst in, crying "Death to the tyrant!" Defending himself with only sword and shield, he put up a much braver show than Almagro had at the end, even killing a man before collapsing on the ground in a pool of blood, run through by his assailants' swords. He seems to have mumbled a confession, drawn a Cross on the floor in his own blood, and then died.

Blood, treachery, and hoped-for salvation—a conquistador's life to the very end.

113

MARY, QUEEN OF SCOTS

ELIZABETH I AND MARY, QUEEN OF SCOTS: TWO QUEENS, ONE REALM

THEY WERE COUSINS AT A TIME WHEN BLOODLINE mattered over almost everything but religion and they were powerful women during a period when most of their sex were expected to stand in the shadows cast by men. There were a number of things beside their common ancestry and status that might have brought them together—their intelligence, humor, beauty, and the realm they shared and loved. "How much better were it that we being two Queens so near of kin, neighbours and living in one isle, should be friends and live together like sisters," wrote Mary, Queen of Scots, to her cousin, Queen Elizabeth I. For her part Elizabeth lamented aloud to her advisors that she wished she and Mary were "but as two milkmaids with pails upon our arms."

It was not to be. Caught up in a power struggle over the bodies and souls of their people, Mary and Elizabeth were destined never to be the "sisters" each longed for them to be and, in fact, became rivals, each plotting the death of the other. Although, as one historian has put it, "it was their royal rather than their human status" that made them vie with each other, it was their humanity that, in the end, makes this story tragic.

"YESTERDAY MY LADY PRINCESS ..." The path that led the cousins to their bloody end began with Henry VIII, King of England from 1509 and 1547, and his desire to have a male heir. His first wife, Catherine of Aragon, had not produced one, although she and Henry had a daughter, Mary Tudor. As time went by without the expected heir, Henry grew impatient and finally became besotted with the young, lithe and spirited Anne Boleyn, one of the queen's entourage. When Pope Clement VII was reluctant to give permission for Henry to annul his marriage to Catherine, Henry, with the help of obliging clergy he himself had appointed, had the twenty-four-year union decreed null and void and his daughter, Mary, declared illegitimate.

The king secretly married Anne when she was a month pregnant, in January of 1533, in the high hopes that she was carrying his longed-for male heir. In fact, on September 7, she gave birth to a girl, Elizabeth, much to the king's anger and dismay. Two further pregnancies ended in miscarriage and stillbirth, and Henry set about the process of vilifying Anne by causing false charges of adultery and incest to be brought against her. In May 1536 she was beheaded. Three months later, Henry declared two-year-old Elizabeth illegitimate—now, like her half-sister Mary, she was no longer a princess, merely a lady—and ordered that she be raised in a separate household. Elizabeth was keenly aware of her uncertain status, even at a young age. A year later, aged only three and a half, she supposedly said to the governor of her household: "How haps it Governor, yesterday my Lady Princess and today but my Lady Elizabeth?"

THE ROUGH WOOING Only twelve days after Anne Boleyn's death, Henry had married Jane Seymour, who at last provided the male heir he sought, Prince Edward, who was born in October 1537. But by this time Pope Clement had excommunicated Henry, who responded by having himself declared "the Only Supreme Head in Earth of the Church of England" and making it treason for anyone to refuse to acknowledge him as such. Thus began the English Reformation, which resulted in the founding of the Anglican Church. It was also a period of persecution of English Catholics. Monasteries were suppressed and had their property confiscated by the Crown, while dissenting clergy were tortured and executed. In the meantime, because Henry had been excommunicated, the country was considered by the pope and the heads of Catholic countries such as France and Spain to be legally without a ruler, which made England a legitimate target for attack.

Partly because of this, Henry VIII sought to consolidate his hold on the British Isles. He annexed Wales, and then, looking about him, saw the perfect opportunity for bringing Scotland under English sway. In December 1542, the Scottish ruler, James V, died, leaving behind a six-day-old infant daughter, Mary Stuart, whose mother, also Mary, was from the noble French family of Guise. James's father had been married to Henry's Aunt Margaret, which made infant Mary a Tudor granddaughter. What better than to betroth his young son Edward, now six, to Mary Stuart, thus joining the two realms?

Typically, Henry ignored a few problems, the main one being the fact that the child Mary—and much of Scotland—was Catholic and considered Henry a sinner and apostate. Henry also set a condition that Scotland break its strong ties with France, something Mary of Guise naturally refused to do. She hid her child for months after her birth, until she could be crowned Queen of Scots in Stirling

POLITICAL VIRGINITY

Was Queen Elizabeth I, the famous "Virgin Queen," really a virgin? The answer is, probably. There were very good reasons for remaining so. One was the simple fact that childbirth was dangerous. Puerperal fever was common; the pregnancy of Elizabeth's beloved stepmother, Queen Catherine Parr, ended with her dying of the fever, and this must have made a profound impression on the teenaged Elizabeth. Also, her mother, Anne Boleyn (as well as another stepmother, Catherine Howard), had been executed in part because of charges of sexual licentiousness, which, at least in Anne Boleyn's case, were simply untrue.

Elizabeth's adolescent experience with Thomas Seymour, whose wooing of her ended with his execution, showed her the need for political caution when it came to sex. Like Seymour, the men she was attracted to, particularly her Master of Horse, Lord Robert Dudley, whom she genuinely and passionately loved, were ambitious and aggressive figures who aroused resentment and jealousy, two malign emotions of which there was already ample supply in the Elizabethan court.

Elizabeth was to walk a sexual tightrope throughout her long reign, resisting the urging of advisors to marry while keeping the door open, just, to the possibility.

Castle when she was nine months old. At this point, Henry began what has been called the "rough wooing" of Scotland to force the country to allow the marriage. It consisted of a series of military attacks on Scotland—they continued until 1551— which were bloody and costly in the extreme to both countries.

Although Henry did not get his way, it was considered safer to remove Mary, Queen of Scots, from the country, and when she was only five her mother took her to be raised in the French court.

"THE FINEST SHE THAT EVER WAS ..." In France, the young Mary was betrothed to the Dauphin Francis, son of King Henri II, and she married him when she was fifteen. Fifteen months later, Henri died after a jousting accident and Mary became Queen Consort of France. Her family, the Guises, were, as one historian has put it, "magnificent in presence, consummate in charm and energy ... audacious, vindictive and [capable of] abominable cruelty." They were often at odds with the rest of France and the French court. During Francis's rule, a Protestant plot to unseat the Guises was discovered and, so the story goes, one afternoon Mary listened to the torture of fifty of the leaders of this revolt in the courtyard of the castle where she was staying. She apparently sang hymns and chanted psalms to drown out the screams, but it was a typical moment in her life—religion and blood rising together to a horrible crescendo.

Mary's husband, Francis, died of natural causes after reigning for only a year, and Catherine de Médici, who had been married to Henri II and who wanted to see the power of the Guises diminished, decided that Mary was highly expendable—the sooner she was packed off to Scotland, the better for everyone concerned.

And so, in the summer of 1561, Mary made ready to return to a country of which she was officially queen but of which she had little personal experience. She was nineteen years old and possessed a fine education as well as an understanding of the uses of power. She also possessed something else: she was extremely beautiful. Almost six feet tall—an almost unheard-of height for women of the age—with chestnut hair, extraordinarily white skin, and piercing grey eyes, she was called by an English ambassador (who had no reason to love her) "the finest she that ever was." An Italian minister to the French court said that she was "personally the most beautiful [woman] in Europe."

Yet, it was her very beauty—and the passion and recklessness that often accompany unusual physical attractiveness—that was to prove her undoing.

QUEEN ELIZABETH As Mary was preparing to leave France for Scotland she was being watched carefully by another queen, her cousin Elizabeth, some nine years older than Mary and not nearly so beautiful, but possessing a glorious intelligence and the instincts of a true survivor. Henry VIII had died in 1547, when Elizabeth was thirteen years old. Raised by a loving governess and tutored by William Grindal, an extraordinary teacher, Elizabeth's poise and learning were legendary—as a child of eight, she had once entered a room and spoken to French, Italian and Spanish ambassadors, each in his own language, without pause or mistake. Before Henry died, secure in the knowledge that he finally had a male heir, he had placed both Mary Tudor and Elizabeth back in the line of succession to the throne.

Catherine Parr, Henry's last wife, then married Thomas Seymour, who was the brother of the Lord Protector of Henry's heir, young Edward VI, and took Elizabeth into her household. When Catherine died in childbirth, Thomas Seymour, who had previously flirted with the adolescent Elizabeth, now began to woo her in earnest, seeking the power that marriage to an heir to the English throne would bring. Elizabeth was both titillated and frightened by his aggressive advances. In 1549, he was arrested and charged with plotting to marry her and overthrow her brother, and was beheaded. On the occasion of his death, Elizabeth supposedly remarked: "This day died a man with much wit and very little judgment."

The experience scarred Elizabeth and she vowed never again to let a man attempt to use her in this way. Having escaped this predicament because of her youth and relative innocence, she now fell into one that was far more serious. When her brother, Edward, was dying of tuberculosis, aged only fifteen, he overturned the line of succession set up by Henry VIII and named Lady Jane Grey as his successor. Grey reigned for only nine days before she was overthrown and executed by Mary Tudor, whom many in England felt was the rightful heir to the throne, but the Catholic Mary's rule was repressive in the extreme, with English Protestants harried and publicly burned as heretics. One poet wrote, after a public execution of seven Protestants: "When these, at Maidstone, were put to death / We wished for our ELIZABETH."

The popular longing for the young Elizabeth was extraordinary. Mary was aware of it and in 1554 accused Elizabeth of plotting against her. Despite her half-sister's beseechments, the queen threw the terrified twenty-year-old into the Tower, which was usually a prelude to execution. Fortunately, Mary was unable to prove that Elizabeth had committed treason and she also feared executing such a popular figure. Elizabeth was released from the Tower and placed under house arrest for a year, but then gradually restored to her rightful position. By the time Mary died in 1558, she had named Elizabeth her heir.

THE FIRST CLASH The Elizabeth who pondered what to do about the arrival of the cousin she had never met was twenty-seven years old and had been queen for two years. She was extraordinarily popular with the people of England, whom she made a point of cultivating during annual processions around the country, much as a modern politician might visit his or her constituency. Elizabeth had bright red hair, very pale skin, a longish face, and eyes that were an unusually dark hue for someone of her coloring. She was short-sighted and had an endearing habit of leaning towards people when she spoke to them, which seemed

LEFT A contemporary depiction of Henry VIII and his family, this allegory of the Tudor succession by Lucas de Heere shows Henry in the center, with Mary and her husband, Philip of Spain, on the left, and Edward VI and Elizabeth on the right.

to ask them to confide in her. Men found her fascinating and she loved them in return, particularly her childhood friend Robert Dudley, her "dear Robin," who was her Master of Horse. But she kept him, and others, at a distance, preferring to concentrate on ruling her kingdom without interference from a husband. She did, however, surround herself with male advisors, particularly William Cecil and Francis Walsingham, who loyally helped her navigate the treacherous undercurrents of English and Continental politics.

In August 1561, as Mary planned to return to her kingdom of Scotland, she sought Elizabeth's promise of safe passage through English waters. This Elizabeth agreed to—but only if Mary ratified the Treaty of Edinburgh, which stated that Mary would renounce her claim to the throne of England. This Mary refused to do. She knew that Elizabeth had supported Scottish lords who had recently rebelled against her throne, and this angered her. In a sharp display of one-upmanship, she sent a letter to Elizabeth, saying that she had never rebelled against her, although many of Elizabeth's own subjects, who "be not of the mind she [Elizabeth] is, neither in religion, nor other things" were "inclined to hear offers."

In other words, Mary was saying, with the arrogance that Elizabeth would grow to hate, that there were those in England who considered her, Mary, the true queen. As would be typical when it came to dealing with her cousin, Elizabeth vacillated, finally agreeing to safe passage, but Mary had already decided to sail—in her own typical fashion telling all who would listen that should the ship run aground in England, Elizabeth would almost certainly capture and execute her.

"SHE IS TOO HIGH" Mary was given a tumultuous welcome when she returned to Edinburgh, with celebratory cannon thundering and people lining the streets to get a look at her, but she found that the country was not quite as she had left it. For one thing, it had become much more Protestant under the control of her illegitimate brother Lord James Stewart and the influence of the fiery Calvinist preacher John Knox, who met with Mary soon after she arrived in the country and brought her to tears by threatening her with "the greveus plagues of God" for worshipping Catholic idols.

It was a difficult transition for Mary, coming from the warm weather of the Loire Valley to Scotland's less welcoming climate. Her people were fascinated by her—one early biographer claimed that it was as if this lovely presence had "flown in through the air"—but a little suspicious and mistrusting. And Elizabeth continued to joust with her over the issue of succession to the English throne. Mary's minister William Maitland of Lethington visited Elizabeth to warn her that the idea that Mary should be named to succeed Elizabeth was "firmly rooted in her head." Elizabeth claimed to understand this and not dispute it, but went on to say that naming a successor now could be dangerous for her, since others might rally to Mary and plot to unseat her. It would be like "seeing my winding-sheet before my eyes," she said, in a memorable phrase.

It was also a prophetic phrase, because very soon after this Elizabeth became ill with smallpox, a disease few escaped at the time. "Death possessed almost every joint of me," Elizabeth was later to write, and she struggled with fever for a week and then remained in seclusion while her pox scars healed. Her illness may have convinced her that some accommodation with Mary should be arranged, and thus she made an extraordinary suggestion early in 1563 to the Scottish ambassador to her court, James Melville. If Mary would agree to wed Robert Dudley—it must be remembered, this was the man who was probably the love of Elizabeth's life—she, Mary, would "proceed to the inquisition of her right and title to be our next cousin and heir."

Melville was startled to hear this—he assumed that the queen and Dudley were lovers, though this was not the case—but in further conversation with Elizabeth he realized she was serious. He said he would bring the proposal to Queen Mary, which he did, but she dismissed it. Dudley was a Protestant, for one thing, and, for another, who was Elizabeth to be planning Mary's marriages? Still, Elizabeth had taken a liking to Melville and they had a bit of byplay that provides a lighter moment in the Elizabeth–Mary saga.

Who was the fairest queen, Elizabeth asked him teasingly—Elizabeth or Mary?

Melville replied diplomatically that Elizabeth was the fairest in England, Mary in Scotland. Elizabeth then went on to ask which queen was taller, to which Melville could give a more honest answer: Mary was taller, he replied.

On this, Elizabeth pounced: "Then she is too high," she said. "For I am neither too high nor too low."

MARY BROUGHT LOW Having turned down Elizabeth's proposal, Mary proceeded to make a disastrous marriage that would prove the start of her numerous troubles in Scotland. She impulsively wed Henry Stuart, Lord Darnley, a handsome, ambitious and not too bright young man, who also happened to be her first cousin, as well as a pretender to the English throne. Marrying Darnley because she was passionately attracted to him (the exact opposite of what her cousin Elizabeth would do) was a serious mistake: he proved to be a nightmare of a spouse. He demanded more power than she was willing to give him and then, when she was pregnant, physically attacked her, hoping to get her to miscarry.

This proved unsuccessful, but Darnley then sought out Mary's friend and confidant, her secretary David Riccio. Entering Mary's inner chambers, Darnley and a large group of conspirators dragged the frightened Riccio (who was literally cowering behind Mary's skirts) out onto the floor and stabbed him to death, leaving over fifty dagger wounds in his body, all of this under the pretext that Mary and Riccio were having an affair. Mary then seemed to reconcile with Darnley, but shortly after the birth of her son, the future James VI, in late 1566, a gunpowder explosion blew through Darnley's home. When civilians raced to the scene,

BLOODY MARY

Before Elizabeth ascended to the throne, the monarch of England was Mary Tudor, who reigned from 1553 to 1558. Mary was Elizabeth's half-sister, seventeen years her senior, the daughter of Henry VIII and his first wife, Catherine of Aragon. Because Henry divorced Catherine when she could not produce a male heir—setting in motion the chain of events that led to the formation of the Church of England—Mary, once heir to the throne, found herself ousted and humiliated along with her mother.

Once Mary was able to gain the throne of England, she attempted to turn back the clock by restoring Catholicism as the legitimate religion in the land. This might have worked had she allowed room for both Church of England and Roman Church, but Mary was not a woman noted for her tolerance. She began an era of persecution that saw three hundred Protestants executed in what one historian has called "an orgy of burnings." Most of them were ordinary people who refused to recant their religion. Mary, in her fanaticism, had misread the mood of the English people. While they saw the legality of her claim to the throne—many felt that all of Henry's marriages after his first were illegitimate—and while many were Catholics driven underground during Henry's persecutions, they did not want to see these horrors visited upon their fellows. This, combined with Mary's marriage to the Catholic Philip II of Spain, made her a highly unpopular queen. She died in November of 1558, probably of ovarian cancer. She was forty-two years old, and she went unmourned, even by her husband.

they found Darnley dead fifty feet from the house—not killed by the explosion, however, but through suffocation or strangulation. One of his servants lay dead beside him.

Blame was immediately cast upon Mary and James Hepburn, the Earl of Bothwell, the man who would become her third husband. While Mary may not have known the details of the plot to kill her husband, or specifically ordered it, most historians believe that she was aware that the plan was underway and did nothing to stand in its way. But marrying Bothwell three months later was Mary's worst mistake, for it was assumed that she and Bothwell had together murdered Darnley. An army of three thousand Scottish Protestant leaders rode against Mary and Bothwell in June 1567, captured Mary (Bothwell escaped to Norway, where he was later to die in prison, insane) and forced her to abdicate in favor of her ten-month-old son, James. She was held a prisoner in Edinburgh and then Loch Leven castle, where she miscarried twin sons (by Bothwell).

However, Mary's saga was far from done. In May of 1568, with the help of a young admirer, she escaped Loch Leven and raised an army against the Scottish lords who had imprisoned her. She was defeated, but managed to gallop for ninety miles with a few faithful retainers until she reached the Solway Firth and crossed, with only the clothes on her back, into England. She then wrote to her cousin: "I entreat you to fetch me as soon as you can for I am in a pitiable condition, not only for a Queen, but for a gentlewoman."

THE LONG IMPRISONMENT During Mary's troubles Elizabeth had ostentatiously worn a locket containing a picture of her cousin but, in fact, Mary's flight to England caused her no end of trouble. Elizabeth did not want to be seen to be supporting Mary in a civil war and her first desire was to return her. However, the Protestants who now ruled Scotland did not want Mary returned and Elizabeth desired that these men be on her side, especially if France decided to take advantage of the chaos and try to invade Scotland.

So Elizabeth was stuck with her cousin, who engendered conflicting emotions in her breast. On the one hand, Mary got herself into trouble precisely because of the type of headlong impetuousness that she, Elizabeth, had avoided all her life. On the other hand, she genuinely sympathized with the plight of the younger woman, who appealed to her maternal and familial instincts. Mary was clever enough to play on this; while imprisoned in Scotland in 1568, she wrote a sonnet to Queen Elizabeth, which stated:

Therefore, dear sister, should this letter dwell
Upon my weighty need of seeing you,
It is that grief and pain should be my due
Unless my wait should end both swift and well.

Elizabeth would not see Mary, perhaps being afraid that the woman's notorious charm would sway her into making a move that would be contrary to her own self-interest. Instead, she decided to keep her in a genteel imprisonment, at first in Bolton Castle, and then in Sheffield Castle, until she could figure out what to do with her. This caused her a certain amount of guilt—Elizabeth had, after all, been imprisoned herself, and by her half-sister—but on the other hand, it could be worse, for Elizabeth's advisors were calling for Mary to be tried for the murder of her husband. A court of inquiry in late 1568 produced the famous "casket letters"—missives in a silver jewel casket purporting to be in the queen's handwriting and incriminating her in Darnley's death. These failed to convict Mary (most historians now believe these letters to be forgeries) but in the main Mary survived because Elizabeth willed it.

Still, the English queen could not release Mary and hence her genteel imprisonment stretched on for nineteen years. At the same time as she was writing letters begging to be allowed into Elizabeth's company ("I shall discover to you the secrets of my heart"), Mary was sending secret notes to King Philip II of Spain, saying that if he would help her escape, "I shall be Queen of England in three months and Mass shall be said all over the country."

The fact that Mary thought she could so easily supplant such a popular queen shows just how detached from reality she was becoming. Part of this was the simple fact that in what was called "close confinement"—she was able to move about within the castle, but was not allowed outside—she was simply out of touch. Kept company by the Countess of Shrewsbury (wife of Mary's jailer for fifteen years, the Earl of Shrewsbury), Mary did a great deal of embroidery, into some of which she placed secret codes or jokes—as in the piece where an orange-haired tabby wore a crown and threatened a poor mouse. But Mary almost immediately became the focus of serious plots to depose or even assassinate her cousin. The first, in 1569, known as the Revolt of the Northern Earls, was a doomed attempt by the Earls of Northumberland and Westmorland to rise up to try to rescue Mary. This was followed in 1571 by the Ridolfi plot, an attempt by an Italian banker who joined forces with the Catholic Duke of Norfolk and King Philip of Spain to murder Elizabeth and put Mary, married to Norfolk, on the throne of England. This too was stopped and its principals were executed, causing the pope to excommunicate Elizabeth.

Over the years, as these plots and others grew in seriousness, Mary was kept in closer and closer confinement, finally being transferred in January 1585 to a stark Tudor stronghold, Tutbury Castle, where her jailer was no longer the amiable Shewsbury (who, like many another men, had fallen in love with Mary) but Sir Amyas Paulet, an extremely religious Protestant who was not susceptible to her charms. Elizabeth also had Sir Francis Walsingham, head of her intelligence service—and her spies rivaled any that the KGB or CIA could boast today—intercept and read Mary's mail. It was thus that Elizabeth and her advisors became aware of the Babington Plot.

One of the many young Catholic gentlemen inspired by the legend of the romantic and imprisoned Queen Mary (Mary was now forty-two), the twenty-five-year-old Anthony Babington had decided that he would simultaneously use six assassins to attack Queen Elizabeth while one hundred co-conspirators would free Mary. Foolishly, he wrote to Mary, telling her of his plans. Even more foolishly, unaware that the Elizabethan spies were reading her mail, Mary wrote back suggesting that quantities of money and foreign aid might be needed, but assuring Babington that her "good intentions" went with him and his assassins.

"TO THE HURT, DEATH AND DESTRUCTION"

Although there is some controversy as to whether all or part of this plot was dreamed up by Walsingham to entrap Mary, her ready acquiescence to Babington's plans was all that was needed. Mary was put on trial for treason in late October 1586 and found guilty of having "compassed and imagined within this Realm of England divers Matters tending to the Hurt, Death and Destruction of the Royal Person of our Sovereign the Queen."

The sentence for such an offense was execution, but it then became extremely difficult to get Elizabeth to sign the death warrant. Not only was she worried how Europe, in particular Catholic Spain, might take such an action, but she was concerned about the uproar it would cause in Scotland, now ruled by Mary's son, twenty-one-year-old James VI. At one point, Elizabeth even wrote to Paulet, her jailor, and asked him if he might contrive to find some way to secretly murder Mary and make it look like she had died of natural causes. This he refused to do.

Elizabeth's reluctance, her anguish over sentencing her rival to death, shows that her natural sympathies were still in play, despite Mary's numerous betrayals. Finally, on February 1, Elizabeth suddenly sent for Mary's death warrant and signed it. Fearful that she might change her mind, her advisors met and decided to proceed with the execution without talking to Elizabeth about details, as it was "neither fit nor convenient to trouble her majesty any further."

On February 7, Mary, who was now being held in Fotheringhay Castle, was told that she would be beheaded the next morning. She immediately said, "I did not think that the Queen, my Sister, would have consented to my Death ... but seeing her pleasure is so, Death shall be to me most welcome." Even to the very end, Mary determined to die nobly, a martyr for her cause—"wrongfully a prisoner," as she had written to Elizabeth after her trial.

THE EXECUTION On the bitterly cold morning of February 8, Mary was led to a low platform within the castle, accompanied by six of her servants, whom she wanted there to make sure the tale of her execution was carried far and wide. The platform contained a chair for disrobing and a chopping block, all draped in black velvet. Mary herself was dressed in black with a floor-length veil of white linen falling down her back. She carried a crucifix and was immune to the blandishments of the Protestant chaplain assigned to accompany her, telling him she was "firmly fixed and resolved in the ancient Catholic Roman Religion."

Once on the platform she forgave her executioner and then, with the help of her maids, took off her black robe to reveal a crimson petticoat, the deep red symbolizing not only martyrdom, but the sexuality that the Queen of England, her real executioner, had always denied herself. Blindfolding herself with a white cloth, Mary laid her head upon the block, murmuring "In manus tuas, Domine" ("Into thy hands, O Lord"). The first stroke of the executioner's ax missed her neck and sliced into her skull, causing her to groan, "Sweet Jesus!" The second severed her neck.

There are many stories about her death—that when the executioner held up her head, her wig came off, showing her closely cropped grey hair, that her Skye terrier was hidden deeply in the folds of her skirt and would not leave the scaffolding. True or not, they were repeated throughout England as Mary's body was hurriedly embalmed and then buried—not in France, as she requested, but in England. Her dramatic death, which she had carefully planned, bestowed upon her a martyrdom and a power that Queen Elizabeth could never match.

After Elizabeth was told the news of Mary's death she angrily denounced her advisors, claiming that she had never intended for her to die. There was no doubt that she had, but there was also a sense of deep guilt—for Mary was her close "sister Queen," the young woman for whom she, in a sense, had made herself responsible, and who now was dead at her hands. Yet when Philip II of Spain launched his Spanish Armada against England, in part because of Mary's execution, Elizabeth was able to rise up and experience her finest moments as a ruler, uniting a country now under massive foreign attack in a way that she never could have with Mary alive. In a very literal sense, Mary's death offered Elizabeth the chance for a new life.

In a final irony, as she approached her own death at the age of seventy in 1603, Elizabeth would name as her successor Mary's son, King James VI of Scotland, a firm Protestant but a Stuart, nonetheless, who would reign in England as King James I.

THE PAGEANTRY OF THE CHOPPING BLOCK

The execution of Mary, Queen of Scots, was far from the only instance of royal beheading in the period and the drama she created around her own end was only the latest in a long line of what might be called the pageantry of the chopping block. When Elizabeth's mother, Queen Anne Boleyn, was executed by her husband, King Henry VIII, in May of 1536—supposedly for adultery, but possibly because she had whispered that the king was impotent—she was decapitated. Ordinary citizens were generally hanged during this period (heretics were burned), but royalty had their heads cut off, usually after being imprisoned in the Tower of London.

Perhaps because Henry had a soft spot for Anne, despite all, he imported a special swordsman from France to do the deed, rather than having some black-hooded executioner whack away with an ax. Anne was aware of this kindness on Henry's part and appreciated it, although she apparently told more than one person that there should be no problem with her, as "I have such a little neck." On the appointed day, Anne knelt upright (in execution by sword there was no block).

The swordsman was apparently so skilled that onlookers claimed that Anne actually seemed to be unaware that she had just been decapitated.

There was no doubt, however, about the execution of sixteen-year-old Lady Jane Grey in 1554. This was so pathetic that even hardened Londoners recoiled. Jane, like Anne Boleyn, was afforded the privilege of a private execution on Tower Green, inside the Tower of London, rather than have to suffer the spectacle of a public execution on Tower Hill, but reports, of course, leaked out. The young woman had bravely said a prayer, forgiven the executioner, and even tied on her own blindfold. But, once she had it on, she was unable to find the chopping block upon which to lay her head, and staggered around the platform crying, "What shall I do? Where is it?" Finally, a chaplain helped her to find it and she lay down, whispered another prayer, and was beheaded.

BELOW Mary, Queen of Scots, went to her death with dignity and style, wearing a crimson petticoat below her black robe. The executioner's first stroke with the ax cut into her skull and he needed a second stroke to behead her.

CHARLES XII OF SWEDEN VERSUS

PETER THE GREAT OF RUSSIA

CHARLES XII OF SWEDEN AND PETER THE GREAT OF RUSSIA: DEATH STRUGGLE OF THE NORTHERN KINGS

THE FAMOUS WARS OF EUROPE IN THE SEVENTEENTH and eighteenth centuries took place between France and Austria, England, Holland and Prussia, as the emerging nations fought with each other over territory and religion in such struggles as the Eighty Years War and the Thirty Years War. The very titles of these lengthy, slogging struggles, precursors of modern warfare in their despoilment of civilian populations and use of mercenary armies, connote their grim and never-ending natures.

As influential, but far less well known, was a conflict that took place on the cusp of the seventeenth and eighteenth centuries between two great northern kingdoms: Russia and Sweden. Although what would come to be called the Great Northern War would be, for all intents and purposes, settled on a blazing hot day in the Ukraine at a place called Poltava, it was not heat that characterized this struggle, but cold: the cold of the unending northern winters, the crystalline frozen silences of the great northern wastes through which the two armies would struggle. Battles took place in blinding snowstorms; armies attacked across frozen lakes; the Baltic Sea, uproarious with storms, saw naval action on an unprecedented scale.

The opposing armies were led by two kings: Charles XII of Sweden and Czar Peter the Great of Russia, both obdurate, ambitious and strikingly eccentric rulers, but men whom Voltaire called "by common accord, the most remarkable men to have appeared in over two thousand years."

MOTHER RUSSIA At the time the future Czar Peter the Great was born in 1672, Russia was the largest nation on earth, its territory stretching from Eastern Europe to the Pacific, from Siberia to the Black Sea. It was a place of endless dark forests, vast steppe plains, and four mighty rivers: the Dnieper, the Don, the Volga, and the Dvina, the last flowing north into the Baltic Sea.

Russia's god-like monarch, the czar, lived in the Kremlin, a fortress on a hill high above Moscow (*kreml* is the Russian word for "fortress"). The age when kings believed they had been given a divine right to rule was coming to an end in most of Europe, but not in Russia. The czar, as a visiting Englishman wrote in the mid-seventeenth century, like a "sparkling sun darted forth most sumptuous rays," so cloaked was he in gold and precious jewels. Paying proper obeisance to the czar meant you dove to the floor and kissed the very place where he had trod with his jeweled sandals. He was, in a very real sense, God's partner on earth: "Through God and the czar, Russia is strong," went one ancient proverb.

By the mid-seventeenth century, however, Russia was perhaps not so strong. Ruled by Peter the Great's pious father, Alexis, it was crippled by a vast, unmanageable, and corrupt state bureaucracy where wheels turned very, very slowly. Ninety percent of the wealth of the nation lay with the top one percent of the sparse population of eight million—the *boyars*, or nobility. The rest of the country was made up of serfs, who labored in conditions unchanged since the Dark Ages. Indeed, the rest of Europe looked on Russia, with its substandard living conditions, superstitions, and odd, long-bearded patriarchs of the Orthodox Church, as a giant but backward younger brother, one who might never come into his own.

GRAND SWEDEN It may be hard for us today, when we associate Sweden with peace, Nobel Prizes, and progressive thinking, to realize that in its heyday it was the most relentless military power in Europe, ruler of a vast Baltic empire that included the entire northern shore of the Baltic Sea, Finland, Estonia, Ingria, and Livonia, as well as numerous seaports on the northern coast of Germany, rewards for Sweden's participation in the winning Protestant side of the Thirty Years War, which ended in 1648.

Sweden, brimming with evergreen forests, with over ninety thousand lakes, and with valuable iron and copper mines, bustled with trade, its merchants and sailing vessels reaching all the ports of Europe. Yet, in the mid-seventeenth century it had a population of, at most, two million people. How had such a small country gained an empire? The answer lay in the Swedish army and in an extraordinary line of Swedish warrior-kings, beginning with Gustavus Adolphus, known as the Lion of the North, whose gains in the Thirty Years War were bought with his own blood—he died leading a cavalry charge at the battle of Lützen during that war. But he had fashioned the ragtag Swedish army into a well-drilled force, dividing it up into squadrons consisting of four one-hundred-man companies and emphasizing volley fire with muskets, rather than attacks by pikesmen. Swedish kings subsequent to Adolphus carried on this military tradition. Charles XI looked at the small population of the country and came up with a brilliant way of maximizing its resources. He divided Sweden into tiny areas called *rota*, each consisting of roughly ten farmsteads, and made each *rota* responsible for producing a soldier—training, feeding, and clothing him and, if he died or was wounded, replacing him.

This ensured that Sweden had a steady supply of patriotic, motivated men, men who were the finest their communities could provide. A good thing, too. For when Charles XI died in 1697, his son, the extraordinary fifteen-year-old King Charles XII, would need every soldier he could get to battle the country that was Sweden's mortal enemy: Russia.

PETER THE GREAT Russia and Sweden had been fighting since the thirteenth century for control of the valuable ports of the Gulf of Finland. The provinces of Estonia, Ingria, and Livonia, as well as the great fortress ports of Narva and Riga, were all once Russian lands but were now controlled by Sweden, something that enraged the young Czar Peter. Born in 1672 to Czar Alexis and his beloved second wife, the Czarina Natalya, Peter was only three and a half when his father died. His semi-invalid, older half-brother Fyodor became czar but died in 1682. Peter and his sixteen-year-old half-brother Ivan were then named co-czars, but the real power was held by his scheming half-sister Sophia, who would rule Russia for the next seven years.

By 1689, Peter had overthrown Sophia in a bloody coup in which he had many of her advisors tortured and killed—sadistic torture was to be a hallmark of Peter's regime—and by 1694, when he was twenty-two, he had taken complete control of Russia. Unlike his feeble half-brothers, he was an amazing physical specimen: six feet seven inches tall, with piercing green eyes, brown hair that hung halfway to his shoulders, and an energy that could not be contained—he was a young man who refused to sit still, who constantly paced the room. When agitated he was prone to facial spasms that could turn into what may have been petit mal epileptic seizures.

The Russian world was notoriously xenophobic, but Peter made many close foreign friends, reflecting his curiosity about the world and his drive to modernize Russia. He sought to improve the Russian army with the best arms that money could buy and brought in foreign advisors to train an officer corps; he forced his courtiers to cut off their long, archaic beards (or pay a "beard tax" for keeping them); he switched the country to the Julian calendar from the old Russian one. His greatest desire was to bring Russia into regular contact with the rest of the world by making it a great maritime power. Yet his only ocean port was the remote White Sea port of Archangel. To the south the Black Sea was blocked by the immense power of the Ottoman Empire, and to the west Sweden—holding onto what Peter believed to be Russian land—controlled the Baltic.

CHARLES XII Ten years younger than Peter, Charles XII was every bit as amazing a physical specimen. He was a sickly child who, at the age of six, was removed from the care of his mother and the women at the Swedish court in Stockholm and placed in his own quarters with only male servants and courtiers. When he was seven he shot a fox, at ten he killed his first wolf, and at eleven he dispatched his first bear. He was blond, blue-eyed, and slender, a boy who worshipped the achievements of Alexander the Great and quickly grasped language, mathematics, and science, but he was extraordinarily obstinate, the most stubborn person any of his tutors or advisors had ever seen.

In 1697, Charles's father, Charles XI, died of natural causes. Since, by Swedish law, a prince could not become king until he was eighteen, a board of regents was appointed to advise the fifteen-year-old Charles, but they were so hesitant in influencing his decisions that they simply gave up and allowed the adolescent to be crowned king in November of that year. Charles, at this early age, was filled with an amazing self-confidence coupled with an extraordinary physical vigor and sense of adventure. He loved to gallop on frozen lakes, almost daring the ice to break beneath him (once or twice it did); to hunt bears with only wooden pitchforks; to play violent military games with his Drabants, his young officer corps, who followed him everywhere. Like Peter, Charles drank heavily; unlike Peter, he stopped after one particularly humiliating night when he passed out drunk in public.

While Charles was learning to be both man and king, others were plotting against him. In 1699, King Frederick IV of Denmark and Frederick Augustus, Elector of Saxony and King of Poland, made a secret alliance to attack his kingdom. The plan was that Augustus would invade the Swedish territory of Livonia on the east coast of the Baltic Sea, while Frederick attacked the Swedish province of Holstein-Gottorp.

In order to make their plans even more effective, the two monarchs secretly sent a commission to Peter the Great to enlist his aid. Here was his chance to regain Russia's Baltic ports, to turn Russia into the maritime power he had always hoped it would become: he would attack and seize the Swedish fortress of Narva, on the east coast of the Gulf of Finland. Although he was unable to move until September 1700, at last he would be able to open Russia to the Baltic, to seize what he called "the inheritance of our fathers."

THE GREAT NORTHERN WAR
Early in 1700, Charles's enemies struck, with near simultaneous invasions of Livonia and Holstein-Gottorp. Charles happened to be bear-hunting at the time; when he heard the news, he returned to Stockholm and addressed his council. His father had told him, he said, to keep Sweden peaceful unless "you are dragged into war by the hair." Well, now he was being dragged. He told his advisors: "I have resolved never to begin an unjust war, but also never to end a just one without overcoming my enemy."

Charles's enemies had seriously underestimated him. Although he was now only eighteen, his instinct for military matters was sure and swift. Both Frederick

135

and Augustus had expected him to divide his troops and send them to the areas under invasion—instead, Charles mounted an amphibious attack straight into the heart of Denmark, at unprotected Copenhagen. By July 1700, ten thousand Swedish troops had surrounded the Danish capital city and begun bombarding it; King Frederick raced back, but with his troops far away there was nothing he could do but surrender quickly. By a treaty made in August, he gave back the Swedish territory he had invaded and dropped out of the war.

This left Augustus and his Saxons, who were even then attacking the port of Riga, in Livonia. But as Charles planned his next move, ominous news reached him: Russian troops were massing on the borders of the Swedish Baltic province of Ingria. In September, Peter, accompanying these troops, declared war on Sweden and attacked across the border, racing twenty miles to invest the city of Narva. Throwing up huge earthworks across the only road by which a relief force could arrive, the Russians began to bombard the city, which held out bravely despite repeated assaults.

THE FIRST BRAWL Narva was the first time that Charles XII and Peter the Great were to face each other in combat, and each was convinced of the rightness of his cause. Peter was on an empire-building mission, as well as what he considered a patriotic one: to open up the world for Russia by seizing a port that, by his lights, belonged to his country in any event. The young Charles, rigid yet extremely brave and determined, could claim with justice that the Russians had attacked first and now deserved almost any treatment they got. His was a righteous anger, which would be appeased only by victory.

Racing across the stormy Baltic, Charles mustered a force of some ten thousand infantry and cavalry about 150 miles from Narva. When Augustus heard the news that Charles had landed, he withdrew his forces from Riga and headed east, back into Poland. Now with only one enemy left to face, Charles turned towards Narva, despite the fact that the northern winter was setting in.

Charles and his relief force arrived at Narva on November 19 after an arduous march, but Peter the Great had departed the night before. This left Peter open to charges—widely believed in Europe at the time, and certainly believed by Charles—that he was a coward, afraid of physical danger, afraid to face his adversary, although his later behavior at the battle of Poltava would seem to disprove this. It is more likely that Peter thought the Swedes could be easily handled by his appointed general, the Duke du Croy, an officer originally from the Spanish Netherlands, and a force of some forty thousand Russian troops, who outnumbered the Swedes four to one. Peter went on his way to find Augustus and seek an explanation as to why he had withdrawn—a move that had seriously jeopardized the Russian position.

In the meantime, the Swedes would no doubt deploy, set up their lines, perform reconnaissance and, in a week or so, attack. That was the way war was fought at the time. By then, Peter would have returned, possibly with Augustus and reinforcements.

But delay was not Charles's style. On the afternoon of November 20, as snow began to fall heavily, the Swedish army fired signal rockets and charged en masse at the Russian lines, using ladders to cross the trenches the Russians had dug to stop such an assault, and leaping up and over the enemy earthworks. Picking a weak spot in the four-mile-wide Russian line, Charles's forces crashed through and then divided, half going to the left, half to the right, slaughtering the Russians in the trenches.

Taken by surprise, Peter's soldiers began to flee, some of them drowning in the Narva River in their panic. Although certain Russian regiments made a brave stand, the Swedish victory was complete. Eight thousand Russians were killed or wounded; the rest were forced to lay down their arms and march out of the city in humiliation. Peter lost hundreds of artillery pieces and large ammunition stores. The victory was so total that Charles could not help but crow: "There is no pleasure in fighting the Russians for they will not stand like other men but run away at once ..."

"AN AGENT OF GOD" Peter had not gone far when word of the stunning Russian defeat at Narva reached him. His immediate fear was Moscow— for now there was almost nothing to stop Charles taking his army and marching directly into the Russian capital. However, Peter, like Charles, was never one to falter in the face of adversity. He immediately began a rebuilding program for his army, frantically raising ten new regiments of dragoons and seeking desperately to find a way to replace the artillery he valued so highly (eventually, as a result of the loss of cannon at Narva, Russians began to cast their own cannon). He also bought forty thousand modern flintlocks from England; by 1706, Russia was also making its own rifles.

From the disastrous ashes of the battle of Narva, the Russian army rose up, phoenix-like, although in this he had help from Charles XII, whose single-mindedness, for once, was not a virtue. Charles had said at the outset of the war: "I intend to finish first one of my enemies and then will talk with the other." As far as he was concerned, Augustus, King of Poland, needed to be dealt with first and then he would turn to Russia. In the spring of 1702, Charles invaded Poland, seeking the total defeat of Augustus. This was where Charles's puritanical nature got in the way. He was not just out to defeat an enemy—he wanted to wreak an almost biblical retribution on him. One of Charles's generals wrote: "He believes that he is an agent of God, sent to punish every act of faithlessness." But the war in Poland turned into a quagmire as the Swedish king chased Augustus and his forces through endless tracts of forests and miles of bogs, all the time fighting off the attacks of partisan groups (Charles's cruel response of burning entire villages and slaughtering their inhabitants did not endear him to the populace).

FOLLOWING PAGES
The battle of Poltava was a decisive victory for Peter the Great, whose defeat of his rival Charles ended Sweden's dominance of northern Europe and established Russia as a power of the future.

This slogging war in Poland lasted until the winter of 1707, when Charles forced Augustus to abdicate and placed a puppet king on the Polish throne. During this time Peter had not been idle. With his rebuilt army he struck at the Baltic ports in Charles's rear, finally capturing the mouth of the Neva and building his long-hoped for seaport of St. Petersburg.

In August 1707, as Charles made preparations to invade Russia, Peter, as zealous as Charles but more practical, wanted to sue for peace. Charles refused to hear of it and so Peter went to the French king, Louis XIV, seeking to have him act as an intermediary. Peter would pay Sweden a hefty sum to keep the port of Narva and he wanted St. Petersburg, as well. The rest of the eastern Baltic provinces were Sweden's.

Charles would not accept this. "The czar is not yet humiliated enough to accept the terms of peace which I intend to prescribe," he said, and in August 1707, he marched an army of forty thousand men from Saxony, putting them on the road to Moscow.

HIS GREATEST ADVENTURE So began what one historian has called Charles's "greatest adventure." He intended to ride straight into the capital city of his adversary and dictate terms to him. Peter, for once, seemed daunted by the Swedish king's fanaticism. As Charles moved closer to Russia, the czar was laid low by fever and prone to frequent bouts of rage in which he physically beat those close to him. Still, at the same time, he had prepared. He sent marauding Cossacks into western Poland to lay waste the country—now a reluctant ally of Sweden—poisoning the wells with corpses and burning crops and villages, so that Charles would be met with nothing but scorched earth.

But Charles kept on coming. In late December 1707, he crossed the frozen Vistula. In the summer of 1708, campaigning hard for months, the Swedes finally caught up with the Russian forces at the Lithuanian village of Holowczyn, where they attacked and beat them, killing five thousand men, but not before the Russians put up a stiff resistance. It was gradually beginning to dawn on the Swedes that these Russians were not the Russian troops of Narva and that they intended to make a fight of things in their homeland.

After the victory at Holowczyn, the way lay open to the Dnieper River and, ultimately, Moscow, but the hard-campaigning Swedes were finally bogging down in the great stretches of Russia, as the French and Germans would do in succeeding centuries. Unable to live off the land, trailing a great wagon train of supplies, Charles decided in the late summer of 1708 that the only solution was to head south into the Ukraine, where rich crops awaited and where the Cossack leader Ivan Mazepa had promised thousands of troops to help him in the spring campaign against Peter.

It turned out to be a disastrous move. Charles divided his army into two parts, with one force, under General Adam Ludwig Lewenhaupt, guarding the baggage train. Vulnerable to Russian attack, Lewenhaupt was forced to fight for his life, and lost thousands of men as the Russians, marching parallel to the Swedes, harried them into the Ukraine.

Then the coldest winter in living memory spread through Europe. The Seine froze in Paris, windmills froze in their sockets in the Netherlands, and even the Baltic iced over. In the Ukraine there were scenes of horror, as sentries froze solid on guard duty and dragoons died on their horses and became grotesque statues. Swedish field hospitals were filled with men with amputated and frostbitten limbs. Over three thousand Swedes died of exposure.

A WOUNDED KING When the spring of 1709 came it was welcome, but Charles was still in a difficult position, far from home—he had, in fact, not returned to Sweden since 1700, when the war first began—and with the Russians drawing closer. Too, the armies promised by Mazepa had proved illusory: at best, he could muster only three thousand Cossacks.

Both kings sensed that the time for a showdown had arrived. Czar Peter had now joined his forces in the field and, that spring, the two armies began circling each other near the town of Poltava, which lay on a route the Tartar armies of old had taken from the broad steppes either into Crimea or Turkey, or west into Poland. In 1399, a bloody battle had been fought in this heavily wooded, ravine-slashed area between Lithuanians and the forces of Tamerlane. In 1941, Hitler would headquarter his advancing German army here as he sought to invade Russia.

In 1709, though, Poltava was fortified by a small Russian force, which Charles began to besiege in May. The real action would take place not in the town itself, but north of it, when Peter arrived in early June and spread his army in formation along a long open corridor of ground between two heavily wooded areas. The Swedish force, now reduced to about twenty-five thousand men—men who had been campaigning for nine bitter years—were facing about forty thousand Russian troops and an impressive array of artillery. (The Swedes had few artillery pieces as Charles believed these slowed up the rapid movement of an army that depended on speed and shock tactics.) The Russians had also erected a series of log redoubts along the front of their lines.

The position seemed impregnable, but it did have its drawbacks. Charles noted that the Russian back was to a river and a steep bluff, with only one ford where an army could cross. If the Swedes could get behind the Russians and trap them, they could capture the entire army—and the czar himself. The odds, the Swedish king reminded his generals, had been worse at Narva, where the Swedes were outnumbered four to one.

Then something catastrophic happened. Charles, impervious as usual to danger, had been out reconnoitering Russian positions when he was hit in the left foot by a Russian musket ball. The shot went right through his heel and

THE FOUNDING OF ST. PETERSBURG

In the spring of 1703, with Charles occupied in conquering Poland, Peter took an army of twenty thousand and achieved a lifelong dream: he captured the mouth of the Neva River, which flows into the Baltic, thus at last restoring Russian access to the sea. With characteristic immediacy and energy, on May 16 he began to build a fortress, which was called St. Peter and St. Paul, on an island in the center of the river.

The rest of the city rose in the marshes nearby, a superhuman effort on the part of Russian workers, who were forced to import wood and stone from upstream, drive piles into the marshes, lay foundations and dig canals. St. Petersburg has been called "a city built on bones," for thousands of workers—perhaps as many as thirty thousand—died of disease and hardship while wresting the city from the malarial swamps. Prone to flooding and fire, with a population that had to be forced to emigrate there, surrounded by aggressive wolf packs that were known to seize and eat human beings, St. Petersburg was not exactly a vacation spot. Yet the city—its name was changed to Leningrad after the Revolution and then back to St. Petersburg in 1991—has endured attacks by Swedes, French and Germans to remain Russia's Baltic port and a pivotal city, just as Peter imagined it.

exited his foot by his big toe. Although in excruciating pain, he acted as if nothing had happened until he returned to camp, when he fainted getting off his horse. Swedish doctors operated, but a fever set in and twenty-seven-year-old Charles lay on the brink of death for two days, before he finally began to recover. Even then he was unable to mount a horse and had to be carried everywhere in a litter. Charles was so much in personal command of his army that this was a disaster. He had able commanders such as General Lewenhaupt and Field Marshal Count Carl Gunter Rehnskjold, but these two men disliked each other and needed Charles's guiding hand.

In the end, wracked with pain on his stretcher, Charles gathered his men around him and told them to do what the Swedish army did: attack, boldly and with surprise.

ATTACK The Swedish army crept slowly into position close to the Russian fortifications on the night of July 27–28, making sure to keep absolutely quiet. The plan was that the Swedish cavalry would circle around behind the woods on either side of the narrow corridor of open ground up which the infantry would attack. With the Swedish horse charging in from the rear and the infantry attacking from in front, the Russians would be trapped.

Things went wrong almost from the outset. The Swedes lay quietly in the grass, no more than a hundred yards from the Russian lines, but the cavalry got lost in the darkness and did not arrive in position until four in the morning. By that time something else had become clear to the Swedes. In the growing dawn light, they saw that the Russians had hastily built four log forts stretching down from the main line of forts at the top of the corridor, like the stem of a "T." These they would have to get past, and quickly. A hasty plan was made to send in screening forces to fire on these redoubts while the main Swedish forces charged past; no sooner had this been done than the Swedes were spotted, shots were fired, and the battle began.

At first the Swedish infantry, charging up through the long corridor of open ground, were successful. They quickly neutralized two of the four earthen forts at the base of the "T" and swept up towards the main line of Russian defenses, despite the fact that cannon fire did horrible carnage to their ranks. Then the Swedish officer in charge of neutralizing the redoubts became bogged down in attacking them, instead of bypassing them. Lacking his support, Field Marshal Rehnskjold was able to drive through the Russian forts at the top of the corridor but was not able to hold them. The smaller Swedish force, unaided by its cavalry, which had been driven off, was gradually destroyed by Russian reinforcements, which poured in.

This was the first engagement of the long battle in which both Czar Peter and King Charles were present personally. The contrast between the two could not have been more striking. Peter rode a dun-colored Arabian horse, wearing a

LEFT Peter the Great, having just beheaded one of the rebel *streltsy* (foreground), is shown drinking with his nobles in this painting from c. 1700. The next victim is shown on the left, awaiting his fate.

PETER THE GREAT AND TORTURE

Peter the Great's reputation as a modernizer and empire-builder is at odds with another part of his reputation—that of a man who not only believed in sadistic torture to get what he wanted, but who also enjoyed it. When, early in his reign, the *streltsy*—the guardsmen and musketeers who were a professional army class in Moscow—rebelled against him, Peter ordered an orgy of torture, which included beating victims with sticks or knouts (heavy whips), roasting them over fires, or putting them on the rack and pulling their arms and legs out of their sockets. Yet those *streltsy* who were tortured put up with these horrible punishments, in the main, with equanimity (one of them even confessed to Peter that a secret "torture society" existed—its members practiced torturing each other in preparation for this very eventuality). Enraged, Peter turned to the expedient of having certain of his nobles execute victims themselves, to prove their loyalty. The czar was almost always present at these bloody scenes; some say he beheaded a dozen victims himself, although this remains unproven.

Peter's worst excess, however, remains the torture and death of his son, Alexis, who had run away to Italy with his pregnant lover. In 1717, Peter wrote to Alexis, saying "I promise to God and His judgment that I will not punish you" if Alexis returned to Russia. Foolishly, Alexis believed him, returning to Russia and to the paranoid Peter's fears that the boy was leading a secret rebellion against him. Peter had Alexis tortured, under which duress Alexis admitted, "I wish for my father's death." That was all Peter needed to hear. Alexis died—no one knows quite how—but probably he was whipped to death.

tri cornered hat and exposing himself to fire almost recklessly, so much so that a bullet lodged in his saddle and a spent round was later found in his scarf. Charles, in the meantime, had to be carried in a litter, holding his unsheathed sword by his side. He was near the thick of the fighting, surrounded by his officer corps of elite Drabants, many of whom were killed as they formed a human wall protecting their king, but he could not see, could not direct his forces, could not lend his indomitable spirit to the fray.

In the end, the lack of Charles and the grand presence of Peter made the difference. Badly mauled, the Swedish army began to retreat, but more than twenty thousand men were taken into captivity in Russia; few ever returned. Rehnskjold and Lewenhaupt were captured as well, and brought to dinner with the

BELOW The body of Charles XII is carried home for burial after he was shot in the head by an enemy sniper at the siege of Fredriksten in southern Norway. His constant wars had exhausted Sweden and his death was not mourned.

czar that very night. He treated them kindly, offering them food and many toasts to their bravery, but he kept repeating: "Where is my brother Charles?"

Charles had managed to escape. With a small group of officers, he had been able to escape across the Dnieper and they finally made their way to the Ottoman lands in Turkey, where they were given asylum.

A WORLD CHANGED FOREVER One day's battle had made a permanent change in Europe. Instead of creating a Russia controlled by Sweden, which would have made it the world's greatest empire, Poltava had added a new player to the European stage: Czar Peter's Russia, a Russia with a Baltic port and ambitions to change the shape of the world.

Charles XII did not give up. He spent five years in Turkey, trying to foment a war between the Ottomans and Russia. Tired of his machinations, the Turks finally tossed him out, and in 1714 he made his way back to Sweden in a lightning ride, traveling thirteen hundred miles in less than two weeks. The king made a dramatic re-entry to a country he had not seen in fifteen years, but the mood in Sweden had changed. Charles was seeking revenge, but the country was war-weary and wanted only peace. Even so, the king planned a new military offensive in 1718.

Older now and somewhat wiser, Charles decided that the czar's position in the Baltic was now too strong to attack directly. Instead, he launched an assault on Russia's ally and Sweden's age-old enemy, Denmark. Deciding to seize southern Norway first, he besieged Fredriksten, a fortress stronghold there. On the evening of November 30, peering over a trench at the enemy lines despite the entreaties of his officers, Charles was shot in the head by an enemy sniper and instantly killed. He was thirty-six years old and unpopular, and rumors, probably untrue, spread that he had been killed by his own men to end the war.

When he died, his country did not mourn him, so weighed down were they by the burdens of war, but Peter, his great rival, did. When he heard the news he exclaimed: "My dear Charles, how much I pity you!" He ordered the Russian court to wear mourning clothes for a week. Nevertheless, with Charles out of his way, Peter was at last able to bring Russia into the modern world. By the Treaty of Nystad, signed in 1721, the Great Northern War was finally over and Peter received, in perpetuity, access to the Baltic, western Europe, and the world. Russia would now, and henceforth, be a force to be reckoned with.

BENEDICT ARNOLD

BENEDICT ARNOLD AND HORATIO GATES:
A CLASH FOR CONTROL

WHEN GENERAL HORATIO GATES AND MAJOR General Benedict Arnold joined forces to fight the British in northern New York in the fall of 1777, they were supposedly the finest officers the Continental Army had to offer: Arnold fresh from a heroic, though futile, attempt to capture Quebec and Gates a decorated officer who was a shrewd and experienced campaigner. But the mercurial thirty-four-year-old Arnold and the plodding fifty-year-old Gates (his opponent, the British General John Burgoyne, called him "the old midwife") were oil and water. Their clash over how to win the battle of Saratoga—and who should take credit for the victory, which was the turning point in American fortunes during the war—would have serious repercussions for the country in the years to come.

SON OF A SERVANT It is a commentary on the chaotic and turbulent eighteenth century that Horatio Gates should have ended up in an American uniform. He was born in England in 1727—his mother, Dorothy, was a servant in the employ of the Duke of Leeds and his father, Robert, was a former smuggler turned customs official. There was some speculation that Horatio Gates was actually the son of the duke, for the duke seemed to take an inordinate interest in the infant Horatio. Plus, a certain resemblance can be seen between Leeds and Horatio in adult portraits—both have a schoolmasterly, sharp-nosed look.

There is no way to prove this, but speculation on his origin haunted Horatio for years—perhaps one reason why when he joined the British army he gave his date of birth as 1729, rather than 1727. The Duke of Leeds died in 1729, a fact that would have made it impossible for him to be Horatio's father. After the duke's death, Dorothy went to work for the Duke of Bolton in Greenwich, where he had established a sumptuous residence for his mistress, the actress Lavinia Fenton. Horatio was thus raised in a genteel atmosphere; mingling with Lavinia's three children, he learned how to speak the language of the English upper classes. A mixed blessing, perhaps, for someone who was not actually to the manor born—one American would later characterize him as "a snob of the first water ... with an unctuous, pious way about him"—but it did get him into the best schools someone in his situation could hope to attend.

In 1745, through the good offices of the Duke of Bolton, young Horatio Gates was commissioned a lieutenant (see page 191 for the system of purchasing commissions) and sent to fight on the Continent in the War of Austrian Succession.

A BOY FOR GLORY In 1741, just a few years before Gates received his commission, his nemesis, Benedict Arnold V, was born in Norwich, Connecticut, the last of his mother's eleven children. Of them all, only two—Benedict and his sister Hannah—would survive childhood. His father, Benedict III, was a barrel-maker who had married Hannah King, the widow of a shipowner and merchant, and inherited the merchant's vessels, goods, and shipyards. After this stroke of fortune, Benedict III (now known locally as Captain Arnold) became a wealthy and respected man.

Benedict V (a Benedict IV had been born before him, only to die in infancy) was a tough, resilient, and scrappy boy with regular, handsome features and mesmerizing dark blue eyes. He became a leader of the boys around the Norwich waterfront and was known for his fearlessness, as well as for his physical strength and titanic temper. At the age of twelve he challenged a local police officer to a fight after the latter had caught him in a childish prank. Both fellow children and local adults sensed that young Arnold had some larger purpose—that he was, as one writer has put it, "a boy bound pell-mell for glory."

Unfortunately, Captain Arnold began drinking seriously, perhaps because of the grim ill-fortune of fathering so many dead children, and his business deteriorated. In 1754, as Benedict turned thirteen, his father was arrested for debt and thrown into prison. The young Benedict was then apprenticed to a wealthy apothecary, who was one of his mother's cousins, but the life was too quiet for him. The French and Indian War—the North American stage of the Seven Years War—had broken out in 1754. At the age of sixteen, Arnold ran away to enlist with colonial forces fighting with the British; his mother had him forcibly returned, but the next year he left again to campaign against the French. At this point his mother became ill and, with his father little more than the town drunk, Benedict returned to care for her. When she died, in the summer of 1759, he went back to campaigning, but he had missed out on most of the momentous aspects of the war—the successful British sieges of Louisbourg, Ticonderoga, Crown Point, and Quebec.

The glory he so longed for would have to wait—for now.

GATES IN AMERICA Fifteen years older than young Benedict, Horatio Gates was having a very different experience in the French and Indian War. Having fought on the Continent in the War for Austrian Succession, when he became a staff officer and then his regiment's adjutant, Gates had decided to make the army his career. In the words of one biographer, he had trained himself "to be a good hand at cards, a jolly drinking partner, and an adept at barracks ribaldry"— a regular, aristocratic fellow, in other words, not a commoner in disguise. However, his finances were a problem.

In 1749, after he was posted to Halifax, Nova Scotia, he could not afford to purchase his promotion to captain. Then, back in England and wishing to marry young Elizabeth Phillips, he heard that a captain stationed in the colony of Maryland wanted to sell his commission and would be willing to part with it on credit.

Gates jumped at the chance, got married, and in March 1755 joined his new company in America. He arrived just in time for the opening shots of the French and Indian War. Gates—along with future American military officers George Washington, Charles Lee, and Daniel Morgan—took part in an expedition, led by General Edward Braddock, to attack the French at Fort Duquesne, in the Ohio River Valley. Their column was ambushed by the French and their Indian allies in July of that year. Braddock was killed and his forces virtually annihilated. Gates himself was shot in the chest, but survived when a private carried him away from the battlefield where the Indians were killing and scalping the wounded.

Afterwards Gates served with distinction in the war, seeing action in the West Indies during the British capture of Martinique and managing to secure promotion to major. However, perhaps sensing that his position would always be precarious in the British Army, he resigned at the end of the war and moved with his wife and son, Robert, to America, where he settled on a plantation in West Virginia.

"ARE THE AMERICANS ALL ASLEEP?" After the French and Indian War, Benedict Arnold established a successful apothecary shop and expanded into West Indian trade, selling his family home and buying a forty-ton sloop, the *Fortune*, the first of a three-vessel fleet he would own. Plying the Caribbean waters, trading in salt and cotton, by 1766 he had become a highly successful young man. He was also gaining a reputation as a man who retaliated for the slightest insult, at one point fighting a duel with a British captain who had mocked him (he wounded the man and forced him to apologize).

Arnold soon began taking part in the increasingly volatile political situation in America. Great Britain, deeply in debt after the Seven Years War, began to tax the American colonies, forcing them to pay for the cost of the British soldiers now garrisoned in America and Canada after the French defeat. Arnold became a member of the New Haven chapter of the Sons of Liberty, a radical organization

LEFT The Continental Congress, shown in session, acted as the provisional government for the colonies after hostilities broke out with the British. Arnold was aggrieved that it denied him the promotions he thought he deserved.

that demanded independence from Great Britain. When the infamous Boston Massacre occurred in 1770—unarmed American protestors were killed on Boston streets by British troops—Arnold was in the West Indies, but he wrote: "Good god, are the Americans all asleep and tamely giving up their liberties ... that they don't take immediate vengeance on such miscreants?"

By 1775 Arnold, now married to his first wife, Margaret, and with two children, had become the most powerful leader for American independence in Connecticut. When word first came that spring that the Americans had clashed with the British at the battles of Lexington and Concord, near Boston, Arnold decided to respond with a bold stroke.

Joining forces with a Vermont rebel leader named Ethan Allen, on May 10, 1775 Arnold and his militia made a dawn assault on the British-held fort of Ticonderoga on the border of New York State and Vermont. The surprised garrison surrendered quickly and the Ticonderoga cannon were then hauled away, carried overland, and used to help break the British siege of Boston.

Despite this signal victory, Arnold—too brash, arrogant and angry to be well connected politically—was infuriated when the Continental Congress sent another commander to replace him: he was to be the new commander's subordinate. Enraged, he resigned his commission and disbanded his regiment. Heading home, he heard that his wife, Margaret, only thirty years old, had died suddenly, leaving him with three boys.

"I SHALL BE ... HAPPY IN YOUR FRIENDSHIP"

Settled on his plantation in West Virginia, Horatio Gates became a slaveholder and amassed hundreds of acres of land. He also became a lieutenant colonel in his local militia and kept in close touch with patriot leaders, including George Washington, as hostilities with the British began to seem inevitable. Like Benedict Arnold, Gates was galvanized by the fighting at Lexington and Concord in the spring of 1775. He first heard about it on May 29; by June 2 he had arrived at Washington's home in Virginia, offering his services to his former comrade-in-arms, who was about to become commander in chief of America's Continental Army. Washington recommended that the Continental Congress commission Gates as a brigadier general and adjutant general of the army—this meant that he was in charge of the details and routine of organizing the army, a task at which he excelled.

Stationed with Washington in Cambridge, Massachusetts, in mid-summer of 1775, Gates had his first encounter with Benedict Arnold. Arnold had only been able to keep his vow to retire for a few weeks. Anxious to be back in the war, he presented George Washington with his bold plan to invade Canada and attack the British stronghold of Quebec via a little-known route through northern Maine. Washington was impressed by Arnold, as was Gates—the tall, ruggedly handsome young man from Connecticut had an energy and a fearlessness that was inspiring. Washington gave his permission, even though it was late in the season to be invading Canada, and Gates helped Arnold organize.

Arnold's snowbound invasion—plagued by misfortune and starvation—became famous in America as a tragic attempt to do the impossible. After trekking hundreds of miles through impassable wilderness, leaving bloody footprints in the snow, Arnold's men attacked the citadel of Quebec and were repulsed, with Arnold badly wounded in the leg. Nevertheless, in recompense for his efforts, Washington nominated Arnold for brigadier general. Before Arnold was to return to America in early June he wrote Horatio Gates: "I shall be ever happy in your friendship and society" and pledged that he would not give up the fight.

"YOUR BEST FRIENDS ARE NOT YOUR COUNTRYMEN"

The next few months saw some of the most desperate fighting of the war. Washington was driven from New York by the attacking forces of the British under General William Howe—in fact, by December he would be pushed back through New Jersey and across the Delaware River into Pennsylvania. The only thing that sustained the colonies that dark summer was another incredible effort by Benedict Arnold. Even though still recovering from his wounds, he proposed to Washington and Gates that he build a fleet to sail on Lake Champlain to blunt the thrust of British forces coming south from Canada, as Howe's forces were attacking from the east and north. Gates supported this plan, far-fetched though it might sound, writing to Congress: "General Arnold, who is perfectly skilled in naval affairs, has most nobly undertaken to command our fleet upon the lake."

As Arnold attempted to build his fleet that summer, he harassed Gates constantly for more supplies, until Gates snapped at him: "Believe me, dear sir, no man alive could be more anxious for the welfare of you and your fleet." But Arnold was not happy. "When you ask for a frigate," he wrote a friend, "they give you a raft."

Already their rivalry was growing, with Gates taking the credit for the growing fleet, acting as if it were his idea and minimizing Arnold's role. Worse was to come, as Gates, apparently trying to curry favor with the Continental Congress, refused to support Arnold when an investigation began into his failed expedition to Quebec and charges that he had allowed his men to loot. However, Gates, the politician that Arnold could never be, let Arnold believe that he *had* supported him and Arnold was taken in by this charade, at first, even though a friend wrote to him, in a thinly veiled hint: "Your best friends are not your countrymen."

The upshot was that, even though Arnold would fight a brilliant delaying action against the British on Lake Champlain in the battle of Valcour Bay in October—essentially halting their northern invasion—he was denied his promotion to brigadier. He did not learn about this from Gates—he read about it in the newspaper.

THE ROAD TO SARATOGA On March 17, 1777, Gates was named Commander of the Northern Department, replacing his direct superior, General Philip Schuyler, who was a supporter of Benedict Arnold. In April, Arnold, his personal debts mounting along with his anger, rode to Philadelphia to personally confront Congress about his failed promotion. Since he was the senior officer in Philadelphia at that moment, he even tried to take command there, but once again Congress appointed a more junior officer to take the role. And, once again, on July 11, 1777, Arnold resigned his commission. "Honor is a sacrifice no man ought to make," he told Congress, whose straight-laced, puritanical politicians had always hated his posturing and braggadocio. One of them sneered that Arnold "has conducted himself almost without blemish ... if a man may be said to do so because self-love was injured ..."

This was going too far for George Washington. Before Congress could accept Arnold's resignation, he wrote them urgently to reconsider, asking them to appoint Arnold to the Northern Department, where British forces under General John Burgoyne had just retaken Fort Ticonderoga and were preparing to move down through upstate New York in an attempt to cut the colonies in half along the Hudson River. Congress relented, although they did not restore Arnold's seniority, and he agreed to serve in his country's time of dire need.

Thus, in early September, Arnold was again on campaign, joining forces under Horatio Gates along the Hudson River, just north of the town of Saratoga.

"A VOICE THAT RANG CLEAR AS A TRUMPET"

In the late summer and early fall of 1777, the future of the new American nation was seriously at risk. General Howe had finally captured the capital, Philadelphia, causing Congress to flee, and the British commander, General Burgoyne, having conquered Fort Ticonderoga, led a force of seven thousand regular British troops and German mercenaries, as well as hundreds of Loyalist militia and savage Indians, from the north, aiming straight as an arrow down the Hudson River. When Arnold joined Gates, the latter had seven thousand troops, but most of them were militia, with raw recruits untested against the steel of British bayonets. But Gates had two things going for him: the services of Arnold and those of the brilliant Daniel Morgan, the leader of a brigade of sharpshooters and frontiersman that was one of America's most formidable units.

Morgan and Arnold had been together on the Quebec expedition and thought alike: the only way to defeat the British was to lure them into fighting American-style, in the wilderness, where their cavalry and artillery were of less use. Accordingly, they convinced Gates to set up his defenses along Bemis Heights (named for a local tavern owner), a high bluff on the Hudson, with the river running to the right, or east, of the Continental lines and forests and gullies falling away to the west. Without the boats necessary to pass on the river, Burgoyne would be forced to try to outflank the Americans through the wild country on the west, where the British formations would be broken up and they would be less able to employ their big guns.

BELOW The British under General Burgoyne surrender after the second battle of Saratoga in October 1777. Although Gates claimed credit for the American victory, Burgoyne attributed it to Arnold.

Gates listened to this plan and approved it, and so the Americans dug in behind earthworks and waited. Gates did not trust the quality of American troops against regular British forces and wanted to fight a defensive action—to simply force the British to come to them. Arnold disagreed. He wanted, he told Gates, to "march out and attack" the enemy, for if one simply allowed the British all the time in the world to organize, they would eventually be able to draw up their heavy artillery and blast away at the American defenses. This dispute became so heated that Arnold was banned from Gates's staff meetings.

On the morning of September 19, as "the sun burned off the mist and melted a light frost into dew," Burgoyne's troops were sighted approaching. Arnold was beside himself with his trademark anger and energy. Approaching Gates, he badgered him into giving permission for him to send out four hundred of Morgan's riflemen to set an ambush in the woods to the west.

At first, Morgan's men surprised the British and drove them back, but soon they were in trouble as they ran into the main force of Burgoyne's army. A battle raged over a 350-yard cleared field known locally as Freeman's Farm, and Arnold fed in reinforcements. He was now in his martial element, standing in front of the American lines, one observer wrote, "his eyes flashing, pointing with his sword to the advancing foe, with a voice that rang clear as a trumpet and electrified the lines."

The battle of Freeman's Farm ended in what was technically a victory for the British, for Arnold, under pressure of a savage Hessian bayonet attack, was forced to withdraw from the clearing that evening, but it was a victory the British could ill afford. They lost 600 of their men dead, wounded or taken prisoner, to 380 Americans.

Back in the American lines, Arnold was enraged with Gates, who had not sent reinforcements during the evening's attack by the Hessians. Gates claimed that he was short on ammunition, but Arnold disputed this furiously. The next day Gates sent a report to Congress in which he took credit for the victory, without even mentioning Arnold and the men he had led that bloody afternoon.

"YOU HAVE NO BUSINESS HERE" On September 22, Gates went a step further, ordering Daniel Morgan's division to report directly to him for orders—essentially removing them from Arnold's command. Arnold could take it no longer. He burst into Gates's headquarters unannounced—a serious breach of protocol in itself—and harangued Gates about Morgan's removal. Their argument was so loud that it could be heard throughout the building, with Arnold "ridiculed" by Gates, who employed "high words and gross language" in putting down his subordinate. Gates told Arnold that as soon as General Benjamin Lincoln arrived, he planned on taking over Arnold's division. He further said that Arnold was of so little use to the American forces that, if Arnold liked, he would write him a pass to leave the army—on the spot.

The next day, demanding to know why he had been treated with "affront and indignity," Arnold requested just such a pass to leave the camp, and Gates provided it to him. Their dispute had disheartened the fighting men of the American army, who knew that Burgoyne was only licking his wounds as he prepared for another attack, and knew as well that Arnold was the fighting general they needed to lead them.

Rather typically, Arnold did not actually leave, instead brooding about the camp and sending more notes to Gates ("I have reason to think your treatment [of me] proceeds from a spirit of jealousy"), telling him that by his inaction in the face of Burgoyne he was setting up the army for failure—even now, a fleet of British ships under Sir Henry Clinton was making its way up the Hudson River from New York, in a diversionary attack. Arnold had the gall to write to his superior officer: "Let me entreat you to improve."

This was too much. On October 1, as Lincoln arrived in the American lines, Gates had Arnold relieved of command. In the meantime, Burgoyne had finally decided to bestir himself to attack the Americans and hook up with Clinton's forces. On October 7 he sent a column of about seventeen hundred men on a reconnaissance in force towards the American lines, seeking a breakthrough. Gates ordered Morgan's men to begin shooting from the trees. As the battle heated up and the British were driven back to their fortified positions, Arnold still felt Gates was too passive, too willing to let Burgoyne retreat without destroying him.

Swallowing his pride, he went to Gates and begged to be let in on the action. Gates replied, "I am afraid to trust you, Arnold." Arnold persisted and finally Gates shouted at him: "General, I have nothing for you to do. You have no business here."

"VICTORY OR DEATH" Now, in one of the most extraordinary moments of the Revolutionary War, Arnold mounted his horse, cast one last disdainful look at Gates, and charged into the battle, shouting "Victory or Death!" Gates screamed for an aide to stop Arnold; the man chased after him, but it was too late. Arriving among the Continental troops at the very front of the line, he asked them what regiment they were from. He found out that they were Connecticut troops and cried: "Come on, boys! If the day is long, we'll have them in hell before night."

Arnold, searching for a break in the British fortifications, sent his grey charger racing along the length of the British lines as bullets whizzed around him, although some British troops were too astonished even to fire. He found a weak spot and led his men through it. Just as he did so, a Hessian fired at him, hitting him in the same leg that had been wounded at Quebec. Seven more bullets killed his horse, which fell on Arnold's wounded leg. As Americans rushed by him, driving the British back, Arnold writhed in agony. Ironically, Gates's aide now, finally, caught up with him, with the order to return to headquarters.

THE BEAUTIFUL MISS SHIPPEN

Margaret Shippen, known to one and all as Peggy, was a Philadelphia belle who was considered by most British officers to be the most beautiful young woman in the colonies. She was born in 1760, the daughter of Judge Edward Shippen IV and his wife, Peggy. The Shippens were one of the richest and most politically connected families in America and they have often been portrayed as Tory sympathizers, but the picture is a bit more complex. After the British captured Philadelphia in 1777, the Shippen home played host to numerous high-ranking young British officers, including Major John André, who was smitten with the slight, delicate-featured, sloe-eyed Peggy, writing poetry to her and playing the flute for her amusement. Yet before the British capture, Edward Shippen had entertained high-ranking American officers, including George Washington, and he personally owed Washington a debt of gratitude, for after Shippen's son, Edward, who had rashly joined the British army, was captured by the Patriots, Washington personally saw to his release.

When the British evacuated Philadelphia in June of 1778, Benedict Arnold became military governor of the city. Barely recovered from wounds suffered at Saratoga, he cut a dashing figure, the crippled hero who, all knew, had saved the day. He, too, was struck by Shippen, who at eighteen was half his age, and she by him and his "oft-repeated stories of gallant deeds [and] traits of generosity and courage." Although Peggy Shippen's own sympathies were definitely Loyalist and her father opposed the union, she and Arnold married in 1779.

Despite her protestations, Peggy Shippen certainly knew of Arnold's decision, sometime in May 1779, to defect to the British, and probably even connected him with Major John André. Still, Peggy was able to convince George Washington to allow her to return to Philadelphia from West Point after Arnold fled, helped in part by a letter from Arnold to Washington himself (sent from a British ship) claiming that Peggy was "as good and innocent as an angel." After Philadelphia, she joined Arnold in British-held New York and from there went into exile with him in Great Britain and Canada.

Peggy was to live three years longer than Arnold, dying of cancer at the age of forty-four in 1804. Their life in exile was not an easy one, but Peggy stuck loyally by her husband. However, after her death, it was discovered that she had a locket that contained a wisp of John André's hair. According to family legend, Benedict Arnold never knew of its existence.

BELOW Margaret Shippen, second wife of Benedict Arnold, and child. Margaret, from a Loyalist Philadelphia family, remained loyal to Arnold and followed him into exile.

One indication of how high feelings ran against Benedict Arnold after he betrayed his country was a plot concocted by George Washington and his adjutant, Henry "Light Horse Harry" Lee, to kidnap and kill Arnold. In October 1780, as Arnold actively recruited his own Loyalist force from New York City, Lee ordered one of his smartest and most loyal troops, twenty-three-year-old Major John Champe, to "desert" to Arnold, kidnap him, and bring him to Washington to be hanged.

Champe's defection was perfectly staged and Arnold met the quiet but intense young man, invited him for a drink, and eventually recruited him to be his senior non-commissioned officer. Champe noticed that Arnold took a walk around his grounds late each night before retiring. He was sure, he notified Lee, that he could kidnap Arnold and take him across the river to New Jersey.

However, on December 11, 1780, the night when this kidnapping was scheduled, Arnold unwittingly foiled it by ordering his troops to embark on board ship for an expedition to fight the Continentals in Virginia. Unable to get another chance to snatch Arnold, Champe deserted back to the Patriots several weeks later.

But Arnold's decisive actions that day were to finally spell defeat for Burgoyne, who now withdrew and surrendered his forces—under extremely generous terms dictated by Gates—on October 17th. Gates claimed that Arnold was "the greatest poltroon in the world" and had merely taken advantage of a situation set up by him, but Burgoyne later told Parliament that he had lost this second battle of Saratoga (known as the battle of Bemis Heights) because "Arnold chose to give rather than receive the attack," thus surprising the British so they were unable to launch a counterblow.

"INDELIBLE INFAMY" Now began the battle after the battle, with Gates seizing much of the credit for the victory—the most important result of which was that it had emboldened the French to join the war on the side of the Americans. Congress even struck off a gold medal honoring Gates. His supporters downplayed Arnold's achievements and even spread the rumor that his valor at Saratoga was due to drunkenness, a rumor that persisted into the twentieth century. The wounded Arnold would never lead American troops into battle again. Made governor of Philadelphia after Howe's British forces retreated from the capital, he wooed and married the lovely Loyalist sympathizer Peggy Shippen.

With Congress refusing to consider his promotion, with his debts growing because of foolish financial schemes, and with a court-martial for malfeasance brought against him by his political enemies, Arnold finally had had enough. He considered himself the victor of the most important battle to date in the history of the new country, and now he was treated like a common criminal.

In the summer of 1780, he asked for and received a posting as commander of the crucial American military fort of West Point, north of New York City on the Hudson. Perhaps influenced by his beautiful Tory wife, he now contacted the British and plotted with them to turn over West Point in return for a commission as brigadier general and twenty thousand pounds. His plan failed when his contact with the British—Major John André, a former suitor of Peggy's—was captured, and Arnold fled to New York City and put on a British uniform.

Horatio Gates, for his part, was refused Washington's position but was finally given command of American forces in the south. There he engaged the British under Lord Cornwallis at Camden, South Carolina, and, without an Arnold present, was soundly defeated in August 1780. Charges of personal cowardice followed him and he was never to hold a combat command in the American army again.

Hearing of Gates's defeat at Camden, Arnold wrote to a friend, sarcastically calling Gates "that hero" and saying that his retreat in the face of the enemy would "blot his escutcheon with indelible infamy." This was an extraordinary statement from a man who was planning to betray his country, and whose own "escutcheon" would soon become synonymous with the word "traitor"—but for Arnold it was always about personal honor and bravery, less about country. In that sense, perhaps, his critics in the Continental Congress were right all along.

THE DEBACLE AT CAMDEN

Horatio Gates was in command not only during the greatest victory of American forces during the Revolution, but also during their worst defeat. In July 1780, Gates arrived to take command of American forces in South Carolina, where they were being threatened by British regular troops and Loyalist militia under Lieutenant General George Cornwallis. Gates immediately made a series of stunningly bad decisions. He decided to march his three thousand men to attack the British-held town of Camden, South Carolina. Gates wanted to maintain secrecy but, against advice, chose a route that led through terrible swampland, where there was little food for his troops. Because he disapproved of their scruffy appearance, he refused the valuable aid of American irregular troops under the command of guerilla leader Francis Marion, the renowned "Swamp Fox." Gates even dismissed his cavalry, claiming that they would do him little good on the southern terrain.

The British became aware of Gates's movements and Cornwallis led a force out to meet him. The two armies literally ran into each other in the dark on the morning of August 16, and then settled back to await daylight. Although Gates's force was equal in numbers to those of the British, two thousand of them were inexperienced militia. His officers advised him to retreat. Instead, he placed his men in battle array and waited. When the British regular forces made a bayonet charge against his militia, the terrified men broke and ran, some without even firing a shot. Despite brave fighting on the part of the Continental regular troops, it appears that Gates fled soon after the militia, leaving his other men to their fate. Although no exact record of his movements exists, Gates managed to be in Charlotte, North Carolina, sixty miles away, only a few hours after the battle.

ABOVE Horatio Gates might look the part of a successful general, but his final command was a disaster and he appears to have fled the battleground at Camden, leaving his men to their fate.

ALEXANDER HAMILTON

AARON BURR AND ALEXANDER HAMILTON : THE DUEL THAT CHANGED AMERICAN HISTORY

TODAY WEEHAWKEN, NEW JERSEY, IS A BUSTLING urban area on the high Palisades cliffs directly across the Hudson River from the island of Manhattan. Weehawken is home to a thriving working class of perhaps twenty thousand people; many thousands more travel through the town each day, for Weehawken contains the western terminus of the Lincoln Tunnel, one of two commuter tunnels under the river heading into Manhattan. The onomatopoetic name means "place of gulls" in the local Lenape Indian dialect, and gulls still sweep over Weehawken's high cliffs as they did two hundred years ago, when Alexander Hamilton and Aaron Burr took separate boats across the Hudson on a hot July day to fight a duel.

Their Weehawken dueling place—a narrow ledge partway up the cliff and accessible only at low tide—has long since vanished, but Aaron Burr and Alexander Hamilton have not. They are, of course, not the only famous rivals in American political history, but theirs was the only rivalry to end with one antagonist killing the other. If the particulars of the duel are still hotly debated—and even why it occurred in the first place—its place in American history is undisputed. Alexander Hamilton was America's first Secretary of the Treasury, the man who established a national banking system and, as he put it, "introduced order in the finances" of a new nation debt-ridden after the Revolutionary War. Aaron Burr was a brilliant politician, America's fourth vice-president and a man who nearly became president. They were early patriots who might have worked together to further the growth of the country. Instead, they destroyed each other.

THE MYSTIQUE OF BURR AND HAMILTON

Historians, to this day, cannot agree on who these gentlemen were. A recent biography sympathetic to Hamilton refers to Burr as charming, unprincipled, and vacant: "He was like an empty refrigerator—bright, cold and empty." Yet a new biography of Burr relates that, "in moral terms, it is arguable that [Burr] behaved with greater honesty and directness than Hamilton."

Hamilton is considered by some to be a political schemer out only for his own ends—yet others see him as the man who saved a foundering United States with his philosophy of a strong central government (a courageous stance at a time in the new country when authoritative central government was suspect). Burr is portrayed as a man devoid of political philosophy, out only to make his ends justify the means. Yet other writers describe him as a visionary whose dreams of expansion into the western territories were no different from those of Thomas Jefferson—yet it was Burr who was tried for treason when he attempted to create a western kingdom.

One theory has it that the two men were simply too much alike. Both were handsome, brilliant, short of stature, and sexually promiscuous. They were politicians operating in what was then a very small political arena, in which the seismic shock of the American Revolution had released fratricidal passions. Yet, the final and fatal quarrel between these two men, rivals for twelve years, came at a time when both were out of office, or about to be, and heavily in debt. All they had left was their honor, which, for eighteenth century gentlemen, meant their lives.

"THE BASTARD SON OF A SCOTCH PEDDLAR"

John Adams, America's second president, hated Alexander Hamilton with a passion and referred to him as "a Creole bastard," the "bastard son of a Scotch peddlar," and "a man devoid of every moral principle—a bastard." In those days, illegitimacy of birth counted a good deal towards who you were in the world, and there is no doubt that Hamilton's parents were not married. He was born on the island of Nevis, in the Caribbean, in 1757, the son of James Hamilton, a ne'er-do-well scion of a wealthy Scottish family, and one Rachel Lavien. When Alexander Hamilton was eight, his father abandoned the family, leaving Rachel to support them by running a small store on the island of St. Croix; in 1768, both Hamilton and his mother came down with malaria. Hamilton survived; his mother did not.

At the age of ten, he was thus effectively orphaned, and his misfortunes continued when a cousin who adopted him committed suicide shortly thereafter. But Hamilton was an astonishingly bright and informed boy who wrote well and kept the books for a merchant, impressing so many in his community that they collected money to send him, in 1772, to the American colonies for further schooling. There he attended King's College in New York City and fell under the influence of the patriotic fervor sweeping the colonies prior to their armed rebellion against the British crown. Joining a New York militia unit, he raised an artillery company of sixty men and fought the British in 1776 at the battle of Harlem Heights in New York. He so distinguished himself during the retreat of George Washington's army that Washington made him a lieutenant colonel and, in March 1777, invited him to serve on his staff.

"ONE GIVEN TO ME FROM THE DEAD" Although Aaron Burr had a more distinguished bloodline than Alexander Hamilton, his childhood was also marked by tragedy and displacement. Born in New Jersey in 1756, he was the son of the Reverend Aaron Burr, Sr., president of Princeton College, and Esther Edwards, who was the daughter of the famous Calvinist theologian Jonathan Edwards. A sickly child, who nearly died when he was only eight months old, causing his mother to write in her journal: "I look on the Child as one given to me from the dead." He lost both his parents by the time he was two years old. Like Hamilton, he overcame his disadvantaged childhood. He graduated from Princeton in 1772 with a degree in theology but decided to switch to law, where he proved a brilliant student, but, again as with Hamilton, the war intervened.

In 1775, Burr took part in General Benedict Arnold's notoriously difficult winter expedition into Canada that failed to capture Quebec (see page 152). However, Burr distinguished himself for his courage in action and would continue to do so. Like Hamilton's, Burr's bravery came to the notice of George Washington, who wanted to appoint Burr to his staff, but Washington and Burr clashed—some historians say they took an instant dislike to each other—and after further heroic service at the battle of Monmouth in 1778, Burr retired from the army, studied law in Albany, New York, and opened a private practice in Manhattan.

EARLY ADVERSARIES Hamilton, in the meantime, had risen to become Washington's chief of staff, drafting the general's orders and letters, although he continued to seek active field command and led a daring charge at the battle of Yorktown during the American victory there. He left the army at the war's end and moved to New York where he, too, became a lawyer. He and Burr rose to become the finest young litigators in New York and began to clash in courtrooms— Burr, the cool and intellectual blueblood with strangely mesmerizing black-violet eyes, and Hamilton, illegitimate son of the islands, with his Scottish red hair and profound impatience, speaking passionately from the heart.

The two men became political adversaries as well, in the charged and fractious politics of New York in the 1780s. Here Hamilton rose to far greater prominence. As a friend of George Washington's, he was elected to the Continental Congress and began writing a series of papers (along with John Jay and future president James Madison) that would influence the writing of America's Constitution and the shape of the government. The Federalist Papers, as they are called, postulated a strong central government with the power to tax and raise armies, issue currency,

LEFT Alexander Hamilton (standing), Secretary of State Thomas Jefferson, and President George Washington in consultation c. 1795 during Hamilton's tenure as Secretary of the Treasury.

and create a national bank. From this philosophy rose the Federalist Party; in 1789, George Washington, the nation's first elected president, named Hamilton his secretary of the treasury.

Burr was not without political influence, the same year becoming New York's attorney general. Even though Hamilton's prestige was far greater, he seems to have been threatened by Burr in some deeply personal way and went out of his way to attack him. In 1792, Hamilton's father-in-law, General Philip Schuyler, lost his bid for re-election as a New York senator and the post was offered by Shuyler's political enemies to Aaron Burr. Hamilton already disliked Burr but, seeing him rise as a member of the Republican Party to a position that might, possibly, push him into national prominence, he went on the attack, starting a letter-writing campaign calling Burr an "embryo Caesar" and claiming that he had heard "rumors" that Burr was "unprincipled as a private and public man."

This latter charge, Hamilton would use again and again against Burr. The imputation, in the veiled language of the time, was that Burr was, privately, a sexual debaucher. Burr had married a woman ten years older than himself, Theodosia Prevost, a sickly woman by whom he had one daughter, his beloved

Theodosia. It was known that Burr had many sexual affairs (historians were later to discover a secret diary, written in code, detailing these) but Hamilton was not a man who should have been throwing stones. In what became infamous as the "Maria Reynolds affair," the secretary of the treasury—married now, with children who would eventually number seven—had an affair with a woman who was secretly working with her husband to blackmail Hamilton. And even after the blackmail was revealed Hamilton continued to see her. When this sordid affair was made public, Hamilton admitted to it in print, in a *mea culpa* read by all of America. Some admired him for his frankness. Others were horrified that he would expose his family to this type of embarrassment (but Hamilton would also have an affair, or at the very least a deep infatuation, with his wife's sister, Angelica Church).

Hamilton suspected that Aaron Burr had had a hand in bringing this affair to light. Burr was Maria Reynolds's lawyer in later litigation and certainly enjoyed seeing his rival's embarrassment, but there is no hard and fast evidence that he conspired to make public Hamilton's private fiasco.

"NO MEANS TOO ATROCIOUS" As the 1790s continued, Hamilton immersed himself in the art of American political attack. He managed to make powerful enemies, even among the members of his own party, in particular John Adams, against whom he continually schemed. By 1795, as Adams was about to become president, Hamilton's growing debts—he was building a grand house in Manhattan—and the enmity he had incurred caused him to resign from his position as secretary of the treasury and go back into private practice. But, of course, he did not leave politics. When the contested presidential election of 1800, featuring Federalist John Adams against Republican Thomas Jefferson, began, Hamilton's hatred of Adams caused him to write an extraordinary letter entitled *Letter from Alexander Hamilton Concerning the Public Conduct and Character of John Adams*, fifty-four pages of what one historian has called "unremitting vilification." "If we must have an enemy at the head of the government, let it be one whom we can oppose ... who will not involve our party in the disgrace of his foolish and bad measures," Hamilton wrote.

Hamilton was attempting to get members of his own party to vote against their own candidate, a high-stakes gamble that helped put Adams second in the vote total, behind two men who were tied: Jefferson and none other than Aaron Burr, who had seized on this division in the Federalist Party to make his run for the presidency. The election was thrown into the House of Representatives, where members would vote to break the tie. Even though Hamilton disliked Thomas Jefferson, he hated Aaron Burr far worse, and once more his poisoned pen came out. "Jefferson or Burr?" he wrote to one politician. "The former without a doubt ... Burr's elevation can only promote the purposes of the desperate and the profligate ..." To another important Federalist, he wrote: "I ... am sure there is no means too atrocious to be employed by [Burr]."

In the winter of February 1801, the House voted Thomas Jefferson as president. Aaron Burr, as runner-up in the vote total, became his vice-president. It is interesting that the New England-based Federalist Party would vote for a Virginia Republican over the New Yorker Burr—many, including Burr, attributed this to machinations on the part of Hamilton. In the next few years Burr, who had come within a few votes of attaining the highest office in the land, saw his fortunes fall precipitously. Politically, he and Jefferson were never close and Jefferson marginalized his vice-president, leaving him with little or nothing to do. (Jefferson's attitude towards his vice-president was not helped by anonymous pamphlets that were appearing in New York at the time, accusing Burr of scheming to wrest the presidency from him—pamphlets Burr assumed were written by Hamilton or someone in his employ.)

Also, Burr, having made certain poorly conceived business deals, was deeply in debt and his wife, Theodosia, had died. By 1804, Thomas Jefferson had made it clear that he would not pick Burr as his vice-president for another term. Burr cast about for another political sinecure and decided to throw himself into the New York governor's race, but the candidate backed by Alexander Hamilton, Morgan Lewis, beat Burr badly in a dirty electoral contest that saw Hamilton again casting aspersions on Burr's character.

THE CHALLENGE Sometime in April 1804, during the New York gubernatorial race, Hamilton attended an Albany, New York, dinner party where one of the guests was a Dr. Charles D. Cooper, a prominent Federalist. At this party, according to a letter sent to an Albany newspaper by Dr. Cooper, Hamilton had remarked that Burr "was a dangerous man", who was "not to be trusted with the reins of government." Even more offensive, from Burr's point of view, was another line written by Cooper: "I could detail to you a still more despicable opinion which [Hamilton] has expressed of Mr. Burr."

Burr did not learn about this letter until June and what bothered him was the word "despicable," which at the time had the connotation of meaning "sordid," or unusually debauched. No one knows exactly what Hamilton said about Burr at that dinner party to earn Cooper's use of the adjective. Historians have speculated that he may have called Burr a sodomite or even have accused him of having an incestuous relationship with his daughter, Theodosia. Burr himself did not know, but he was enraged when he read the letter. At the time, he was suffering from "ague"—possibly severe sinusitis—and his patience may have been at low ebb. He summoned his aide, William P. Van Ness, and told him that "Hamilton has at different times and upon various occasions used language and expressed opinions highly injurious to my reputation." He then sent Van Ness to Hamilton's law office with a letter demanding that Hamilton provide "a prompt and unqualified acknowledgement or denial" of the charges contained in Cooper's letter.

This Hamilton refused to do, essentially saying that he and Burr had been rivals for so long that almost anything he, Hamilton, said was not a matter of honor but a matter of mere politics: "I deem it inadmissible ... to consent to be interrogated as to the justice of the *inferences*, which may be drawn by others, from whatever I may have said of a political *opponent* in the course of fifteen years competition" [italics in original].

Hamilton could merely have said that he did not recall making any such remarks and it is possible that Burr would have let the matter go, but this aggressive and slightly mocking reply was too much for him. His face wrapped in warm rags to still his pain, he replied that "political opposition can never absolve Gentlemen from the necessity of a rigid adherence to the laws of honor and the rules of decorum." In private, he had already told Van Ness that he felt that Hamilton "had a settled and implacable malevolence" towards him. "These things must have an end," he said.

Van Ness delivered Burr's challenge of a duel to Nathaniel Pendleton, a former comrade-in-arms of Hamilton's who would now act as Hamilton's second in the matter. Pendleton would later write that when Hamilton received the actual challenge, on June 27, he seemed stunned—he may have fooled himself into thinking that Burr would stop short of an actual duel, but Burr's hatred was not to be assuaged in any other way. Hamilton was forced to accept, even though he was clearly reluctant.

DUELING Neither Hamilton nor Burr was a stranger to dueling. Such matches were outlawed in New York, which was the reason why gentlemen from Manhattan fought in New Jersey (where duels were against the law as well, but the penalties were much lighter).

Duels, which had descended from the judicial combats of the Middle Ages (whoever won was the man willed by God to win), had become a part of English society in the seventeenth century and were, therefore, a part of what American gentlemen considered proper behavior in order to right a slight against their honor. Duels in America were mainly fought with pistols, according to strict rules—the Irish Code Duello, drawn up in 1777, was the one used by most Americans. Duels were not, necessarily, injurious to one's health. It has been estimated that only twenty percent of the duels of the time ended in fatalities, because of the extreme inaccuracy of the smoothbore pistols even at twenty to thirty feet, the usual distance. (There is another study that claims that only one in fourteen duelists died.) When both duelists fired and both missed, they could— and often did—claim their honor satisfied.

Both Hamilton and Burr had, as younger men, come out against dueling, but both had been involved in duels. Burr had, in fact, fought one against Hamilton's brother-in-law John Church at Weehawken in 1799, with Hamilton acting as Church's second. Neither man was injured and they had called it a day. Hamilton

"THE LAST HIGH-TONED DUEL"

While dueling was, in the main, quite a serious business, it sometimes had its comic aspects. One such moment occurred in 1826, when the fiery Virginia Senator John Randolph accused Henry Clay, Speaker of the House of Representatives, of having secretly conspired to throw the election of 1824 to President John Quincy Adams. In fact, he referred to Clay as a "blackleg," slang for a cheating gambler.

This was too much for Clay and he challenged Randolph to a duel. The two met at a secret dueling spot along the Potomac River near Washington, but a comedy of errors ensued. Randolph accidentally discharged his gun and had to be given another. Then both Clay and Randolph shot—and missed. The men reloaded and Clay fired first. His bullet passed through Randolph's jacket without hurting him. Randolph then eyed Clay speculatively for a moment, and deliberately fired his pistol in the air. "I do not fire on you, Mr. Clay," he said.

The two men shook hands and left the dueling ground together. Senator Thomas Hart Benton, present as a second, remarked dryly that it was "about the last high-toned duel" he ever saw.

himself had challenged future president James Monroe to a duel, but wiser heads had interfered.

Perhaps most tragically of all, Hamilton's eldest son, nineteen-year-old Philip, had been killed in a duel at Weehawken just three years before, an event that had profoundly depressed Hamilton. He had told Philip at the time that the boy should "reserve" his fire—fire in the air—apparently because he believed Philip had given his opponent provocation to fight the duel. However, this was against the Irish Code Duello, which stated that if a man felt he had given offense, he should simply apologize. Sadly, Hamilton's advice to Philip may have helped get him killed.

One would think that, with the example of his son fresh in his mind, Hamilton would have done anything to avoid a duel. Unfortunately, Hamilton had seen a recent example of what could happen to a man who backed away from a point of honor. His dear friend Robert Troup had the previous year been involved in an altercation with Colonel William Stephens Smith, a customs official at the Port of New York and also the son-in-law of former President John Adams. Smith had challenged Troup to a duel and Troup, deeply in debt, physically unwell, and with a wife and six children to support, had abjectly apologized rather than shoot it out with Smith.

Smith laughed in a letter to his friend Aaron Burr that Troup's reputation "is blasted in society." Troup soon developed an ulcerated tongue and mouth that

THE DEATH OF PHILIP HAMILTON

There is no record of Alexander Hamilton's thoughts as his boat approached the New Jersey shore and the Weehawken dueling grounds on July 11, 1804, but one wonders if he could help thinking about his eldest son, Philip, who had been killed in a duel at that very spot three years before.

On November 20, 1801, nineteen-year-old Philip, a recent Columbia College graduate, and his friend, Richard Price, had drunkenly insulted a twenty-seven-year-old lawyer by the name of George I. Eacker. Insults could not be tolerated by gentlemen, and thus a duel was arranged. First, Eacker and Price squared off on the Weehawken heights; each fired twice at the other, missing, and honor was declared satisfied. Next it was Hamilton's turn. His father had urged him to miss deliberately—to fire his pistol in the air. When the two men met at Weehawken and the second cried "Present!", neither man raised his pistol for a full minute. Then Hamilton raised his pistol and Eacker had no choice but to respond. Hamilton's shot went wild; Eacker's ball hit him in the body. He died twenty-four hours later, in agony, with his mother and father clutching him.

made it almost impossible for him to speak and sank deeper into misery. Seeing this, Hamilton knew that though he, too, had a wife and family and debts, there was no way he could live with himself if he evaded Burr.

LAST WILLS With their seconds still wrangling over the date of the duel, the two men went about wrapping up business affairs. On July 4, exactly a week before the duel, Hamilton and Burr attended the same social event: a gathering of the Society of Cincinnati, a group composed of ex-officers of the Revolutionary Army and their male descendants. Meeting at the famous Fraunces Tavern (which still stands in downtown New York), the men drank, sang songs, and celebrated the nation's Independence Day.

Burr and Hamilton sat next to each other, but did not speak. Hamilton seemed almost overly merry, at one point even standing up on the table to sing an old marching song, while Burr appeared sunk in gloom, occasionally glaring at Hamilton. He left early and Hamilton retired to his downtown home on Cedar Street and sat down to write a letter to his wife, Eliza, who knew almost nothing about what would happen in a week's time. The letter was not to be delivered "unless I shall first have terminated my earthly career," but he told her how much he loved her, attempting, no doubt, to atone for his indiscretions of the past. On Sunday, July 7, as his son John Church Hamilton later remembered, Hamilton called everyone to sit with him on the grass in front of the Grange, staring at the stars. Later that night, uncharacteristically, Hamilton called John to his room and said, rather plaintively: "Won't you come sleep with me tonight?"

On that Monday, Aaron Burr impatiently wrote William Van Ness and told him that he must "get on" with picking a date. Meeting with Nathaniel Pendleton that afternoon, they finally chose the early morning of Wednesday, July 11, two days hence. On the night before the duel, Burr, alone in his home except for his three slaves, wrote a last will and testament, which he enclosed in an envelope with a covering letter to his son-in-law, Joseph Alston. "If it shall be my lot to fall," he said, "I commit to you all that is most dear to me—my reputation and my daughter." Hamilton, also alone in his Cedar Street home, wrote another letter to his wife. Earlier he had completed his will. Significantly, he also wrote a letter saying that he would "withhold" his fire, whether Burr fired at him or not. Some historians take this as genuine; others see it as another scheming attempt to defame Burr should Burr kill him in the duel.

Then both men attempted to sleep in the muggy New York heat.

WEEHAWKEN, JULY 11, 1804 At about 5:00 a.m. the next morning, Burr and Van Ness took a boat across the Hudson River to the dueling ground in Weehawken. Climbing up the cliff path, the two realized that they had arrived first and set about clearing the underbrush from the ledge—it was apparent that no one had dueled there in some time. The ledge was the perfect dueling place, six feet wide and eleven yards long, it was partially hidden by a large boulder and a cedar tree.

About an hour later, Hamilton, Nathaniel Pendleton, and a physician, Dr. David Hosack, arrived. While Hosack waited with the boatsmen (so that he could legally claim not to have witnessed the duel), Hamilton and Pendleton climbed to the ledge. The two seconds huddled together, conferring over the rules of the duel—both men would stand about ten paces (thirty feet) apart and fire on the command: "Present!" They had already agreed to use the set of pistols belonging to Hamilton's brother-in-law John Church—the same pair of custom-made English pistols that had been used in the duel that killed Philip Hamilton. Usually, dueling pistols were about .50 caliber; these were .544 caliber, firing a ball weighing a full ounce. The guns were, as one writer has put it, "heavy enough to shoot horses." Each had a hair-trigger adjustment, if the shooter desired a very quick trigger release, but this entailed the possibility of less accuracy.

The two seconds flipped a coin to see who would have choice of position. Pendleton won and placed Hamilton with his back to the cliff. Unfortunately, this meant the glare of the sun off the river (by this time it was about 7:00 a.m.) glanced into his eyes. It is possible that Pendleton thought Burr would be a better target, outlined by the light, but he seems to have made a poor choice. After each man was handed his pistol (Pendleton asked Hamilton if he wanted the hairspring set, to which Hamilton replied in the negative) Hamilton asked for a pause, squinting into the light. He told the men present that the "direction of the light" made it hard for him to focus and he finally took glasses from his pocket and put them on.

With this, the men were asked if they were ready, to which they both said: "Yes." They took their dueling stances—right leg stretched in front of the left, right arm extended, stomach sucked in. The idea was to try to present as little body surface as possible for a bullet to strike.

Pendleton cried "Present!" and both men fired. Predictably, Pendleton thought Burr fired first and Van Ness thought that Hamilton did. In the split-second that followed, Pendleton saw Hamilton's arm jerk up as his gun went off, and realized that he had been wounded. Holding onto his pistol, Hamilton hit the ground face-first. Burr, too, seemed to stumble under a bullet's impact, but it turned out he had stepped on a stone and was not hit—Hamilton's bullet had whistled through the tree above him. Seeing Hamilton lying on the ground, he went forward, as if to help him, but he was stopped by Van Ness who grabbed him and led him down the path to the river, just as Dr. Hosack, who had heard the shots, was coming up. Although Burr insisted that he wanted to speak with Hamilton, Van Ness quickly got him into the boat and they set off for Manhattan.

When Hosack arrived, he found that Hamilton, now being held in Pendleton's arms, had been shot on his right side, above his hip. The bullet had gone through his liver and smashed his vertebrae. Hamilton had no feeling in his legs.

"This is a mortal wound, Doctor," he said.

BURR'S WESTERN ADVENTURE

Part of Aaron Burr's notoriety stems not from his duel with Alexander Hamilton but from an attempt either to establish an empire of his own in the west or to invade Mexico—like so much in Burr's life, exactly what he was doing remains unclear.

After the expiration of his vice-presidential term, Burr began telling people that he planned "a grand expedition" in the uncharted lands west of the Mississippi—the territory purchased by Jefferson from France in what had become known as the Louisiana Purchase. Great Britain's ambassador to America, Anthony Merry, would later say that Burr had asked him for money to "effect a Separation of the Western Part of the United States." At the same time, he plotted with James Wilkinson, governor of Louisiana, to invade Mexico, then part of the Spanish territories. Burr's expedition got under way in December 1806 with a thousand men recruited from upstate New York. With this force, he headed down the Mississippi River in the direction of New Orleans. Wilkinson, who—it was discovered much later—was actually a spy in the employ of the Spanish, decided that the situation boded ill for Spain and, therefore, revealed Burr's plans

to President Jefferson. Burr was arrested in early 1807 and charged with treason—in fact, Jefferson, angry and embarrassed by his former vice-president, claimed that Burr was guilty "beyond question." However, at the trial in Richmond, Virginia, in May—Burr attended, dressed in black silk, along with his daughter, Theodosia, her son and her husband—Burr was found innocent of treason, probably because the main witnesses against him, such as Wilkinson, were so widely mistrusted and disliked.

Was Burr guilty of treason? Possibly not. He explained that even his remarks to the British ambassador had been made to conceal his true and secret intention of invading Mexico and, indeed, Wilkinson's actions in betraying him would seem to support this, for Wilkinson, the Spanish spy, was seeking to protect Spanish territory from invasion. Yet, while he was perhaps not a traitor, Burr's plan to invade Mexico was irresponsible and megalomaniacal in the extreme—it could have ignited a broader war against Spain and its ally France, something the young American government did not need.

LEFT Aaron Burr defends himself at his trial for treason in Richmond, Virginia, in May 1807. He was accused of attempting to create an independent state in the American west.

THE END OF THE AFFAIR Hamilton died about twenty-four hours later, drugged with laudanum, having been able to say goodbye to his wife and children, and still insisting that he had fired his shot in the air. "Pendleton knows," he murmured, "that I did not intend to fire on him." This point has been debated for over two hundred years, and was debated the morning after Hamilton's death, with Van Ness claiming vehemently that Hamilton had aimed to kill Burr and Pendleton claiming the Hamilton intended to throw his fire away.

While this dispute will never be settled, one does wonder why Hamilton made such a show of putting on his spectacles and complaining about the light if he intended merely to fire in the air. It is possible this was his intention and Burr merely shot more quickly, but under the rules of dueling at the time, Burr's behavior was completely proper.

Not that it mattered. There was a huge outpouring of grief for Hamilton, even on the part of those who had never been particular fans of his, and Burr soon realized that his life had changed forever. Still the vice-president of the United States, he was forced to flee New York, which was attempting to bring an indictment against him for murder, even though the duel had taken place in New Jersey. (The indictment was eventually dropped.)

Burr stopped first in Philadelphia, where he spent some time with a former lover. ("If any male friend of yours should be dying of ennui," he wrote Theodosia, "recommend him to engage in a duel and a courtship at the same time.") He then went to South Carolina, where he stayed with his son-in-law. On leaving the vice-presidency after the election of 1804 (which went to Thomas Jefferson and George Clinton), Burr made an attempt to establish a western empire, which resulted in his being tried, but acquitted, of treason. He spent years wandering around Europe, notorious now all over the world as the man who shot Alexander Hamilton, but he never apologized for his act. His personal life was marred by the death of Theodosia in a shipwreck in 1812. Returning to New York, he set up a successful practice as a lawyer and died at the ripe old age of eighty, on September 14, 1836. A Protestant minister with him tried to get him to discuss (and repent) the duel, but all the dying Burr would say was: "I was provoked to that encounter."

Perhaps. But it seems obvious from the exchange of letters between Hamilton and Burr that an angry and depressed Burr, his political career falling apart, decided to press through his grievances against a man who had harried him all his life—Alexander Hamilton. Perhaps he thought this might assuage his anger—and possibly resurrect his reputation as a warrior. If so, it did not work. Alexander Hamilton remains famous, but Aaron Burr is now only notorious.

NAPOLEON BONAPARTE VERSUS

THE DUKE OF WELLINGTON

NAPOLEON BONAPARTE AND THE DUKE OF WELLINGTON: SO ALIKE, SO VERY DIFFERENT

NAPOLEON BONAPARTE AND ARTHUR WELLESLEY, Duke of Wellington, were the primary geniuses of the battlefields of early nineteenth century Europe, although their genius revealed itself in different ways. Wellington, while capable of bold moves, was a defensive strategist of the first order, while Napoleon's surprise attacks won him battle after battle across Europe and the Near East. They only met each other in combat once, at Waterloo, and after that pivotal battle they could not have been more scathing about each other.

"Bonaparte's whole life, civil, political, military, was a fraud," Wellington later wrote.

"[Wellington] has no courage," Bonaparte said. "He acted out of fear. He had one stroke of fortune and he knows that such fortune never comes twice."

Yet, after Wellington's victory at Waterloo over a curiously dispirited Napoleon, the two men would still be entangled, like tired pugilists who cannot disengage themselves from a clinch. Wellington would sleep with two of Napoleon's mistresses during the French emperor's last exile and, outliving his opponent by twenty years, would fill his rich homes with Napoleonic memorabilia. And although, in fact, Wellington had saved his life in the immediate aftermath of Waterloo, Napoleon would revile the British leader, even leaving ten thousand francs in his will to a man who had tried to assassinate Wellington.

Theirs was eventually to become a rivalry over the verdict of posterity. Who, in fact, was the greater general—the tall, hook-nosed, stern, and reactionary Wellington or the short, rotund, and volatile Napoleon?

"FRIVOLOUS AND CARELESS PERSONAGES"

Arthur Wesley—the family would later change the spelling to Wellesley—was born in Country Meath, Ireland, on May 1, 1769, just over three months before Napoleon's entry into the world. He was the third of five surviving sons of the Earl of Mornington, a member of the Anglo-Irish ruling class, and his wife. Arthur's brother Richard would describe their parents as "frivolous and careless personages" and, in fact, they were too busy frittering away the earl's inheritance to pay much attention to their sons, sending them off to public school—in Wellington's case, Eton—and then ignoring them.

By the time young Arthur was eighteen, he had still not been able to find anything to do with himself in the world. The story goes that his mother spotted him at a London theater one night and whispered to her companion, "I do believe there is my ugly boy, Arthur. What can I do with him?" Surprised, apparently, to see him underfoot among her society friends, she decided to arrange a commission for him in the infantry. After short service in Ireland, Wellesley arrived in British India. There his career really began, at the advanced age, for the time, of twenty-seven. He had saved his money and managed to purchase a colonelcy (up until the Crimean War—see page 191—British officers could buy their own commissions) and he thrived in India. He was not a typical British officer given to gaming, polo (although he was an excellent horseman) and drinking. Instead, the slim, austere young man—who might have been handsome except for what one historian has called "an astonishing large and ugly proboscis"—read books on philosophy and military strategy and awaited his chance for combat, then, as now, the only way for a military officer to really get ahead in his chosen profession.

That chance came in 1799, as the British sought to conquer the southern Hindu state of Mysore. Leading the Thirty-third Indian Army Regiment, plus thousands of sepoys (native Indian troops), Wellington captured the fortress of the Sultan of Mysore, Tipu, killing him and seizing a treasure valued at over 1,100,000 pounds. The British government rewarded Wellesley by making him governor of Mysore and giving him 4,000 pounds out of Tipu's treasury. The young man who had made such an inauspicious start was on his way.

"THE LITTLE CORPORAL"

On August 15, 1769, Napoleon Buonaparte was born on the island of Corsica, which had become a French possession only the year before. His father, Carlo, was a lawyer from minor Italian nobility, but he had had little material success despite many grand schemes. His mother, Letizia, a stern and unemotional woman, was nonetheless the heart of the family of eight children, one of whom died before Napoleon was born. In May of 1779, Napoleon's father secured him a scholarship to the Royal Military School at Brienne-le-Château, a small town near Troyes, France. Like Wellington, he was simply left there for the next five years. At first Napoleon had a difficult time. He was very short in stature and what little French he spoke was tinged with a brusque Corsican accent, making him a target for teasing by the other boys.

The young Napoleon was notable for his arrogance and stubbornness. When some French boy would mock him, he would shake his (quite tiny) fist and shout: "I'll make you French pay, one day!" Once, as a punishment, he was ordered by his schoolmaster to eat dinner kneeling. "I'll eat standing up, Monsieur," he shouted at the man. "In my family we kneel only before God!" He then seemed to have a fit that left him shaking, sobbing, and finally vomiting. The punishment was rescinded and he was taken to the infirmary.

Napoleon graduated from the Royal Military School in 1785 and was admitted to the prestigious Ecole Militaire in Paris where he was adjudged by an examiner to be "capricious, haughty and frightfully egotistical ... [yet] proud, ambitious and aspiring to everything." Napoleon graduated a second lieutenant in the artillery at the age of sixteen. Within a few years, he became embroiled in the tumultuous French Revolution. In 1793, now a major fighting with the new republican army of France, he drove off the British who had sent troops to Toulon to aid a royalist uprising there. Wounded in the successful action, he was promoted to brigadier general. Two years later, he cleared the Paris streets of royalist forces with what he famously called "a whiff of grapeshot."

In 1796, lionized by the new government of France and by the press, the "Little Corporal"—as he became known for his closeness to his adoring troops—set off with an army on his very first conquest, that of Italy.

"BONAPARTE WILL COME THIS WAY" Arthur Wellesley had entered India at the age of twenty-seven with very little to show for himself. When he returned home, in 1805, it was as a major general and a Knight of the Order of Bath, a figure of national renown in England. His first order of business—and not very successful business, at that—was to marry the wealthy Kitty Pakenham, a young woman who had rejected his first marriage proposal in 1793. Conscious of his newfound prestige and reputation, Wellington had proposed to her long-distance from India and she had accepted. To his dismay, when he saw her for the first time in years, he realized that the young and glamorous London society girl had aged quickly and badly. To his brother he said: "She has grown ugly, by Jove." Honor demanded that he go through with his proposal but theirs was an unhappy and distant marriage, the strains of which Wellington relieved by seeking outside female companionship.

Wellesley soon had more pressing business, however. Napoleon Bonaparte had risen to become the most powerful man in France, after an astonishing series of military campaigns that saw him conquer countries from Italy to Egypt. Although the British, under their famous naval hero Lord Nelson, had demolished the French fleet at the Battle of the Nile, near Alexandria, in 1798, Napoleon's forces still controlled vast amounts of territory. In 1799, he returned to France and seized power; in 1804, he had himself proclaimed emperor. And his military successes continued. In the next two years, although he again lost a naval battle to Admiral Nelson at Trafalgar, he was able to inflict massive defeats on the armies of Britain's coalition partners Austria and Russia. There were real fears in Britain that Napoleon would invade the country. Mothers sang a lullaby to their babies that began:

> Baby, baby, naughty baby
> Hush you naughty thing, I say,
> Hush your squalling or it may be
> Bonaparte will come this way.

In 1808 Napoleon ordered his forces to capture Portugal (which would not cooperate in the Continental Blockade he had instituted against England) and installed his brother Joseph on the throne of Spain. Britain now knew it had to fight an all-out land war against the man whose hunger for conquest exceeded that of anyone in the world (it is no coincidence that one of Hitler's first acts, upon entering the conquered city of Paris in 1940, was to visit Napoleon's tomb).

THE PENINSULAR WAR By November 30, 1808, Napoleon had captured the Portuguese capital city of Lisbon, closing it to British shipping. He then sent 120,000 French soldiers into Spain, declaring that he was a "liberator." But while he had easily overcome the Spanish army, the Spanish people were another matter entirely. They formed guerilla groups and fought a war against the man they considered an oppressor, not a liberator. Napoleon now entered the peninsula himself, bringing an army and slaughtering thousands of Spanish rebels, but the fighting spread like wildfire across the Iberian Peninsula. In 1809, Napoleon was forced to return to France to deal with Austria, which was again preparing to go to war against him.

That same year, Wellesley was appointed commander in chief of British forces in the peninsula. Consistently outnumbered by margins of as much as three to one, it was here Wellesley earned his reputation as a brilliant defensive strategist. After the British took back Lisbon, he had the British army and their Portuguese allies set up a fortified line along Portugal's mountainous frontier with Spain. Time and time again, he defeated the best of Napoleon's generals—Michel Ney, André Masséna, and Nicolas-Jean de Dieu Soult. Wellesley told his subordinates: "They may overwhelm me but they will not outmaneuver me."

Wellesley's victories were the first the English and their allies had been able to score on land against the Napoleonic armies. Partly, as Wellington put it, this was because most of Napoleon's opponents were terrified by his reputation: "I suspect all the continental armies were more than half beaten before the battle began—I at least will not be frightened beforehand."

THE NAPOLEONIC CODE

While many see Napoleon as a malign influence in European history, the legal code he set up while emperor has been called by historians "one of the few documents which have influenced the whole world."

The French legal system was a jumbled variety of near-feudal laws that recognized the rights of the rich over the poor in almost every instance. Napoleon's code, drawn up at his behest by legal scholars, prohibited this sort of patchwork justice, setting up laws that judges throughout the entire country must abide by. It abolished secret laws, which were a staple of the *ancien régime* in France, as well as laws that made offenses criminal after the fact. Heresy, sacrilege, and "witchcraft" were no longer crimes, as they had been from medieval days.

The most lasting contribution of the code was the tenet that a person was innocent until proven guilty and should not be remanded in custody for a long period without trial. While people were still held for lengthy periods, especially in serious crimes such as murder, the code helped set a precedent for fairer treatment of defendants, especially those without connections and money.

Wellesley never had more than eighty thousand men, while the French, during certain periods of the Peninsular War, could muster three hundred thousand. Despite this, by 1813, Wellington's forces had driven the French out of Spain and entered southern France—the first time the British had done so against Napoleon. In the meantime, Napoleon had badly miscalculated by invading Russia in June 1812. He entered the vast country that summer with five hundred thousand men. By the time he returned home, in the desperate early winter of 1813, he had one hundred thousand. "My star was fading," he would later write of this time. "I felt the reins slipping out of my grasp and there was nothing I could do about it."

Sweden, Great Britain, Russia, Prussia, and Austria were arrayed against him. By the fall of 1813, his forces were retreating all over Europe. By the end of March 1814, coalition forces marched down the Champs-Elysées in Paris and on April 12 Napoleon abdicated his throne. The Treaty of Fontainebleau exiled him to the tiny Mediterranean isle of Elba, and Louis XVIII, brother of Louis XVI, was installed on the throne of France, supported by the coalition powers who wanted a stable monarchy in that country. Peace, it seemed, had at last arrived.

"THE DEVIL HAS BEEN UNCHAINED" Arthur Wellesley was now covered in glory. He was made Duke of Wellington, awarded thousands of acres of property and hundreds of thousands of pounds, and he returned home to a hero's welcome. He was the most prominent member of his generation in Britain, the most renowned general the country had. The British government sent him as their ambassador to the new royal court in Paris in the August of 1814, but assassins loyal to Napoleon tracked him everywhere, literally leaping out of dark alleys to shoot at him, and it was finally considered too dangerous for him to be there. He was sent on to Austria, as the British representative at the Congress of Vienna; it was there, in March of 1815, that he heard the shocking news that on February 26 Napoleon had escaped from Elba.

Napoleon was not officially a prisoner on Elba—in fact, he was emperor of the island's 120,000 inhabitants—but British warships patrolled the waters off the island's beaches, keeping on eye on him. Napoleon's spies told him that the new monarchy in France was floundering, the economy was on the skids, and that many people longed for his charismatic leadership. On a personal note, he was cut off from his wife and son, enraged that Louis XVIII had refused to pay him the sizeable sum of money guaranteed him under the Treaty of Fontainebleau, and aware of rumors that the French court was seeking either to kill him or have him banished to a remote island in the south Atlantic.

So he escaped, giving the slip to the British warships. An army of his old veterans, led by his old general Marshal Ney, was sent by the French court to stop him. Instead, he convinced them to join him. Two weeks later, he entered Paris in triumph as Louis XVIII fled in panic.

"The Devil," wrote one Austrian diplomat, "has been unchained."

NAPOLEON AND WELLINGTON

For once, however, Napoleon's timing was poor. Even as he entered Paris, Great Britain, Prussia, Russia, and Austria were deciding at the Congress of Vienna how to divide up the spoils of their victory over Napoleon. Normally, it might take all these powers months to form a coalition, but with representatives of each government present and with the urgency of the threat, they immediately allied themselves against Napoleon, forming the Seventh Coalition. Their goal was to surround his forces, march on Paris, and destroy him.

By May, the Duke of Wellington had an allied force of 68,000 men in Belgium and was waiting to be joined by 70,000 Prussian troops under General Gebhard von Blücher, whose stated goal was to capture Napoleon and have him shot immediately. In June, Napoleon moved north. His goal was to capture Brussels, the capital of Belgium, but also to prevent Blücher and Wellington linking up to form an army that would be twice the size of his. On June 16, in a stunning victory, Napoleon defeated Blücher's forces at Ligny, driving them back.

So it was that on the morning of June 18, just outside the Belgian village of Waterloo, the Allies and the French faced each other over a piece of farmland two miles wide and about two-thirds of a mile across. On the north side, drawn up along and behind a ridge, was the Army of the Netherlands, an Anglo-Belgian-Dutch force of 68,000 men that contained only 28,000 British soldiers but was led

ABOVE Napoleon and his troops escaped from the island of Elba, off the coast of Italy, in February 1815. He managed to avoid the British warships patrolling the area and landed in France in an attempt to regain his empire.

by the Duke of Wellington. On the other side was Napoleon Bonaparte and an army of just over 72,000, some of whom were from his Grand Army of the old days, but many of whom were old men or raw recruits.

Now, at last, Napoleon and Wellington were to face each other in combat. Wellington was forty-six years old, Napoleon forty-five. Both had started off in their respective armies humble in rank and both had risen high, although Napoleon's ascent was the greater—to become emperor, to write the Napoleonic Code, to own most of Europe. The two rivals had, however, developed vastly differing command styles.

Wellington, who went into battle in a civilian grey frock coat, was ever-present on the front lines and accorded very little responsibility to staff officers. "There is nothing I dislike so much," he said, "as those extended operations which I cannot direct myself." Being unable to delegate authority was not one of Wellington's best qualities—for one thing, it made his presence while lead was flying around essential, leading to numerous horses being shot out from under him and at least one battle wound that put him to bed for a week. "I began to feel as if God has his finger on me," he said once, a dangerous attitude for a soldier to take. However, his men loved him for the danger he placed himself in—they called him "Old Hookey" or "Old Nosey" for his outsized nose—and had supreme faith in him.

Napoleon, while certainly brave and not averse to personal risk in combat, was more of a theorist—he drew up his battle plans and expected his subordinates to carry them out. He was a gallant figure and, to many French soldiers in the past, a god-like one. However, he was as arrogant now as he had been when he was a young military school cadet. He had not bothered to make a study of Wellington's command style, sneeringly calling him "the Sepoy General" (meaning he was only good to lead native troops). As morning dawned on June 18, he told his commanders that the day's battle would be a "picnic." Indeed, it appeared to be his main concern that Wellington not escape.

WATERLOO It was too bad that Napoleon had not bothered to study Wellington's previous campaigns, because he would have understood that Wellington was superb when it came to positioning troops in defensive positions. On the morning of June 18, most of his men were arrayed not at the top of the low ridge that Napoleon faced, but just behind the crest. Wellington was one of the first commanders to understand the value of using the rear slopes of hills and ridgelines to protect his men from artillery and also to disguise his total numbers. Wellington had personally reconnoitered and chosen this position.

Unlike Napoleon, Wellington had studied his opponent and he knew that the French commander loved to outflank his enemies whenever possible, and so Wellington's lines were drawn up along a broad front, to minimize this possibility. But flanking was not what Napoleon had in mind this day. He knew that Blücher's defeated Prussian forces were not destroyed—were, in fact, coming on to link up with Wellington—and that he, therefore, needed to move quickly. What he decided upon was the bluntest of blunt attacks: a frontal charge to punch a hole through Wellington's lines and then turn and roll up the Allied forces before Blücher could arrive. After that, as he told his staff, they would all be dining in Brussels that night.

Napoleon's actions belied his confident words. On the morning of June 18, after noting that the previous night's rainstorm had made the ground too muddy to maneuver, he delayed his attack. This alone was a clue that he was not himself—previously, a muddy field would have been no more than a minor hindrance, especially as time was of the essence for him to make his attack. But he was not physically well: he suffered from hemorrhoids, which had become painfully prolapsed. It is possible that he was also afflicted by cystitis, a bladder infection that makes urinating painful and causes high fever and which is worsened by cold and wet conditions.

There was also something else afflicting Napoleon. Later, he would say that he had the sense, that morning, that "fortune" had abandoned him. Another commander might make a strategic retreat, might regroup for another day, but not Napoleon. At 1:30 p.m., he ordered his eighty-four guns to open up on the English positions, unleashing a thunderous barrage, but Wellington had ordered his men to lie down on the rear slope of the hill and the cannonballs did far less damage than the French thought they would. At two o'clock, Napoleon ordered his massive frontal charge, sending three divisions directly at the spot in the line held by Wellington's Belgian troops, whom Napoleon considered the most likely to break. But two of these divisions made a mortal mistake: their officers ordered them to proceed in columns, rather than on a broad front, making them a massed target for Allied artillery and musket fire from Wellington's troops, which had now risen up from behind the slope and assumed their positions on the crest of the ridge. One observer noted that under the hail of fire, the French troops "appeared to wave like high-standing corn blown by sudden gusts of wind ... their caps and muskets ... flying in the air."

It was the beginning of a very deadly day. The Belgians did indeed turn and run, leaving a gap in the center of Wellington's lines, but because of the deafening noise and the shock of the carnage, the brave French troops veered to the right and became entangled in a double row of hedges defended by a division of Scottish infantry. Three thousand Scottish rifles opened up all at once at a distance of perhaps twenty yards, stunning the French. Still, incredibly, they came on, until the charge was finally broken by a British cavalry attack.

Fighting now centered around three isolated stone farmhouses and their outbuildings which stood on the battlefield—Hougoumont, La Haye Sainte, and Papelotte, natural defensive positions that changed hands numerous times. After the blunting of the initial French attack, Napoleon sent Marshal Ney to capture La Haye Sainte and the French infantry, sustaining ferocious casualties, wrested

FOLLOWING PAGES
The Battle of Waterloo saw Napoleon's and Wellington's armies clash in a battle that resulted in enormous carnage. The Duke of Wellington, surrounded by his staff, is shown directing his troops on the right.

it from the British. When Ney asked for reinforcements in order to capitalize on his breakthrough, Napoleon refused him. For Blücher's Prussian forces had now been spotted coming from the east—the reinforcements that spelled doom for Napoleon and victory for Wellington.

Even so, despite the fact that he was very evidently defeated, Napoleon now prepared the last attack of his career, using his elite forces, the Imperial Guard. He lied to those around him and claimed the approaching force of Prussians was actually a French force under Marshal Grouchy (who had been supposed to stop Blücher, but had failed to do so). Inspired by what they thought was victory snatched from the jaws of defeat, the bearskin capped Guards, seven battalions strong—"a dark, waving forest of them" in the early evening gloom—attacked, shouting "*Vive l'Empereur!*" As Napoleon watched, forty thousand Allied troops—at the personal instigation of Wellington, who was in the front lines waving his hat— launched a devastating counterattack. Even the brave Guards could not stand this. They broke and ran, and with them went Napoleon Bonaparte's last chance. Seeing that all was lost, he fled. Forty thousand corpses from both armies lay behind on the stinking battlefield.

"HIS DEATH BLOW" Although the battle was what he referred to as a "near-run thing"—had Blücher's forces not arrived, Napoleon might indeed have triumphed—Wellington knew right away that he had dealt Napoleon "his death blow." He said in astonishment: "Napoleon did not maneuver at all; he just moved forward in the old style, in columns, and was driven off in the old style." As Napoleon fled to Paris, however, Wellington saved his life. The crusty old Prussian General Blücher wanted to shoot Napoleon the instant he was found. "Blücher wants to kill him," Wellington said. "But I advised him to have nothing to do with so foul a transaction ..."

Napoleon abdicated again on June 24 and was captured by the British as he attempted to flee to America. This time he was exiled far, far away, to the tiny island of St. Helena, in the south Atlantic. From there, he recovered himself enough to launch personal attacks on Wellington (whom he had still never met), saying that it was only through pure luck that his rival had won at Waterloo. He died in 1821, a broken man, while Wellington went on to become prime minister of Britain, one of the men who shaped the post-war, more reactionary Europe.

Certainly, it would seem that Napoleon lost this rivalry. Posterity gives him the nod as the far more brilliant general—and certainly the more interesting personage—but it was Wellington's simplicity of tactics and sensible maneuvering that saved the day at Waterloo.

THE MYSTERY OF NAPOLEON'S DEATH—SOLVED?

Napoleon Bonaparte died on the lonely island of St. Helena on May 4, 1821, at the age of fifty-two. During an autopsy performed at the time, doctors discovered that his stomach was extensively ulcerated, with one lesion penetrating the stomach wall and entering the liver. It was also filled with dark material that looked like coffee grounds, a sign of internal bleeding. Since Napoleon had lost twenty pounds in the last six months, and since his father had died of stomach cancer, the nineteenth century physicians quite reasonably decided the emperor had succumbed to the same fate.

Yet, ever since, rumors have persisted that Napoleon was poisoned with arsenic; in 1961, scientific examination of a lock of his hair reported levels of arsenic as much as six hundred times greater than normal. Some scholars have even picked his murderer: Tristan de Montholon, a close advisor to whom Napoleon surprisingly left the bulk of his fortune and who may have killed him to hurry his access to the money.

In 2007, however, a team of researchers from the University of Texas Southwestern decided the diagnosis of stomach cancer was the correct one after all, although Napoleon probably developed it from a stomach ulcer exacerbated by the highly salted foods he ate during his campaigning years. Had Napoleon died of arsenic poisoning, such telltale signs as hemorrhaging in the lining of his heart or discoloration of his fingernails would have been discovered. The size of the lesions in Napoleon's stomach alone—one was about four inches across—point instead to a classic case of gastric cancer.

ABOVE A group of English officers gather round Napoleon's coffin on the island of St. Helena, while a priest looks on. Napoleon was reportedly buried inside three coffins, one of iron, one of lead, and an outer one of mahogany.

THE EARL OF LUCAN

THE EARL OF LUCAN AND THE EARL OF CARDIGAN: THE CHARGE OF THE LIGHT BRIGADE

JAMES THOMAS BRUDENELL, THE SEVENTH EARL of Cardigan, and George Charles Bingham, the third Earl of Lucan, were among the richest, handsomest men in Europe in the mid-nineteenth century. They had everything—vast estates, women, social prestige, and glamorous commands in the post-Napoleonic era British army. However, they were also pompous, vain, as obstinate as two-year-olds and, at least in the case of Cardigan, extremely dim-witted. Plus which, they hated each other with a passion.

Spoiled British aristocrats feuding? What else is new? Well, the problem was, Lucan and Cardigan carried their feud to the Crimea in 1854, on a British expedition to punch upstart Russia in the nose. The two men, wrote a fellow officer, were "like a pair of scissors who go snip and snip and snip without doing each other any harm, but God help the poor devil who gets between them." Unfortunately, in this case, the poor devil in the middle was a whole handful of devils, the famous six hundred men of the proud and glorious Light Brigade. In part because of the long-held grudge between Cardigan and Lucan, those men were sent charging down the aptly named Valley of Death to be blown to smithereens.

THE EARL OF LUCAN George Bingham, future third Earl of Lucan, was born in 1800, the scion of an English family who had ruled vast Irish estates in County Mayo for centuries, and with an iron hand. It was a Bingham who had ordered a thousand shipwrecked survivors of the Spanish Armada butchered as they washed ashore in 1588. It was Binghams who enriched themselves while the Irish peasants who were their tenants gnawed at potatoes in thatched huts.

The Binghams were also a military family, and when George was born his father and mother naturally expected him to follow these ancestral footsteps. This he was happy to do. He was an amazingly handsome young man, with curling dark hair and piercing eyes, and quite intelligent, to boot. When he was sixteen, his father purchased a commission for him in a regiment of infantry; within ten years, further purchases had made him the lieutenant colonel in command of the renowned Seventeenth Lancers, one of the finest regiments in British history.

The "purchase system," as it was called, had been in place in the British army for many decades—both the Duke of Wellington and Horatio Gates (see pages 149 and 171) had followed the practice of purchasing their initial officer's commission and then paying for each subsequent bump up in rank. This system ensured that well-educated officers from noble, or at least upper middle class, families received plum sinecures and populated almost all officer ranks. To further discourage poor but ambitious young men, officers' salaries were mere honorariums. Most officers were expected to have the private means not only to pay for their own uniforms and mess, but also to provide extras for the regiments under their command.

Although the inequities of the purchase system were evident and attempts had been made in Parliament to abolish it, they had so far failed miserably. This was partly because the British army had just come from years of glorious victory in the Napoleonic Wars and was filled with officers who had bought their rank, the Duke of Wellington, the most worshipped figure in England, chief among them.

In any event, Lucan as a young colonel stinted nothing in providing for his regiment, but he was also a petty tyrant, a man with whom even his aunt remonstrated for his "martinet zeal." Soon his reputation became so damaged that he decided it might be time to see the world a little. In 1828 he took leave from the army and managed to get himself attached to the staff of the Russian Prince Woronzov—at this time the Russians were fighting the Turks—where he acquitted himself with bravery.

When he returned to England, Bingham did something even more fateful than going to war. In 1829 he married Anne Brudenell—an aristocratic young woman the queen sardonically described as "worldly but not over-wise"—who just happened to be the youngest sister of James Thomas Brudenell, soon to be the seventh Earl of Cardigan.

"THE MELANCHOLY TRUTH" Born in 1797, Brudenell came from a family even richer and more distinguished than Bingham's. He was raised on a vast country estate—the Manor, in Buckinghamshire—the spoiled brother of seven adoring sisters. Brudenell, too, was quite handsome, although fair rather than dark, and he was also a crack shot and horseman and had a pleasant disposition. His one drawback, writes the historian Cecil Woodham-Smith, was that he was "unusually stupid ... the melancholy truth was that his gorgeous head had nothing in it."

Unfortunately, young Brudenell's pleasant disposition disappeared after he was thrown from a horse and landed on his head at the age of fourteen. When he recovered, weeks later, he had become peevish and given to sudden, violent mood swings and fits of rage. And one more thing—he became known for never, ever letting go of a grudge.

Unlike Bingham, Brudenell did not immediately enter the army, but instead set about leading the life of a handsome, extremely wealthy young playboy. He spent a great deal of time in Paris carousing and it was there, in 1823, that he met and eloped with a married woman named Elizabeth Johnstone, the wife of a Brudenell family friend, Captain Johnstone. This was the first scandal of what were to be many for Brudenell. Johnstone sued him in court for alienation of affection and won one thousand pounds. After the trial, a vengeful Brudenell sent a messenger to Captain Johnstone offering to "give him satisfaction" (fight a duel) but Johnstone merely laughed and replied: "Tell Lord Brudenell that he has already given me the satisfaction of having removed the most damned bad-tempered and extravagant bitch in the kingdom."

Now, as a married man, Brudenell did need a profession and so he began purchasing commissions until he obtained the colonelcy of the Fifteenth Hussars, a cavalry regiment that was one of the proudest in the English army. It was said that this command cost him forty thousand pounds.

THE FEUD BEGINS It was probably inevitable that Brudenell and Bingham would be rivals. They were natural competitors, both rich, handsome, and now in charge of their own regiments. Their rivalry only needed a spark, which flared when Bingham insisted on making Brudenell's sister Anne live on his remote Irish estates, taking her away from London society and from Brudenell, who doted on her. For, in 1837, Bingham (who became Earl of Lucan in 1839 when his father died) decided to resign his commission in the army and devote himself to making money. He did this mainly by means of the infamous "land clearances" by which Irish peasants were driven from their homes so that Lucan and other English landlords could consolidate holdings into larger parcels—this was a practice that, during the Famine years of the 1840s, resulted in thousands of dead Irish.

Unable to accept so remote a life, Anne rebelled and finally she and Lucan began to lead separate lives, an occurrence for which Brudenell blamed Lucan. However, by this time Brudenell had his own problems, which included his being one of the most unpopular men in England. This had come about because of his treatment of the Fifteenth Hussars, the regiment whose command he had purchased. Like Lucan, Lord Cardigan (for he, too, had now received his title) was a martinet, but unlike his brother-in-law he was given to towering rages over what even a commanding officer called "trifles." He was obsessed with the appearance of his soldiers as well as that of their horses, ordering that the animals be clipped and groomed twice a week. He purchased new stable jackets for the men to wear when grooming the horses, and when this met with protest because the jackets were uncomfortable and superfluous, he actually had a Captain Walthen court-martialed for refusing to make his men wear them. This trial met with such universal contempt, in an era when a populist movement was challenging the entrenched and arrogant airs of such Tories as Cardigan, that not only was Walthen acquitted, but Cardigan was scolded in the Court's decision and removed from command.

THE "BLACK BOTTLE" AFFAIR

One would think this might have been enough for Cardigan, but two years later, using his immense wealth and influence, he purchased another command, this time with the Eleventh Light Dragoons. Cardigan was not only stupid, he was, as a contemporary put it, "innocent as a horse" and simply could not understand why all the commoners who surrounded him simply did not knuckle under when he told them too. It seemed like a perfectly natural thing, to Cardigan, to have an officer arrested for not having wine decanted before being brought to the table at the officers' mess—the infamous "black bottle" affair. He also fought a duel with a former officer of the regiment, seriously wounding him, and had another young officer arrested for not vacating his room quickly enough when a friend of Cardigan's wanted to stay there.

The officers of his regiment banded together, realizing that the only way they could stop this petty tyranny was to go public with their complaints. When the newspapers began to publish accounts, Lord Cardigan was booed and hissed when he made public appearances. At one theater, the crowd gathered under his box, shaking their fists at him and crying "Shame!" and "Turn him out!" until he was forced to leave.

Finally, in 1841, he was put on trial for the duel he had participated in—dueling was officially illegal in England—but was found not guilty on a technicality. Such was his arrogance that, shortly afterwards, he had a soldier flogged on Easter Sunday, causing even more uproar. Because of his connections, and despite many internal reprimands from his superiors, Cardigan was allowed to keep his post in the army. Throughout the 1840s, while Lucan became one of the most despised men in Ireland, his equally despised brother-in-law managed to keep his regiment and even turn them, with the brilliant uniforms he had had designed for them cherry-red pants, blue jackets scalloped with gold, capes edged with gold lace, tall fur caps—into the envy (sartorial at least) of the rest of the regiments in the army.

"The incredible tightness of their cherry-coloured pants," wrote the *Times*, with perhaps just a touch of derision, "defies description."

THE CHANCE OF A LIFETIME

By the early 1850s, with both Lucan and Cardigan in their fifties, one would think that they might have been approaching some measure of staidness and satisfaction with life. This was not so. Anne Brudenell and Lucan had finally separated, causing Cardigan to heap abuse on Lucan's head, claiming that he had abused her, kept her short of money, and isolated her from her family. Lucan, in the meantime, insisted to one and all that Cardigan was unfit to command a squad, let alone a regiment, even if he did spend ten thousand pounds a year on their uniforms alone. It was known in London society that one should never, ever, for whatever reason, invite the two men to the same dinner party, but there the matter would have stayed had it not been for the little matter of a war in the offing.

Czar Nicholas I of Russia, seeking a warm-water port to expand his country's sphere of influence into the Near East, declared war on Turkey in October 1853 and immediately seized the port of Sebastopol on the Black Sea. This enraged Great Britain—an ally, along with France, of Turkey—and it, in turn, declared war on Russia in 1854. All of Britain was swept by patriotic fervor. It must be remembered that, despite some fighting in Afghanistan and India, Britain had not been in a "proper" war since the Duke of Wellington defeated Napoleon at Waterloo in 1815. The officers who fought in Afghanistan were the only commanders in the British army who had recently experienced combat, but these were looked down on as "Indian" officers (just as, ironically, Napoleon had sneered at Wellington as "the Sepoy General") and actively discouraged from joining the army now being organized to fight in the Crimea.

This type of criminal arrogance marked the behavior of the British officer corps in general in 1854. The commander in chief of the British Expeditionary Force to the East, as it was called, was Lord Raglan, sixty-five years old and an intimate of the Duke of Wellington. He had lost an arm at Waterloo and still had the disconcerting habit of referring to the French as "the enemy" (staff officers had to remind him numerous times that the French, this time, were English allies). Among the many aging officers who now vied to go to the Crimea for their last (and often first) chance at war was Lord Cardigan who, despite failed marriages and the fact that he suffered from chronic bronchitis, desperately wanted to prove himself. Raglan was connected to the Cardigan family and—despite the universal contempt in which Cardigan was held by the men of the Eleventh Hussars (as the Light Dragoons had been renamed)—he gave Cardigan command of the Light Brigade of British cavalry, of which the Eleventh Hussars was a regiment.

Moreover—in a move that caused much head-shaking—he made Lord Lucan commanding officer of the entire cavalry division. Thus, in the spring of 1854, the British set out for the Crimea with an aging general staff whose experience of war, if any, was over forty years old, and with two men who hated each other's guts in charge of the superb British cavalry.

"MY DEAR CARDIGAN" The British army sailed first to Scutari on the Asian coast of the Bosphorus, then to Varna, on the Black Sea. From Varna, it was a two hundred mile journey across the Black Sea to Sebastopol, on the tip of the Crimean Peninsula. The British intended to use Varna as a base camp, but cholera raged there, decimating the ranks of British soldiers as well as the hundreds of soldiers' wives who had accompanied the expedition—for the expedition was seen, at least until its arrival in the Black Sea region, as a sort of lark.

In the meantime, Lord Cardigan had decided that, even though Lucan was his nominal commander, he would not pay any attention to him. Thus, he embarked ahead of Lucan for Varna with his entire force, without mentioning it to his former brother-in-law but clearing it first with Lord Raglan. Lucan began to write frustrated notes such as this: "My dear Cardigan: It is obvious that service cannot be carried on as it should be ... if a subordinate officer is allowed to pass over his immediate and responsible superior and communicate direct with the General Commanding ..."

Belatedly, Raglan sent Cardigan a note expressly reminding him that Lucan was his superior and needed to be consulted directly on all matters. Cardigan's response to this was to decide that he would obey Lucan's orders *to the letter*, but no less and certainly no more. In the meantime, before leaving Varna, Lord Lucan had resorted to his usual nitpicking, sending out orders such as: "The Major General observes that officers do not wear their gold sword knots as prescribed by regulations."

While this was happening, cholera continued to ravage the camp. When the British sailed from Varna on September 7, men aboard the more than six hundred transports were dying right and left of the disease. At night, their bodies were tied with weights and dumped overboard but, because the weights were too light, the bodies rose again as gases expanded in them, and the troopships were followed by the ghastly spectacle of corpses, kept upright by the weights, bobbing along with just their heads and shoulders out of the water.

LORD LOOK-ON The British army disembarked on September 14 in the aptly named Calamita Bay, just north of Sebastopol, and marched south to engage the Russians through steppe country that was so short of water that many men, weakened by disease, died of thirst en route. With them were their allies, the French. Although they were marching off to the greatest adventure of their lives, Lucan and Cardigan kept bickering. Faced, all of a sudden, with thousands of Russian cavalry, the British cavalry lined up, ready for their first action against the enemy, but then found themselves delayed as Lucan and Cardigan argued bitterly over the proper alignment of the regiments. By the time they were ready, more Russian cavalry had arrived and Lord Raglan decided he did not want to risk his cavalry in a charge when they were so outnumbered.

The members of the division were forced to retreat, and the cavalrymen, their pride wounded, blamed it all on Lord Lucan, although in truth Raglan was the one who refused to give battle. No matter. Lucan's name, it was decided by the men of his division, would henceforth be Lord Look-On.

THE GLORIOUS MRS. DUBERLY

War seemed such a picnic to the British officers first sailing to the Crimea that many of them brought their wives with them. One such officer was Captain Henry Duberly, paymaster of the Eighth Royal Irish Hussars, part of the Light Brigade. His wife's name was Fanny, but one and all knew her as Mrs. Duberly. Twenty-five years old, she was, as one historian has written, "vivacious, daring ... and a splendid horsewoman."

Mrs. Duberly was a special favorite of Lord Cardigan. When Lord Raglan announced that under no circumstances were women to accompany the men from the staging area in Turkey to the Crimea—and even paced the dock to make sure this order was enforced—Mrs. Duberly snuck aboard Cardigan's own ship disguised as a Turkish woman. Once in the Crimea, she became one of the first women to view modern war close up. As Russian forces arrived to begin the battle that resulted in the famous charge, Captain Duberly sent his wife a note that read: "The battle of Baklava [sic] has begun and promises to be a hot one. I send you the horse. Lose no time but come up as quickly as you can. Do not wait for breakfast."

Hungry but steadfast, Mrs. Duberly watched the entire battle from the heights with much of the British officer corps and later wrote about it in her book *Journal Kept during the Russian War*. She was close enough to see a lot of death and dying: "Even my closed eyelids were filled with the ruddy glare of blood," she wrote memorably.

Mrs. Duberly was frowned upon by London society after this escapade—genteel women did not accompany armies like so many camp followers, and her book was also a source of much gossip on the Lucan-Cardigan feud—but she continued her adventures with her intrepid husband, going on to India and even inadvertently taking part in a cavalry charge during the Sepoy Mutiny of 1856, when her horse bolted.

RIGHT In this early photograph, Mrs Duberly is shown on horseback, a characteristic pose for this adventurous and unconventional woman. Her husband, Henry, stands before her.

There would be fighting aplenty for the British army, however. On September 20, they engaged a far superior force of Russians near the Alma River and defeated them in a battle that proved the extraordinary courage of the British forces, who charged entrenched Russian positions on cliffs with complete disregard for their own safety. Since the British war correspondent William Howard Russell was on the scene reporting for the London *Times* via the new technology of telegraph, people back in London heard about it immediately and Alma became a very popular name for baby girls born at this time.

Yet even in the midst of this triumph, Cardigan and Lucan were bickering so badly that Lord Raglan felt forced to write them each an appeal that began: "The Earl of Lucan and the Earl of Cardigan are nearly connected. They are both gentlemen of high honor and elevated connection in the country apart from their military rank ... [I] earnestly recommend them frankly to associate with each other."

It did little good.

THE NOBLE YACHTSMAN The British were now in position to take Sebastopol but, greatly weakened by the fierce battle and by the twin plagues of cholera and dysentery, they were forced to pause while the army was re-supplied through the nearby port of Balaklava. With Cardigan and Lucan fighting like "two spoiled children," as another officer put it, Raglan finally separated Cardigan's Light Brigade of cavalry (more lightly armed and faster) from the Heavy Brigade personally commanded by Lucan, although Lucan still retained overall command.

Now it was Cardigan's turn to earn a nickname, for on October 14 his gorgeous yacht, the *Dryad*, which had sailed expressly from England to care for him, came cruising into Balaklava Harbor. On board were his French chef and his wine cellar. Cardigan now began spending evenings there, returning to his regiment during the day. The troops chortled at this, naming him the Noble Yachtsman.

In hindsight, it seems inevitable that two such men in charge of a division of cavalry in enemy country would sooner or later contribute to some great disaster—in fact, the officers and men of the entire cavalry division expected no good to come of the situation and held both their commanders in great contempt. One wrote back home: "Lord Cardigan has as much brains as my boot. He is only to be equaled in matters of intellect by his relation, the Earl of Lucan. In my opinion, two such fools could hardly be picked out of the British Army. And they take command! But they are Earls!"

"WE MUST NOT STIR FROM HERE" Since the English had failed to make a decisive attack on Sebastopol, the Russians decided at the end of October that now was the time to move in force against the enemy positions and relieve the siege. Their goal was to cut the English off from their supply lines at

Balaklava. On October 25, the Russian army approached with a force of eleven thousand infantry and cavalry and about 140 guns, moving directly down the plain of Balaklava. This was three miles long by two miles wide and divided into two valleys, North Valley and South Valley, interrupted by a line of ridges known as the Causeway Heights. To the left of the Causeway Heights, from the British point of view, was another group of low hills called the Fedyukhin Heights. Behind the British lines was a high escarpment called the Sapoune Heights.

The Russians easily overwhelmed the Turks manning gun emplacements along the Causeway Heights and kept on coming. It was a crystalline and beautiful fall day and Lord Raglan and his staff and numerous onlookers, including the journalist William Howard Russell, stood on the Sapoune Heights, some seven hundred feet above the valley, and watched the Russians approach. It was as if, wrote one historian, they were watching the impending battle "from a box in a theater." The massive Russian force attacked, but was repulsed by the Ninety-third Highlanders, who stood their ground against the enemy onslaught although vastly outnumbered; watching from the Sapoune Heights, Russell was astonished to see the red-coated infantry with their bayonets—what he called "a thin red streak tipped with a line of steel," although the phrase has come down in history as "the thin red line"—swallowed up whole by the Russians but somehow able to push them back.

Then Lord Lucan's Heavy Brigade of cavalry, led by General James Scarlett, made an extraordinary uphill charge against the Russians, five hundred British horsemen clashing with three thousand Cossacks. Cavalry hacked away at each other with sabers in a cloud of dust—the British, frustrated by the thick coats the Russians wore, resorted to running their sabers through the enemy's face. From the heights where Raglan and his officers stood, all seemed confusion—but then, slowly, the boiling mass of men and horses separated and the Russians began to flee. The Heavies were too exhausted to follow their enemy as they raced back down the valley, but Lord Cardigan's Light Brigade was there. In fact, it had been there all along, with Cardigan not raising a hand to help in the fight, only commenting: "Those damn Heavies will have the laugh on us this day."

His men implored him now to attack the retreating enemy—a perfect target, if ever there was one—but Cardigan merely replied: "No, no, sir, we must not stir from here." A phrase for Cardigan's behavior—passive-aggressive—was coined in a later century. Since he had received no specific orders from Lord Lucan, he would not move from the spot, even though the enemy was in flight before his very eyes.

"ATTACK, SIR? ATTACK WHAT?" From the heights, Lord Raglan watched in frustration as the Russian cavalry escaped back up the North Valley. To make matters worse, he could see retreating Russian infantry scrambling along the heights on either side, where they were now attempting to pull away cannon captured from the Turkish emplacements on Causeway

Heights—cannon that were actually British naval guns. Raglan sent the first of a series of four orders from his vantage point on Sapoune Heights to Lord Lucan in the valley, telling him to attack the guns with his Light Brigade.

But to Lucan—already impatient with Raglan for his support of Cardigan and his refusal, until recently, to allow the cavalry to engage the enemy—these orders were confusing and unclear. Attack what Russian guns? Without Raglan's birds-eye vantage, the only guns Lucan could see were the heavy Russian emplacements a mile down the valley, on either side, and those at the very end. It would be suicide to attack these with cavalry, in his estimation.

An hour and a half passed with Lucan attempting to get clarification from Raglan and Raglan becoming more and more impatient. Finally, fed up, Raglan dictated a note that read in part: "Lord Raglan wishes the cavalry to advance rapidly to the front—follow the enemy and try to prevent the enemy from carrying away the guns." The note was given to a Captain Lewis Edward Nolan, one of the finest young cavalry officers in the British army, a man who had written a book on cavalry tactics and who was thought to be one of the best riders in the world.

Unfortunately, he also hated Lucan, despising him as a man who lacked guts and ability. Riding pell-mell down the steep cliff to the valley, he arrived in front of Lucan and impatiently delivered the message to attack the Russian guns.

Angered by Nolan's arrogance, Lucan replied: "Attack, sir? Attack what? What guns, sir?" And Nolan, instead of pointing at the guns along the Causeway, flung his arm in the direction of the Russian emplacements a mile and a quarter down the valley: "There, my lord, is your enemy, there are your guns!"

THE CHARGE OF THE LIGHT BRIGADE There was little to do now but attack, as far as Lucan was concerned—and since he could not see the guns above him on Causeway Heights, he assumed the attack was to be straight down at the Russian emplacements at the end of the valley. He ordered Lord Cardigan into his presence and told him that he must attack the Russian guns with his Light Brigade. Lucan would follow with the Heavies.

Cardigan stared at his brother-in-law and saluted. "Certainly, sir. But allow me to point out to you that the Russians have a battery in the valley in our front and batteries and riflemen on both sides."

Lucan replied, staring directly at Cardigan: "I know it, but Lord Raglan will have it. We have no choice but to obey."

It may have been the most human—even, by stiff upper lip British aristocracy standards, the most empathetic—conversation the two men had ever had. Had they actually been on speaking terms with each other, they might together have figured out exactly what guns they were supposed to attack, perhaps by querying Nolan more closely. Instead, there was no doubt each thought this conversation was their last. As he turned around, Cardigan was heard to mutter: "Here goes the last of the Brudenells."

Cardigan formed his 673 cavalrymen up into two lines, but Lucan, as was
his annoying habit, interfered and made him break them up into three. Lord
Cardigan then took the lead, five horse-lengths ahead of his front line. He raised
his sword, a trumpet sounded, and the charge of the Light Brigade began. At first,
Cardigan, wearing a resplendent uniform of red and royal blue, riding his favorite
charger, Ronald, and sitting stiffly erect in his saddle, kept his men moving
at a trot, but the British had only traveled perhaps a hundred yards when the
first Russian artillery salvo rang out. Strangely, it immediately killed Captain
Nolan, who had ridden out in front of the British lines, much to Cardigan's
irritation, in what was probably an excess of zeal but may have been an attempt
to direct the charge at its true target. But with Nolan dead—his body, upright on
its panicked horse, galloped back through the ranks of the Light Brigade—the
last man in the valley who knew where the charge was truly supposed to go
had disappeared.

As the lines of the Light Brigade passed within range of the Russian artillery on Fedyukhin and Causeway Heights, it was exposed to a withering crossfire. "Round shot passed through us and the shells burst over and amongst us," one British private later wrote. "I felt the wind from [a cannon ball] as it passed by me. I later found I was bespattered by [a fellow soldier's] flesh." Still Cardigan kept the men going at a stately pace. However, as the heavy fire continued and more and more men fell, riderless horses became a serious problem, breaking into the ranks of the men and tearing up their cohesion. One officer later said that "at one time I had as many as five horses on my right and two on my left, cringing in on me as round shot came bounding by them."

Lord Lucan, following behind with his Heavies, could see the futility of the Light Brigade's position and made an instant decision. "They have sacrificed the Light Brigade," he told his aide. "They will not have the Heavy if I can help it." He turned his regiment back down the valley. The Light Brigade was now on its own.

INTO THE VALLEY OF DEATH

Only eight or so minutes had passed since the beginning of the charge, but it seemed an eternity to the men battered by Russian gunfire. They were now at the end of the valley but the Russian guns there blazed away at them, yellow streaks of fire shooting through the clouds of white smoke. Cardigan could no longer hold the men back and they charged at a gallop for the Russian gunners, who let loose a final salvo from only eight yards out, decimating their ranks. But then the Light Brigade was on them, swinging their sabers and hacking their enemy down. It is a little known fact that the Light Brigade actually reached its objective—or perceived objective—and managed to capture Russian guns and kill their crews, and even drive away Cossack cavalry gathered beyond the guns.

Lord Cardigan had continued ahead of the Light Brigade and—despite having a cannon fire directly at him from a few yards away—was now in the rear of the Russian lines. By an extraordinary coincidence, he was spotted by a certain Prince Radziwell, who had been an acquaintance of his in London and Paris; the prince sent his Cossacks to capture, rather than kill, Cardigan, and this probably saved his life. Evading the enemy cavalry, Cardigan simply turned, rode through the smoky chaos of the guns, and headed back down the valley to the British lines, as erect as ever.

Cardigan had made an extraordinarily brave charge—stupid or not, he "had the heart of a lion," as Lord Raglan put it—but, now considering that he had discharged his duty, he did not stop to look to the welfare of the men fighting around him and simply continued on back. The survivors of the Light Brigade, finding their position untenable, retreated later to find that Cardigan was already back in safety. This later led to the rumor that he had not even taken part in the charge. A false rumor, of course—he was there, but he was Cardigan and so he had done it in his own way.

A "TRUMP CARD-IGAN"

When Lord Cardigan returned to England and basked in his (rather brief) period in the sun, even the clothing he wore became famous—in particular, the soft wool jacket, buttoned down the front, that he wore in the Crimea. It was dubbed a "Cardigan" and the craze for it was so great that manufacturers could not keep up with the demand. Everywhere one went in England, according to published reports, one saw men and women wearing their Cardigans quite proudly. The humorous newspaper Punch published a picture of Lord Cardigan wearing one, calling it a "Trump Card-igan."

The craze for Lord Cardigan was so great that he also donned the resplendent uniform he had worn in the Crimea when he made a dramatic speech about the charge in London. Afterwards, the crowd plucked hairs from his horse's tail as souvenirs. He went around England making the same speech, during the course of which, according to reports, Cardigan would often "be so overcome that he was unable to proceed."

As more and more Crimea veterans returned with the real story, Cardigan's role was called into question, but his name continues to live in on his simple, button-down sweater.

THE LADY WITH THE LAMP

Along with the end of the purchase system, the Crimean War also resulted in a better system for taking care of sick and wounded soldiers. British casualties in the Crimea were extraordinarily high, and a good many of them came from diseases such as typhus, cholera, and dysentery. An end to such unnecessary deaths was to came about through the efforts of one woman: Florence Nightingale.

Nightingale was born in 1820 of an upper class English family. When she was seventeen, she experienced a religious awakening and, horrified by the plight of the indigent in England's poorhouses and hospitals, became an advocate for improved medical care and conditions. After news came back from the Crimean War, partly through the reports of William Howard Russell, of the conditions of the sick and wounded, Nightingale rushed a group of forty nurses to Turkey, where the sick and wounded had been taken from Balaklava. The conditions were horrible. The army cared little for these casualties: there were few medicines and little nutritious food, and the sanitary conditions were terrible. Hospitals were death traps, with overflowing sewers and latrines and little or no ventilation. Ten times as many soldiers died there of illness as of wounds from the battlefield.

Although Nightingale was able to do little immediately to lower the death toll in Turkey, she became famous in England as "the lady with the lamp," the tireless nurse who walked through the wards of the wounded at night, ceaselessly caring for them. In fact, she became convinced, well ahead of her time, that hygiene was the key to making many of these men well, and when she returned to London she pioneered a sanitary approach to nursing in hospitals and in the army. As a result, death tolls in future would be greatly reduced. By the time she died in 1910, she had founded the modern profession of nursing.

LEFT Florence Nightingale took a group of nurses to Turkey to care for the wounded during the Crimean War. Her recognition of the importance of hygiene and sanitary practices would eventually save the lives of millions.

Of the 673 cavalrymen who had headed down the valley, 195 returned. The charge had lasted all of twenty minutes.

FAME AND ILL-FORTUNE Thanks to William Howard Russell and the telegraph, the charge of the Light Brigade became famous almost immediately. Reading about it in his morning *Times*, Alfred Lord Tennyson, Poet Laureate of England, was so moved by the bravery of the men and the futility of the action that he wrote "The Charge of the Light Brigade," the poem which made the incident famous throughout history.

The war did not end until 1856 but Cardigan, taking "sick leave," found his way back to England in early 1855 and was treated like a conquering hero—at least until returning veterans of the war started to set the story straight about what one historian has called "his callous lack of responsibility for his men." Tennyson had written in his poem "tho someone had blundered," and now the British public placed the blame on Cardigan and Lucan. (Lord Raglan died of cholera while still in the Crimea.)

Cardigan weathered the crisis while pursuing the latest love of his life, Miss Adeline de Horsey, daughter of his old friend Spencer Horsey de Horsey. Cardigan was sixty years old, Adeline thirty-three, and there was also the little matter of Cardigan's still being married, but ... the earl pursued Adeline vigorously all the same. When, at last, his wife died, he raced to Miss Adeline de Horsey, went down on bended knee, and gasped to her: "Dearest, she's dead ... let's get married at once."

Cardigan was to die at the age of seventy-one, fittingly enough by falling off a horse. In the meantime, Lucan, embittered by the blame cast his way, retired to his Irish estates, where he lived to the grand old age of eighty-eight.

Many good things came of the awfulness of the Crimean War. The "purchase system" was finally abolished after it was seen what a botch aristocratic officers had made of things in the Crimea, while the role of the enlisted man—his bravery and suffering—was highlighted, resulting in an attempt to bring better food and medical care to the fighting man in the field. The likes of Lucan and Cardigan, Lord Look-On and the Noble Yachtsman, will never come again—one hopes, anyway.

BENJAMIN DISRAELI

BENJAMIN DISRAELI AND WILLIAM GLADSTONE: GREAT STATESMEN, GREAT HATERS

DISRAELI AND GLADSTONE HATED EACH OTHER for at least thirty long years, with a hatred that burned like a bright fire. It was said by an observer that Disraeli "has the power of saying in two words that which drives a person of Mr. Gladstone's temperament into a state of great excitement." Gladstone in turn claimed Disraeli had destroyed his own political party with his unprincipled stances.

The two men were the great British statesmen of the Victorian era, Disraeli twice prime minister, Gladstone four times. Although they were on different sides of the aisle—Disraeli a Tory or Conservative, Gladstone a Liberal—they were divided as much by personal differences as political issues. As Lord Granville, a Liberal, commented to Queen Victoria in 1880: "Lord Beaconsfield [Disraeli] and Gladstone are men of extraordinary ability; they dislike each other more than is usual among public men." Strangely for a Conservative, Disraeli was all dash and flash, and stabbing wit, a brilliant social figure, while Gladstone, a staunch Christian, was far more stolid and unimaginative, although certainly intelligent and fiercely ambitious. That the two just simply rubbed each other the wrong way—and would have had they been fellow fishmongers or haberdashers—can be seen in this anecdote: Gladstone's nickname, bestowed by his affectionate supporters, was Grand Old Man, or GOM. Disraeli claimed that the initials stood for God's Only Mistake.

A YOUTH OF BYRONIC INTENSITY Benjamin Disraeli was born in 1804, the son of Isaac and Maria D'Israeli (Benjamin would later change the spelling of the name). Isaac was from a Jewish family that originated in Arabia;

Maria was of a prominent family of Italian Jews. Isaac was a literary figure of some repute, a man who wrote poetry and criticism, and Benjamin grew up in a loving middle-class family, especially close to his sister, Sarah, two years older. Disraeli's Jewishness would be a central fact of his life. In an era when Jews were not allowed in "polite society"—although this would change, to some extent, with the rise of the great Rothschild banking family in mid-century—the young Benjamin would almost certainly have been unable to pursue the career he did had not his practical father had him baptized an Anglican when he was thirteen. Disraeli is still the only British prime minister of Jewish birth.

Even so, Disraeli felt keenly all his life—even after Queen Victoria made him an earl, Lord Beaconsfield—that he was an outsider. Yet he did not hide his Jewish background; in fact, he mythologized it, claiming that he was from a Sephardic family forced to emigrate from Spain during the Inquisition. This was not true, but what was true was that, as one biographer put it, "he felt himself innately superior, an aristocrat by instinct." His father sent him to middling good schools to train as a lawyer, but the law was not for Disraeli. He was Byronic in countenance—thin, large-headed, dark-haired, with slightly olive skin, and burnished dark eyes. Since he was sickly—asthma plagued him all his life—his father took him abroad on a tour of Europe in 1824. When he returned, with typical impetuousness, he threw himself into financial speculation. Newly recognized republics in South America were selling shares in silver mines. Disraeli joined a number of other men, including publisher John Murray, in buying shares, and he and Murray formed a newspaper, the *Representative*, in order to convince more speculators to do the same. In 1825, the market in silver mines crashed (most mines turned out to be worthless or even non-existent) and Disraeli, aged twenty-one, was left financially ruined and facing a bleak future.

"A RISING YOUNG MAN" William Gladstone was born of Scottish heritage, but in Liverpool, England, in 1809, the fourth of six children. His father, Sir John Gladstone, was a wealthy merchant who was able to give his four sons the best in the way of education. Unlike his future rival, William was what one historian has called "a quintessential member of the rich upper middle class." He was educated at Eton and Christ Church, where he excelled, taking a prized "double first" in Classics and Mathematics and graduating in 1831. Like Disraeli, he took a tour of Europe with his father, but when he returned home he stood for Parliament as a Tory. He was elected a MP for Newark in 1832 at the age of twenty-three, although not without some help from the Duke of Newcastle, whose son was a friend of his.

Interestingly enough, at this time Gladstone was an ultra-conservative. He spoke out strongly against the abolition of slavery (in part because his father owned plantations worked by slaves in the West Indies) and against other democratic reforms. Even at his young age he was an accomplished orator, a handsome, dark-haired man of medium stature who was not afraid to speak passionately about any subject he believed in. He caught the eye of Prime Minister Robert Peel, who called him "a rising young man," and was given a series of Cabinet posts, first junior lord of the Treasury, then under-secretary of state for the colonies. When Peel's government was voted out in 1835, Gladstone lost his post but retained a seat in the House. Like Disraeli, Gladstone prided himself on his writing, but his long, somewhat turgid works were unlike the torrid novels Disraeli would write. Gladstone's first work was called *The State in Its Relations with the Church*, which was mainly about how Britain should work to protect and extend the influence of the Church of England—the perfect book for the staid (and now respectably married, to Catherine Glynne) young former government minister to have written.

TURNING TO POLITICS

As Gladstone was earning honors at university and working his way up the political ladder, Disraeli was experiencing a period of deep emotional distress following the collapse of his newspaper and share venture. He decided to turn his hand to writing and in a very short time produced his first novel, *Vivian Grey*, which was a success, but not quite in the way he wanted—the society figures he lampooned in the book naturally turned against him and ridiculed him. Broke, he fell into a state of nervous exhaustion—Disraeli's health was always closely tied to his mental state—from which he was rescued when two friends, the married couple Sara and Benjamin Austen, took him back to France, Switzerland, and Italy on a tour of the places where the famous poet Lord Byron had stayed. Disraeli was probably in love with Sara, in a romantic and unrequited way (seeking solace, as he wrote self-pityingly, in the "smile of a married woman"), but his trip with the Austens in 1826 did get his creative juices flowing and, when he finally returned from Europe, he was to pen several more novels in quick succession.

Another trip abroad in 1830—this time to the Near East and Albania—was more of a maturing experience. Traveling in the company of his sister's fiancé, William Meredith, shy Disraeli had his sexual initiation (with prostitutes, where he picked up a venereal disease) and took part in a seamier sort of sojourn, replete with long nights of drinking in Albania and Egypt. Unfortunately, Meredith came down with smallpox in Egypt and died, sending Disraeli back home determined now to make something of his life. He had always been torn between literature and politics, and when he returned in 1832 the great debate in England was over a series of Reform Acts, which made major changes to the British electoral system, giving more men the vote (although women were still disenfranchised) and opening up the vote in certain boroughs that had been "in the pocket" of wealthy patrons.

Disraeli supported reform, but here he had his first taste of political reality. Running for Parliament as an Independent Radical, he lost three times, before finally having himself elected to the House of Commons in 1837 as a Tory.

"THE CLUB OF CLUBS" When Disraeli entered it (a year before Queen Victoria's coronation, in 1838), the House of Commons was, despite the reforms, still a place for English gentlemen—the "club of clubs," as it was known. Disraeli, the young novelist of Jewish origin, faced formidable difficulties in assimilating himself into this group—something he dearly wanted to do. William Gladstone fitted in much better with the members, who lounged on their benches, cracking nuts and tossing the shells on the floor, and ordering drinks from the waitresses and steak or pork-pie from Bellamy, who famously was in charge of the member's dining room (when William Pitt died, his last words were: "I think I could eat one of Bellamy's pork-pies"). Gladstone was on the opposition bench now, although his mentor Robert Peel would be re-elected prime minister in 1841, and there is no doubt that the twenty-nine-year-old veteran of the House and the newcomer of thirty-four eyed each other cautiously.

Disraeli made a horrendous maiden speech, which was so elaborate, over-long, and affected that it was met by hisses and catcalls, but his last words were: "I sit down now but the time must come when you will hear me." Gladstone, along with Robert Peel, laughed at Disraeli—he seemed, for now, a minor and rather foppish politician who would pose little threat to them. When Peel became prime minister again, Gladstone would be appointed president of the Board of Trade and then colonial secretary. Disraeli, who had attempted to cultivate Peel, to no avail, was furious that he had not been given a government post, and he never forgave Peel—and, by extension, Gladstone—for this.

It is easy to see why Disraeli rubbed some the wrong way—he was known to change his principles to gain political support; he had just married a woman twelve years his senior, Mary Anne Wyndham Lewis, widow of a close friend, and people supposed it had to be for her money (it may have been, but the two turned out to be very happy together); and he was an obvious social climber. But his opponents, Gladstone among them, underestimated him. In 1846, Disraeli found his issue. Gladstone and Robert Peel favored repeal of the Corn Laws, which were tariff statutes that protected the British market from being flooded with cheap grain (mainly from America) and thus driving down the prices British farmers could get for their goods. Repeal made sense, not only because of the famine beginning in Ireland—some (although definitely not all) British politicians felt it was important to get grain to the starving there as soon as possible—but also because Peel felt free trade would eventually stimulate the British economy.

Peel was able to force through the repeal of the Corn Laws, but the battle shattered the Tory Party, dividing it into "Peelites," or "free traders," and the "protectionists." Because almost every experienced politician followed Peel, Disraeli was left by default to emerge as the leader of his party, looking, as one contemporary politician put it, "like a subaltern in a great battle whose every superior officer was killed or wounded."

"SINGLE COMBAT" In 1851, Benjamin Disraeli's Protectionists came into power with Lord Derby as prime minister, Robert Peel having died in 1850. It was to be a government full of undistinguished politicians. When the elderly Duke of Wellington, a staunch Tory, was told who the ministers of the Cabinet were, he put his hand to his ear and said impatiently. "Who? Who?" and thus Derby's ministry received its nickname. Benjamin Disraeli was appointed Chancellor of the Exchequer, quite a stretch, given that his personal finances were always in disarray and he knew little about national economics.

It was during Disraeli's first post as a cabinet minister that what the London *Times* later described as "single combat" began between Gladstone and Disraeli. On December 3, 1851, Disraeli rose in the House to present his budget. His speech took five hours and contained a very controversial point—the lowering of taxes for three major British industries (agriculture, shipping, and sugar) by way of compensation for lifting protectionist laws and subjecting them to free trade. This, of course, enraged the Peelites and their allies and sparked afresh the argument between protectionism and free trade. As Disraeli made his speech, lightning and thunder crashed outside Parliament, providing a suitably dramatic accompaniment to the shouts and catcalls.

Disraeli also took the opportunity to make personal attacks on numerous Peelite rivals, one of whom he described as a "weird Sibyl." When he was done, at one in the morning, Gladstone stood up, so agitated that for a few moments he could not even speak. Observers said that his "usually calm face ... was livid and distorted with passion," not just because of the attempt to subvert free trade, but because of Disraeli's personal attacks. He scolded Disraeli, saying: "Whatever he [Disraeli] has learned ... he has not yet learned the limits of discretion, of moderation, of forbearance, that ought to restrain the conduct and language of every member of the House."

Disraeli was enraged that he had been lectured publicly by the younger man. Even worse, Gladstone took apart his budget, piece by piece, so that by three in the morning it was clear that it would not be passed. Derby's government fell, Disraeli along with it. Gladstone's speech was thought to have single-handedly brought down a government. A coalition government of Whigs and Peelites now took over the reins and Gladstone was named Chancellor of the Exchequer, presaging a petty quarrel between the two rivals. Disraeli refused to give Gladstone his chancellor's robe, which by tradition was passed between chancellors, because it had once been worn by William Pitt, whom Disraeli greatly admired.

It was the first, but not the last, time the two men would stoop to such displays of pettiness.

"A TONE OF MORAL SUPERIORITY" The same *Times* article that had described Gladstone and Disraeli's speeches as "single combat" went on to point out the differences between the two men's styles—Disraeli's style of speaking was "clear, nervous, brilliant and epigrammatic," while Gladstone (whom the *Times* preferred) had "a tone of moral superiority ... and earnest sincerity." It was precisely that "moral superiority" that Disraeli and numerous others disliked about Gladstone, whose Christianity had a sense of mission about it repugnant to those less religiously inclined—and there were those who felt that it was hypocritical, as well.

Gladstone was so devoted to the Anglican Church that when his sister Lucy, whom he had supported through a long history of opium addiction and mental health problems, became a Catholic he abandoned her. One observer noted wryly that "if Gladstone were soaked in boiling water and rinsed until he were twisted into a rope, I do not suppose a drop of fun would come out," while Disraeli—acerbic as ever, especially after his recent defeat—wrote that Gladstone "had not one redeeming defect."

Nonetheless, Gladstone was a talented and astute chancellor who paid attention to detail, cutting down on government expenditures by changing much of the paper stock to postcards—some say he invented that form of communication. He had intended to abolish income tax, but when his prime minister, Lord Aberdeen, became disastrously involved in the Crimean War, he was forced to raise it, to much dissatisfaction. Aberdeen's government fell and, in the game of musical chairs that these two rivals often played, Disraeli once again became Chancellor of the Exchequer—only this time, he was able to bring his own robe with him.

"THE GREASY POLE" The year 1868 was pivotal for both Disraeli and Gladstone. Disraeli, the de facto leader of what had now become the Conservative Party, had brilliantly outmaneuvered Gladstone and his Liberals (as the Peelites and their allies the Whigs were now known) on a new electoral Reform Bill in 1867. This actually went much further than what the Liberals, the party of reform, had wanted, so that he stole their thunder and got complete credit for the bill. Gladstone, watching this display of Machiavellian genius, appeared "to be in awe of [Disraeli's] diabolical cleverness," one observer said. Even his grand oratorical manner fell apart, and he became given to "a kind of suppressed and bitter laugh," while gesticulating impotently with his arms.

When Lord Derby resigned his office of prime minister in early 1868, Disraeli became prime minister of England. He had, as he said, "climbed to the top of the greasy pole." One of his tasks, while at that height, was handling Queen Victoria, whom one might have expected would look askance at the flamboyant prime minister (a night's evening dress for Disraeli might be green velvet trousers, a yellow waistcoat, and "low shoes with silver buckles") of Jewish origin, but in fact the two became fast friends, with Disraeli providing a bulwark for the disconsolate queen (in lifelong mourning for her Prince Albert). "The present Man will do well," she wrote to one of her daughters, "and will be particularly loyal and anxious to please me in every way."

GLADSTONE'S LADIES OF THE NIGHT

William Gladstone had an extraordinary avocation of attempting to rescue prostitutes from the London streets—and he involved himself in a very personal way. Gladstone patrolled the streets of London at least twice a week, late at night, meeting women and offering to help them get away from their profession and from the pimps or bullies who controlled them. He told them that he would take them to a place—such as the Church Penitentiary Association, which he had founded—where they could get three meals a day, a safe place to sleep, medical care, and vocational training.

There were rumors, of course, that his relationships with the women he saved were improper—many at the time accepted this as fact—but it was almost certainly not the case. In fact, he spent in total about 94,000 pounds of his own money in his efforts. Some of these prostitutes were children as young as ten or eleven, kept by brothel keepers or pimps because of a belief by some Victorian men that sex with a young virgin could cure venereal disease.

Gladstone kept up his work for some forty years, saving the lives of numbers of uncounted young women.

However, Disraeli faced tough times ahead. His Conservatives were still a minority in Parliament and the very Reform Bill he had championed so cleverly called for new elections before 1868 was out, in order to allow newly enfranchised voters the opportunity to cast a ballot. The election of 1868 proved a fierce battle between Gladstone and Disraeli. Now the boiling issue was whether to have the Anglican Church remain the official church of Ireland, and Gladstone, taking a page from Disraeli's own playbook, stole the issue away from Disraeli. Despite his own staunch Anglican beliefs, Gladstone supported disestablishment, thus endearing himself to Irish Catholics. In the end, the Conservatives were soundly defeated and Disraeli was ousted, and, once again, there was embarrassment. It turned out an expense account at the disposal of the prime minister was overdrawn by sixteen hundred pounds; this, it turned out, was not Disraeli's fault but that of one of his secretaries, but it caused him great embarrassment. As one of Disraeli's friends said: "If it was not Gladstone and Diz it would not matter in the least." But, as it was, Disraeli was mortified.

THE AUTHOR AND THE PRIME MINISTER William

Gladstone, taking control in 1868, had one agenda and that was reform. He set about it with a will, modernizing the army, the civil service, and the judicial system, and working to establish a system to halt the outrages perpetrated by corrupt landlords in Ireland. In the meantime, in May of 1870, Disraeli published his first bestseller, a thriller called *Lothair*, which went through eight editions within a year and earned its author ten thousand pounds. Disraeli retained his seat among the Conservative Party minority in the House of Commons and, as smart as ever when sitting on a Parliamentary bench, needled and goaded Gladstone without attempting to get into a major confrontation with him. Gladstone, some felt, was already feeling the pressure of his ambitious agenda and showed "a mixture of anger and contempt" when he rose to speak.

Disraeli, for his part, always answered the prime minister with a glacial calm, as if to further underscore the differences between the two. During one exchange, an observer noted, "[Gladstone] was like a cat on hot bricks ... and presented a striking contrast to Disraeli, for Disraeli cuts up the Minister with as much sang-froid as an anatomist cuts up a frog ..."

Still, the Conservative Party felt it was time for a change and attempted to replace the now sixty-seven-year-old Disraeli as party leader in 1872, only to find a remarkable public outpouring of affection for the man. Demonstrations and marches were staged in his honor, surprising him. He had long been famous but was never quite sure of his popularity, ever viewing himself as an outsider, especially among the common people. Taking advantage of this wave of good will, the Conservatives swept to victory in 1874, with Disraeli as their prime minister. Moving quickly, Disraeli instituted a series of social reforms that made improvements in public housing, health, the safety of food and drugs, workplace

conditions, and the like. It was Disraeli's favorite political move—attacking the opposition by stealing their issues and making them his own—and he crowed about it.

THE MIDLOTHIAN TRIUMPH
William Gladstone had retired (briefly) as head of the Liberal Party after Disraeli's victory, but those who knew him understood that he was itching for an issue to use to oust Disraeli and return to power.

He published a pamphlet in 1876 called *Bulgarian Horrors and the Question of the East*, which described the brutal repression of a Bulgarian rebellion by the Ottoman Empire and what Gladstone believed to be the Disraeli government's outrageous moral indifference to the atrocities. Disraeli—he was now Lord Beaconsfield—made a tactical error in claiming that the reports of these atrocities were exaggerated, when numerous eyewitness accounts attested to them.

ABOVE A debate in the House of Commons in the early 1860s, with William Gladstone sitting in the left foreground while Benjamin Disraeli sits on the other side of the House, in opposition.

In November 1879, seeking re-election—he had given up his previous seat in the House—Gladstone traveled by train throughout the Midlothian constituency in Scotland, giving a series of speeches on the issue. These speeches are what one historian has described as Gladstone's "finest hour as a popular orator and politician." He spoke to thousands of working-class Scots, using the Bulgarian issue to denounce the Disraeli government for its wars in Afghanistan and against the Zulu, where "ten thousand ... innocent people [were] slaughtered." A single speech sometimes lasted five hours. Despite the fact that Disraeli referred to these passionate attacks as "drenching rhetoric" from "the Impetuous Hypocrite," they were enough to rally the Liberals and drive the Disraeli government out of office.

The Midlothian campaign has been called "the first modern political campaign." In an era when it was considered undignified for politicians to campaign, Gladstone took his pleas directly to the people and—also very modern—used a single issue, greatly distorted, to pillory his opponent. With cleverness born of his long rivalry with Disraeli, Gladstone also made sure to hit home again and again at what he called "Beaconsfieldism," which vaguely meant that all issues, domestic and foreign, were the fault of a Disraeli who had now risen above his station and abandoned the common people to become an earl.

In 1880, Disraeli resigned as prime minister and Gladstone took his place. This time there were no incidents as they exchanged places at 10 Downing Street. However, when Disraeli was asked whether his old rival had beaten him, he answered vehemently that "the distress of the country is the cause & the sole cause of the fall of the government over which I presided."

To the very end of his political life, Disraeli would rather proclaim the country wretched than Gladstone a victor on his own merits.

"SO HE DIED"
Benjamin Disraeli's health grew exceeding feeble—he suffered from gout and his asthma had become much worse—and while he watched the Gladstone government from retirement, he was to take no part. Queen Victoria sent letters imploring him to come and visit her (after receiving one such missive, he said to a friend: "I had better not. She would only ask me to take a message to Albert"). Finally, after a long illness, he passed away on April 19, 1881. There was a huge public outpouring of grief at his death, but the mourners did not include William Gladstone. When he discovered that Disraeli's will directed that he have a private funeral, as opposed to a state one, Gladstone—who felt this directive was a false show of modesty—remarked to his private secretary: "As he lived, so he died—all display, without reality or genuineness."

As prime minister it was Gladstone's job to give the parliamentary eulogy on Disraeli's death, a task he agonized over so much he made himself ill. On May 9, he delivered it, claiming that Disraeli had "in a degree undoubtedly extraordinary, strength of will, long-sighted consistency of purpose, remarkable power of government ... and great parliamentary courage."

When he was done, Gladstone—who would serve out two more terms as prime minister and live to be eighty-nine—told a friend that delivering this eulogy had been the hardest task he had ever set himself to in his life.

LADY CARDIGAN AND DISRAELI'S BREATH

Despite the fact that he was nearing seventy, Disraeli was a prime commodity on the widower market after the death of his wife and he soon attracted the attention of the Countess of Cardigan, née Adeline de Horsey, widow of that Lord Cardigan who was famous for the Charge of the Light Brigade (see page 203).

Lady Cardigan was eccentric, to say the least—she was fond of wearing the uniform Lord Cardigan had worn during the infamous charge—and although she claimed to Disraeli that she had had "twelve offers of marriage" since the death of her husband, he was not interested. Lady Cardigan got her revenge when she wrote her memoirs. In them she claimed: "That morning I was much exercised in my mind about a proposal of marriage I had just received from Disraeli. My Uncle, Admiral Rous, had said to me, 'My dear, you can't marry that d—d Jew,' but I had known Disraeli all my life and liked him very well. He had, however, one drawback, as far as I was concerned, and that was his breath."

Disraeli was dead by this time, but he certainly never proposed marriage to her, halitosis or not.

FRANCISCO "PANCHO" VILLA

VERSUS **EMILIANO ZAPATA**

FRANCISCO "PANCHO" VILLA AND EMILIANO ZAPATA: NO COMMON CAUSE

PANCHO VILLA AND EMILIANO ZAPATA ARE EXTRAORDINARY, larger-than-life figures of the Mexican Revolution—and their reputations are not just confined to Mexico. Many books have been written about them, and movies have been made romanticizing their legends. (Villa even made a personal appearance in a 1914 film, *The Life of General Villa*, by the American director Raoul Walsh.) They had some similarities, but many differences. Villa was the outsized bandit, grinning through his moustache at the cameras, Zapata the smoldering revolutionary with black eyes staring suspiciously at one and all. Both desired an end to the repressive policies of the Mexican government of Porfirio Díaz and at least a beginning of freedom for the peasantry of Mexico.

The two men appeared at virtually the same time on the stage of the first major revolution of the twentieth century and, had they been able to share power, Mexican history might have changed. The fact that they were unable to make common cause was, as one historian has put it, "one of the great tragedies of the Mexican Revolution."

"NO RE-ELECTION" In the late nineteenth century, Mexico seemed to have at last thrown off the dictators who had always ruled over it—first the Spanish, beginning in the early sixteenth century, and then the French from the mid-nineteenth century. In 1876, Porfirio Díaz, who had been a heroic general in the war to oust the French and was now a liberal Mexican politician promising land reform, defeated the incumbent Mexican president and became head of the republic.

In a number of ways, Díaz was good for Mexico. He helped industrialize the country, building factories, dams, and better roads, and this brought in a flood of foreign capital, from the United States especially. But most of the money went to members of the already wealthy elite families, while the mass of peons, or peasants, labored under brutal conditions. To make matters worse, Díaz broke the promise that his election had been predicated upon. Decreeing that no peasant could hold land unless he held a formal, legal title to it—something that most peons, even if their families had worked the same patch of earth for centuries, did not possess—he parceled out much of the richest farm lands to the ruling oligarchy or to foreign companies.

Another broken promise was Díaz's vow of "no re-election," which meant that he believed that no Mexican president should serve more than one term consecutively. But Díaz ruled for thirty-five years, rigging elections and using the army to terrorize people into voting for him. He claimed he knew what was best for the people of Mexico: a strong hand, "Order followed by Progress."

But the Mexican people began to disagree. In 1910, a politician named Francisco Madero (who presented himself as liberal, but was in fact almost as conservative as Díaz) ran against the long-time president for re-election, promising land reform. Díaz had him jailed, but Madero escaped to the United States, where he declared himself the winner and then, on November 20, 1910, called on the Mexican people to rise up in revolt. Among the Mexicans already preparing themselves for war were two men, one from the north, and one from the south.

"LAND AND LIBERTY" Emiliano Zapata was born in August 1879 in the tiny Mexican state of Morelos, about fifty miles south of Mexico City. Zapata was a mestizo, which meant that he was half white and half Indian; mestizos made up half the Mexican population but were the objects of racial prejudice. As Zapata grew up under Díaz's regime, he, like many of those who lived in Morelos, seethed with anger as the rich owners of the sugarcane plantations kept expanding their land and taking more and more of the ancestral farms of the villagers. When he was three years old, the owner of one hacienda, or huge plantation, attempted to steal his village's water supply. The hacienda owner had the secret help of an elder of the community and, when this was found out, the villagers cut off their elder's head and left his body in the street.

Zapata's family were minor landowners but saw their property taken up piece by piece, for as the railroads came closer and closer, armed thugs employed by the huge landowners simply took the land. One of his earliest memories was seeing his father weeping because an orchard that had been in his family for a century had been taken by the *hacendados*, or plantation owners.

By the time Zapata was sixteen both his mother and father had died. Although many of his ten brothers and sisters supported Díaz, he vowed to take his revenge on the president who allowed the *hacendados* to steal land with impunity. His life changed in 1906 when an itinerant schoolteacher and bookseller came to the village and, through him, Zapata learned about the theories of Russian anarchists such as Peter Kropotkin. He began to imagine himself a revolutionary. He would seem, at first, an unlikely figure in this role. Despite his powerful intellectual abilities, he was a bit of a dandy, who as a young man loved to dress up in a suit with flashy coins sewn onto it. He was also a superb horseman, and was once invited to become the manager of the stables of a rich horseowner in Mexico City. Zapata spent one month there, seeing that the stables were more opulent than the homes of poor people back in Morelos, and quit.

Back in his village, he was more determined than ever to help the peons who had lost land. Elected as village chief at the age of twenty-eight, he spent eight days studying all the deeds in the village office and was then able to successfully mount legal challenges to the land usurpation by the *hacendados*. But these challenges took a long time, and many of the courts were corrupt, bribed by wealthy families. And so, as change and revolution hung in the air in 1910, Zapata took a group of armed guerillas and began a revolt in southern Mexico, simply seizing land. The battle cry of what Zapata called the Liberation Army of the South was "Land and Liberty!"

THE BIRTH OF PANCHO VILLA Francisco "Pancho" Villa
was born Doroteo Arango in June 1878 in the northern Mexican state of Durango, an area very different from where Emiliano Zapata grew up. It was a rugged land, of the Sierra Madre mountains, of great plains, huge cattle ranches, and mining towns, much like the American southwest portrayed in cowboy films. Doroteo was born to a sharecropper family; his father died young and Doroteo and his brothers and sisters were forced to labor at a huge nearby ranch owned by the wealthy Negrete family.

At sixteen, Doroteo became an outlaw. According to oft-repeated legend—it is hard now to ascertain the complete truth of this—he came home one day in 1894 and discovered that a member of the Negrete clan had tried to rape his sister. Villa's own account has him shooting the man in the foot and then taking off into the nearby Sierra Madres, afraid that Negrete would have him killed. (Another version has it that he killed the man.) It was then that the sixteen-year-old outlaw changed his name to Francisco "Pancho" Villa, his grandfather's name. After nearly dying as a fugitive, he found other outlaws like himself in the mountains—refugees of all sorts running from the Mexican police and army. Villa joined a large group of these bandits run by Ignacio Parra and they began robbing the wealthy miners and landowners and running back into the refuge of the mountains with posses and police hot on their tails. Despite the fact that he later changed his life story to pretend that he was a kind of Robin Hood at this time, Villa probably kept most of the money he stole to spend on women in the remote little towns near the bandits' hideout.

In 1901, after Parra had been gunned down by police, Villa was caught, down on his luck, trying to steal two mules. In Díaz's Mexico, this was a hanging offense, but he was saved because of his connections with a powerful black marketeer, who had the judge in his pocket—Villa was sentenced only to a year in the army, from which he deserted as soon as possible. He then fell upon hard times, working as a miner, a butcher, a cattle rustler, a hired gun guarding the huge payrolls of American railroad companies, and even as a mason and bricklayer.

Then, in 1910, in Chihuahua, Villa met Abraham Gonzales, who was a representative of future Mexican President Madero and the future governor of Chihuahua. There was something in the rough-hewn, barely literate Villa that appealed to Gonzales. He became Villa's mentor, teaching him how, if one looked at it in a certain way, what Villa had been doing was acting as people's hero, stealing from the rich (even if not exactly giving to the poor). Villa thereafter joined the revolution of Francisco Madero against Porfirio Díaz. He was a bandit turned revolutionary; historians still speculate as to which side of him predominated.

Whatever he was, he was a fighting man. By early 1911, as the revolution Madero had called for spread across the land, Villa joined forces with other rebels such as Castulo Herrera under the overall command of Pascual Orozco. Leading a force of perhaps five hundred men, Villa made daring raids against Díaz's federal forces, striking fast and hard in guerilla fashion. He then forced Herrera out of command and took over Herrera's men himself, becoming second only to Orozco. His exploits—such as walking into a federal-held town with only one companion and shooting his way out—made for great press coverage in both Mexico and the United States. At the May battle of Ciudad Juarez, near the American border, Villa moved his troops by train, the first time he had used a tactic he would employ for swift movement throughout the war. Villa's army beat back the federals while U.S. citizens watched the battle from El Paso, Texas, newsreel cameras turned, and reporters furiously took notes for the American press.

And so, in a sense, Pancho Villa was born. He was thirty-two years old at the time, muscular, with a stocky build and curly black hair. He had brown eyes that could mesmerize you, people said. In fact, reporters continually described him in animal terms—as a wolf or a cougar. He did not drink or smoke but loved to dance and sing—yet his volcanic temper could explode at any moment and he could be extraordinarily cruel. (Modern analysts have speculated that he was manic-depressive.) Villa was a crack shot and a great horseman who was known as "the centaur of the north" for his ability to ride for hours at a time, Mexican style, standing up straight with his legs in the stirrups. Women flocked to him (and when some did not come to him voluntarily, he forced himself on them).

Soon, Villa, Orozco, Madero and his men pushed Díaz out of office (the Mexican president fled to his former enemies, the French, with a large fortune), but the first of the revolutionaries to enter Mexico City was not Villa, but the firebrand from the south, Emiliano Zapata.

THE "WIVES" OF ZAPATA AND VILLA

Although Emiliano Zapata and Pancho Villa were unalike in many ways, they shared a love of womanizing and a very strange idea of what "marriage" constituted. Each was married once, legally: Zapata to Josefa Espejo, by whom he had two children, both of whom died in childhood, and Villa to Soledad Holguin.

In the case of Villa, there was another and far more squalid side to his womanizing, and that is the issue of rape. When Villa saw a woman he took a fancy to, he would often kidnap her, arrange a fake "marriage" with a "judge" (usually one of his cronies) and then rape the terrified girl. Although Zapata did not have a reputation for rape, he did indulge in the practice of fake marriages. He "married" Juana Mola Mendez, one of his first mistresses, in this fashion, and he and his brother had a fake double marriage to a pair of sisters.

After the deaths of Zapata and Villa, the Mexican courts were filled with suits and countersuits filed by women who claimed to have been married to these great leaders of the revolution.

VIVA ZAPATA Zapata's movement towards the Mexican capital from the southern part of the country had been a very different affair. For one thing, it resembled a class revolution far more than the fighting in the north. Zapata, far more so than the Russian revolutionaries who would follow him a few years later, was a so-called "anarchist communist," in the sense that while he believed in a communistic sharing of land and wealth, he did not essentially believe in any type of central government at all, even a communist one. He believed in literally killing all landlords—understanding, as one historian has put it, that "the differences between [peons and *hacendados*] were irreconcilable"—and letting people decide for themselves what they wanted to do. In late 1910 and early 1911, his revolution spread like wildfire up the southern Mexican states, his peasant fighters dressed all in white and carrying banners with pictures of the Virgin of Guadalupe, crying "Viva Zapata!" as they attacked the federals in their forts and police stations.

The Zapatistas, as they were called, were led by this determined man, whose ideology made it unlikely that he would compromise. His battles against the federals were bloody and uncompromising. No quarter was given on either side; peasants and army soldiers blasted away at each other at point-blank range or hacked each other to death with bayonets. Prisoners were killed. On May 13, after the great battle of Cuautla, in which his four thousand troops destroyed an elite Mexican regiment, Zapata was able to enter Mexico City in triumph, as famous in the south as Villa was in the north.

At this time, both men still subordinated themselves to Francisco Madero, who became president of Mexico in November 1911, but it soon became apparent to Zapata that Madero was not the revolutionary he claimed to be. He kept stalling on the land reforms he had promised Zapata, who had no patience with these delays and soon fled to the mountains, where he reformed his Liberation army into an anti-Madero army.

In the chaotic atmosphere that would become a trademark of the Mexican Revolution, the commander in chief of Madero's army, Pascual Orozco, staged a counter-revolution against Madero, only to have Pancho Villa, fighting alongside General Victoriano Huerta, defeat him. But Huerta, seeing Pancho Villa as a threat, trumped up charges against him and—for the first but not the last time in Villa's life—placed him up against a wall to be shot by firing squad. At the last moment, a telegram arrived from Madero in Mexico City, saving Villa's life, but Huerta then entered Mexico City with a sizeable force, had Madero murdered, and proclaimed himself president.

VILLA AND ZAPATA In the swirling currents of the highly unstable revolution, Villa and Zapata both hated Huerta—Villa's hatred became worse after Huerta ordered the execution of his mentor, Abraham Gonzales in 1913—and joined forces with other revolutionaries, including Alvaro Obregón and Venustiano Carranza, to fight against him. Carranza, supported by new U.S.

President Woodrow Wilson—who wanted Heurta ousted—became the new head of the Mexican government after forcing Huerta into exile in Spain. Villa was now at the height of his powers—he had confiscated gold from banks in the north of Mexico, armed his men, bought railroad cars and mobile hospital units, and won a series of victories—but, predictably, both Carranza and Obregón feared him.

Zapata, too, had seen the dangers of the Carranza government, which he refused to recognize in any event because it had not been elected by the people. The one thing in the world that Carranza and Obregón feared most was an alliance of their former allies, Villa and Zapata, and, in fact, Zapata and Villa were seeking this very thing. In the fall of 1913, Zapata sent a secret emissary north to seek out Villa and sound him out about a joint Mexican government featuring the two of them; Villa seemed to empathize with Zapatista goals. The two men, who had never met, began corresponding with each other. A group of their aides then met, seeking to iron out agreements between the bandit-revolutionary and the socialist-anarchist-land reformer, and it seemed as if an alliance was in the offing.

The two men finally met on December 4, 1914, at a school in the town of Xochimilico, in front of a packed group of aides and onlookers. People there

ABOVE Pancho Villa rides at the head of his men after a victory at Torreón in October 1913. The wagons included quantities of arms and mobile hospital units, purchased with gold he had confiscated from banks.

immediately saw the physical dissimilarities between the two—Villa weighed 180 pounds and towered over the 130 pound Zapata. Villa, who was an indifferent and sometimes eccentric dresser, wore a strange combination of pith helmet, heavy brown sweater, and khaki riding trousers, while Zapata dressed in a lavender shirt, with two brightly colored silk neckerchiefs, and narrow black trousers with silver buttons down the outside seams. The differences between the two could clearly be seen in their troops—Villa's looked like almost any army's soldiers, in drab khakis, whereas Zapata's men wore their traditional white cotton shirts and sandals and were far more poorly armed.

BELOW Villa and Zapata in Mexico City on January 2, 1915, after their defeat of Obregón and Carranza. Villa sits in the presidential chair, while Zapata, in collar and tie, sits on the right.

The two men seemed to be almost shy with one another, saying very little for about half an hour, until Villa made an insulting remark about Carranza, which brightened Zapata considerably. "I always told them Carranza was a son-of-a-bitch," he said. The two men then talked at considerable length about their points of view. Villa did agree with the necessity of land reform but, never as politicized as Zapata, was vague about how he might achieve it, although he cautioned: "we shall not give up the Mausers that we hold in our hand" even after land equity was achieved. He feared, he said, a counter-revolution.

Zapata spoke passionately about his peasant followers. "They feel so much love for the land," he said. "They still don't believe it when they're told 'This land is yours.' They think it's a dream."

After this public meeting, the two men met secretly to discuss the coming campaign against Carranza and Obregón. Here, unfortunately, the problems between the two men really arose. Villa wanted Zapata's agreement that, he, Villa, would be commander in chief of the forces of both men—it was the only way to beat their powerful common enemy he said, sensibly enough. But Zapata, also sensibly enough, did not really trust Villa with both armies. "I don't go north," he said to Villa. "And you don't go south."

"But, General," Villa replied, "keep in mind that these people are very strong."

Zapata said that he would deal with Carranza if Villa would deal with Obregón. "Well, if you can guarantee it," Villa said unhappily.

Two days later, in an extraordinary scene, both men entered Mexico City at the head of armies totaling fifty-five thousand men and rode, side by side, to the presidential palace. Obregón and Carranza had, for the moment, fled. As a joke, Villa sat down on the presidential chair first, and then got up and smiled for Zapata to take his turn.

Zapata refused. "I didn't fight for that. I fought to get the lands back," he said. "We should burn that chair to end all ambitions."

This exchange showed the difference between these two men who, although they respected each other, had world views that diverged widely. It was ironic—Villa had the much stronger army but no really coherent political goals, while Zapata had a true vision he wished to enact but a far weaker army. Had they been able to come together here, Mexico would have been spared much bloodshed.

"DIE KILLING" With the failure of these two men to form a real alliance, the Mexican Revolution turned into a civil war. Obregón, an able general, pushed Villa back in a series of fierce battles in the north, the bloodiest being the first and second battles of Celaya, in the spring of 1915. Obregón lost an arm in that clash, but Villa was soundly defeated, for the time being. The United States government, assuming now that Carranza had won the war, officially recognized him as president of Mexico in early 1916. In revenge, Pancho Villa crossed the

One reason why the ten-year-long Mexican Revolution was so bloody was the advent of two modern weapons. The first one was the machine-gun and the other was dynamite, with its explosive power.

Machine-guns are descendants of the Gatling gun, invented by the American Richard Gatling. Although they were used in combat in the late nineteenth century, these rapid-fire automatic weapons did not go into wider production until the Russo-Japanese War in 1905. All the varying factions in the Mexican Revolution depended on machine-guns, mounted on boxcars or above trenches, and they took a huge toll.

After 1910, a staple of American writing and film making about the Mexican Revolution featured a Mexican peasant in a wide sombrero lighting a stick of dynamite with a cigar and tossing it at his enemy. This was not just—or all—stereotyping. Dynamite was a favorite weapon. It was easy to make from nitroglycerine mixed with a powdery substance to stabilize it, and it was then placed in a tube and lit with a fuse. In other words, it was a primitive, but effective, way of blowing the hell out of your enemy—that is, if you did not blow the hell out of yourself first.

THE MANY DEATHS OF PANCHO VILLA

Pancho Villa, like so many other prominent figures of the Mexican Revolution, died a violent death—in his case, gunned down after he dropped his guard and left his lavish hacienda for a visit with an old mistress. Nine bullets pierced him, killing him instantly as he drove his Dodge saloon car back home.

Immediately legends grew. One was that Villa said to his comrades in the car: "Don't let it end like this. Tell them I have said something." Given that he died immediately and that seven out of the nine people in his car were dead in a few minutes, this is certainly apocryphal.

Another story about Villa is that grave robbers decapitated his corpse and that, somehow, his skull found its way in 1926 to the infamous Yale University secret Skull and Bones Society, where it rests today alongside other famous skulls, such as the one of the Indian chieftain Geronimo supposedly stolen in his youth by George H. W. Bush, president of the United States from 1988 to 1992. There is no way of ascertaining the truth of this, however.

United States–Mexico border in a rage and raided a New Mexico town, killing eighteen Americans. A vengeful American government, who considered Villa a bandit, nothing more, sent forces under General John J. Pershing into Mexico in hot pursuit of him—Pershing's men included Douglas MacArthur and George Patton. Despite the fact that they used airplanes, they were never able to catch up with Villa and eventually had to withdraw.

The bloody chaos in Mexico now was incredible—Zapata and Villa were fighting Obregón and Carranza, while the Americans chased Villa. When General Obregón was asked one day what his goal in the war was, he replied starkly: "Die killing."

Zapata himself waged a guerilla war of attrition in the south, using a new strategy to attack infrastructure—railroad, factories, bridges—in the hopes that foreign observers might be moved to step in and help get rid of Carranza, especially since much of the property being demolished belonged to America and other countries. Vengefully, Carranza launched wave after wave of vicious reprisal attacks in the south. If one villager was known to have helped a Zapatista, the entire village died. A bounty was put on Zapata's head and he was forced to travel everywhere with a bodyguard of fifty men.

Despite pressures like this, Carranza stayed in office, and in 1917 even created a constitution for Mexico (which had the main result of increasing his own power). As time went by, the forces of both Villa and Zapata were weakened by their never-ending battles and, in 1919, Zapata was desperate enough to let down his guard. He had approached a crack federal cavalry officer, Colonel Jesús Guajardo, asking him to defect. When Guajardo's superior heard about it, he gave Guajardo a choice: plan a trap for Zapata or be shot. Guajardo chose the former and told Zapata that he wanted to defect. Zapata tested this resolve by telling Guajardo that he must shoot and kill about fifty ex-Zapatistas who had defected to the federals and, in fact, Guajardo executed these men.

When Zapata went to see Guajardo, he was met by the smiling colonel, who had provided a guard of honor for his distinguished visitor. As a bugle sounded, the men presented arms—and then shot Zapata at point-blank range, killing him instantly.

THE END OF PANCHO VILLA
With Zapata's death went any real hope that the revolution in Mexican would end up benefiting the Mexican peasants. Carranza remained president until the following year, when the ruthless Obregón rose up and assassinated him on May 20, 1920. Villa was still too strong to destroy militarily, so Obregón offered him a deal: if he retired from politics to his massive hacienda in Chihuahua, Obregón would leave him alone. This Villa did, returning to the land holdings (163,000 acres) brought by money gained during the revolution and, ironically, leading the life of a wealthy *hacendado*. Obregón also gave Villa U.S. $100,000, which further cushioned his existence and helped him turn his hacienda into an armed camp—because, of course, Obregón was not to be trusted.

In the end, Villa provoked his own death. Although he had no real desire to get back into politics, he told a reporter that he could still raise forty thousand armed men if he wanted to, a statement of typical braggadocio that Obregón took as a threat. He told Villa to hold a press conference to deny it, but Villa refused to do this. And so Obregón waited until Villa let his guard down, which occurred in July of 1923. Villa was going to attend a christening in a local village and also see one of his mistresses, and he felt safe enough to travel without his usual fifty-man bodyguard. On the way home, an ice-cream vendor (in a pre-arranged signal to the assassins) called out "Villa, Villa!" and waved at the great Mexican revolutionary. Villa, driving his own car, waved back—and Obregón's hidden men opened up, killing Villa and seven of the nine people with him.

And so it was over. A ten-year-long revolution that cost as many as a million lives could have been greatly shortened if two men had been able to understand that, out of all the figures of the Mexican Revolution, they were the most alike—under the skin, that is.

ADOLF HITLER

VERSUS **ERNST RÖHM**

ADOLF HITLER AND ERNST RÖHM:
THE NIGHT OF THE LONG KNIVES

ADOLF HITLER AND ERNST RÖHM: BOTH THESE MEN were scarred, physically and emotionally, in the seething cauldron that was the Western Front in World War I, and afterwards both fought to salvage something from the ruin of their country. By joining paramilitary organizations and radical political parties that drew on old dreams of fervent nationalism they gained a sense of power.

Röhm and Hitler were misfits and loners and that they met each other at all is one of the great malevolent accidents of history. But once they did, their relationship helped form the brutal state that would become the Third Reich—that is, until the Führer launched the operation known to history as "the Night of the Long Knives." With the blood of his former blood brother on his hands, Hitler at last was in a position to reach for ultimate power.

"A GROTESQUE BABY" Ernst Röhm was born in Munich in 1887, one of three children of aristocratic parents. The Röhm family had a long history of military service, and Ernst joined the small German armed forces in 1906, at the age of only nineteen. When World War I broke out, Röhm, like so many millions of young men of his generation, jumped at the chance to fight for his country in what he considered to be a just cause—but the war was to change him permanently and destroy his ideals. At the very beginning of the conflict, while fighting in Flanders in September 1914, the young Captain Röhm was horrendously wounded by shrapnel that destroyed much of his face. Plastic surgeons of the era did their best to put him back together, but any picture of him shows the result: a man whose visage is horribly scarred, puffy with swollen tissue, and whose snout-like nose is obviously an artificial construction. One historian has written that Röhm looked like "a grotesque baby." Contemporaries likened him to a pig.

Despite his scars, Röhm returned to the front and continued to fight. Twice more he was wounded. After the second time, at Verdun, he was invalided out of the service and began to work for the Bavarian War Ministry as a supply officer. In some ways, this was as transformative an experience as combat itself, for Röhm was able to observe first-hand how corrupt bureaucrats operated, while thousands were dying daily at the front. And he learned how organizations worked, something that would soon stand him in very good stead.

ADOLF HITLER Adolf Hitler was born in Austria on April 20, 1889, the fourth child of six. His mother's name was Klara; his father, Alois, was a customs inspector who had changed his last name from the coarser and more rural-sounding Schicklgruber to Hitler for reasons that are not completely known. (Historians have discounted the rumor, once a staple of Allied propaganda, that Hitler had a Jewish grandparent.) Adolf—the name derives from Old High German, meaning "noble wolf," and "Wolf" was one of Hitler's favorite nicknames for himself—grew up in a comfortable middle class home, although he was beaten often by his father, a stern disciplinarian with a bad temper. Hitler's mother (who would watch four of her six children die of childhood diseases) was loving to the point of overprotectiveness.

Because of Alois's job, the family moved around a good deal, eventually settling in Linz. Alois died there in 1903, and in 1906, at the age of sixteen, Adolf dropped out of school for good, deciding to be a painter. Supported by his doting mother, he twice failed to gain admittance to the Academy of Fine Arts in Vienna, but he continued to live in that city even after Klara died of breast cancer in 1907. By 1909 he had run out of money and by the following year was living in a homeless shelter. Hitler later claimed that it was during this period that he became an anti-Semite— Vienna had a large and prosperous Jewish population, whom Hitler resented—but his furies may have stirred within him even earlier, since he was known to have had fallings out with Jewish schoolmates as far back as grammar school.

Like Röhm, Hitler was swept up in the great fervor at the beginning of World War I, which gave the drifting and aimless young man direction. He served as a corporal in a Bavarian regiment, acting as a runner delivering messages, a dangerous job that won him two Iron Crosses. In 1916, at the battle of the Somme, a shell exploded near him, killing several of those around him and wounding him in the leg. In 1917 he returned to his regiment and in October 1918 was partially blinded by mustard gas near Ypres.

The war was over for Hitler—and almost over for Germany.

"THE GREATEST VILLAINY …" In what Hitler would call in *Mein Kampf* "the greatest villainy of the century," Germany negotiated peace with

RIGHT Soldiers and policemen in Eaglesham, Scotland, inspect the wreckage of the Messerschmitt ME-110 in which Rudolf Hess, deputy leader of the Nazi Party, made his solo flight to Scotland.

RUDOLF HESS

One of the saddest figures from the early days of the Nazis was Rudolf Hess, an SA member who, along with Ernst Röhm, was imprisoned with Adolf Hitler in Landsberg Prison. Another veteran of World War I, he took down Hitler's dictated *Mein Kampf* and soon became his private secretary. Much more so than any of the other Nazis of the period, Hess was completely devoted to Hitler, showing him an almost slavish loyalty.

Hess was named deputy party leader in 1933, but his title was almost entirely ceremonial. One of his tasks was to announce Hitler at mass meetings. Eventually he was named second successor to Hitler, after Hermann Göring, but he was given very little real power and eventually lost out after a power struggle with Martin Bormann.

The saga of Hess really begins on May 10, 1941. With Hitler locked in a life or death struggle with Great Britain, Hess, an expert flyer, decided to take a Messerschmitt ME-110 to Britain on a self-styled "peace mission" to the Duke of Hamilton, whom he had met briefly. Incredibly, he dodged British air defenses and managed to bail out of his plane within thirty miles of the duke's manor in Scotland.

Hess told British interrogators that if they would leave Hitler alone in Europe, he would stop warring against Great Britain. But Hess's captors soon realized that their captive was mentally unstable—indeed, his main value was in propaganda, in having humiliated Hitler and his henchmen—and he was dumped in a POW camp. In 1945, he was placed on trial at Nuremberg with the rest of the Nazis, despite the fact that he had begun to talk to himself and was becoming more and more paranoid, and sentenced to life imprisonment. Held in Spandau Prison in West Berlin, he gradually lost his mind and memory, perhaps a fitting fate for the last Nazi alive of Hitler's original elite group. Hess committed suicide in prison in 1987, at the age of ninety-two.

the Allies, ending World War I in November of 1918. Germany's military had been defeated, its economy was bankrupt, and millions of men had died or been wounded (1.75 million soldiers were killed or disabled by the influenza epidemic in the summer of 1918 alone). But the Treaty of Versailles, which followed, was unwisely draconian on the part of the Allies: Germany was rendered almost completely impotent, allowed to have only a small standing army and forced to pay war reparations. The battle-hardened veterans of the Western Front, including Ernst Röhm and Adolf Hitler, were outraged.

Certain they had been betrayed by their own countrymen—the generals and politicians they called the "November criminals"—Röhm and Hitler and thousands like them returned radicalized to a country that had begun to disintegrate. Inflation made the German mark all but worthless, unemployment was endemic, as was hunger (people in major cities such as Berlin had begun resorting to cannibalism to survive), and Communist agitators (Bolsheviks) were everywhere. Munich, in the early spring of 1919, was temporarily controlled by Communist committees, but these were ousted by paramilitary organizations like the Freikorps (Free Corps), which Ernst Röhm joined upon his return to civilian life.

Röhm, with his aristocratic upbringing, was horrified that the German monarchy had been dissolved and that the country had been declared a republic. The Freikorps was a loose organization of different groups—monarchists like Röhm, nationalists, imperialists, and angry and displaced soldiers of the German Reichswehr (the severely weakened German army). Armed by the Reichswehr, the Freikorps staged pitched battles against the Bolsheviks, particularly in Bavaria. Röhm, with his combat and supply experience, quickly rose to become commander in chief of the Munich Freikorps and it was in Munich, in 1920, that he was to meet the former Reichswehr corporal named Adolf Hitler.

NAZIS After the war was over and he left the hospital, Hitler remained in the army for a short time and returned to Munich. There he became a spy for a branch of military intelligence and was sent, in 1919, to infiltrate a minor political group called the German Workers Party (Deutsche Arbeiterpartei), or DAP. Instead, in a sense, DAP infiltrated Hitler. He found himself enamored of DAP's anti-Semitic, anti-Marxist ideas and of its call for a type of "non-Jewish" national socialism.

At the same time, Hitler met Dietrich Eckart, one of the early founders of the occult Thule society, who became his mentor, even teaching him what type of clothes to wear (long leather trench coats became his habitual garb) and how to speak in public. Very shortly, Hitler became a featured speaker of DAP and, by late 1920, had left the army and taken control of the party, which he renamed the National Socialist German Workers' Party (National-Sozialistische Deutsche Arbeiterpartei, or NSDAP). Members of the party were soon called "Nazis," from the German pronunciation of the beginning of the word "National."

Ernst Röhm had been a member of DAP and remained a member in the new Nazi party. Hitler probably first met him in the fall of 1919 and soon realized how valuable he was. Röhm had extensive paramilitary connections and knew all the leading members of the confusing patchwork of military groups in the Weimar Republic of postwar Germany. More importantly, he was able to build up a sizeable cache of small arms (forbidden, of course, by the Treaty of Versailles), so much so that the scar-faced young man was known as "the machine-gun king," and it was he to whom the various thugs and brigands of these mercenary groups came for guns and ammunition.

Adolf Hitler and Ernst Röhm took an instant and genuine liking to each other. Both respected the other's service in the war, both had the same bitter hatred of Jews, Marxists, and the republic set up by the Treaty of Versailles. Moreover, each had a separate sphere of influence, so that—at first, at any rate—they did not clash. Hitler led the political arm of the Nazi party, Röhm its military wing. By 1921, Röhm had taken members of his old Freikorps and formed a new group called the Sturmabteilung, or Stormtroopers, more generally known as the SA. These brownshirted thugs were Hitler's enforcers as he began to preach his radical National Socialist philosophy in Bavarian beer halls. Brawls broke out everywhere, but Hitler was protected by Röhm and henchmen like Rudolf Hess and Edmund Heines. Invoking a heroic, nationalistic past to a people starved for both material goods and spiritual sustenance, Hitler gradually became a force to be reckoned with in Bavaria.

THE BEER HALL PUTSCH

In 1923, emboldened by the fact that he had made a serious ally in the respected General Erich Ludendorff, Hitler attempted to take control of Bavaria. On November 8, he stormed a public meeting in a beer hall at gunpoint and demanded that the local government support him in "marching on Berlin" to take control of the country. At the same time, Röhm and his SA attacked and briefly held the Munich police station. The next day, the police retaliated by attacking Hitler and his followers. Sixteen Nazis were killed and Hitler, Ludendorff, and Röhm were put on trial. Hitler was sentenced to five years in Landsberg Prison, but his uprising had made him a popular hero. Röhm spent time in the same prison, further strengthening his bond with Hitler. Both were released early, at the end of 1924, as part of a general amnesty of political prisoners.

Hitler had made good use of his prison time by dictating his memoirs, *Mein Kampf*, to Rudolf Hess. Part vitriolic diatribe, part invented autobiography, part clarion call for a new German nation-state, *Mein Kampf* spelled Hitler's entrance into the national German consciousness, selling over two hundred thousand copies in a few years. Although both the Nazi party and the SA were officially banned, Hitler sought ways around this. He had decided to play by the rules and seek power through elected office; something he called "the strategy of legality."

HOMOSEXUALITY IN NAZI GERMANY

There is no denying that many of the early members of the Nazi party and the SA were homosexuals. It was an open secret that Ernst Röhm, his adjutant Edmund Heines, and numerous young officers in the SA had gay parties and lived in the swirling gay underground of Berlin. When Heines was rousted out of bed on the Night of the Long Knives he had a teenage boy with him, one of the reasons why he was among the first to be shot.

Even before the turn of the twentieth century, Germany had a fairly free and open gay population, especially in Berlin. The very first organization for gay and lesbian rights, the Scientific-Humanitarian Committee, was formed in Berlin in 1897, in part to combat a law on the books, the infamous Paragraph 175, which made homosexual acts illegal. However, with the advent of Nazism, gays began to be persecuted. Nazis claimed that gay men offended the sacred purity of the Aryan family, which they were pushing as the centerpiece of their new political philosophy. For a time, as persecution of the general population of gays and lesbians began, Röhm and his gay SA cronies were protected, but as soon as Hitler decided to get rid of Röhm, the fact of his homosexuality became one of the chief rationales for doing so.

In 1935, at Hitler's direction, the Reichstag amended Paragraph 175. Now men convicted under the law could be castrated, and "chronic homosexuals" could be sent to concentration camps, where some were subject to experiments, including testosterone implants, to change their sexual orientation. Most homosexuals in the camps were forced to wear a pink triangle to identify them as such; their lives were even more difficult than those of the average inmate.

It is hard to estimate how many pink triangle gays died in Hitler's concentration camps. Ten to fifteen thousand is the number generally given. The death rate of gay men in the camps was three to four times higher than that of any other non-Jewish group, and gays did not even have the satisfaction of seeing their persecutors brought to justice at the Nuremberg war crime trials, possibly because of homophobia on the Allied side, and possibly because the infamous Paragraph 175 was still on the books in Germany and would, in fact, remain so until 1969.

RIGHT The perimeter fence of the Nazi concentration camp at Auschwitz, Poland. In 1935 the notorious Paragraph 175, which made homosexuality illegal, was amended so that homosexuals could be sent to concentration camps.

Until the end of the 1920s, Hitler spent his time consolidating his power within the National Socialist Party, as well as disarming challenges from other party members, such as Joseph Goebbels, whom he converted into allies.

But when, fearful that the SA would get him arrested again with its brawling tactics, Hitler tried to turn this paramilitary organization into an innocuous-seeming recruiting department for young men, Ernst Röhm laughed at him. He referred to Hitler as "Adolphe Legalite," lampooning his "strategy of legality." In 1925, the warlike Röhm could no longer take it. Fed up with what he called the "castration" of the organization that had been his brainchild, and now veering away from National Socialism—which increasingly meant rule by one man, Hitler—Röhm quit his post and decided to go to Bolivia as an advisor to the Bolivian Army.

"THE PRIMACY OF THE SOLDIER" Röhm stayed in South America for five years, eventually becoming a lieutenant colonel in the Bolivian army. Little is known about most of his sojourn there, but while he was away, Hitler experienced both success and problems. Members of his party increasingly won seats in the Reichstag, the German parliament—in September 1930 they pulled in nineteen percent of the national vote. It seemed Hitler's attempt at respectability was beginning to work, but he had trouble within his organization, as the SA leaders in Röhm's absence were unable to control their men. In the meantime, a new Nazi organization, the Schutzstaffel, or SS, had been formed as a kind of elite personal bodyguard for Hitler and, led by icy-cold Heinrich Himmler, it was gaining power within the party.

In October of 1930, Hitler sent Röhm a gracious letter, asking him to come back to Germany to become the new chief of staff of the SA. Hitler needed Röhm to help form the SA into an organization that would be able to intimidate more and more people into voting for Hitler, but change its image at the same time. Röhm returned in January 1931 and immediately began reshaping the SA. In just one year, 1931, he increased the organization from 88,000 to 260,000 men. He put down rebellious elements within the SA, while scrubbing it clean—now, instead of battling in beer halls, groups of the SA would march in lockstep to church each Sunday. But Röhm still insisted on what he called "the primacy of the soldier." This meant that, as far as he was concerned, the SA should no longer be controlled by the political wing of the party. Naturally, this caused friction with Hitler, who began to realize that Röhm, while invaluable, now had control of a large army of men who were utterly loyal to him.

To make matters more difficult, Röhm began to feud with Heinrich Himmler and his growing cadre of SS. Partly it was a class difference—despite his own aristocratic upbringing, Röhm's SA was a working-class army, while most of the SS considered themselves the elite of society. By the beginning of 1934, with the SA growing to nearly three million men, Himmler and Hermann Göring began to scheme to oust Röhm. And Ernst Röhm's lifestyle made their job a little easier.

"THE MORAL EDUCATION OF GENTEEL YOUNG LADIES"

In a time when most gay men were in the closet, Ernst Röhm made relatively little secret of his homosexuality, in particular his proclivity for young men. In 1925, he had brought charges of theft against a seventeen-year-old male prostitute who had stolen luggage from him and who may have been trying to blackmail him (the boy had told police that Röhm "asked me to engage in an abhorrent form of sexual intercourse"). While in Bolivia, Röhm openly wrote letters to friends complaining about the lack of male companionship: "So here I am, poor fool, not knowing what to do with myself. I think sadly back to beautiful Berlin, where a man can be so happy."

Back in Germany, Röhm lost no time in establishing a lifestyle that, rumor had it, encompassed orgies. Certainly his chief deputy in the SA, Edmund Heines, as well as numerous others who joined Röhm in the "new" SA were homosexuals, and some critics began to complain to Hitler that Röhm was using the SA as a kind of gay recruiting society. In May 1932, General Ludendorff told Hitler that he had "documentary evidence of grave abuses inside [the SA] stemming from the homosexual proclivities of ... Röhm and Heines." But Hitler would not listen—in fact, so valuable did he consider Röhm to be that he issued an official statement that read, in part: "The SA is not an institute for the moral education of genteel young ladies ... an [SA officer's] private life cannot be an object of scrutiny."

Still, Röhm's enemies began to close in on him, helped by his own growing ego. Even as Hitler became Chancellor of Germany in 1933 and the Nazi party finally came fully into power, Röhm was distancing himself from his old comrade. Hitler had finally been able to win over the Prussian military elite of the country, those who controlled the Reichswehr, but Röhm hinted that Hitler had betrayed the principles of the German "revolution," and had thrown himself in with bourgeoisie who could never understand a true fighter. He said publicly that "the German Revolution has been won, not by philistines, bigots and sermonizers, but by revolutionary fighters"—that is, the SA. He told an acquaintance: "Hitler can't walk over me as he might have done a year ago. I've seen to that. Don't forget that I have three million men, with every key position in the hands of my own people."

THE NIGHT OF THE LONG KNIVES

Röhm—with a force that could overwhelm both the Reichswehr and the SS, if he chose to unleash it—had finally become too big an obstacle for Hitler to ignore. To make matters worse for Röhm, Himmler and Göring came to Hitler with a story that the French had offered Röhm twelve million francs if he would overthrow Hitler. They told him that Röhm was planning a coup in which the SA was going to take over Germany. Both of these stories were fabrications. Hitler may not have believed that France was paying Röhm such an outlandish sum, but it appears he took seriously the threat that Röhm was going to oust him. This is understandable, given Röhm's own braggadocio and the fact that the SS and the Gestapo, the German secret police, had been compiling fake "dossiers" on various SA members to support their claims.

At one meeting in which the SS convinced him of Röhm's perfidy, Hitler was described by onlookers as so enraged that spit dripped from his mouth as he screamed that he would have Röhm and all his SA leaders shot. Convinced by the SS that he had little time to spare before the SA struck, Hitler put a plan into place quickly. On June 28, 1934, Hitler ordered that Röhm and his chief officers attend a meeting with him in Bad Wiessee, Bavaria, in the late morning of June 30th. Around 6:30 a.m. on the 30th, Hitler himself, carrying a whip and a pistol and followed by armed men of the SS, pulled up in front of the Hotel Hanselbauer, where Röhm, Heines, and other SA leaders were sleeping. Storming into the hotel, Hitler barged into Röhm's room, pointed the gun at him, and accused him of being a traitor, a charge Röhm vehemently denied. But it was too late. The Night of the Long Knives—a line from a popular German song—had begun. It was only a night figuratively speaking, for it stretched over an entire twenty-four-hour period, but it spelled the end of Ernst Röhm and the SA.

Röhm and his officers were carted off, complaining loudly, to Stadelheim Prison in Munich. Hitler, in the meantime, in a towering rage, gave orders for the immediate execution of six of the SA officers, putting crosses next to their names on a list. They were taken out of their cells, told, "You have been condemned to death by the Führer. Heil Hitler!," then put up against a wall and shot. Across the country, other murders were taking place, as death squads sent by the SS gunned down political opponents of every stripe. One hapless man, a music critic, was killed by mistake when the SS mistook him for an old adversary of Hitler's.

Finally, it was Röhm's turn. Hitler at first told observers that he would not have his old comrade shot because of "his services to the Movement," but in the end he was convinced by Himmler that Röhm had to go. Hitler made his decision on Sunday, July 1, but insisted that Röhm be made to take his own life, as if to expiate for his own sin, and possibly to assuage any guilt Hitler may have been feeling. Three SS men drove to Stadelheim and gave Röhm a pistol. They waited outside the cell for ten minutes, but when no shot was fired, they re-entered, pistols drawn. Röhm, bare-chested, attempted to say something, but they waved him off and opened fire, killing him instantly.

The next day, the Gestapo burned all files having to do with those killed during the Night of the Long Knives. In all, perhaps ninety, but possibly as many as two hundred, people had been slaughtered.

"I ORDERED THE LEADERS OF THE GUILTY SHOT" Two weeks after Röhm was shot, on Friday, July 13, Adolf Hitler made an address at a special evening session of the Reichstag held at the Opera House, in Berlin. He was surrounded by black-shirted SS men and his speech was broadcast to the German nation—and the world—over the radio.

LEFT Hitler (center, standing) addressing the German Reichstag at the Kroll Opera House, Berlin. He made a similar staged speech after the Night of the Long Knives, justifying his actions on the grounds that Röhm had "violated every decency."

HITLER'S GIRLS

Like his fellow dictator, Josef Stalin, Adolf Hitler preferred very young women—girls, really—whom he could manipulate and control, at least as long as their hero-worship of him lasted.

The first of these women was sixteen-year-old Mimi Reiter, whom Hitler met in 1926 while vacationing in Austria. Mimi was a Catholic boarding-school student to whom Hitler introduced himself in a park one day, only about two weeks after her mother had died suddenly. The vulnerable young girl began accompanying Hitler on long rides in the country, calling him "Wolf," his chosen nickname for himself. In this idyllic setting, they would kiss passionately, according to Mimi's postwar account. But soon Hitler disappeared back to Munich, leaving her lonely and so love-struck that she would treasure his memory all her life.

Perhaps the most notorious of Hitler's girls during this period was Geli Raubal, who was the daughter of Hitler's half-sister, Angela. In 1928, when Hitler was thirty-nine years old, he called Angela in Vienna and asked her to keep house for him in Munich. She brought along the vivacious twenty-year-old Geli. Geli soon began appearing in public with Hitler and gossip about the relationship between "Uncle Alf" and his niece became common in Munich. It is not known for certain if their relationship was sexual. However, Hitler did have—possibly for the first and only time in his life—at least a deep infatuation with Geli. He became extremely dominating with her, controlling her life to the point of having her escorted everywhere she went. "My uncle is a monster," she told a friend. Finally, in September 1931, Geli apparently tried to break away from Hitler, possibly to see a Jewish musician she had fallen in love with in Vienna. Hitler refused to let her go. On Friday, September 18, she went to Hitler's apartment while he was not there and shot herself in the heart with his pistol. Rumors persist to this day that she had been savagely beaten and her nose broken, possibly by Hitler himself. On hearing of her death, however, he fell into a deep depression; intimates thought he was going to have a nervous breakdown.

Hitler took Eva Braun—some twenty-three years his junior—as his mistress the following year (Braun would attempt suicide twice during their relationship) and stayed with her the rest of his life, marrying her a few hours before they jointly took their lives in 1945. But he would never forget Geri.

In his speech he described the events of the Night of the Long Knives, without, however, going into gory details. He would, he said, "maintain a few reservations imposed by the interests of the Reich and by a sense of decency." Most people, however, had read in the newspapers or heard through the rumor mill about the executions, about the gay SA officers in bed with their young lovers.

"It was no longer simply a question of Röhm's intentions," Hitler said in his speech, "but also of his attitude, which reflected his growing alienation from the Party ... The life the Chief of Staff and a certain number of other leaders had begun to lead was intolerable from the point of view of National Socialism. The question was no longer that he and his friends had violated every decency, but rather that the contagion was widespread, and was affecting even the most decent elements."

In the starkest of terms, Hitler then said: "I ordered the leaders of the guilty shot. I also ordered the abscesses caused by our internal and external poisons cauterized ... The action was completed during the night of Sunday, July 1, and normal conditions have been re-established."

As Hitler finished his speech, applause rang through the Opera House and could be heard from the streets outside, where onlookers had gathered to hear the speech broadcast over loudspeakers. Hitler stepped outside to the salutes of his deputies and the cheers of the crowd, got into a black limousine, and drove off into a future that would include the total downfall of his country but not, at least, Ernst Röhm.

JOSEPH STALIN

JOSEPH STALIN AND LEON TROTSKY: THE DOER VS. THE DREAMER

ADOLF HITLER WAS FOND OF SAYING IT WAS MUCH easier for him to turn "a Communist into a Nazi" than to perform the same trick with a proponent of democracy, meaning that scratching a Bolshevik and finding totalitarian tendencies was not very hard. Of course, Hitler is hardly an unbiased source in this matter. Communists hated both him and fascism with a passion, and his defeat in the Soviet Union in 1941–42 was a turning point in World War II.

But—he had a point. Take a look at Leon Trotsky and Joseph Stalin, two original Bolsheviks who rose to power in Russia during the revolution and became rivals to the death. Neither of them cared much for the common people—although Stalin was better at pretending he did—both maneuvering to take control of Russia and place it as far from a socialist utopia as possible. Both men were indeed revolutionaries—we still know them, not by their real names, but by their Bolshevik *noms de plume*—but both were seduced by power. The difference between them was that Stalin knew how to get power, while Trotsky floundered when it came to the moment to grab it.

SOSO Joseph Stalin was born Iosif Vissarionovich Dzhugashvili in Gori, Georgia, on December 21, 1879. His twenty-year-old mother, Ekaterina, had previously given birth to three children, all of whom died. His father, Vissarion, was a shoemaker given to brutal rages. Iosif was a sickly boy who contracted smallpox when he was seven, scarring his face for life. Other scars were inflicted by his father, who beat him often, instilling in him a lifelong hatred of authority. When Vissarion died in 1890 Stalin was only eleven, but the man's death was a relief.

As his illiterate mother took in washing to make ends meet, her son grew, despite his small stature, into a talented young man who wrote poetry and painted. Ekaterina saved enough money—a truly monumental feat in the wretched poverty in which they lived—to send Soso, as he was nicknamed (Georgian for "Joe"), to elementary school, from which he graduated at the age of fourteen in 1893. In the summer of 1894, the local parish priest was able to arrange a scholarship for Soso at the Theological Seminary in the Georgian capital of Tiflis (now Tbilisi). There he had his first taste of revolution.

Russia, under the czars, had spent much of the nineteenth century conquering the Caucasus region, of which Georgia was a part. By the time of Soso's birth, Georgia had completely lost its independence and its people were treated as little better than slaves by the Russian authorities, who considered Georgians backward and ignorant. While at the Theological Seminary, supposedly studying to be a priest or teacher, Soso joined a secret organization whose goal was to free Georgia from the Russians. These nationalist aspirations, however, were soon succeeded by Marxist ones. Soso became a Social Democrat and, in 1899, was expelled from the seminary for trying to convert his fellow students to his cause.

THE PLIGHT OF RUSSIA As the twentieth century began, Russia was still ruled by czars, as it had been for centuries. These august leaders did very little for the common people, with the result that almost all the land in Russia was owned by a small percentage of the population. The feudal institution of serfdom had been abolished in 1861, but it did not really matter—peasants still worked long, arduous hours, lived short lives, and owned nothing. But as the reign of Czar Nicholas II began in 1894, change was in the wind. The Industrial Revolution, late in coming to the country, had sent millions to the swelling cities in search of work, just as the radical theories of Karl Marx—who pointed out the evident evils of capitalism and raised the notion that the wealth of the world should be shared—were being disseminated.

The result was that Marxist groups began to form, led by men such as Vladimir Lenin, a St. Petersburg lawyer turned radical, who was arrested by czarist police and sent into exile in Siberia. Released in 1900, he lectured throughout Europe, preaching the evils of the czarist system and the glories of Marxism, or Social Democracy, as the movement was being called.

Another member of these groups was Lev Bronstein, born on November 7, 1879, who would come to be known to the world as Leon Trotsky.

TROTSKY Lev Bronstein was born in different circumstances from those of his great rival, Stalin. His father, David, was a small landowner in southern Russia and his mother, Anna, was a housewife who took care of Lev and his siblings (two brothers and a sister would survive childhood out of eight children born to the family). The Bronsteins were Jewish, a fact that would influence Trotsky's later fate. They were not wealthy—they had, Trotsky would later write, "a bleak sufficiency," no more—but from the very beginning note was taken of Trotsky's talent: his ability to read, speak, and, above all, to write.

The handsome, blue-eyed, bespectacled boy with the high forehead and curly dark hair was also arrogant. He went through the local Jewish primary school and was then able to attend a state high school in Odessa, where he was expelled for a year after disagreement with a teacher but still managed to graduate at the top of his class. However, he had difficulty managing relationships with people. He was so competitive, a classmate said, that "everywhere and always he had to be first." He had no close friends, although he did gather admirers of his eloquence and ability, even on a tight budget, to dress well.

Although he had once denounced Marxism, Bronstein was influenced by its tenets as the plight of workers and peasants—whom he saw daily, barefoot, dressed in rags—became worse and worse. Along with some former classmates, he formed a Social Democratic group called the South Russia Workers Union, which tried to unionize dock workers in the Black Sea town of Nikolayev in 1897. However, the group was amateurish and was soon infiltrated by czarist police. Lev was arrested and spent two years in an Odessa prison while his crime was being investigated. After that, he was exiled to Siberia.

Exile and jail—the true makings of a revolutionary. While spending three years in Siberia, Lev—who had taken the name Leon Trotsky as ironic tribute to one of his jailers in Odessa—married a young woman who gave birth to two daughters, but, as far as he was concerned, his family was expendable to the cause. Leaving them in Siberia, he escaped in September 1902. He eventually found his way to London, where he joined Lenin and other revolutionary exiles, who were writing and publishing a Social Democratic newspaper there. Soon, calling himself Pero, or "the Pen," Trotsky began writing as well.

COMRADE KOBA In the meantime, Soso—who had begun using the alias Koba—was also following the revolutionary's path. After organizing a workers' strike at a Rothschild-owned oil plant in Baku, Azerbaijan, he was arrested, jailed and exiled to Siberia, but he escaped, returned home and went underground. Unlike Trotsky, he wrote little, instead choosing a more violent way to aid the revolution. Joining forces with a man named Simon Ter-Petrossian, he planned bank robberies which eventually netted millions of dollars for the cause, even though enough innocent people were killed that the Bolsheviks—as the majority party of Social Democrats was now calling itself—condemned such actions in 1907.

Although Koba was careful not to risk his own neck in the robberies, they gave him a reputation as a man of action, a loyal party functionary who would do anything to advance the revolution. He was small, but broad-chested and powerful, and quickly intelligent, despite the impression he sometimes gave of being stolid and a little ponderous. The young revolutionary had numerous girlfriends, some of them schoolgirls in their early teens, who were attracted to his boldness and his unusual yellow-brown eyes. Between arrests, he met Vladimir Lenin, who would soon refer to him as "that splendid Georgian" and invite him to the Fifth Party Congress taking place in London in 1907. It was there that he and Trotsky first met. They were a study in contrasts. Trotsky, who had become indispensable to Lenin (although the two frequently had strong political differences), was everywhere, speaking eloquently on the cause of world revolution. Soso/Koba (who called himself "Ivanovitch" at the Congress) spent the entire three weeks without saying a single word.

He returned to Georgia and eventually moved to Moscow, where he became editor of the Bolshevik underground newspaper *Pravda*. For this, czarist authorities arrested him and he was sentenced in 1913 to permanent exile in northern Siberia, where he met and married a thirteen-year-old girl by whom he had two children. It was here he began calling himself "Stalin," which means "man of steel."

During his exile, World War I began and the fortunes of the Bolshevik party changed dramatically. Taking advantage of the disintegration of czarist power during the war, Lenin, Leon Trotsky, and other Bolsheviks seized power in St. Petersburg in October 1917. The Russian Revolution had begun.

"FROM AN UNDERGROUND EXISTENCE" After he had taken over in Russia, Lenin told Stalin that "to pass so quickly from an underground existence to power makes one dizzy." Stalin, however, did not play a large role in the events shaping the revolution of 1917–18. He was released from exile in March 1917 and, with Lenin and Trotsky still in exile, supported the moderate provisional government of Aleksandr Kerensky, a political mistake he hastily rectified when Lenin returned to Russia in April of that year and began planning the October uprising in St. Petersburg, soon to be renamed Petrograd. While Stalin would later rewrite his role in Soviet history books to make it seem as if he had been a planner of these epochal events, it was really Trotsky who, having returned from a lengthy stay in England and America, showed considerable organizational skill in fomenting the Bolshevik uprising.

While Stalin seemed to many to be a minor political functionary at the time (one Bolshevik wrote that he was "a grey blur, looming now and then dimly and not leaving any trace"), Trotsky was in his element. It was taken for granted by all concerned that he was Lenin's number two man and heir apparent. Trotsky became commissar of foreign affairs and then, in March 1918, after he helped negotiate a peace with Germany that resulted in the Treaty of Brest-Litovsk—a very costly peace to the new Russian government, but a necessary one—Trotsky became commissar of the army. The Russian Civil War had just begun, in which czarist sympathizers (the so-called White Army), actively supported by America, France and England, fought the Red Army across Russia for two bloody and violent years.

"A PRODUCT OF PARTY MACHINERY" Considering

his lack of military experience, Trotsky did very well, turning the poorly armed and poorly motivated Red Army into a cohesive fighting machine. He punished deserters ruthlessly—the Red Army was suffering massive defections—and also insisted on using former czarist officers, simply because they had the most experience in the field.

This caused a division between himself and Stalin, who had been made a commissar in charge of supplying the army in the south of Russia and did not want to use anyone associated with the former regime. By this time, Trotsky was aware of Stalin but did not consider him important. Trotsky would see him at meetings and party events in Moscow, smoking his pipe and listening silently. Trotsky later noted that "there was no sign of friendship" in the man's eyes when he looked at Trotsky, but he considered Stalin little more than "a product of the party machinery."

Underestimating Stalin was a grave error. The Georgian had apparently sensed weakness in Trotsky, a weakness he could use to help move himself up the party ladder. He resisted Trotsky's orders continuously, going around him to complain to Lenin (over the use of the czarist officers) and also demanding absurdly large amounts of supplies, which he knew Trotsky could not produce. Trotsky himself now complained to Lenin: "Stalin's actions are disrupting all my plans."

Lenin refused to take sides and would not remove Stalin from his position, to Trotsky's frustration. Even more interesting, Stalin would keep Trotsky off balance by making small gestures of friendship and even publishing an article in *Pravda* giving Trotsky credit for the successful October uprising of 1917:

> *All practical work in connection with the organization of the uprising was done under the immediate direction of Comrade Trotsky ... it can be stated with certainty that the party is indebted primarily and principally to [Trotsky].*

Trotsky, from the high intellectual eminence he occupied, had still not caught on that "the unremarkable Caucasian" was a serious foe.

"THE FUNERAL IS ON SATURDAY" In August 1918 Vladimir

Lenin was shot and nearly killed by a woman named Fanya Kaplan, a disillusioned Social Democrat. He recovered from the shooting, but with two bullets lodged in his body. A brutal repression ensued, with Stalin calling for "open and systematic mass terror" to be used against anyone disloyal to the regime. Between 1918 and 1920 perhaps twenty thousand were executed, a foreshadowing of things to come in the 1930s. Then, in May 1922, Lenin suffered a stroke, probably brought on by the bullet still lodged in his neck, which left him partially paralyzed on his left side. By December he had suffered another stroke, which caused him to retire from his active role as head of the Politburo, the Soviet Union's top executive organization.

STALIN'S GANG

Joseph Stalin, back when he was known as Comrade Koba, was one of the most daring bank robbers of his time, and his successful raid on the State Bank of Tiflis in Georgia in 1907 ranks with any of the wildest episodes of the James Gang of the old American West.

Stalin, fresh from seminary school and ready to prove his worth as a revolutionary, began robbing banks and feeding the money back to his Marxist comrades in St. Petersburg and abroad. With his usual love of jargon, Stalin called these "expropriations." Stalin was the mastermind of such operations, but the man who carried them out was Simon Ter-Petrossian, whose nickname was Kamo.

Kamo was born in 1882, the handsome son of a wealthy Armenian merchant. Early on, he fell under the sway of the young man whom his father referred to as "that good-for-nothing". Stalin, however, taught Kamo at least some Russian, playing on the young man's desire to be assimilated into mainstream Russian society. From there it was but a matter of a few months to teach him Marxism and show him how to handle a gun. Kamo proved a ready learner and a master of disguise—his adventures were such that one historian has called him "a Bolshevik superman." He was also not averse to violence: in his first robbery in February 1906, he killed the driver of a mail coach and made off with fifteen thousand rubles.

The most famous robbery of Stalin's gang took place on June 25, 1907, in the Georgian capital of Tiflis. That morning, in the middle of the bustling square at the center of the town, two mail coaches were delivering money to the State Bank. No one noticed two small carriages carrying a couple of young men and their ladies, as well as a mustachioed army officer. The officer was Kamo; the others were terrorists recruited by Stalin.

All of a sudden chaos erupted as the terrorists sprayed gunfire and hurled ten bombs at the mail carriages. As shrapnel cut down bank guards and innocent bystanders alike, the robbers escaped with sealed linen bags containing more than a quarter of a million rubles—about 3.4 million dollars in today's currency. The money was smuggled into Finland, to expatriate Bolsheviks there, and the terrorists scattered. As usual, Stalin himself took no part in the actual execution of the robbery, and apparently disowned Kamo's group after the London Fifth Party Congress condemned such actions, both because of the loss of innocent life and because, as it turned out, many of the five hundred ruble notes were marked by czarist authorities—Lenin himself was nearly caught trying to change one.

After his exile, Trotsky would try to reveal Stalin's role in masterminding this infamous robbery—"One wonders," he wrote, "why the official biographies are too cowardly to mention this?"—but, as usual, Stalin was successful in whitewashing his past.

BELOW Mug shots from 1912, showing the revolutionary soon to be known as Joseph Stalin, at the time when he was editor of the newspaper *Pravda*. They are from the file on Stalin held by the St Petersburg imperial police.

A further stroke in March 1923 left him unable to speak, until a fourth and last stroke finally killed him on January 21, 1924. After he first retired from politics, Lenin wrote a letter that has been called "Lenin's Testament." In it he called Trotsky "probably the most capable man in the current Central Committee," while at the same time asking those in power to "think about removing Stalin" from his current post as general secretary of the Communist Party because he could not be trusted to use power wisely.

Both Trotsky and Stalin were aware of this testament before Lenin died and it is interesting how each reacted to it. Trotsky, seeing that it practically anointed him as Lenin's heir apparent, simply went about business as usual, expecting that power would come to him when Lenin died, but Stalin began maneuvering behind the scenes. His first real power play was simple. When Lenin died, Trotsky happened to be Tiflis. Stalin sent him a telegram that Lenin had passed away and Trotsky replied that he would return to attend the funeral.

Stalin's telegram back read: "The funeral is on Saturday, you won't be in time. The Politburo thinks that in your state of health [Trotsky had been feeling unwell] you should go to Sukhumi [a resort city on the Black Sea]."

In fact, the funeral was on Sunday, January 27th. This apparently caring and concerned telegram was a clever salvo in Stalin's war against Trotsky. Believing his rival's lie, Trotsky did not show up at the funeral, which in the atmosphere of suspicion pervading Soviet politics was seen as a serious sign of disrespect for Lenin and possibly a sign that Trotsky was on the outs with the party elite. His decision not to attend was a foolish one; a more wily politician would have seen through Stalin and headed straight for Moscow. One historian has called it "perhaps the decisive moment leading to Trotsky's defeat."

BANISHMENT In the ensuing years, Trotsky's weaknesses and Stalin's strengths were starkly exposed. Trotsky could still move people with his speeches and his writing, but in his intellectual arrogance and coldness was unable to put together the infrastructure of support that every politician needs. Stalin, on the other hand, could easily play the hard-drinking, back-slapping politician, and he had far fewer scruples than Trotsky. Events began passing Trotsky by; he still clung to his leftist roots, which called for a world communist takeover, whereas Stalin had moved to the center and was interested mainly in consolidating power in Russia, where he eventually destroyed everyone who had once been close to him.

Stalin waged an unrelenting propaganda war against Trotsky, exposing articles that Trotsky had written as far back as 1913, during some of his disagreements with Lenin, and using these to prove that Trotsky had been disloyal. In 1925, Trotsky was relieved of his job as military commissar, probably at the behest of Stalin, who did not want Trotsky turning the Red Army on him—but that was something Stalin might do, not Trotsky. Trotsky was now sidelined into minor positions, while Stalin in his position as general secretary grew ever more powerful. Hopelessly on the defensive under what his second wife, Natalya, later described as a "storm" of attacks, Trotsky found himself stripped of his party membership in 1927 as a "divisive" element. According to Stalin, Trotsky had tried to seize Lenin's authority after the revolution, he was a secret capitalist, and he was an instrument of terror. Trotsky was featured in anti-Semitic cartoons in newspapers and personified in posters as a Jewish demon who consorted with wealthy Western industrialists.

Stalin began killing and imprisoning Trotsky's supporters; he did not dare do this yet to Trotsky himself, but in 1929 he did exile him.

MISERY Trotsky's first stop was Turkey, where he stayed for four years. After that, he spent time in France and Norway before finally arriving in Mexico, in 1937, continually dogged by the spies of Stalin's secret police, the OGU and the NKVD. He became the voice for international revolution, the voice against Stalin in the world. Stalin, in the meantime, had fully consolidated power in the Soviet Union under his own rule, and had began the killings of the Great Terror. Trotsky's family was a prime target. Although his brother Alexander renounced him publicly, he was shot in 1938. His older sister had died of cancer in 1924, but his younger sister was executed by Stalin's secret police in 1941. Both her sons, Trotsky's nephews, were shot in 1936.

Trotsky's elder son, Lev, was poisoned by Soviet agents while recovering from appendicitis in a Paris hospital in 1938. His younger son, Sergey, was arrested in Russia in 1937 and simply disappeared. (Sergey's wife, speaking bitterly of Trotsky, said: "He brought misery to everyone he came in contact with.") Even the children of Trotsky's first wife were not forgotten. His younger daughter, Nina, died of tuberculosis but her end was probably hastened by the fact that Stalin had her husband shot. The elder, Zina, killed herself in Berlin, unhinged by the incredible vengeance Stalin was aiming at Trotsky.

Despite this, Trotsky continued to write and speak out against Stalin. He wrote a history of the Russian Revolution and an autobiography, and spoke out in interviews in the world press against the totalitarian dead-end into which Stalin had directed the revolution. The Moscow show trials of the 1930s were a particular target—Trotsky published two books, *The Revolution Betrayed* and Stalin's *Crimes*, which attempted to expose the trials as shams. This enraged Stalin, who, in the late 1930s, understood the threat raised by Hitler's Nazi Party and wanted support from Western powers such as Great Britain and America. Deciding that Trotsky must be dealt with once and for all, he instructed the NKVD to assassinate him.

Trotsky's house in Mexico City was surrounded by high walls and guarded by bodyguards, but Soviet agents dressed in police and army uniforms launched a daring assault on it at 4:00 a.m. on May 24, 1940, blasting the bedroom where Trotsky and Natalya slept with machine-gun fire. Over two hundred bullets pocked the walls, but ended up missing their targets as they huddled in terror in a corner, Natalya covering Trotsky's body with her own.

THE GREAT TERROR

Once Stalin had exiled Trotsky and consolidated his power—by 1930—he was able to begin purging his opponents. Trotsky's family, almost completely wiped out by Stalin's police, was just the tip of the iceberg. Former czarist supporters were the first to go, followed by those who had supposedly betrayed Communist ideals. These were tried in kangaroo courts in great "show trials" intended to show the Soviet people—and the world—that Stalin's enemies were legion and needed to be eliminated. Their crimes were vague: "lack of faith in the Soviet state" was one common charge. Confessions were wrenched out by torture and the "guilty" disappeared into gulags in Siberia—when Stalin died in 1953 there were twelve million people in the concentration camps—or were executed with a bullet to the back of the head.

It was not just the show trials, of course. By forcing collectivization on millions of farmers, Stalin starved to death ten million Russians and Ukrainians in just a few years. As Robert Conquest pointed out in his pivotal book *The Great Terror*, published in the 1960s and the first major work to expose the evil workings of Stalin's regime, perhaps twenty million people in all died while Stalin was lionized by leftists in the West. There were "gulag-deniers" just as there are now "holocaust-deniers," prominent among them the famous philosopher Jean-Paul Sartre. In the end, though, the evidence is incontrovertible: Joseph Stalin perpetrated one of the greatest crimes in human history.

ABOVE Russian women using crude rakes to gather up the hay harvest on a collective farm outside Moscow in August 1941. Stalin's policy of forced collectivization of farms resulted in food shortages and millions of deaths.

TROTSKY'S ASSASSIN

His full name was Jaime Ramón Mercader del Rio Hernandez and he was a passionately committed Communist—that much was understood at the time of Trotsky's death. Mercader carried a letter in his pocket at the time of the assassination stating that he had become disillusioned with Trotsky because Trotsky had told him that he intended to go to Russia and kill his old comrade, Stalin. No one at the time suspected that this letter had been written by the NKVD, the Russian secret service, and that Mercader was a full agent of the NKVD, carrying out Stalin's express orders to kill Trotsky.

Jaime Mercader was born in Barcelona in 1914, the son of a businessman and a beautiful but unstable Cuban mother, Eustacia. During the Spanish Civil War, Eustacia left her husband and five sons, joined the Communist Party, and eventually became an NKVD agent. It was through her that Jaime himself became an NKVD operative. The NKVD inserted him into Trotskyite circles in 1938 and he began his seduction of twenty-eight-year-old Sylvia Agelof, a New York-born adherent of Trotsky who served as his secretary. The Trotsky household guards got used to seeing her handsome boyfriend, who called himself Frank Jacson, drop her off and pick her up after work. Gradually, Trotsky got to know Mercader and liked the young man, who professed himself to be an admirer.

And so, on that fateful day in August 1940 when he showed up with a raincoat over his arm, looking nervous, no one thought too much about it. The letter found in his pocket led to his being dismissed as the kind of solitary and disgruntled nut who often commits assassinations. During the twenty years he spent in a Mexican prison (five of them in total solitary) Mercader never varied from his story that he was the only one involved. In fact, he had been directed by his handler, the NKVD Colonel Naum Eitingon, who told him "Mexico is the ideal country" in which to assassinate Trotsky because it did not have a death penalty if he were caught. And Mercader's own mother was involved, waiting in a car just outside Trotsky's villa with Eitingon. They sped away when it became clear Mercader had been trapped by Trotsky's guards and would not escape.

In 1960, Mercader was released from prison and deported directly to Moscow where he was made a hero of the Soviet Union, one of only twenty-one non-Soviet citizens to be given the honor. Mercader eventually moved to Cuba, where he died in 1978.

BELOW A trio of pictures published in *Time* magazine on September 2, 1940: Trotsky lies fatally wounded in hospital (left), the reaction of his widow (centre), and his attacker, Ramon Mercader, a Stalinist agent, who was wounded by Trotsky's bodyguards.

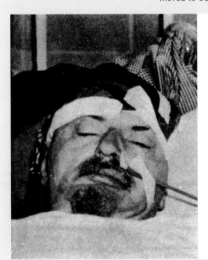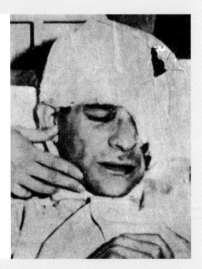

Astonishingly, Communists fed the press the story that Trotsky had arranged this attempt on his own life in order to smear Stalin.

THE DEATH OF LEON TROTSKY

Trotsky survived, but not for long. Working on yet another book about Stalin that summer, he made the acquaintance of a young man who had become engaged to marry his secretary and who professed great admiration for him. The man called himself Frank Jacson but his real name was Jaime Ramón Mercader; he was an assassin in the employ of the NKVD. On Tuesday, August 20, 1940, he arrived, suspiciously carrying a raincoat over his arm on what was a very hot day. Still, no one looked askance at him as he engaged Trotsky in conversation, then followed him into his study and asked him to take a look at an article he, Mercader, had written. As Trotsky bent over his desk to examine it, Mercader took out a cut-down mountaineer's ice ax from under the raincoat (not an ice pick, as has been so often cited) and jammed it into the base of Trotsky's brain.

He had been told by his NKVD handlers that this would kill Trotsky instantly, but instead Trotsky screamed—a cry that was heard all over the house—and rushed at Mercader, grabbing at him and biting his hand. Mercader was captured by Trotsky's bodyguards and turned over to the Mexican police. Trotsky had the strength to tell his bodyguards to stop beating his assassin: "He must not be killed; he must talk." Despite the best efforts of his doctors, Trotsky died the next day at the age of sixty.

Ironically enough, Mercader was later to say that "terrorism is necessary in the struggle for Communism." He was quoting Trotsky himself. While Trotsky, the eternal revolutionary, was violently opposed to Stalin, he probably would have pursued similar policies, especially when it came to the enforced farm collectivization of the 1930s, which left millions of Soviet peasants dead of starvation. In the end, however, Stalin was the doer, Trotsky the dreamer, and the brilliant orator and writer paid for it with his life.

CHIANG KAI-SHEK

CHIANG KAI-SHEK AND MAO ZEDONG: BATTLE FOR A NATION

E ARLY ON A SNOWY MORNING IN DECEMBER 1936, Generalissimo Chiang Kai-shek—leader of the Nationalist Chinese forces, self-proclaimed ruler of over 450 million people—awoke in a lovely palace complex that had been built, during the Ming dynasty, around hot springs outside the northern Chinese city of Xi'an. The complex had a lotus pool, an ornate bathhouse and numerous decorated pavilions with curved roofs. Past emperors had entertained their concubines there, but Chiang was in residence for a very different reason. On this morning, December 12, he was about to order his Nationalist forces to launch an all-out attack on a major Communist base to the north of Xi'an—the base where the ragged Communist army had come to rest after their Long March of 6,000 miles that had lasted 369 days and cost thousands of lives.

Chiang was finally poised to crush his arch-enemy, Mao Zedong, the man who had harried and harassed him for the last ten years. Now that final victory was at hand, Chiang had made a point of personally coming to direct the attack that he publicly referred to as "the last five minutes" of his war to annihilate Mao and his army. But, unknown to Chiang, victory was about to be snatched from his grasp.

The previous day, in the Communists' cave headquarters, Mao's secretary had handed him a cable written in a secret code the secretary was unable to decipher. Mao took one look at it and smiled. "There's good news on the way," he said.

As Chiang began his morning exercise ritual, gunfire broke out around the palace complex. A force of about 120 soldiers had arrived in four trucks, shot and killed Chiang's sentries, and begun to fight with his bodyguards as they attempted to get closer to his quarters. Still in pajamas, the fifty-year-old Chiang leaped over a ten-foot wall, fell into a disused moat, and then, limping, made his way up the mountain that rose behind the complex. Bullets whizzed by him; two of his bodyguards dropped dead and others were wounded. At last, he and a few men bruised and shivering, found refuge in a cave. Outside, they could hear the enemy soldiers closing in.

CHINA: DYING TO BE REBORN From 1934 to 1949, Mao Zedong and Chiang Kai-shek went head to head in a struggle that left no part of China untouched, and powerfully altered the geopolitical balance of the twentieth century. Each man loathed the other, but they had numerous similarities. Both came from country villages (and made much of that fact), married first wives chosen for them by their mothers, worshipped Chinese reformer Sun Yat-sen, were supremely nationalistic, and distrusted the foreign alliances they were forced to make. Both men were made of steel—were, as one observer wrote, "persistent, merciless and highly ambitious." Each man was convinced to an extraordinary degree that he, alone, personified his country. And each man knew that theirs was a contest that could only end in the complete destruction of the other.

The historian Jonathan Spence has written of Mao that "his visions of social and economic change became hopelessly enmeshed with violence and fear," and the same holds true of Chiang, although he envisioned a capitalist republic, not a socialist utopia. It is estimated that, between 1926 and 1949, thirty-five million people died in China through war or famine. Millions of these deaths can be attributed directly to the bitter struggle between Mao Zedong and Chiang Kai-shek.

Chiang was born in 1887, Mao in 1893, into a China undergoing one of the bleakest periods in its history. Most of the population was rural, illiterate, and profoundly impoverished. Although the nineteenth century was drawing to a close, old customs and superstitions abounded. Trial magistrates accepted hearsay testimony from ghosts; periodic panics arose as witch hunts took place for "evil characters." Convicted criminals were subjected to draconian punishments, including stoning, beheading, and being placed in cages to die a slow death from exposure and malnutrition. It was commonplace for droughts, floods, and cholera epidemics to kill many thousands of people every year.

The Qing dynasty, which had ruled for 250 years, was corrupt and tottering. The country was being eaten away by foreign powers. The Japanese, victors in a short, bloody war in 1894, had staked claims in Manchuria and annexed the island of Taiwan. The Germans had taken over areas in north China, the British were expanding their holdings in the central part of the country, and the French were moving in from the southwest.

Change was in the air. Particularly in the coastal cities, a new middle class had begun to emerge: doctors, lawyers, and merchants with Western education and a sense that political and social transformation was necessary to advance China into the twentieth century.

CHIANG Chiang Kai-shek was born in the eastern seaboard province of Zhejiang. The Chiangs, who claimed to come from nobility, owned a salt shop in their village of Xikou and Chiang was schooled by a tutor, in part because he was often in bad health. As a boy, he was well known for being imperious, controlling, reckless, and also seeking to be the center of attention—traits that would follow him into adulthood. During childhood play, Chiang later told a journalist, "I was frequently exposed to the risk of being drowned or burnt to death or else severely cut or wounded." He once put chopsticks down his throat to see how far he could push them, and another time nearly drowned by thrusting his head into the tight neck of a large water jar. Yet he was a leader. A contemporary remembered that, in their boyhood games of war, "[Chiang] liked to be at the head of the children."

Chiang's father died when he was seven, and the salt store had to be sold. Now without influence, the widow Wang, as she was called, was forced to take in sewing to make ends meet. At one point, tax collectors imprisoned Chiang until his mother could pay their bill, an injustice that Chiang would always remember. In a privately circulated memoir he wrote as he turned fifty, he said: "My family, solitary and without influence, became at once the target of insults and maltreatment." After his ten-year-old brother died, Chiang became his mother's sole hope in life. When he was fourteen, she arranged a marriage for him to a young, illiterate village girl named Mao Fumei, but the marriage was not a successful one—he (and his mother) mistreated her, even refusing to allow her to laugh and speak in the house, and Chiang beat her and at one point dragged her across the room by her hair. Chiang, far more than Mao Zedong, was imperious when it came to social class; his wife received the treatment a Qing nobleman might accord a servant. Chiang valued—more than merit or talent—total obedience by those he considered his subordinates. (It was why he ultimately surrounded himself with corrupt lackeys, while Mao, in his own way equally autocratic, managed to find men of quality to serve under him.)

At the age of sixteen, Chiang left his village to attend Phoenix Mountain School in the district capital, where he led a protest calling for better teachers. Around this time he read a book that inflamed his imagination. Written by an anonymous author, *The Revolutionary Handbook* called for a mass revolt of the Chinese people and the establishment of a constitutional republic based on that of the United States. By the time he was eighteen, Chiang had decided to go to military school, where he could learn how to fight and lead men in combat. Young Chinese men of Chiang's generation knew that the best military training was to be had in Japan, which had now defeated both Russia and China in war, and which had a forward-looking industrialism that was very different from China's backward economy. In 1905, cutting off his queue, or long pigtail—a symbol of submission to the imperial dynasty—he went to Japan to attend military college. His relatives were alarmed at his radical actions, but his mother, ever faithful, sold possessions to pay for his trip and schooling.

MAO Mao Zedong was born in the rural province of Hunan, where his parents owned a three-acre farm, considered a very decent size by the Chinese standards of the time. (Mao would later exaggerate the poverty of his upbringing for, although his parents could be classed as peasants, they were in fact members of a comfortable lower middle class.) Mao had six brothers and sisters, although only he and two brothers would survive childhood disease and live to adulthood. Like Chiang, Mao was quite close to his mother, a devout Buddhist, whose love, he would later write, "was extended to all, far and near." There are few records of Mao's childhood. He was not close to his father and appears to have lived with his grandparents during a large portion of his early life, since his father served for long periods as a soldier in the provincial army, and was often away.

At the age of fourteen, Mao—able now to read and use an abacus—left school to keep books and accounts for his father, with whom he did not get along. "The first capitalist I struggled against," he told American journalist Edgar Snow in 1936, "was my father." He was married—like Chiang's, his union was arranged by his mother—to a nineteen-year-old girl named Lo-shi from a neighboring clan. Their marriage lasted two years, until her death from causes unknown in 1909, at the age of twenty-one. They did not have children and Mao in later years denied the marriage, claiming that his second wife was his first. Yet it is possible that the shock of Lo-shi's passing forced Mao to look outward, to think of the world beyond his family and village.

Around this time, a cousin sent Mao a book that would have a dramatic impact on his life. Called *Words of Warning to an Affluent Age*, it was written by Zheng Guanying, a merchant with extensive foreign contacts, and warned against the danger of the Japanese, English, and Americans taking over the country. The book urged Chinese to modernize in order to meet this threat, and it made the extremely radical suggestion that parliamentary government should be introduced to China. *Words of Warning*, Mao later told a journalist, "stimulated in me a desire to resume my studies." He moved, first to neighboring Xiangxiang, a bustling market town, and then, in 1910, at the age of seventeen, to Changsha, the provincial capital of Hunan. Armed with a letter from a former teacher, he was admitted on scholarship to a school for young rural men, and began to learn something of the wider world. He read a pamphlet called "The Dismemberment of China," and always remembered its opening line: "Alas, China will be subjugated." But, during his study of the American Revolution, he was equally impressed by a sentence in a textbook that read: "After eight years of difficult war, Washington won victory and built up his nation."

REVOLUTIONARY BEGINNINGS It was the political radical Sun Yat-sen's uprising of 1911 that gave both Chiang and Mao a first taste of revolution and set them on a collision course. At that time the country was being ruled by regents, on behalf of the six-year-old Emperor Pu Yi. The exiled Sun

Yat-sen had secretly built up an infrastructure of activists in the Qing army and court. In the spring of 1911, at a signal from Sun, an uprising was launched in Guangzhou and then spread to other cities. By October, there was a massive military mutiny in Wuhan. In February, the Qing regents abdicated and China became a republic.

Mao cut off his queue in solidarity with the rebels and was so inspired when he heard a member of the revolutionary army address his school that he decided to leave Changsha immediately and join the mutiny taking place in Wuhan, which was not far away. He was delayed, however, because he could not find his galoshes—and Wuhan was known to be a rainy city. By the time he located them, the uprising in Wuhan was over. (This is a comical bit of history and underscores Mao's extreme practicality, but according to historians it is also quite possible that Mao had doubts about his course of action, once his passions died down a bit.)

Chiang took a far more active role in the events of 1911 than Mao. Along with a follower of Sun Yat-sen's named Chen Qimei, who became his closest friend, Chiang returned from Japan to Shanghai to lead an artillery regiment that helped defeat Qing forces. By the spring of 1912, China was, suddenly, a republic, led by Sun Yat-sen, who had returned from exile. Afterwards, Chiang and Chen stayed in Shanghai, where Chiang met Sun Yat-sen and quickly became one of his close advisors. Chiang and Chen also forged links with the Shanghai underworld, particularly with a gang boss called Big-Eared Du, leader of the Green Gang (so-called for their supposed love of jade). For the next twenty years Chiang would call on Du whenever he needed kidnapping, robbery or extortion undertaken.

By the fall of 1912, Sun Yat-sen had formed the Nationalist Party, or Kuomintang (KMT), but he was pushed out of power by a former Qing general named Yuan Shikai who, with the aid of a rich American businessman, declared himself the new monarch of China. Chiang, Chen, and Sun led a series of revolutionary actions against Yuan's regime. In retaliation, Yuan had Chen assassinated and drove Chiang and Sun into hiding. Finally, the two were successful in pushing Yuan out, although the KMT was too weak to take and hold power. Thus an era of civil war began, as the country was torn apart by battling warlords who were either former generals in the imperial army, locally powerful landlords with ambitions, or underworld gangsters trying to carve out as big a piece of the pie as they could. Chiang served his apprenticeship in this vicious world of Chinese power politics and then he was ready for the next step: to conquer China and make himself ruler.

Mao, meanwhile, had left Hunan to study at Beijing University. His own revolutionary ideals were shaped not by bullet and sword, but by studying Adam Smith, Charles Darwin, John Stuart Mill, and Jean-Jacques Rousseau. To those around him (including his father, who stopped sending him money) he seemed aimless—a daydreamer who spent all his time in the library among his books while epochal events were happening around him. Once, when students at the university clashed with authorities, Mao hid in a toilet. By 1918, and possibly before, he had read Marxist theory and had joined a group of students inspired by the Bolshevik victory in Russia. He was now twenty-five and fell in love—with his teacher's daughter, eighteen-year-old Yang Kaihui. Together, they traveled to Shanghai to live together, and eventually they were married. Mao ran a successful bookstore there.

By 1921, Mao had joined the Communist Party. Aided by the Russian Comintern, which had infiltrated numerous student cells and study groups, he traveled around China, looking at working conditions in factories and coalmines. He then became a professional revolutionary organizer, having learned how to coordinate strikes of thousands of workers. Because of Mao and other party members, powerful unions began to form in Shanghai and other major cities.

In 1925, Sun Yat-sen died of cancer and Chiang Kai-shek emerged as leader of the Nationalist forces, by dint of having most of his rivals killed—he personally shot and killed one competitor while the man lay sick in a hospital bed. But before his death, Sun had merged the KMT with the growing Communist Party, thinking the two forces could band together when the day came to face the inevitable Japanese invasion.

So it was that in 1926, when Chiang and Mao met for the first time, they met as allies. Mao was head of the Propaganda Department of the KMT and attended a June meeting where Chiang, along with his loyal cadre of army officers, planned the joint KMT–Communist offensive against the warlords who controlled the northern part of the country. Unlike their second, much-recorded meeting in 1945, neither man left a written account of this earlier encounter, but it is impossible to imagine they had much in common. Despite the similarities in their upbringing, the two had already embarked on very different courses. The thirty-three-year-old Mao was a lanky, awkward young man with country ways—including a love of hot, peppery food and plump peasant girls—still clinging to him. Seven years older, Chiang—who had seen combat, killed men, and was far worldlier—was a ramrod-straight figure with a shaved head and wearing a military uniform. He was surrounded, an observer noted, by a "fanatically loyal cadre of young officers [already] growing rich by black market deals sanctioned by a leader who turned a blind eye."

Chiang's goal was to change China into a republic, open it up to the West, and thereby have it advance into the twentieth century in military might and industry. Mao's deep desire, stated at the time in a letter to a revolutionary comrade, was to "act energetically to carry out the great union of the popular masses without delay. The world is ours, the state is ours, society is ours."

One thing they still had in common: the desire to be in total and complete control of China.

THE BARREL OF A GUN At first, the so-called "United Front" operated effectively in the Northern Expedition against the warlords who were dividing the country. In August of 1926, the combined KMT–Communist forces had swept through Hunan, winning battle after battle, but by the spring of 1927 the United Front had fallen apart. Chiang watched as the Communists gained more and more power—they had 57,000 members by the end of 1926—and as the labor unions in the large cities began to assert themselves. Fearing a Communist takeover, Chiang decided to strike first. Allied with the Green Gang, and with the financial support of Americans who also feared the growing Communist power, Chiang rounded up and killed thousands of Communist labor union members in Shanghai.

One of Chiang's targets was Mao, who barely escaped Shanghai and was forced to leave his wife, Yang, and three small children behind. He fled to the northern city of Wuhan, enraged by Chiang's actions. In a report he sent to the Comintern in Moscow, Mao described the KMT as "an empty house, led by no one"—a deliberate disparagement of Chiang's leadership. Yet, at the same time, he pointed out that Chiang had risen by "grasping the gun." In the next sentence, Mao went on to pen his famous dictum: "We must know that political power is obtained from the barrel of a gun." He immediately set about building an army, but of the thousands of Communist Party members, only a few were willing to join him in open warfare against Chiang. In the first skirmishes his poorly trained factory workers and peasant farmers were consistently beaten by Chiang's Nationalist army, and Mao retreated deeper into the countryside, to the rugged mountains of Kiangsi Province.

In the meantime, Yang, with the three children, had escaped Shanghai to Changsha, the capital city of Hunan, where she and Mao had met. By 1930, they were living there in very low profile, out of touch with the isolated Mao, trapped in the mountains by Chiang's army. Because of attacks in the Changsha area by local Communists, the KMT mounted a series of reprisals, executing Communists wherever they could find them. Yang was discovered. When she refused to betray Mao's whereabouts—it is almost certain she did not know precisely where he was, in any event—she was beheaded at the orders of a Nationalist general. The three children were saved by a neighbor, although they lived a hand-to-mouth existence for years. The youngest died, but the two oldest boys were finally rescued and taken to Moscow by the Russian Communist Party, and Mao was reunited with them in 1946.

Even before Yang's death, Mao had taken up with He Zizhen, the woman who would later become his third wife, but he was grief-stricken when he heard about the death of Yang and the uncertain fate of his children. The preponderance of evidence is that Chiang did not personally order Yang's execution, but it is also likely that Mao believed he did. After finding out about Yang's death, Mao became ill with various mysterious ailments and was almost removed from the leadership by the party. He wrote to his younger brother, Mao Zetan, telling him that he had dreamed about "the death of the Generalissimo."

CHIANG'S WOMEN …

Chiang Kai-shek and Mao Zedong were desperate rivals, but were similar when it came to their dramatic relationships with women.

Chiang was married three times. His first marriage, to Mao Fumei, was arranged by his mother in his home village. He abandoned Mao by 1920 and she died in a Japanese air raid in 1939.

He married his second wife, Chen Jieru, in 1921. They lived together in Shanghai and Canton while Chiang fought his way to the top of the Nationalist party, at which point he dumped her, sent her to America, and later denied that they were married at all.

He did this because he wanted to enter into a politically advantageous marriage to Meiling Soong, the beautiful, American-educated, younger sister of Sun Yat-sen's widow. Madame Chiang, as she became known to an adoring American public, acted as the Generalissimo's interpreter and knew how to charm everybody, journalists, especially. (One correspondent described her as "quite dishy—it isn't fright that sends shivers down your spine when you shake hands with her.") Madame Chiang also wanted to influence American electoral politics. During a trip to Washington in 1943, she had an affair with would-be Republican presidential candidate Wendell Wilkie. She told Wilkie backer Gardener Cowles that she did not trust current President Franklin Roosevelt and would be willing to spend large sums to elect Wilkie.

It was, as Cowles later noted, "a totally mad proposal," but "I was so mesmerized by clearly one of the most formidable women of the time that this evening I would not have dismissed anything she said."

ABOVE Chinese Nationalist leader Generalissimo Chiang Kai-shek and his third wife, Meiling Soong, who became known to the world as Madame Chiang, in a photograph from the early 1930s.

… AND MAO'S WOMEN

Mao's mother arranged his first marriage, to Lo-shi, a young girl who was also distantly related to him. She died of undisclosed causes soon thereafter. In 1924 he married Yang Kaihui, the daughter of his professor, in Shanghai, but in 1927 he had to flee to the mountains to escape Chiang Kai-shek's Nationalist army, and there he began an affair with a beautiful Chinese Communist poet named He Zizhen. A few years later, Yang was executed by Nationalist forces and Mao married He Zizhen.

In 1939, at his cave headquarters in Yan'an, Mao was introduced to Jian Qing and shortly thereafter divorced He Zizhen and married Jian. Jian was a lovely, vivacious Shanghai film actress, but after Mao's total victory, she, like Madame Chiang, let power go to her head. Madame Mao, as she was called, ruthlessly suppressed evidence of her past, killing film directors and actors she had worked with. She spent a great deal of time playing cards and repeatedly watching *Gone with the Wind*. Sensitive to noise, she forced servants in the Beijing palace to wear sheepskin clothes to muffle sound.

After Mao died, however, her enemies had their revenge. Madame Mao was tried and convicted for being part of the so-called "Gang of Four," traitors to the revolutionary cause. She was sentenced to death, although the sentence was commuted to live imprisonment. She was released to house arrest in 1991 and died in 1993, some say by her own hand.

From 1930 to 1934, Chiang Kai-shek launched repeated assaults against Mao in his mountain fortress, the Kiangsi Soviet. Unlike Mao, Chiang did not often accompany his army to the field, preferring to command from afar, but there is no doubt that he saw Mao as a stubborn symbol of resistance against his regime. By this time, he was firm friends with the American government and American business interests, and he told a press conference that "Mao and his army are all that stand in the way of peace and a united China," as he had either vanquished the opposing warlords, or bribed them into being his allies. He continued to play up Mao's very real connection with Russian Communism and Joseph Stalin, repeating to more than one journalist that Mao was "Stalin's puppet."

The Luce media empire, in particular, loved Chiang, and he was often featured on the cover of *Life* magazine. The press saw Chiang's rigid self-control, but did not witness his truly volcanic temper or his bouts of debauchery with alcohol and women, particularly Shanghai "sing-song girls." Chiang had long since divorced his first wife. Showing his opportunistic nature, he had proposed to Sun Yat-sen's widow almost immediately after Sun died. When she refused him, he married her younger sister so he could position himself as Sun Yat-sen's brother-in-law.

As Chiang became sleeker and more well groomed, Mao in his mountain redoubt was the opposite: shaggy and shambling, a foreshadowing of the bear-like man he would later become physically. Where Chiang exhibited self-control, Mao was folksy and expansive, but he had a politician's touch of seeming to take anyone he talked to into his confidence. At the same time, he had ruthlessly eliminated his enemies within the Communist Party, and he went through women nearly as rapidly as Chiang.

At the moment, Chiang was in the ascendancy, Mao on the run, but the tables were about to be turned.

THE CAPTIVE GENERALISSIMO
Mao held out as long as he could in Kiangsi, but when his position became untenable under Chiang's repeated attacks, he decided he had to abandon his base. In October 1934, he began what would become known as the Long March. A column of almost ninety thousand Communist troops, including Mao and his pregnant third wife, He Zizhen, headed north. The march was nightmarish and brutal. The Communists were harried the entire way by KMT troops at one point a devastating artillery and bomber attack caused nearly forty thousand casualties. He Zizhen was nearly killed in a bombing raid; when she gave birth, to a daughter, the girl had to be left behind with a local peasant family, and was never found again.

By the fall of 1935, only fifteen thousand starving Communists reached a base in northern China, near Yan'an, which had caves for them to hide in and ample provisions. But Mao was now cornered, and Chiang moved in for the kill, for that "last five minutes" before total victory. That was when Mao pounced on his rival.

OPPOSITE PAGE Mao Zedong (left) pictured with fellow Communist leader Zhou Enlai in 1935, during the Long March north from Kiangsi to Yan'an to escape Chiang's Nationalist forces.

For the first time, Chiang was personally within Mao's grasp. Harried into a remote corner of China, having lost tens of thousands of his followers, including his younger brother (who had died fighting a rearguard action), as well as his second wife and, for all he knew, four children, Mao had a debt to settle with Chiang. Much later, he told a gathering of Chinese students that Chiang's arrival to join the KMT forces was "heaven-sent"—odd language for a Communist, but such was his desire to even the score.

Mao's heartiness and politicking had paid off, for he and his Communists had secretly wooed the former warlord of Manchuria, General Zhang Xueliang, who had been forced out of his homeland by Japanese forces but who still had a large army. Chiang thought General Zhang was on his side, but Zhang had gone over to Mao and his men. On December 12, Zhang sent his forces against the palace complex at Xi'an, to capture the Generalissimo and take him captive.

After the attack on the palace complex around the hot springs, Chiang hid in his cave for as long as he could. Finally, surrounded and freezing, he gave himself up and was taken to Zhang's military headquarters. It was too risky for Mao to be present, lest the KMT mount a massive rescue assault (in fact, Nationalist generals had to be restrained by Madame Chiang Kai-shek from bombing Zhang's headquarters). Instead, he sent Zhou Enlai, his able lieutenant, to discuss the options with Zhang. Mao's initial desire, as he later described it to a reporter, was "to kill the man who had done so much evil to the people," but his wish was thwarted for a number of reasons.

The ever-paranoid Joseph Stalin told Mao that he was certain Zhang was a "tool of the Japanese"—that he had kidnapped Chiang at the orders of the Japanese in order to eliminate a potent enemy against their advance through China. Pressure, too, came from the Americans. The American ambassador dismissed Zhang as "a first class Chicago gangster," and the pro-Chiang *Life* magazine dubbed him "villain of the week." Chiang, too, was active. With Zhang wavering under pressure, Chiang was able to give an interview to an American journalist, in which he described Mao as a "red puppet" and vowed that, even if he were killed, the Nationalist cause would triumph.

Although it must have been hard for him to resist shooting the man who had been out to destroy him for so long, Mao was a realist. In a brilliant propaganda ploy, he announced that he would release Chiang if the latter promised to lay down his arms against the Communists and join forces with them in a "Second United Front" to attack the Japanese, who were advancing through Manchuria. Should Chiang fail to do this and civil war resume, he would be "solely responsible" for the outcome.

Chiang was forced to agree to Mao's terms in order to win his release. Of course, he intended to attack the Communists again as soon as possible, but the kidnapping was a shock to him—he fell ill afterwards and it took him weeks to recover—and the final assault against Mao and his men was postponed, and then

炮 打 司 令 部
（我的一张大字报）

无产阶级文化大革命全面胜利万岁

postponed again. It was all the breathing room the Communists needed. They were able to regroup and, with help from the Russians, re-arm. Moreover, Mao's victory over Chiang had given him a boost in stature in the eyes of the Chinese people. In 1939, the first Mao posters began to appear, showing Mao moving heroically at the head of a marching column of troops.

THE SINO-JAPANESE WAR Many years after the war, when Mao was ruler of all China, he received a delegation of Japanese visitors who were there to apologize for their country's conduct in China. They were surprised when Mao laughed and told them not to bother—if it had not been for the Japanese, he would still be living in a cave in the wilderness. This was an exaggeration, but only a slight one.

In fact, both Mao and Chiang made highly pragmatic use of the 1937–1945 war against the Japanese. Mao and his forces actually did relatively little fighting, preferring to keep to the vast deserted areas inside rural China and harry the Japanese in guerrilla actions. Chiang also shaped the war to his needs, but in

ABOVE During Mao's struggles of the 1930s it would have been difficult to predict the god-like status he would eventually have within China, as reflected on this banner from August 1967, during the Cultural Revolution.

a different way. In 1939, Shanghai and then Nanjing fell to the Japanese. Even though it was hopeless, Chiang had put up a military defense of the cities and suffered 250,000 casualties. Some observers wondered why, but there was a reason behind it. Chiang wanted to show the West that the Nationalists would not give in to the Japanese, would keep on fighting and tie down as many of the enemy as possible in China. After Pearl Harbor, the Americans sent Chiang Land Lease armaments, advisors, and millions upon millions of dollars. Very few Americans—General Joseph Stillwell was one who did—realized that Chiang's real plan was to stockpile war materiel, not to fight the Japanese.

Both he and Mao were preparing for the inevitable civil war once the Japanese were defeated. They were determined, once and for all, to crush each other.

A FINAL MEETING When the war ended, each side took stock. The country was in a state one observer called "numbing wretchedness." Millions of civilians had died and millions more were refugees. Parts of China were suffering the worst cholera outbreak since 1932. Had Mao and Chiang banded together to fight in a true "United Front" against the Japanese, the war might have ended sooner, with less bloodshed, but they were so intent on saving their resources for the final battle to destroy each other that all of China suffered—and would suffer more as the two armies circled each other, waiting for full resumption of the civil war.

In mid-June 1945, as it became more and more apparent that Japan would go down in defeat, Mao made a series of speeches that amounted to a concerted verbal assault on Chiang Kai-shek and any pretensions he might have to be leader of the Chinese people. Chiang, according to Mao, was a "corrupt bandit and traitor," whom Mao would "settle accounts with." Mao also met privately in Yan'an with the American ambassador to China, Joseph Hurley. Far from being more conciliatory in person, Mao called Chiang "a turtle's egg," an insulting Chinese epithet. At the same time, Mao told the Russian ambassador that Chiang was "a dictator, a butcher and a half-wit."

Chiang, for his part, was ready to destroy Mao. His coffers had grown fat with American dollars, and he and his wife, Madame Chiang, were the darlings of the American public after numerous visits to the United States during the war. Visiting San Francisco in the spring of 1945, he told a lecture audience, with Madame Chiang interpreting, that Mao Zedong "was the evil thorn puncturing the side of China."

There was one last attempt by Washington to avert civil war. At the behest of American intermediaries, Chiang and Mao agreed to meet at the end of August 1945, in the wartime capital of Chongqing, for talks to seek a non-violent solution. It was a strange meeting between the rivals, one held mainly for display—as Chiang's biographer Jonathan Fenby has written, "both sides needed to show an eagerness for national unity after the long conflict with Japan."

Distrust was rampant. Mao was suspicious that the meeting was a trap and insisted that Ambassador Hurley accompany him on the plane, causing Chiang to crow in his diary: "Never imagined that [Mao] could be so chickenhearted and shameless." In public he toasted Mao with the hope that they could "go back to the days of 1926," when they were so briefly allies. In his diary he wrote: "I promised [Mao] to resolve all our differences in a spirit of fairness and magnanimity. He asked for 48 divisions."

Mao ate heartily at every meal, smoked incessantly, commented to the press on his very first plane ride ("Very efficient," he called it) and seemed to take a shine to Chiang, something that was almost certainly a part of his folksy act. "Long live President Chiang Kai-shek," he called out, at one cocktail party. To which Chiang replied sardonically: "Look—isn't he a prize exhibit?"

The conference ended with bland assurances on both sides that a peaceful solution would be sought—something almost no one believed. As one English observer wrote: "Neither Mao nor Chiang trusts one another. Each wants territorial, military, civil, political control. Yet each claps hands for democracy, unity, freedom [and] nationalisation."

When Mao returned to his base at Yan'an, he fell uncharacteristically ill—one of his advisors wrote that he "lay on his bed prostrated, his body trembling. His hands and legs twitched convulsively, and he was bathed in a cold sweat." Despite his cool exterior at the conference, an interpreter who had been with him there felt that Mao had realized that, finally, the end of his fifteen-year battle with Chiang was at hand.

TOTAL VICTORY, TOTAL DEFEAT

In March 1946, the Russians withdrew from the parts of Manchuria they had occupied after the Japanese defeat, leaving Mao's Communist forces with a cornucopia of captured Japanese weapons—700,000 rifles, 14,000 machine-guns, and 700 military vehicles, including tanks. By mid-April, the civil war had begun. At first, things went well for the Nationalist forces. Chiang's army took all the major cities in south and central Manchuria and seemed to be defeating the Communists—who had renamed themselves the PLA, or People's Liberation Army—on all fronts. But, here, Chiang's relationship with America finally became his undoing. Despite misgivings, he agreed to allow Truman's envoy, George Marshall, to again attempt to work out a peace between the warring parties. Two truces were called during the spring and summer of 1946 as Mao's envoy, Zhou Enlai, bargained with Chiang's representatives at American-arranged meetings. However, the only effect of the truces—and it was a major one—was to allow Mao and the PLA to regroup after the Nationalists had pushed them to their limits. And—as was so often the case—Chiang's strength was not as deep as it appeared. Inflation raged through the middle classes and official corruption was rife. Chiang's secret police cracked down severely on protestors who were alienated from the Nationalist regime—in

one case, in Beijing, thirty students who were merely protesting a lack of textbooks were buried alive.

Mao's forces finally began to attack. When they crossed the Yellow River in the fall of 1947, Chiang's response was to change the flow of the river to flood PLA bases. This drove the Communists off temporarily, but also made 400,000 people homeless, thus further weakening Chiang's government.

The fiercest battles took place in Manchuria, where the PLA seized city after city, costing the Nationalists hundreds of thousands of casualties. By early 1948, the PLA controlled all of Manchuria and was moving south towards Beijing and the port city of Tianjin, singing a song about "driving the thief Chiang to his doom" as they marched.

Chiang Kai-shek attempted to form a National Assembly and give his country at least the semblance of a democracy, but everyone—including the Americans, whom Chiang had failed one too many times—saw it as the puppet government it was. As U.S. aid was withdrawn from him, city after city fell to Mao and his PLA. War correspondents in late 1948 reported that villages for hundreds of miles in large swathes of China were ablaze. In some besieged cities, civilians ate human flesh, which sold for U.S. $1.20 a pound. On December 8, 1949, with the Nationalist forces crumbling all through China, Chiang Kai-shek fled with his government to Taiwan.

The final war between Mao and Chiang had cost five million lives in addition to the three or so million people who had died in their earlier campaigns. Would history have been different had the two of them not been so opposed to each other, so personally contemptuous? Almost certainly. Without their stubbornness, a compromise might have been worked out and China might have been spared the millions more dead under Mao's ruthless purges. People noted time and time again that Chiang and Mao refused to do anything except pay lip service to compromise, even when an alliance might have been in their best interests. It always seemed that they were seeking a way to continue their feud. As one historian has written: "Chiang and Mao preferred, even in the end, the fight to the death [that] had shaped their lives."

Mao died in 1976, at the age of eighty-three. Shortly before his death, he told his colleagues that, of all the things he had done in his life, only two were really important. One was "to ask the Japanese to return to their ancestral home," a polite way of saying that he had defeated the Japanese in war. When it came to describing the second most vital event of his life, he was less indirect: "I chased Chang Kai-shek to that little island," he said emphatically, meaning Taiwan.

Chiang Kai-shek had passed away on "that little island" the year before, but he has not given up, even in death. At his orders, his body has not been buried, since to be buried anywhere but on the Chinese mainland would be to admit defeat. It lies in a marble casket near his country home, above ground, waiting.

With Mao's giant portrait still hanging on Tiananmen, the Gate of Heavenly Peace, at the heart of Beijing, it would seem that he, after all, was the victor in this epic competition. But, who knows? It is possible Chiang could have the last laugh. China in the early twenty-first century, after decades of revolution, has reached out to the foreigners of whom Mao was so deeply suspicious and is as capitalist a country as there is in the world today. So it is not impossible—in fact, is a delightful irony to consider—that the two rivals may some day rest side by side in their native land.

GENERAL VASILY CHUIKOV

VERSUS FIELD MARSHAL FRIEDRICH PAULUS

GENERAL VASILY CHUIKOV AND FIELD MARSHAL FRIEDRICH PAULUS: PEASANT VS. BUREAUCRAT

O N AUGUST 5, 1942, THE CITIZENS OF STALINGRAD looked up to see, far out in the western steppes, huge tornadoes of dust, almost biblical in their intensity, approaching the city. But this was far more sinister than even the most ominous weather system, for these clouds were man-made, raised by the armored vehicles of the massive German Sixth Army.

The pillars of dust represented doom for most of those watching, for the battle of Stalingrad that would soon consume the city would be, quite possibly, the bloodiest in human history. During a five-month period at least one million people died—possibly many more. Casualties for the armies involved (including killed, wounded, and missing) reached 700,000 for the Russians, 400,000 for the Germans, and a total of 350,000 for the German allies: the Italians, Hungarians, and Romanians. Although the city was eventually evacuated, the civilian death toll numbered some 40,000. And then there were the deaths of the POWs taken by both sides: these extended into the hundreds of thousands.

The battle took place in rubble, in the shadows of huge, half-destroyed factories, in sniper duels, in the stairwells of blasted apartment buildings. The bravery on both sides was incredible, the hardship astounding. Much of the fighting was captured by cameramen and still photographers; the images of the dead, wounded, and terrified sear the imagination still.

Two photographs represent the spirit of the battle. One shows General Vasily Chuikov. The squat, peasant-born Russian commander squints at the camera, his battered face showing absolute and implacable determination. The other picture is of German Field Marshal Friedrich Paulus, who has just surrendered. Paulus is tall, gaunt, unshaven, in a worn overcoat, and his face is grim and haunted.

RUSSLAND IST KAPUTT! When Operation Barbarossa, the surprise German invasion of Soviet Russia, began in June of 1941, Hitler commented: "The eyes of the world will be watching!" and he was right. After sweeping through Europe (but failing in his attempt to bomb the British into submission) Hitler had now turned his ambitions eastward. Observers from Asia to America knew that if he could conquer Russia, he would be in a position of absolute power in the world.

And how could the Russians stop him? The German invasion forces included a million and a half soldiers and extended from the Baltic to the Black Sea. They were divided into two parts. Army Group North headed for Leningrad, while Army Group South struck out for the Ukraine and, after that, Russia and the rich oil fields of the Caucasus. Thousands of demoralized Russian soldiers began to surrender almost immediately. Joseph Stalin, the Russian premier, went into a state of shock and was unable to communicate for days at a time. His hard-drinking generals, mainly cronies, were of little use. Wehrmacht soldiers began to tell each other *Russland ist kaputt*—Russia is finished.

But Russia was not quite *kaputt*. In the north, Leningrad held out against the Germans, at the beginning of the siege that would last nine hundred days. Stalin appointed General Georgy Zhukov, later to become the hero of Leningrad, to protect Moscow, one of Germany's main targets, and although advance units of the German Panzer divisions could see the spires of the city, Moscow held out as the Russian winter set in. The Germans—poorly prepared for freezing weather, since they thought the war would last only a few months—were pushed back.

Enraged, Hitler relieved Field Marshal von Rundstedt as Commander, Army Group South, and replaced him with the hardened Field Marshal von Reichenau. With von Reichenau came his longtime aide, General Friedrich Paulus.

"MORE LIKE A SCIENTIST THAN A GENERAL"

Friedrich Paulus was born in Breitenau, Germany, in 1890, the son of a schoolteacher, and joined the German army in 1911. He took part in World War I, but mainly as a staff officer—one of his habits, even as a boy, was drawing precise scale maps of famous battles—and rose to the rank of captain. Because of his lower middle class upbringing, Paulus felt that he was discriminated against by the aristocratic officer corps of the Kaiser's army and became obsessed with his appearance—his aversion to dirt was legendary and he changed uniforms several times daily—so much so that his friends jokingly called him *"der Lord."* After the war Paulus, an admirer of Hitler, rose steadily through the ranks to a high position in the Wehrmacht General Staff.

In 1940, now a major general, Paulus worked closely with General von Reichenau as the Sixth Army drove through France and Belgium with record speed. Paulus was intimately involved in the planning for Operation Sea Lion—the invasion of Britain—but when that failed to come off, he joined von Reichenau in planning Operation Barbarossa. The two appeared the perfect pair—the tall, fastidious, aristocratic-seeming Paulus with the shorter, vulgar, and more ruthless von Reichenau. In the early winter of 1942, von Reichenau had firmed up German positions and was holding off Soviet attacks, waiting for spring to renew his offensive, when he was suddenly stricken by a heart attack and died.

Hitler then chose Friedrich Paulus as his replacement. The man who had never commanded an army was now head of an entire army group. Although he struck some officers as "more like a scientist than a general" (even on this campaign he relieved his tensions by drawing, to scale, maps of Napoleon's campaign in Russia), he was considered hard working and talented. An inveterate smoker, he stayed up late, pored over maps, made decisions, and then handed them down to his subordinates with a politeness notably lacking in many German officers.

THE ATTACK ON STALINGRAD

In the early summer of 1942, Paulus renewed the attack against the Russians, driving them back with great success and at one point encircling and destroying a Russian army of two hundred thousand. Initially, the Germans were not even supposed to be attacking Stalingrad, the city on the west bank of the Volga; their plan was merely to bomb it to destroy its industrial capabilities, and then to head south to hook up with the Panzer divisions already attacking the Caucasus.

Hitler, however, had heard reports that Stalingrad's defenses were poor and decided he wanted to steal the city that bore the Russian leader's name. He directed Paulus to change plans and aim directly for Stalingrad, and the loyal general did, even though one of his Panzer divisions was to be detached and sent to the Caucasus oil fields, something that made him extremely nervous. He wanted to get to the Russian army before they retreated into Stalingrad—to, as he put it, "hit the Russian so hard a crack that he won't recover for a very long time." But the Russians did not allow this. Instead, they retreated steadily before the German army in the forty miles between the Don and the Volga rivers. Even so, the German soldiers, as they sighted Stalingrad on the banks of the Volga, felt victorious. They were covered with dust and grime—no rain had fallen in the area for two months and the heat was sweltering—but, as one German soldier later put it, "we were the victors … we thought that we could capture the city in a few days."

Stalingrad had begun four hundred years before as a town named Tsaritsyn (it is now called Volgograd) but had been renamed after the Russian Revolution and turned into an important industrial center. Sprawling for twenty miles along the Volga, with a population of half a million, it contained an industrial park with huge plants that manufactured tractors, metal, and chemicals.

On August 23, a massive German aerial bombardment turned the city into rubble. It was then that forty thousand civilians were killed and the Soviet command began to evacuate the survivors across the Volga, although Luftwaffe

THE BLACK CROWS

Field Marshal Walther von Reichenau, Friedrich Paulus's immediate superior, was a confirmed Nazi who wholeheartedly believed in Hitler's propaganda about a master race. As the German army invaded Russia, he made sure that Hitler's "commissar order" (which called for the immediate execution of any Russian political officers captured) was put into effect. Reichenau also enthusiastically gave his own orders to the Sixth Army. One, the so-called "severity order," said that "the [German] soldier must learn fully to appreciate the necessity for the severe but just retribution that must be meted out to the subhuman species of Jewry."

This "retribution" was effected by what one historian has called "a motley collection of homicidal maniacs," divided into Einsatzgruppen, or Special Extermination Squads—probably three thousand executioners in all—who passed through the Russian towns and villages after the Sixth Army went through, rounded up Jews, and shot them. These men wore black uniforms and became known to terrified villagers in Russia as the "Black Crows." Their work had a strange effect on the morale of the Sixth Army. There was almost a carnival atmosphere at the executions, as Sixth Army soldiers chattered and took pictures while Jews were shot and pushed into mass graves. This was too much even for Reichenau, who issued an order in August 1942 forbidding any soldier "who has not been ordered by an officer" to take part in, observe, or photograph any of the executions.

Occasionally German officers sought to intervene. That same August, Colonel Helmuth Groscurth, chief of staff of an infantry division, learned that ninety Jewish orphans ranging in age from infancy to seven years were to be shot the next day. He protested to Sixth Army headquarters, but Reichenau refused to halt the killings. However, he did make one change. The shooting of the children was done by Ukrainian militiamen, in order to safeguard the sensibilities of any Black Crows who might be upset by so evil a deed.

RIGHT German General Walter von Reichenau, Paulus's superior and commander of the Sixth Army, who enthusiastically gave orders for the extermination of any Russian political officers or Jews encountered during the invasion.

RIGHT During the battle of
Stalingrad small groups of
Soviet soldiers were placed
in the ruined buildings, using
them as bases from which to
fight the German troops as
they attempted to infiltrate
the city.

fighters killed more in strafing attacks. By the beginning of September, the Germans had entered the city and were engaged in vicious hand-to-hand fighting among the smoldering, stinking ruins.

"WE DO NOT DARE LOSE THE CITY" The commander of the beleaguered Soviet forces in Stalingrad was the extraordinary General Vasily Chuikov, whom one historian has called Friedrich Paulus's "mirror image." Born in 1900, the son of Russian peasants, Chuikov was a mechanic who doubled as a bell-hop in the hotels of the czarist era, before joining the Red Army in 1918 and fighting in the Russian civil war as a private in a unit commanded by Joseph Stalin. (One of the first towns Chuikov helped wrest from the White Army was Tsaritsyn.)

After the civil war and Stalin's seizure of power, Chuikov, with extraordinary determination, educated himself and then applied for and received admittance to the elite Frunze Military Academy in 1925. He then had the good luck, skill or cunning to survive Stalin's purges, in which many of his fellow officers died or were sent to the gulags. By 1942, he had become the deputy commander of the Soviet Sixty-fourth Army. Unlike Paulus, Chuikov was a man of action to whom manners meant little. He had an extraordinary temper and was known, on occasion, to strike subordinates with his walking stick. His appearance, too, was a contrast to that of his German rival. Chuikov was short and stocky, with a furrowed face and a row of gold teeth that gleamed when he smiled.

As the Germans invaded Stalingrad, Chuikov, who had been stationed near Moscow, was summoned to the city by the overall commander of the Stalingrad Front, General Yeremenko. The former commander of the Sixty-second Army, which was fighting to hold the city, had just been dismissed because of his defeatist attitudes. Yeremenko now offered the job to Chuikov. He told him that Stalin had ordered that the Russians "not take another step back," and that the NKVD was shooting anyone who tried to leave the city. It was a desperate situation. Could Chuikov handle it?

Chuikov replied: "We dare not lose the city."

"THERE IS NO LAND PAST THE VOLGA" On the same day that Chuikov took command, Paulus flew five hundred miles west, back to the Ukraine, where he met with Adolf Hitler for a conference on how the attack was going. Paulus told Hitler that he was sure that Stalingrad would fall in a matter of days. His chief concern was that the armies holding the German lines northwest and south of the city belonged to "satellite" nations—Italy, Hungary, Romania— whose soldiers were poorly trained, unmotivated, and could not be trusted. What if the Russians launched a counterattack and swept in on Paulus's flanks? Hitler said that he would see what he could do about reinforcing these units and the two men parted company on good terms.

ABOVE Soviet machine-gunners fire at German troops who have barricaded themselves into the houses opposite during street fighting on the outskirts of Stalingrad in January 1943.

THE SNIPERS OF STALINGRAD

During the battle of Stalingrad, much of the city was reduced to rubble, rubble that made perfect lairs for snipers. On the Soviet side, these snipers became folk heroes, and none was greater than Vasily Zaitsev. Zaitsev had originally been a shepherd in the Ural Mountains, where he learned to shoot. He was conscripted into the Soviet army and sent to help defend Stalingrad. In his first ten days there, he killed forty Germans. Zaitsev then opened his own sniper school in an abandoned chemical factory and taught other Soviet soldiers, including women, the art of sniping from concealment.

The Soviet press made a great deal of propaganda hay over Zaitsev, something that the Germans naturally desired to counter. So they sent for the head of their Berlin Sniper School, one Major Konings—some accounts have him named Heinz Thorvaald—to hunt down and kill Zaitsev. The Russian found out from a German prisoner that Konings was there, but his presence would have been revealed anyway—more and more Russians were dropping with neat bullet holes in their foreheads. Finally, Zaitsev and his spotter, Nikolai Kulikov, went out looking for the German. For three days they searched for him in the rubble of no-man's-land, until Zaitsev thought he saw a suspicious movement beneath a sheet of iron lying on some bricks.

The next day, he and Kulikov returned to their positions, but waited until the sun was setting behind them. When he saw the rays of the sun glitter on something beneath the sheet iron, Zaitsev told Kulikov to raise a special dummy's head he had created with a helmet on top of it. This Kulikov did and it was immediately hit by a bullet. Just as quickly, Zaitsev fired—and put a bullet right through Major Konings's head.

Vasily Zaitsev went on to kill anywhere from 250 to 400 Germans in the course of the war and was named a Hero of the Soviet Union. Although Zaitsev reports the story of Major Konings in his biography, some historians think it was Soviet propaganda—to this day, no trace has been found of Konings in German records.

Back in Stalingrad, Chuikov had just entered the city to take control. He was met by throngs of women and children begging for water and hordes of wounded stumbling back towards the Volga. It was still summer, but all the leaves had fallen from the trees, token of the tremendous pounding Stalingrad had received. Chuikov's command post was a trench dug into the slope of a hill and covered with branches and earth. On the day after he arrived, German troops attacked in force and Chuikov's makeshift defenses barely held. Still, the Germans were pushed back and Chuikov devised a plan.

Knowing that he could not possibly match German firepower, Chuikov wanted to get his men as close to the Nazis as possible, where the German artillery would be useless. He divided fifteen hundred militiamen with whom he was in immediate contact into squads of ten or twenty—"storm squads"—and placed them in the ruins of buildings throughout the city. These brave squads were sent out to attack the Germans and help funnel their infantry and tanks down certain streets which had been pre-registered for Russian artillery fire. Ironically, the very bombing attacks that had destroyed the city now, in a sense, helped to save it, for Chuikov's men were able to create hidden machine-gun nests and artillery emplacements in the rubble, decimating the Germans as they advanced. An entire company of snipers was deployed, the crack marksmen taking a toll on German lives and morale.

The combatants were so close that the Russians could hear the Germans yelling: *Rus! Rus! Volga bul-bul!* (Russians will drown in the Volga!) On Maemev Hill, where formerly lovers had picnicked, a vicious battle took place where the noise was so intense, one soldier recalled, that it was like two steel needles pressing into his eardrums.

But still the Russians held. Perhaps it helped that Chuikov was with them, and that he had issued a ringing order that began: "There is no land west of the Volga." They needed to fight or die.

STALINGRAD GEFALLEN! Despite his reassurances to Hitler, Friedrich Paulus was becoming nervous. Although by the end of September the Sixth Army was able to raise the German swastika over the government buildings in Stalingrad, the fighting was by no means over. At his headquarters forty miles west of Stalingrad, a worried Paulus chain-smoked, looked at his maps, and played Beethoven records endlessly on his gramophone. He had begun to be afflicted by mild dysentery, which kept his stomach perpetually upset. The German press was present, waiting for the inevitable victory, and they kept asking Paulus if they could announce it. "Any time now, any time!" he told them.

Some German newspapers, taking this as a yes, printed a special edition with the headline *Stalingrad gefallen!* but Goebbels's Propaganda Ministry held up distribution until they checked with Paulus, who had to tell them no, Stalingrad had not fallen.

ABOVE Amid the ruins of the city, Soviet troops storm an apartment block held by the Germans during the battle for Stalingrad.

Gradually, however, the Germans were pushing the Russians back, until almost ninety percent of the city was in German hands (although by no means completely secured). Now Paulus knew he needed to attack the northern part of the city, the factory district. So far the cost to the German army had been appalling—almost eight thousand Germans dead and thirty-one thousand wounded. Paulus begged Hitler for reinforcements, but they were slow in coming. His general staff began to notice that Paulus had developed a tic, the left side of his face fluttering nervously.

As the Germans began to attack the great industrial zone of Stalingrad, Chuikov, too, was falling prey to nervous tension. His body was covered with oozing eczema sores; his hands were wrapped in bandages to keep the lesions from becoming infected. If Paulus thought his losses were bad, they were nothing compared to Chuikov's—in a month the Russians had lost seventy thousand men

killed, wounded, or missing. Reinforcements and supplies had to come in across the Volga River by ferry—ferries that were under constant German artillery fire—or by makeshift bridges that the Russians would rebuild every time the Germans destroyed them. Green recruits brought into the city were forced at gunpoint by political commissars to continue into the holocaust facing them—the glow of the burning city could be seen for miles around the region, and the terror of marching into that inferno must have been indescribable.

On October 2, the Germans unleashed a huge barrage on the industrial sector, where Chuikov had been forced to move his command post. The post was directly under supposedly empty oil tanks near the Red October tractor plant, but Chuikov and his staff found out the hard way that the tanks were full of oil—German shells exploded them, sending a blazing torrent of oil down on the command dugout. Chuikov and his fellow officers were nearly burned to death.

WAR OF THE RATS Hitler, by now grown impatient, ordered Paulus to attack the factories with everything at his disposal— by October 20 he wanted Stalingrad completely in German hands. On October 14, the attack began with hundreds of Stuka dive-bombers bombing and strafing the ruins. Next came two hundred tanks, the behemoths crashing through Soviet lines and bursting into the ruins of the tractor factory, where German and Russian troops fought each other along the assembly lines and in the offices and cafeteria. Within forty-eight hours, five thousand Russian soldiers were killed there. In four days, Chuikov lost thirteen thousand men out of his army of fifty-three thousand.

And still the Russians held. Dissension arose in the German ranks. Paulus had to deal with the complaints of General Freiherr von Richthofen, who commanded the Luftwaffe and felt that the openings his dive-bombers had made in the Russian defenses were not being taken advantage of by Paulus, whom he thought too timid. Paulus complained in return of troop and ammunition shortages that kept him from breaking through Russian lines. Richthofen told an aide: "What we lack is clear thinking and a well-defined primary objective."

If so, it was as much Hitler's fault as Paulus's, since Hitler was the one who had insisted on attacking Stalingrad while at the same time dividing his forces to push into southern Russia. Even now, Hitler refused to think of withdrawing from the city, which, as far as he was concerned, would mean a loss of face to his hated enemy Joseph Stalin. So his soldiers fought and died in the sewers and cellars of the factory district, crawling among the rubble, fighting what they called *Der Rattenkrieg*—The War of the Rats.

In the middle of all of this, the heavy fall rains that Stalingrad had been experiencing turned to snow, and the weather became colder in a harbinger of the harsh Russian winter to come. Still Hitler urged Paulus to attack. On November 10, Paulus launched another major offensive against the Russian factory works, only to be driven back, although his men reached to within two hundred yards of Chuikov's command post.

Then what Paulus had feared all along occurred—the Russians outside Stalingrad launched a major counteroffensive against his forces' exposed flanks. On November 19, Soviet forces attacked the Italian and Romanian armies northwest of the city; the next day, another Soviet army assaulted the Fourth Romanian army south of Stalingrad. In a brilliantly planned, brilliantly executed pincer movement, the Soviet forces tore through the enemy and were able to link up with each other on November 23, west of Stalingrad. Paulus and his men were now completely encircled.

"NOTHING I CAN DO BUT OBEY" Hearing the thunder of artillery and aware of what the Russians were doing, Paulus made an urgent request to Hitler that he be allowed to withdraw the Sixth Army from Stalingrad and move it a hundred miles back to the west. Hitler refused and, in fact, ordered

Paulus to move his own headquarters to within ten miles of Stalingrad, so that he, too, was within the encircling armies. Hermann Göring, head of the Luftwaffe, had assured Hitler that he could supply the city via an airlift, but this was absurd. Many of the planes were shot down by Russian fighters, which increasingly prowled the sky; the Russian winter weather also began to make flying impossible on many days. The supplies that got through were less than twenty percent of what Paulus needed. "We can't fight on what they're giving us," he complained to an aide. "Nor can we live on it."

His staff officers urged him to ignore the Führer's orders, to simply break out and present him with a fait accompli, but Paulus resisted this idea, saying, "There is nothing I can do but obey." Some might agree with this blind loyalty, others might not, but Paulus refused to go against orders. By early December, German soldiers had begun to die of starvation.

Then, suddenly, Hitler changed his mind—in a way. He decided to allow Field Marshal Erich von Manstein, in charge of the Eleventh Army, 280 miles west of Moscow, to send a relief force of Panzers into Stalingrad to carve out a corridor and link up with Paulus, but at the same time he still wanted Paulus to defend Stalingrad. When Manstein received this order, he notified Paulus, who sent him a handwritten note that showed the general was breaking down. It was plaintive in tone: "Both my flanks were exposed in two days ... In this difficult situation, I sent the Führer a signal asking for freedom [to withdraw] ... I have received no direct reply ... On the other hand, even if anything like a corridor is cut through to me, it is still not possible to tell whether the daily increasing weakness of the Army will allow [for a withdrawal] ..."

"SINGLE COMBAT WITH HITLER" As Paulus began to lose hope, Chuikov became even more aggressive. He wanted desperately to destroy the Sixth Army. Even his wife wrote him, saying; "Dear Vasili, I at times imagine you have entered into single combat with Hitler. I know you for twenty years. I know your strengths. It's hard to imagine that someone like Adolf Hitler could get the better of you."

Chuikov did not think so either, although he chafed at the lack of supplies getting through to him, radioing his superiors: "... with every soldier wanting with all his heart and soul to broaden [the fight] so as to breathe more freely, such economies seem unjustified cruelty." Still, he continued to mount "storm patrol" attacks against the Germans, harassing them relentlessly, giving the already frozen and hungry soldiers no rest.

The only hope for the Germans was the approaching relief column of Erich von Manstein, who was fighting his way through to Stalingrad and facing heavy resistance. With radio links down, the only way Manstein and Paulus could communicate with each other was by teletype machine, and Manstein asked whether Paulus might be able to break out to the west—that is, to meet Manstein as his Panzers arrived. Paulus protested that he did not have enough fuel to make such a breakout—something Manstein considered ridiculous. Given the desperate situation facing him, Paulus needed to use what fuel he had to attempt *something*, for otherwise he and the Sixth Army were doomed. Manstein sent a top secret bulletin to Hitler and urged him to order Paulus to break out on his own to the southwest. He ended it by saying that "according to an Army report, the mass of horses cannot be used because they are starved or else have been eaten."

Hitler refused to order this. Perhaps it was *Realpolitik*—he knew Paulus and knew that his commander was not the aggressive type Chuikov was, not the type who at all cost would smash through an encirclement. And he was right. Even though Manstein's Panzers got to within eighteen miles of Stalingrad—and Manstein, counter to Hitler's orders, demanded that Paulus break out, the defeated general claimed that it would take him days to prepare the army to disengage. Paulus, and the Sixth Army, were indeed doomed.

There was nothing Manstein could do to convince him. Their last teletype messages went:

Manstein: Well, that's the lot. Good luck, Paulus.

Paulus: Thank you, sir. And good luck to you, too.

Manstein's Panzers then turned their backs on the burning city, and headed west. It was 27 December, 1942.

"YOU ARE TALKING TO DEAD MEN" Winter had set in

with a vengeance and Paulus's men were now dying of cold as well as starvation—twelve thousand Germans died in December alone. In early January, Chuikov had thousands of leaflets dropped on German positions, claiming that any German who surrendered would receive food, a warm bed, and medical treatment. These were lies, but the Germans inside Stalingrad ignored them anyway. When no one surrendered, Chuikov unleashed upon the city a massive seven thousand gun barrage and an infantry attack that captured one of the Germans' two useable airfields. Airlifted food slowed to a trickle. A Luftwaffe officer who bravely landed a plane full of supplies found a command in disintegration. No one had cleared wrecked planes from the runway or filled in shell holes. When he went to see Paulus, he found the gaunt, ill commander in a rage. Paulus began screaming: "The Führer gave me his firm assurance that he and the whole German people felt responsible for this army and now the annals of German arms are besmirched by this terrible tragedy ... We already speak from a different world than yours, for you are talking to dead men. From now on, our existence will be in the history books."

The Luftwaffe officer flew out of Stalingrad, shaken. In the next ten days, resistance from the Germans was sporadic at best. Most of the troops in the city now hid in cellars and bunkers and surrendered when the Russians moved in on them. Several members of Paulus's staff either committed suicide or went out on

OPPOSITE PAGE Field Marshal Friedrich von Paulus, commander of the German Sixth Army, on February 1, 1943, after surrendering to the Soviets at Stalingrad.

CAMEL MEAT

Hundreds of thousands of Germans, Italians, and Romanians were captured by the Russians after the surrender. The Russians were not prepared to cope with such numbers, as they had little enough food for themselves, let alone their hated enemies. At some of the camps the prisoners were taken to, they were simply not fed at all. At others, Russians pulled up, dumped a truckload of rotting cabbages out on the ground, and let the prisoners fight over them.

Naturally, thousands began to die—and these became a prime source of food for the other prisoners. Slices cut from these frozen corpses were called "camel meat," and it was easy to tell who was eating it—their complexions showed a pinker pallor than the gray-green of the prisoners who were completely without protein. At some camps, the Soviets formed "anti-cannibalism" teams made up of prisoners armed with crowbars. If they saw any of their fellow POWs engaged in eating human flesh, they were to kill them. But very often, this would simply result in other cannibals descending upon the corpses for fresh meat.

Gradually the Russians began to feed the prisoners better, at least marginally so, and many POWs noticed an unexpected phenomenon. The bigger and stronger the person, the more likely it was that he would die first. This was because the amount allotted for each person did not take into account his weight and size. The smaller, thinner person needed less food to get by, and tended to survive the longest.

BELOW A zigzag line stretches to the horizon as German soldiers are marched away from Stalingrad to prison camps. Also visible are destroyed German fortifications and captured artillery and trucks.

suicidal missions against the Russians. On January 30, hoping that Paulus would fight to the last man and then commit suicide, Hitler promoted him to the rank of field marshal.

No field marshal in German history had ever surrendered. As Hitler said later, he expected Paulus to commit suicide or die fighting. "I wanted to give him this final satisfaction," the Führer said of his most loyal soldier. "He could have freed himself from all sorrow and ascended into eternity and national immortality. Instead, he prefers to go to Moscow."

On January 31, Paulus surrendered, saying: "I have no intention of shooting myself for that Bohemian corporal."

THE GLITTERING GOLD SMILE
Friedrich Paulus had finally become wise to the "Bohemian corporal," but it was far too late. His loyalty and his tentativeness proved, in the end, that he was wrong for command of the army group that had come so far, only to perish at Stalingrad. When Paulus actually surrendered, it was to a young Soviet lieutenant named Fyodor Yelchenko, who happened to be standing in the turret of a tank with its gun pointed right at Paulus's headquarters. He was then taken to meet General Mikhail Shumilov, the most senior officer nearby, who asked for identification, to make sure Paulus was who he said he was. The picture that captures the grimy field marshal—the one who so loved to keep his uniforms clean—was taken as he left that humiliating encounter.

When Vasily Chuikov heard of this, he was intensely disappointed, for he had wanted to personally capture Paulus. (After the war, a fairly large group of Soviet general officers claimed to have taken the field marshal's surrender, so great was the honor considered to be.) But Chuikov had to make do with a parade of senior German staff who came before him, some of them weeping. To all of them he offered tea and food, and watched as they devoured it hungrily.

Chuikov would go on to lead one of the Soviet armies that would capture Berlin—to him went the honor of accepting the surrender of that beleaguered city, while Paulus was held in house arrest in Moscow until 1953. When he was released it was to East Germany, where he served as a police inspector in Dresden. Half a million Germans, Italians, Romanians, and Hungarians would not get such gentle treatment from the Russians—400,000 of them died from March to April of 1943, as they were taken to prison camps. In the end, Chuikov's glittering gold smile and fierce battle spirit trumped Paulus's gentle manner and precisely scaled maps, as they would have to, in an inferno like Stalingrad.

GEORGE S. PATTON

VERSUS **BERNARD LAW MONTGOMERY**

GEORGE S. PATTON AND BERNARD LAW MONTGOMERY: THE WARRIOR AGAINST THE PLANNER

YOU CAN TELL WHAT KIND OF PEOPLE THESE TWO pivotal Allied generals of World War II were just by listening to them talk.

Here is Field Marshal Bernard Law Montgomery, head of the British Eighth Army, complaining to a friend during the North African campaign:

I know well I am regarded by many people as being a tiresome person. I think this is very probably true. I try hard not to be tiresome; but I have seen so many mistakes during this war, and so many disasters happen, that I am desperately anxious to try to see that we have no more; and this often means being very tiresome.

In the space of three sentences the word "tiresome" is repeated three times. "Tiresome" is indeed what Montgomery—known to one and all as "Monty"—could be, focusing obsessively on detail, extremely systematic and careful, and convinced that were it not for him the whole Allied war effort (be it in North Africa, Sicily, or France) would fall apart. And yet his dogged determination paid off in glittering Allied victories.

Now here is George S. Patton addressing his American G.I.'s before the invasion of Normandy in June of 1944:

You may be thankful that twenty years from now when you are sitting by the fireplace with your grandson on your knee and he asks you what you did in the great World War II, you won't have to cough, shift him to the other knee and say, "Well, your granddaddy shoveled shit in Louisiana." No, Sir, you can look him straight in the eye and say, "Son, your granddaddy rode with the great Third Army and a son-of-a-goddamned bitch named Georgie Patton."

That is the voice of George Patton—dramatic, profane, brimming with confidence and convinced that were it not for him the Germans would be winning the war. Here were the two most talented commanders the Allies had fighting against Adolf Hitler's vaunted Wehrmacht, Luftwaffe, and Panzer divisions, and not only was each certain that he was the most valuable general alive—Patton wrote in his diary: "On reflection, who is as good as I am? I know of no one."—but each hated the other passionately. What a wonderful way to fight a war.

PRAYING TO ROBERT E. LEE
George S. Patton, Jr., was born in 1885 on his family's 1,800-acre ranch just outside Pasadena, California. His roots were in the American south, however, and he was descended from a long line of Confederate soldiers. Two great-uncles had fought for the Confederacy, one of them dying during Pickett's famous charge at the battle of Gettysburg. His paternal grandfather had also fought for the Rebel cause and been killed at the second battle of Winchester by the saber slash of a Union cavalryman. Patton's mother, Ruth, kept pictures of Confederate generals Robert E. Lee and Stonewall Jackson on the walls of their comfortable home, and Patton, as a young child, mistook them for God and Jesus and directed his prayers to them.

"Georgie," as he was called by his family and later by a small circle of friends, was raised in affluence in a sprawling adobe house protected from the blazing California sun by eucalyptus trees. George and his sister had half a dozen servants and a governess to look after them, and ponies to ride in the family stables. Yet from a very early age Patton was consumed by martial adventures. He had memorized passages from the *Iliad* by the time he was seven years old. At the age of eleven, at a private school in California, he had already decided he wanted to be a soldier. When he was eighteen, he attended the Virginia Military Institute, then transferred to the United States Military Academy at West Point. In 1909, he graduated forty-third in his class of a hundred and three and was commissioned a second lieutenant in the United States cavalry. He was a crack shot as well as a brilliant horseman, and thus was a natural to compete for the United States in the first ever modern pentathlon, coming in fifth.

But war was what Patton hungered for, and he found it in the 1916 American incursion into Mexico (the same one where Douglas MacArthur saw his first combat—see page 313). In this wild and woolly frontier war, young Patton, an aide to General John J. Pershing, commanded fifteen men who traveled in three Dodge touring cars. Ambushing the bandits who were their enemy, they killed three. With what would become trademark Patton grandiosity, he strapped the bodies of the dead Mexicans to the hoods of the cars and drove them triumphantly back to base. For this exploit, Pershing dubbed him "Bandito."

"THE REBELLIOUS ONE" Bernard Law Montgomery was born two years after Patton, in 1887, and five thousand miles away, in London. He was the son of an Anglo-Irish Anglican priest who was made bishop of Tasmania, which is where the family—eight brothers and sisters aside from Bernard—moved when Bernard was only two. Although the Montgomerys were far from well off, they came from a distinguished family, with Monty's paternal grandfather being Sir Robert Montgomery, a British official in Punjab in the nineteenth century. His maternal grandfather was Dean Frederic Farrar, a prominent clergyman and writer.

Montgomery's father was good-natured but somewhat ineffectual, while his mother was iron-willed and the disciplinarian in the family, particularly when it came to Bernard who was, as he later admitted, "the bad boy in the family, the rebellious one. As a result, I had to learn to stand or fall on my own." The family fortunes took a turn for the better when his father accepted a prestigious position back in England when Bernard was thirteen, and the boy was sent as a day student to the elite St. Paul's Academy. Seeking escape from his repressive home life, he decided while at St. Paul's that he would make the army his career. He entered the Royal Military Academy Sandhurst in 1907, at the age of twenty. There he worked hard, but was considered, as one historian has written, "a gauche figure," by the other students, many of whom were from Britain's upper classes. A bit of a "grind," in the parlance of the day, the small, whippet-thin Montgomery was a young man of outsized opinions, who never hesitated to argue with superior officers—in fact, he was told by one Sandhurst teacher that, with his attitude, he would "never get anywhere in the army."

AN OPEN GRAVE World War I, a conflagration that made Patton's skirmishes in Mexico seem like child's play, was the real first test of both Patton's and Montgomery's mettle. Patton arrived in France with the American Expeditionary Force in 1917, as an aide to Pershing, but sitting in the rear was not his style. He asked for and received a combat command.

Now that his beloved cavalry could play no real part in modern war, Patton became lieutenant colonel in charge of the U.S. Tank Corps. The job of these behemoth machines, first developed by the British, was to lead infantry attacks, to cross open ground under machine-gun fire, smash barbed wire, and bridge trenches. At least that was the idea. As Patton quickly found out, these early tanks were given to mechanical breakdown and prone to getting stuck in the mud. At the battle of Saint-Mihiel, in September 1918, Patton was wounded attempting to help the crews of other tanks that had stalled in the soggy ground, but not before he had bravely led a charge against heavy enemy machine-gun fire. Three people close to him were killed, another was wounded, but Patton kept on going, imagining all the time, he said later, that he was watched "from a cloud by my Confederate kinsmen and my Virginia grandfather." He was awarded the Distinguished Service Cross and given a battlefield promotion to full colonel.

Bernard Montgomery, like Patton, acquitted himself courageously. During one attack, when he was armed only with a sword, he saw a German soldier aiming a rifle at him. He tossed aside his sword, leaped on the man, and kicked him "as hard as I could in the lower part of the stomach." In 1914, Montgomery was shot by a sniper in the right lung while preparing to lead an attack. He would have been killed, but a soldier who went to help him was shot dead and fell on top of him, so that his corpse shielded Montgomery from several more bullets, although one eventually hit him in the knee. As it was, he was considered mortally wounded and a grave was dug for him, but he managed to pull through and was sent back to England to recuperate, although the lung would bother him for the rest of his life. He, too, received a decoration—the Distinguished Service Order, or DSO—and a promotion, to captain. Afterwards, he went back to France as a staff officer and rose to the rank of lieutenant colonel.

BETWEEN WARS After the end of the war, Captain George S. Patton—now reverted to his peacetime rank—tried to stay with the Tank Corps but found, to his dismay, that Congress had only granted five hundred dollars to subsidize the funding of an armored force for the United States. Bitterly disappointed, Patton accepted various assignments—one was serving under Army Chief of Staff Douglas MacArthur (each man became a lifelong admirer of the other)—and wrote numerous articles for military journals extolling the advantages of mechanized warfare. He spent time posted in Boston, Washington, and Pearl Harbor, the last in early 1935. (Patton's experience in Hawaii led him to write a highly prescient article speculating on the idea of a Japanese surprise attack on Pearl Harbor, six years before the event happened.)

But Patton was, in 1935, fifty years old and had only risen to lieutenant colonel in rank. He appeared to be going nowhere, and his brash style had made him enemies among certain senior army officers, although he had his supporters, as well—as one friend put it, he was either hated or loved: "there was no middle ground for such a personality."

Bernard Montgomery had a more successful post-war career. He went to the British Army's Staff College at Camberley—a prerequisite for any ambitious officer—and then became a brigade major with the Seventeenth Infantry Brigade, which was garrisoned in Cork, fighting the Irish Republican Army. It was the kind of war Monty hated—house-to-house fighting with guerillas, assassinations, bombs blowing up cars on peaceful streets—but he did his job well. Posted back to England he was given a position teaching army tactics at the Staff College he had attended six years earlier, and people within the military suddenly began to listen to what this funny little man, so voluble and so tightly wound (George Bernard Shaw would later call Monty "that intensely compacted hank of steel wire"), had to say.

Monty preached that the World War I battlefield tactics of simply pounding the hell out of your enemy with artillery fire and then attacking into the teeth of blazing machine-guns were obviously counterproductive: even if you did finally carry the day, the victory was almost always Pyrrhic. One needed to use intelligence far more carefully, to reconnoiter the enemy, to pinpoint weaknesses in his defensive positions, and then to muster forces for an all-out attempt to break through his lines at the most vulnerable spot.

Montgomery was then posted to Palestine and Egypt, and by 1937 had been sent back to Britain to become brigadier in command of the Ninth Infantry Brigade. While he was taking a well-deserved vacation at the beach, his beloved wife, Betty, was bitten by a mosquito. To Montgomery's shock, the bite became infected and she died quite suddenly of septicemia. Many people felt that this stable, vivacious woman was the person who kept Monty from going over the edge, kept him human: "added balance," as one biographer put it, "to his lopsided, narrow character." The army was everything to him, now.

Soon, however, Monty and Patton would be caught up in the biggest crisis of their professional lives, one that would change their fortunes utterly: World War II.

"FINISH WITH THIS CHAP ROMMEL" In 1939, Adolf Hitler proved beyond a doubt the advantages of tank warfare as his troops blitzkrieged across France in record time, and the U.S. Army now belatedly tried to catch up. Congress provided the needed funds, and George Patton—now recognized as a voice that had been crying out in the wilderness for some time—was made commanding general of the Second Armored Division.

Patton took over the division's training in the deserts of Nevada and drilled his tank commanders on his theories of concerted tank attack. The training took place in Nevada for a reason, because the United States was about to launch Operation Torch, a surprise invasion of North Africa, with Patton commanding the Western Task Force of the army. The Americans landed in the desert countries of Morocco and Algeria in November of 1942, quickly overwhelmed the French Vichy defenses, and then moved on to join up with the British Eighth Army.

A few months before this, in August of 1942, Bernard Law Montgomery, now a lieutenant general, had been sent to Egypt to take command of the Eighth Army and stabilize the British war efforts there. Erwin Rommel's vaunted Afrika Korps had pushed the British back through Libya and Egypt and was now not far from Cairo. It was only a stroke of bad fortune that got Monty the command there—Winston Churchill's candidate for the job was killed when his plane was attacked by German fighters. But Monty, with typical single-mindedness, transformed the Eighth Army. He coordinated army and air headquarters, which made for easier ground–air communications in combat, and made sure his commanders knew that now was no time for retreat: every contingency plan for withdrawal was to be burned.

Monty also spent a good deal of time with his troops, something the previous general staff had not done, and the morale of the front line soldiers, who tended

to love him, increased accordingly. In a well-publicized speech, Montgomery said: "We are going to finish with this chap Rommel once and for all. It will be quite easy. There is no doubt about it."

At the very end of August, Rommel attempted to encircle and destroy the British Eighth Army but, aided by top-secret ULTRA reports (decrypted German radio transmissions) that allowed him to know Rommel's movements ahead of time, Monty was able to stop him. In October 1942, Montgomery led British forces, including the Australian Ninth Division, as they pushed the Afrika Korps back and won the pivotal battle of el-Alamein, the first large-scale Allied victory of the war. Suddenly, Montgomery was lionized, knighted by the king and promoted to full general. His confidence, never at low ebb, knew no bounds.

"AN OLD MAN OF ABOUT 60" In Monty's opinion, American intervention had come just as he was pushing the Germans back—too little, too late—and, in any event, American units detached to help the British had fared miserably. The battle of Kasserine Pass had been a humiliating disaster, which saw American troops fleeing in terror before the Afrika Korps. George Patton was sent to remedy this and he stepped into legend when he arrived as Commander

ABOVE General George S. Patton uses his baton to emphasize a point while discussing strategy in Africa. As Commander of II Corps he did much to transform the inexperienced American troops but added to tensions between Americans and British.

301

OPPOSITE PAGE General Eisenhower and Field Marshal Montgomery, with Air Marshal Sir Arthur Tedder (rear), observe maneuvers during field exercises on Salisbury Plain, prior to D-Day.

IKE AND MONTY

Monty and Patton were not the only generals of the Allied high command to be rivals—there was not a great deal of love lost between Monty and Dwight Eisenhower, either. Eisenhower, as Allied Supreme Commander, was Monty's boss (as he was Patton's) but the two men clashed frequently, so much so that Eisenhower, who prided himself on his congeniality, once exclaimed: "Damnit, Montgomery is the only man in either army I can't get along with."

One of the issues that Montgomery had with Eisenhower was that the American commander was, admittedly, a great organizer, but had never commanded in combat. "Nice chap; no general," Monty said of him, contemptuously. Monty, of course, resented the attitude of some American officers, who felt that they had come in and saved the British in North Africa. This was not an attitude reflected by Eisenhower; however, as head of the American war machine, he took the brunt of Monty's anger. Things only got worse in Europe. Monty, whom Eisenhower temporarily put in charge of Allied ground forces in the field during the invasion of Normandy, was promoted to field marshal (a rank that does not exist in the American army) by the grateful British. He thought this made him permanent leader of the British and American ground forces, superseding Eisenhower's second in command, General Omar Bradley. When Ike made it clear this was not the case, Monty claimed that Ike had "demoted" him, and relations between the two became increasingly strained.

Finally, when Monty announced to the British press that his troops had saved the Americans at the Battle of the Bulge—with nineteen thousand American casualties and only two hundred British ones, this was hardly likely—Eisenhower decided to relieve him of command. When an aide to Eisenhower informed Montgomery of this, Monty wrote an abject letter to Ike that ended with the words "Your very devoted subordinate, Monty," and Eisenhower relented.

THE "WILD GOOSE CHASE" OF TASK FORCE BAUM

One of the times Patton's impulsive and headstrong nature got him into trouble was in late March 1945, about a month away from the end of the war in Europe. Knowing that there were Americans being held in a Nazi POW camp about sixty miles away from the position of the Third Army, Patton decided to liberate them. Other officers opposed this decision, but Patton overrode these objections and sent Task Force Baum—so named for its commander, Captain Abraham Baum—on its way. However, Baum's force consisted of only three hundred men and fifteen tanks, hardly enough to fight their way through such an overwhelming enemy presence. Still, with incredible tenacity and heroism, Task Force Baum actually reached the prison camp after fifty-two straight hours of fighting and managed to liberate the Americans. It was all for naught, however. The Wehrmacht called in reinforcements and tightened a ring around the Americans; in the end, all but thirty-five men of Task Force Baum were either killed or captured.

News of the operation was made public and it appeared that Patton had an ulterior motive for ordering the attack in the face of military logic. His son-in-law, Lieutenant Colonel John Waters, who had been captured in North Africa in 1943, was in the camp and Patton knew it as early as February 9, when he was informed of this by General Eisenhower. In fact, this is one reason why he deliberately failed to get Eisenhower's approval for the raid, for Eisenhower would certainly not have approved. Waters—wounded during the fighting for the POW camp—was liberated ten days later, along with many of the soldiers of Task Force Baum who had been captured by the Germans. General Omar Bradley claimed that the whole operation was "a wild goose chase that ended in tragedy." Typically unrepentant, Patton said that his only mistake was not sending a larger force to liberate the camp.

of II Corps. Chain-smoking, wearing two pearl-handled pistols, barking orders, he was like no one these G.I.'s had ever seen. Although he forced them to much higher standards of discipline—everyone needed to wear his helmet and officers were forced to don neckties—they respected him for it.

Just before Patton took command, he attended a "study week" given for high Allied Command in February 1943 and run by none other than Monty, in his favorite role as teacher. Montgomery complained that "Only one American has come (the Comd. of an Armored Corps; an old man of about 60)." This, indeed, was Patton, although he was actually fifty-eight and only two years older than Monty. He listened for a while to Montgomery's preaching about preparation, meticulous intelligence, and detailed organizing being the heart of successful warfare. When the class was done, Patton said quite loudly: "I may be old, I may be slow, I may be stupid, and I know I'm deaf, but it just don't mean a thing to me."

Then he left. He complained to Dwight Eisenhower, overall commander of Allied forces, that these British did not know how to fight, but Eisenhower, who had his own problems with Monty, warned him not to publicly criticize the British. But Patton did bring about a transformation in the American forces. By mid-May, with the combined efforts of both the Americans and British, the Germans were pushed entirely out of North Africa.

OPERATION HUSKY The planning then began for the invasion of Sicily—Operation Husky—as a prelude to attacking up the Italian peninsula. Here, Montgomery and Patton really began to clash. The Americans at this point in the war were providing the bulk of the funding for men and materiel for both British and American forces, and Dwight Eisenhower was in command of the armies from both countries (although he liked to ease this a little for the British by saying, "I'm not an American, I'm an Allied."). But Montgomery was unquestionably the general with the most battle experience.

The only problem was, most Americans could not stand him. He was not hated simply because he was British—as one historian has put it, his arrogance, brusqueness, and standoffishness "would have been equally as distasteful in an American." These personality qualities came into play during the planning of Husky. The first plan had George Patton, in charge of the Seventh Army, going in near the capital city of Palermo in the northwest while Montgomery's Eighth Army hit ports in southeastern Sicily. Montgomery—seeing all the headlines going to Patton—convinced Eisenhower to change the attack so that Patton's army group supported the British, while Montgomery made the main thrust.

On July 9, 1943, the invasion began, with Monty's Eighth Army taking Syracuse while the Americans were bogged down under wave after wave of German counterattacks. Montgomery seriously increased Allied intercommand tensions by suggesting that Patton wait—simply "hold firm"—while he, Monty, headed for Palermo to cut off the enemy. Patton replied: "If we wait for them to take this island while we twiddle our thumbs, we'll wait forever." Even Eisenhower claimed that "Monty is trying to steal the show."

Instead, Patton stole it from him. Dividing his army, he headed straight for Palermo with one part of it—without all the accoutrements that Monty insisted on, air support, adequate intelligence, flanks properly guarded—and captured the capital in six days.

Capturing Palermo was not strategically all that important, but it certainly got the attention of the press and infuriated Montgomery. The rivalry between Patton and Monty was now getting highly personal. Monty cabled Patton and told him he was flying to meet him near Palermo, using the Flying Fortress, complete with an American crew, that Monty had won from another American general in a bet and was intensely proud of. He asked Patton if the runway was long enough for such a big plane, but Patton did not quite answer this question, and Monty went ahead anyway.

As it turned out, the runway was too short for the Fortress, which skidded off to the side and was wrecked. No one was hurt, but Monty wrote a friend: "I nearly got killed in my Fortress the other day trying to land at Palermo to see Patton. He said it was OK for a Fortress, but it was far too small."

"THE FINEST DEMONSTRATION" Nearly getting Monty killed did not get George Patton into trouble, but slapping a shell-shocked American soldier did. Patton, visiting an American field hospital in August, found the man huddled and weeping on a bed, slapped him across the face with his gloves, called him a coward, and kicked him out of the hospital. A week later, a similar incident occurred. When the press heard about them, Patton—only a short time beforehand a conquering American hero—was attacked for being a bully. There were calls for his removal. Eisenhower would not agree to this, saying Patton was "indispensable" to the war effort, but he did send him to Britain to prepare for the coming invasion of Normandy.

There, Patton continued to get into trouble. Where his nickname had previously been "Old Blood and Guts," he became known as "General Foot-in-the-Mouth" for suggesting that the British, Americans, and Russians had a "destiny to rule the world." His dislike of Montgomery, whose army was now fighting its way slowly up the Italian peninsula, continued. He liked to refer to him as "a timid little fart," because of Monty's methodical ways, and when he was forced to toast him at a dinner, he wrote in his diary "the lightning did not strike me."

But Monty got the last laugh on D-Day. While Patton's Third Army was held in reserve in Britain, Monty was in charge of Allied forces on the ground and spearheaded the largest invasion the world had ever known on June 6, 1944. While an immensely frustrated Patton fumed, Monty attacked, fighting a slogging, two and a half month battle in Normandy against entrenched German forces. Finally let into the fight on August 1, Patton more than evened up the rivalry. His Third

RIGHT **RIGHT** U.S. tanks of the Ninth Army plough through heavy mud to open the road for the infantry, as the Allied armies advance towards Germany in November 1944.

306

Army sealed off Brittany and then, exceeding their cautious orders, surged inland in what one historian has called "perhaps the finest demonstration of rapid mobile warfare ever seen in military history." For once, he and Monty were working in concert, driving the enemy back through France, with a giant pincer movement ready to snap shut on the retreating Germans at the city of Falaise. Then the Allied High Command ordered Patton to pull back. Patton interpreted this as an attempt to give Monty all the glory, but it had more to do with Eisenhower's caution, with not wanting to overextend the army, than anything else.

In any event, the Falaise Gap, as it became known, allowed thousands of retreating Germans to fight again another day. On August 20, the gap was finally closed, and then Patton continued with his surge, arriving on August 26 in Paris. Patton had gone four hundred miles in twenty-six days and inflicted 100,000 casualties on the Germans. Packs of reporters followed him everywhere. He was back in his glory.

ENDING THE WAR The Allies were now faced with a choice as to the best way to punch into Germany. Montgomery wanted to attack through Holland, while Patton wanted to send the Third Army through what was known as the Nancy Gap, pushing across the Moselle and Sauer rivers. The two men battled with each other over these alternatives before Eisenhower finally chose Monty's approach in an attempt to appease him. "To hell with Monty," an enraged Patton wrote in his diary. The result, Operation Market Garden, launched in September of 1944, was a dismal failure, and after a few months of fighting the Allies settled in for the winter.

Or so they thought—because on December 16, Adolf Hitler took a huge gamble, sending an enormous force of German infantry and tanks in a surprise attack through the Ardennes Forest, hoping to split the Allied forces and make their way to the port of Antwerp. The British were on the north of this German thrust, the Americans to the south. This was exactly the kind of situation where Patton excelled. Declaring that "the Kraut has stuck his head in the meat grinder and I've got the handle," he immediately sent three divisions to the rescue of the Americans of the 101st Airborne Division, trapped in the strategic city of Bastogne, and turned the tide against the Germans. By February they were in full retreat.

Montgomery's troops had fought bravely during the battle but were involved on a far lesser scale than the Americans, who took the brunt of the attack. Unfortunately, Montgomery attempted in a press conference to take credit for the victory ("one of the most interesting and tricky battles I have ever handled," was the way he put it, implying he was in charge). This so enraged many Americans and Britons that Monty's reputation suffered irreparable harm. One high-ranking British official said that he wished someone would "muzzle or better still, chloroform" Monty. "His love of publicity is a disease like alcoholism or taking drugs and ... it sends him equally mad."

PATTON AND MONTGOMERY THE WARRIOR AGAINST THE PLANNER

Undeterred in their rivalry, Monty and Patton set their sights on being the first to capture Berlin. Patton was the first to reach the Rhine—unzipping his pants as he crossed the bridge to pee into the river—but neither he nor Montgomery would grasp the prize of Berlin. The ever-political Eisenhower decided it would be best if the Soviet Army were allowed to sweep through the city, which they did, on April 21. By April 30, Hitler had killed himself. Eight days later, the war ended.

TOO MUCH ALIKE Say what you will about them, both George Patton and Bernard Montgomery were warriors, and warriors never fare too well in peacetime. Patton got into trouble with Eisenhower because of his repeated anti-Soviet tirades—at one press conference he said, "Do you want a lot of Communists in power ... the Nazi thing is just like the Democratic or Republican thing," implying that the Nazis had been like any other political party but the Soviets were a real threat. When he met with Soviet generals another time, one of them asked, through a translator, if he would have a drink with them. Patton replied to the translator: "Tell that Russian sonuvabitch ... that I regard them as enemies and I'd rather cut my throat than have a drink with one of my enemies."

Eisenhower had no choice but to relieve Patton of command of the Third Army, although he did it gently, arranging to give him command of something called the Fifteenth U.S. Army, which was really a motley array of service troops, clerks, and cooks. Patton accepted his demotion, although it depressed him profoundly. On December 9, 1945, on his way to hunt pheasants near Manheim, Germany, his car struck a truck crossing the road in front of him, and Patton was paralyzed from the neck down. He died of an embolism on December 21, 1945.

Monty lived much longer, dying in 1976 at the age of eighty-eight after helping to create NATO, but his old age had been a difficult one. Despite the fact that he was now a viscount, he lived on a modest pension check and had difficulty making ends meet. He died soon after a particularly tragic loss, when someone broke into his home and stole most of his wartime memorabilia.

Patton and Montgomery, even down to the way they died, were quite different. Still, the reason they were rivals is that they might actually have been the same at the core. As Omar Bradley once wrote: "Patton didn't particularly like Monty. Too cocky for him. Possibly too much like Patton himself."

HARRY S. TRUMAN

VERSUS DOUGLAS MACARTHUR

HARRY S. TRUMAN AND DOUGLAS MACARTHUR:
THE PRESIDENT VS. THE GENERAL

THE PRESIDENTIAL PRESS RELEASE, ISSUED TO bleary-eyed reporters in the White House press room at one o'clock in the morning of April 11, 1951, was written in language whose terseness only added to the drama of its message:

> *With deep regret I have concluded that General of the Army Douglas MacArthur is unable to give his wholehearted support to the policies of the United States Government and the United Nations in matters pertaining to his official duties. In view of the specific responsibilities imposed upon me by the Constitution of the United States and the added responsibility which has been entrusted to me by the United Nations, I have decided that I must make a change of command in the Far East. I have therefore relieved General MacArthur of his commands ...*

> *Full and vigorous debate on matters of national policy is a vital element in the constitutional system of our free democracy. It is fundamental, however, that military commanders must be governed by the policies and directives issued to them in the manner provided by our laws and Constitution ...*

One of the most explosive documents in American history was signed simply: *HST*, which stood for Harry S. Truman. The press release set off shock waves in a nation at war in Korea and beset by fears of Communism on all sides. During such perilous times how could the president of the United States relieve his top general, the man famous for his brilliant surprise attack at Inchon, for his reconstruction of post-war Japan, for the "island-hopping" policy that spelled victory for the

United States and its allies in the Pacific from 1941 to 1945? Within forty-eight hours, 125,000 telegrams had poured into Congress complaining about Truman's actions—"Impeach the B[astard] who calls himself President," one read. "Impeach the Imbecile," said another. In New York thousands of workers staged a spontaneous strike over Truman's decision, and in Los Angeles the city council canceled the day's activities to give time to "sorrowful contemplation of the political assassination of General MacArthur." Flags flew at half-mast and Truman was hanged in effigy in numerous small towns. April 11, 1951, was described by a contemporary writer as "one of the bitterest ... in modern times."

How could a president relieving a military commander cause such a firestorm? To understand that we need to go back into the lives of two rivals who were so utterly different from each other that it could be said they lived on separate planets.

DOUGLAS MACARTHUR Douglas MacArthur, born in 1880, in Little Rock, Arkansas, had both the blessing and the curse of being the son of a great American hero. His father, Arthur MacArthur, Jr., had, as an eighteen-year-old lieutenant, led his Wisconsin regiment up Seminary Ridge at the battle of Gettysburg, thus winning America's highest military honor, the Congressional Medal of Honor. Arthur MacArthur remained in the army after the Civil War and Douglas, the youngest of three brothers, said that his first memory was the sound of a bugle.

From the beginning, Douglas was the chosen one in his family. He entered the prestigious West Point Military Academy in 1898, at the age of eighteen, and was accompanied by his mother, who took a suite of rooms near the campus to make sure he had all the comforts he needed. After graduating in 1903, MacArthur was posted to the Philippines, where his father had been sent during the Spanish–American War.

MacArthur's connections proved invaluable, as he then became an aide-de-camp to President Theodore Roosevelt in 1906 and was sent to Vera Cruz, Mexico, in 1914, when the United States was embroiled in an armed dispute with the new government of Mexico. MacArthur, in his first combat, showed a flair for daring when he raced behind Mexican lines to steal three boxcars that the United States army badly needed to transport men and supplies.

MacArthur was brave, but also flamboyant, vain, and not quite to be trusted. He spent some months after his Vera Cruz episode angling for a Medal of Honor (he did not get one) and probably exaggerating his exploits. The thirty-four-year-old major had also taken to wearing an ostentatious cravat around his neck and smoking a pipe—becoming, as one historian has written, "a peacock among pigeons." If he did not quite speak in the royal "we," he certainly acted as if his opinion were the only one that mattered. (In this he appeared to take after his father—Arthur MacArthur's longtime aide reportedly said: "Arthur MacArthur was the most flamboyantly egotistical man I had ever seen—until I met his son.") Unlike his father, whose career had essentially stalled after the Civil War, Douglas MacArthur kept on ascending. Service in World War I would see him win an astonishing seven Silver Stars for bravery (despite a later reputation for being a coward). After the war, he continued to rise through the peacetime army, becoming superintendent of West Point. In 1925, he was appointed major general, the youngest in the army, and he became Chief of Staff of the Army ten years later, as war clouds began looming over Europe and the Pacific.

HARRY S. TRUMAN Interestingly enough, the "S" in Harry S. Truman stands for nothing at all. It was a compromise made by Harry Truman's mother after he was born in Missouri, in 1884. One grandfather's middle name was Shippe and the other's first name was Solomon, so why not please both (or displease neither) by simply using the letter "S"? It was this kind of homespun practicality that Truman would carry with him all his life. His father, John Truman, was a farmer and cattle dealer, and his mother, Martha, looked after Harry and his three siblings. Truman's family was respectably middle class; he grew up playing the piano and reading the classics as well as doing hard farm work. But politics was his early passion—he read everything he could on U.S. presidents and even served as a page at the 1900 Democratic Convention in Kansas City.

After graduating high school in 1910, the diminutive and deceptively mild-seeming young man took a series of clerical jobs and, as America entered World War I in 1918, joined the army, despite having such poor eyesight that he had to memorize the eye chart to pass the entrance exam. Sent to France as a captain in an artillery regiment, he proved a tough officer and good leader, although he had nowhere near the distinguished war record of Douglas MacArthur. After the war, as MacArthur was rising in the military, Truman allied himself with the notorious Kansas City political boss Tom Prendergast. In the 1920s, he was elected to a judgeship; in 1934, he became a senator from Missouri. A strong supporter of President Franklin Roosevelt's New Deal program, intended to bail the American economy out of the Great Depression, Truman had close ties with the Roosevelt administration, which helped him get re-elected to the Senate in 1940, despite the conviction of his mentor Prendergast on income tax evasion charges.

By 1940, Harry Truman was seen by most as a party politician, about as honest as most of them, but not more so, a man who toed the Democratic line and did what he was told. The real Harry Truman had yet to come onstage.

"I SHALL RETURN" When the war began, Douglas MacArthur was in an interesting position. He had officially retired from the army, after bickering with the Roosevelt administration over his hawkish views on Japan and Nazi Germany's military build-up. By 1941, he had accepted an offer from a friend, President of the Philippines Manuel Quezon, to help him create a Philippine army. Thus he was perfectly placed when Japanese planes bombed Pearl Harbor and the Philippines in early December of 1941, precipitating America's entry into World War II. Roosevelt had recalled him to the United States army the previous July and made him commander of the United States forces in the Far East. As the Japanese invaded the Philippines, MacArthur was made a four-star general.

It is here that much of the MacArthur legend and controversy starts. MacArthur was certainly, like the rest of the American military, caught off guard by the Japanese surprise attacks of December 7–8. He was forced to abandon his army in the Philippines to the not-so-tender mercies of the Japanese and flee to Australia. Despite the fact that President Roosevelt awarded him the Congressional Medal of Honor, making him (at the time) part of the only father–son Medal of Honor winning pair in history, the defeat smarted and he announced to the Philippine people and the world: "I shall return."

In an extraordinary rebuilding and organizational feat, he helped launch the counteroffensive against the Japanese in 1942, a counteroffensive that was based on the strategy of cutting off and isolating major Japanese island bases in the Pacific, while ferociously attacking others as the Americans "island-hopped" their way north to within striking distance of Japan. As the invasion of Japan was being planned—an invasion that was forecast to cost millions of casualties, both Japanese and American—the United States dropped two atomic bombs on the cities of Hiroshima and Nagasaki in August of 1945. Douglas MacArthur accepted the official surrender of Japan on September 2, acting as surrogate for President Harry S. Truman, the man who had ordered the atom bombs dropped.

"THE MOON, THE STARS, AND ALL THE PLANETS" Harry Truman's rise from workmanlike senator to president had occurred in a matter of five short years. As the election year of 1944 began, Franklin Roosevelt, unhappy with his vice president, Henry Wallace, chose Harry Truman to be his new running mate. Truman, in his second term in the Senate, had distanced himself from the Prendergast scandals and won a reputation for fairness and probity, earning nationwide praise for chairing the Special Committee Investigating National Defense, which exposed graft in the defense industry. That November, Roosevelt won easily over the Republican Thomas E. Dewey and Truman was carried into the White House as vice president, perhaps the highest sinecure the farm-boy from Missouri could hope to aspire to.

But a few short months later, on April 12, 1945, Franklin Roosevelt died of a cerebral hemorrhage and Harry Truman became president of the most powerful country in the world, locked in the most deadly struggle the world had ever known. He had served exactly eighty-two days as vice president and had little or no knowledge of international affairs. He told reporters: "When they told me [about Roosevelt's death] I felt like the moon, the stars, and all the planets had fallen on me."

"GIVE 'EM HELL, HARRY!"

A few years before his final run-in with Douglas MacArthur, Harry Truman had been involved in one of the most incredible presidential races in American history.

Vice President Truman had ascended to the top job in April 1945 following the sudden death of President Franklin Roosevelt, but following in the outsized footsteps of the popular and charismatic Roosevelt had proven difficult. By the election year of 1948, wartime price controls had been rescinded, inflation was at an all-time high, and Americans' fear of Communist Russia was reaching an almost paranoid level.

Truman had become so unpopular that a joke going around the country went: "I wonder what Truman would do if he were alive." Even his own Democratic Party made overtures to Dwight Eisenhower, the popular war hero, to replace Truman. Eisenhower refused and Truman was left to face Republican candidate Thomas E. Dewey. Dewey was forty-six years old, a crime-busting governor of New York, whose young, efficient aides worked like top staffers of a well-run corporation. Truman was given little chance of winning against this efficient juggernaut, but went all out on a whistle-stop train tour of 31,000 miles and more than 350 speeches—"giving hell," in his own words, to his opponent—while Dewey, afraid of losing his lead, ran a timid campaign.

Even the night before the election, Truman was expected to lose, and the *Chicago Tribune* printed an edition with the bold headline: "DEWEY DEFEATS TRUMAN." But Truman surprised everyone by winning the election by a margin of almost three million votes. It was a glorious victory for underdogs everywhere, and a lesson for frontrunners: never take anything for granted.

Truman was faced with numerous challenges in the next few years. With the war over and defense industries no longer driving the economy, America experienced inflation, severe housing shortages, and wage strikes in major industries. At the same time, the Cold War had started. Russia attempted to build its own atomic bomb and also aggressively tried to extend control in Europe by blocking access to Berlin, a situation Truman resolved by airlifting supplies to the beleaguered city. The Berlin Airlift was one of Truman's signal foreign policy triumphs, but the American people, tired of the stress of battling inflation in a changed, postwar world, did not think Harry was the charismatic leader they needed. By the election year of 1948 Truman's performance on the domestic front was seen as so dismal that "To err is Truman" became a common saying. While Truman ultimately made an astounding comeback against Thomas E. Dewey, he watched himself being overshadowed by numerous figures on the national scene, in particular by Douglas MacArthur, who that year had made a run at the presidency himself.

"I SUGGEST THAT YOU MAKE A VISIT HOME"

Douglas MacArthur excelled as Supreme Commander of the Allied Powers of Japan (SCAP). While many were calling for the execution, or at least forced abdication, of Emperor Hirohito, MacArthur refused, knowing that the Japanese needed this figurehead in their lives as a link to the past. While he did prosecute numerous Japanese as war criminals, he also helped rebuild the nation as a constitutional democracy, extended the vote to women, allowed the formation of labor unions, liberalized school curriculums, and encouraged free enterprise by dismantling huge, state-run monopolies.

As always with MacArthur, there were contradictions. He himself lived like a lord in the so-called Big House, drove everywhere in his Cadillac V-12 sedan with fender flags flying (one the American flag, the other with five silver stars, denoting his rank) and with a license plate that simply read "1." He made few attempts to actually meet the ordinary Japanese he was helping, and several hundred of them lined up daily outside the Dai Ichi building where he worked, simply to get a look at this august presence. In the meantime, the general's press officers were busy bombarding the public back home with favorable press releases about what a great job MacArthur was doing.

Harry Truman, like any politician anxious about a potential rival, had begun to keep a close eye on MacArthur, and was especially irritated when MacArthur made a public announcement claiming he needed only two hundred thousand men in Japan, instead of his current half a million, thus undermining Truman's attempt to establish a peacetime military draft. In 1947, Truman decided that he wanted MacArthur home to have a little chat with him about domestic political realities and sent him a cable politely saying, "I suggest that you make a visit home."

This was not really a suggestion, of course, but an order from MacArthur's commander in chief, but MacArthur, rather incredibly, refused. He claimed that the situation in Japan was "too dangerous" for him to leave, although he refused to specify why he thought so. Truman backed down, but a year later he sent a request through his military attaché to MacArthur, stating that "the President directs me to advise you that he thinks [visiting Washington] would be very appropriate and timely." Once again MacArthur refused, and once again Truman did not force the issue. That same year, MacArthur, encouraged by the fact that a "MacArthur for President" petition had been signed in Wisconsin by 100,000 voters, threw his hat into the presidential ring. It proved to be a brief fling—unwilling to come to the United States, he could not campaign—and after showing dismally in a few primaries, he dropped out.

Truman now secretly attempted to replace MacArthur, but found no qualified officer who would take the job. The stage was set for a confrontation that would test both men, and the United States Constitution, as never before.

WAR IN KOREA In 1945, after the surrender of Japan, America and the Soviet Union had divided the Korean peninsula (formerly controlled by Japan) at the 38th parallel north. Two separate countries were created: South Korea, closely allied with the United States, and North Korea, strongly aided by the Soviets and Chinese Communists, who, under Mao Zedong, had triumphed over Chiang Kai-shek and his Nationalist forces in 1949 (see page 275). On June 25, 1950, the North Korean Imnun Gun army swept out of the mountains and down through the valleys of South Korea, driving the ill-prepared Republic of Korea (ROK) armies before them. The United Nations called on its members to support South Korea (sixteen nations agreed, although the United States provided over ninety percent of troops and funds) and appointed MacArthur as overall commander. Nevertheless, within two months the Imnun Gun had reached the Naktong River and were advancing on the port city Pusan. U.N. forces established a perimeter around Pusan and held it in fierce fighting, but the situation was dire.

In what many historians feel is his finest hour, the now seventy-year-old MacArthur immediately sensed that the way out of the situation was not a massive frontal attack against the North Koreans at Pusan, which would cost thousands of lives, but instead an attack in the enemy's rear. In a dramatic presentation to the Joint Chiefs of Staff, he convinced them (and therefore Truman) that a landing could be made at Inchon, 150 miles northwest of Pusan. The Imnun Gun would be caught between the two U.N. forces and destroyed. Despite the many difficulties of the operation—which included tides that varied thirty-two feet—MacArthur made an amphibious assault on Inchon on September 15 and caught the North Koreans by surprise. Outflanked, the Imnun Gun began to retreat and the U.N. forces broke out of the Pusan perimeter. Linking up with MacArthur's invasion force, they were in Pyongyang, the North Korean capital, by October 20th.

All was going so brilliantly that even President Truman wanted to bask in some of MacArthur's reflected glory and was willing to go halfway around the

world to meet him on Wake Island, two thousand miles south of Japan in the Pacific Ocean.

"IT WOULD BE A SLAUGHTER"
The meeting at Wake, on October 15, 1950, was the only time Douglas MacArthur and Harry Truman were ever in each other's presence. While supporters of Truman insist that he did not have political motives in going to visit MacArthur—now far and away the most popular figure in America—it is apparent that at least on some level the president did. The mid-term November elections were coming up and the Democrats certainly needed some shoring up. MacArthur knew this and was infuriated at Truman for dragging him away from the war, but his rudeness to his commander

ABOVE U.S. marines in amphibious assault craft move towards Inchon to outflank the North Koreans encircling the U.N. forces at Pusan. The plan, initiated by MacArthur, was successful and turned the tide of the war.

319

in chief was foolish and inexcusable. MacArthur arrived on Wake first, but he was not waiting for Truman as the plane's door opened and the president stepped out on the tarmac. When the general did stride up, he did not salute Truman, but instead simply reached out and shook hands.

The two men first conversed privately and later claimed that they had discovered that they really liked each other—this was almost certainly a lie put out for public consumption. As one historian later wrote, "they never wavered in their mutual contempt." In a public briefing, however, Truman did put one question to MacArthur, the one that was on everyone's mind after the triumphant landing at Inchon. Would the Communist Chinese attempt to cross the border and intervene in the war? MacArthur's reply was dismissive: "Had they intervened in the first or second month of the war, it would have been decisive. We are no longer fearful of their intervention. They have no air force ... If the Chinese tried to get down to Pyongyang it would be a slaughter."

ACROSS THE YALU Ten days after the Wake meeting, as ROK and U.N. forces stood on the banks of the Yalu River, the border between North Korea and Manchuria, one hundred thousand Chinese troops, marching only at night, crossed the Yalu bridges and made a massive attack, decimating the regiments that faced them. MacArthur begged for permission to bomb the bridges, but Truman and the Joint Chiefs of Staff gave him only limited options, afraid of stirring up the Chinese too much. The Chinese vanished briefly—the attack was intended to be a warning to the Americans not to get too close to their borders—but MacArthur, in his supreme arrogance, ignored them and continued pushing troops north. On November 25, three hundred thousand Chinese troops attacked across the now frozen Yalu, sending the U.N. troops reeling back and inflicting heavy losses. By December, they were in full retreat.

Truman wrote bitterly in his diary, thinking back on his Wake Island humiliation, that MacArthur had assured him "that victory was won ... and the Chinese Communists would not attack." It was a disaster of epic proportions for the Truman administration and made even worse by the fact that MacArthur, speaking to American reporters, told them that he had been unable to respond effectively to the Chinese attack because his hands were tied by Washington, "an enormous handicap, without precedent in military history." Truman furiously issued a gag order for all military commanders, but this did little good. MacArthur's pride was wounded—the glory that had covered him since Inchon was now besmirched—and MacArthur's pride lay at the heart of who he was. In February 1951, General Matthew Ridgeway of the Eighth Army managed to drive the Chinese back to the 38th parallel, and Truman now sought a way to negotiate an end to what was turning into a long, stalemated war. Enraged by what he considered capitulation, MacArthur sent a public message to the Chinese, demanding that they surrender or face "a decision by the United Nations to depart from its tolerant efforts to contain the war ... that would doom Red China to the risk of imminent military collapse."

"RANK INSUBORDINATION" Truman was infuriated by this statement, issued without clearance from Washington, and more was to come. MacArthur sent a letter to Republican Congressman Joseph Martin criticizing Truman's foreign policy, saying, "If we lose this war to Communism in Asia, the fall of Europe is inevitable." On April 5, Martin read this missive aloud on the floor of Congress, causing Truman to write in his diary: "This looks like the last straw. Rank insubordination." It is a tenet of the American Constitution that the president has complete control of the military. It is not for a general to make or influence foreign policy or, indeed, enter into any politics. This is why, when Abraham Lincoln appointed Ulysses S. Grant to head the Union Army during the Civil War, he told him: "You are not to decide, discuss or confer with anyone or ask political questions ... such questions the President holds in his own hands."

MacArthur added further fuel to the fire by giving interviews in which he called the tactics of the United States in Korea "ludicrous," and this was enough for Truman. He wrote out the famous order, quoted above, firing MacArthur, on April 10th. But an aide told him that if MacArthur got wind of it before it was

LINCOLN AND
MCCLELLAN

The other famous clash in American history between a president and his top general occurred during the Civil War, when President Abraham Lincoln appointed young thirty-four-year-old George McClellan commander in chief of the Union Army of the Potomac. McClellan—Little Mac, as he was called—was handsome and popular with his men, but one of the most terrible generals in American history. He consistently overestimated the strength of his Confederate enemies and moved at such a glacial pace that Lincoln was once moved to write him: "If you don't want to use the army, I should like to borrow it for awhile."

In 1862, after McClellan's overly cautious performance at the bloody battle of Antietam, Lincoln finally had had enough and relieved him of command.

The Democrats saw their chance to challenge Lincoln in 1864, with the still-embittered McClellan as their candidate. McClellan came out swinging, calling Lincoln "Nothing more than a well-meaning baboon ... What a specimen to be at the head of our affairs now!" But Lincoln easily beat McClellan. Much to the former general's disappointment, the Army of the Potomac, which he had bragged would vote for him to a man, went for Lincoln four votes to one.

issued publicly, he would probably resign, to which Truman replied: "That son-of-a-bitch isn't going to resign on me. I want him fired." Thus the press release was given out to stunned reporters at one o'clock on the morning of April 11th.

As the outcry mounted in the United States, Douglas MacArthur—those around him said he seemed oddly calm, as if this was the outcome he had been seeking—flew home to America for the first time in fourteen years. He claimed that he accepted the president's right to fire him, but was humiliated that it was done in so public a fashion (ignoring, of course, his own public attempts to embarrass Truman). When he touched down in San Francisco, there was, as one of his aides said, "an indescribable scene of pandemonium," as half a million supporters thronged the roads leading from the airport to his hotel.

"OLD SOLDIERS NEVER DIE" Republicans naturally sought to use the worship directed at MacArthur to embarrass the Democratic president, and they insisted that MacArthur be brought forward to explain his side of things to a Joint Session of Congress. At 12:31 p.m., on April 19, with millions of people tuning in on radio and the newly popular television, MacArthur stood before both Houses of Congress and talked for an hour and a half, trying to dispel what he called "the unreality" of American thinking on Asia. He claimed that the Truman administration, by not allowing him to carry the war directly to China, was trying to appease the Red Chinese—appeasement being one of the dirtiest words one could throw around in the Cold War. Interrupted by wild applause, the general closed the speech by remembering the lines of the soldier's ballad, which said: 'Old soldiers never die. They just fade away.' And like the soldier in the ballad, I now close my military career and just fade away—an old soldier who tried to do his duty as God gave him the light to see it. Good-bye."

Many members of his audience in Congress began to weep. One senator shouted: "We have heard God speak today!" Another said: "I have never feared more for the institutions of this country. I honestly felt that if the speech had gone on any longer there might have been a march on the White House."

In the White House, Truman and his advisors watched in despair as the entire country seemed to turn against them—Truman had foreseen an outcry when he fired MacArthur, but not the frenzy that greeted the action. Seven million people now lined a parade route as MacArthur went to New York, where he was to take up residence with his wife. Truman tried to fight back, by leaking the notes of his Wake Island meeting at which MacArthur had said that the Chinese would not intervene, but it did little good.

"THE WRONG WAR" On May 3 Congress opened hearings on the conduct of the Korean War, and once again MacArthur was the star witness. But something curious began to happen. Despite the fact that MacArthur's testimony was as magisterial and authoritative as ever, his star was tarnished by other

American generals summoned to speak to the senators, men who pointed out that engaging in an all-out war against China would be pure folly. Attacking China, said General Omar Bradley, Chairman of the Joint Chiefs of Staff, would put America "in the wrong war, at the wrong place, at the wrong time, and with the wrong enemy." He also told Congress that MacArthur's actions in speaking publicly against Truman were "against all custom and tradition for a military man."

By the end of the hearings, one powerful senator was asking out loud if "the deification of this infallible leader" was a mistake. Why had MacArthur pushed his forces so close to the Yalu? How had he expected the Communists to react, after all? *New York Times* columnist James Reston observed: "MacArthur started as the prosecutor and is now the defendant."

The general began a tour of American cities, seeking to make his point about the war, but the American public had now decided that he was not quite the shining god he had been made out to be. Previously talked up as a presidential possibility for 1952, he was quickly shuffled off to the wings as Republicans brought out Dwight D. Eisenhower—a fellow hero from World War II who had once been MacArthur's clerk—as their candidate. Eisenhower's win over the Democratic candidate was an easy one. Harry Truman had decided not to run and, in fact, both he and MacArthur had been damaged by their battles. Truman's inability to restrain MacArthur before the entire affair turned into a public spectacle contributed seriously to the problem.

In the end, both men lived to ripe old age, each in his own distinct way. Truman had not tried to enrich himself as either senator or president and was forced to live on a shoestring back in Independence, Missouri, at least until an embarrassed Congress passed a law awarding him a $25,000 pension. Truman died at the age of eighty-eight, in 1972. MacArthur, who had accepted a $500,000 payment from President Quezon of the Philippines after the war for his services to that country, ensconced himself in a grand apartment in the Waldorf-Astoria. He passed away in 1964, at the age of eighty-four. There are signs he may have mellowed at the end, however. Two years before he died, addressing a graduating class of cadets at West Point, he told them to stay away from political issues. "These great national problems are not for your professional or military solution," he said.

There is no record of what Harry Truman, sitting on his front porch back in Missouri, thought of *that* statement.

GENERAL VO NGUYEN GIAP VERSUS

GENERAL CHRISTIAN DE CASTRIES

GENERAL VO NGUYEN GIAP AND GENERAL CHRISTIAN DE CASTRIES: THE STRUGGLE FOR DIEN BIEN PHU

NOVEMBER 20, 1953 HAD DAWNED WITH A THICK fog hanging low to the ground in the remote valley of Dien Bien Phu, which is in northwest Vietnam, on the Laos border. Aside from the Viet Minh troops who garrisoned the place, there were perhaps thirteen thousand inhabitants near and around the upland valley, which was surrounded by high hills and known not only for its rice production, but also for being a center for the collection and processing of opium—the drug the Viet Minh used to purchase arms on the black market.

By 10:30 or so in the morning, the fog had burned off, leaving the valley in bright sunshine. A rice farmer working near the edge of the valley heard a rumbling noise and, to his amazement, saw the sky fill with large transport planes.

> *All of a sudden they seemed to be everywhere, dropping clouds of white specks that looked like cotton seeds. But they soon opened up and we saw that soldiers were hanging from them. They seemed to cover the whole valley and within a few minutes they were on the ground, forming into groups.*

What the farmer saw was the beginning of Operation Castor, in which the French parachuted nine thousand troops into this distant valley over the space of three days. By the end of the month, there would be six parachute battalions, totaling sixteen thousand men, in a valley afflicted by spring monsoon rains and surrounded by towering, heavily wooded hills that had not been occupied by the French. Astonishing though it may seem, this vulnerable position was where the French high command decided that it would inflict a major defeat on the Viet

Minh, led by their brilliant general Vo Nguyen Giap, and force them to make major concessions at the peace talks even then beginning in Geneva.

Dien Bien Phu was not the beginning of French arrogance regarding their enemy in Vietnam, but it certainly became the end of it.

A BITTER WAR FOR INDEPENDENCE The country that is now called Vietnam was an ancient kingdom known for the ferocity with which it threw off invaders, be they Mongols or Chinese. In the nineteenth century the French were able to colonize the country by siding with one warring faction against the other, and soon Vietnam was one of the most valuable French possessions in Indochina, which encompassed modern Vietnam, Cambodia, and Laos, and which the French ruled from their capital city of Hanoi. However, by the early part of the twentieth century a Vietnamese nationalist movement had arisen. Led by men such as Ho Chi Minh, it sought to convince the French to give the country its independence.

This the French would not do, even when World War II broke out. During that time, the Japanese coopted the government and eventually ruled the country, but the nationalist movement continued to be active. The Viet Minh—named after their leader Ho—was a Communist-inspired nationalist group that, with aid from the Americans, fought an unremitting guerilla war against the Japanese. When the Japanese surrendered to the Allies, the Viet Minh took advantage of the temporary power vacuum and occupied Hanoi, and Ho Chi Minh declared the independence of what he named The Democratic Republic of Vietnam.

The French were having none of this—as far as they were concerned, Vietnam had only been temporarily taken from them. They sent an expeditionary force to join the Vietnamese loyal to them (who included the puppet Emperor Bao Dai) in ousting the Viet Minh. They had initial success against the rag-tag Viet Minh forces, who were driven from Hanoi into the jungles of northern Vietnam. But in 1949, after the Chinese Communists won their battle against the Nationalist forces, the Viet Minh were supplied with American arms captured from the Nationalists, as well as Chinese advisors. By 1950, the Viet Minh had twenty-three battalions of heavily armed and well-trained men and they launched a major offensive. In just ten months, from February to November of 1950, the Viet Minh, led by Vo Nguyen Giap, registered a series of pivotal victories that pushed the French back from the Chinese border to a defensive line they had established from Hanoi to the Red River Delta.

The Viet Minh now held territory from the Chinese border to within about a hundred miles of Saigon. However, the French were able to hold their defensive line, even though Giap threw thousands of men at it in human-wave attacks that were repulsed with great loss on the Viet Minh side. In April 1953, Giap, unable to break this stalemate, changed tactics and attempted to divert the French by invading Laos. Although he then broke off his attack and retreated, the ruse worked. The French were by now convinced they could not win in Indochina and sought to make an honorable exit by negotiating peace from a position of strength. Their new commander, General Henri Navarre, wanted to push the Viet Minh away from Laos while at the same time defeating their regular infantry in a set piece battle. This would allow the French to use their superior air and artillery power to destroy the Viet Minh as they had in the past, only on a more massive scale.

Fortifying the valley of Dien Bien Phu, which lay directly on the routes the Viet Minh used to get into Laos, would be perfect for this, Navarre thought. And he and his deputy commander, Major General René Cogny, thought that the battlefield commander perfect for the job would be Colonel Christian de Castries.

"THINGS THAT WERE NOT BEAUTIFUL" Colonel Christian Marie Ferdinand de la Croix de Castries was born—and looked every inch—a haughty French aristocrat. His ancestors had fought in every war involving the country since the Crusades; they included a field marshal, nine generals, an admiral, and four colonial lieutenant governors. Born in Paris in 1902, de Castries entered the French armed forces not through the military academy, as was the usual way, but by joining the cavalry when he was twenty years old. During the 1920s and 1930s, he led a glamorous, high-profile life. He was a champion rider—he set a world record jump of 7 feet, 10 inches in 1933—and a daredevil pilot. Tall, thin, with a patrician nose and a cigarette dangling from his lip, de Castries specialized in seducing married women. More than once, he was nearly killed by an outraged husband.

Such a reckless life found its natural expression in war, and de Castries served his country well in World War II. After the German invasion of France, de Castries, as a member of an elite commando unit, fought for three days with only sixty men against an entire German battalion. Taken prisoner only after he was wounded, he was sent into Germany to a POW camp, from which he escaped by digging a tunnel under the wire. Making a perilous journey across Germany and occupied France, he found his way to Spain and joined the Free French forces there. He was wounded again in Italy, fighting against the German forces there.

After the war, he joined the French Expeditionary Force battling the Viet Minh and performed ably and bravely as a group commander, being wounded yet again when both legs were fractured by a land mine. He was now fifty, the holder of a Legion of Honor, and had been mentioned eighteen times in dispatches—here was a fighting man who, it seemed, would be perfect for the bloody job of battling the Viet Minh at Dien Bien Phu.

Except for one, disturbing thing. During World War II, the men who served under de Castries had found that when his soldiers were wounded or killed he seemed to "withdraw" into himself, to retreat into isolation, almost to become mute. This did not take away from their respect for his evident personal courage, but it was odd for a commander in war. He avoided seeing his own wounded and

seldom visited them in the hospital. In fact, he later admitted that he disliked coming in contact with "things that were not beautiful."

"THE LONG WAR" As de Castries and his men began fortifying the valley of Dien Bien Phu, his opponent, General Vo Nguyen Giap, was seeing the opportunity of a lifetime spent seizing opportunities. Giap was born in 1912 in Quan-binh province, in what would later become North Vietnam. His family was moderately well-to-do and they were also fierce Vietnamese patriots. Giap was taught French at school, but at home only their native language was spoken. Giap's mother taught him stories of the Vietnamese heroes of old; his father showed him how to write using the traditional ideographs introduced centuries before by the

ABOVE French parachutists watch comrades being dropped over Dien Bien Phu, at the start of the battle the French hoped would be a decisive strike against the Viet Minh.

THE BATTLE OF BACH DANG RIVER

A millennium before Dien Bien Phu, the Vietnamese fought another pivotal battle against a foreign aggressor, winning against the odds because of another Giap-like general.

By 900 AD, the Chinese had dominated Vietnam for a thousand years. They considered the country a southern Chinese province—in fact, the name they gave Vietnam was Annam, or "Pacified South," a name much resented by the Vietnamese. But—as the French and Americans would much later find out to their chagrin—Vietnam was a difficult country to keep pacified. When the Tang Dynasty fell in 906, rebellious Vietnamese led by the patriot Doung Dinh Nghe rose against the Chinese and by 937 were able to drive them out of the country. However, after Doung was killed in a coup by one of his officers, the ruler of the Southern Han Dynasty, Liu Yan, thought the time was ripe to exert control over the Vietnamese again, and in 938 he sent his own son to invade Vietnam by sailing up the Bach Dang River into the heart of the northern part of the country.

The Chinese had not reckoned on Ngo Quyen, son-in-law of Doung Dinh Nghe. Ngo killed the officer who had murdered his father-in-law and united the Vietnamese forces to meet the Chinese fleet as it came up the Bach Dang. Clever strategist that he was, Ngo hammered wooden stakes with pointed iron tips into the riverbed, where they would be hidden at high tide. Then he sent out a fleet of shallow-draft boats filled with warriors to challenge the heavier ships of the Chinese navy. The Chinese, sensing an easy victory, gave chase. The lighter Vietnamese vessels retreated over the spikes as the tide was turning—but the Chinese boats were impaled and trapped. More than half the Chinese were drowned or killed by the Vietnamese.

Except for a brief period in the fifteenth century, the Chinese had been ousted for good.

RIGHT General Vo Nguyen Giap (background left, smiling) and Ho Chi Minh (background, right) discuss tactics with other commanders during a military campaign against the French in 1950.

Chinese, rather than the simplified alphabet foisted on the country by the French in the nineteenth century.

Giap went to an elite school in the ancient imperial capital of Hue and became radicalized very early by reading the writings of Ho Chi Minh (an alumnus of the school) and others. He and others ran afoul of French authorities when they went on strike over the French ban on national newspapers and his name was inscribed, for the first time, on a French police dossier. Giap became a Marxist while continuing through school and eventually earning a doctorate of economics at the University of Hanoi. He became a teacher, but his mind was on revolution, particularly after the brutal French crackdown on starving Vietnamese, who rose against the authorities during the 1930s after the Great Depression set in and living conditions reached new lows.

Early in 1940, Giap's Marxist fervor came to the attention of Ho Chi Minh, then in exile in China, who sent for him to train him as an organizer. After Giap left Vietnam, his wife, a fellow Marxist, was thrown into prison by French authorities. She died there and her sister was shot by a French firing squad. In 1942, Giap returned to Vietnam to organize a guerilla resistance group that opposed both the French and the occupying Japanese forces. He knew nothing about fighting—once, when he found a grenade in the jungle, he had no idea how to arm it—but he learned, and gradually his rag-tag guerillas coalesced into larger groups which did real damage to the Japanese.

In 1945, when the French refused to recognize Ho's new republic, Giap and many others escaped into the countryside to begin "the long war," as they called it. By November of 1953, it seemed to Giap that this war was finally reaching its end point. As the French built up their forces at Dien Bien Phu, he slowly infiltrated thirty-three infantry battalions, six artillery regiments, and a battalion of engineers into the jungle surrounding the French positions.

"TO STRIKE SURELY" While the press would soon be calling Dien Bien Phu a fortress, this was a misnomer, as there was never a continuous line of French fortifications covering the entire valley. Instead, de Castries and his officers set up eight strongpoints, each with artillery, mortars, and machine-guns, all with interlocking fields of fire that were supposed to keep the Viet Minh from infiltrating between them. (Three of the strongpoints, Gabrielle, Beatrice, and Isabelle, were supposedly named after de Castries's current mistresses.)

The valley was a feverish hive of activity, as the existing small airstrip was lengthened and another was created. Grass was cleared, jungle leveled, electricity brought in, and huge water purifiers provided to keep the men from getting amoebic dysentery from the local water. The novelist Graham Greene, who had pulled strings to be allowed to make an overnight visit from Saigon, noted that the French had also brought along forty-eight thousand bottles of vintage wine, a few of which he drank with de Castries, whom he described as having "the nervy,

GIAP'S GUNS

The ironic part of the French defeat at Dien Bien Phu, of course, was the fact that the Viet Minh were able to deploy far more artillery than de Castries and his fellow officers ever imagined was possible.

This was partly because of the Korean War. Mao's China supplied the Viet Minh with forty-eight 105 mm howitzers captured from the Americans. Added to that, Giap had forty-eight 120 mm mortars, fifty-one 75 mm howitzers, thirty-six 37 mm anti-aircraft guns, and sixty 75 mm recoilless rifles. Finally, at the end of the battle, he added the dreaded Soviet Katyusha multi-tube rocket launchers, whose horrifying shriek terrified the French in their bunkers. To counter this, the French had only about sixty heavy artillery guns.

French experts later estimated that the Viet Minh fired about fifteen hundred tons of ammunition into the French perimeter during the fifty-six day siege. It also shows what an amazing organizer Giap was. All of this ammunition—as well as tons of food supplies—had to be transported by porters through an area with few, if any, passable roads, from as far as two hundred miles away.

histrionic features of an old-time actor." In fact, de Castries was at this stage quite confident. He told one reporter, "I'm going to kick General Giap's teeth in, one by one."

De Castries, as well as Navarre, was certain that the Viet Minh would soon attack in massive human waves, which could be destroyed by French firepower. After all, Giap had done this before. But Giap was now deciding to take a different tack. By the middle of January, his forces numbered fifty thousand men, spread out in the hills surrounding Dien Bien Phu, outweighing the French forces that opposed them by four to one. Chinese advisors who accompanied Giap urged him to simply overwhelm the valley with human-wave attacks. In fact, one such operation was planned, when Giap suddenly canceled it. He knew that now, at this pivotal moment, he could not risk defeat. As he recalled later: "... we came to the conclusion that we could not secure success if we struck swiftly. In consequence, we chose the other tactics: to strike surely and advance surely."

As one soldier at the battle remembered later: "Now the shovel became our most popular weapon. Everyone dug tunnels and trenches ... we gradually surrounded Dien Bien Phu with an underground network."

Giap also made another decision, perhaps the decisive one for the battle to come. The French knew that the Viet Minh had artillery (although they underestimated just how much) but they assumed Giap would place his guns on the far sides of the hills surrounding the valley, where the howitzers would lob shells over in a high arc, directed by forward artillery spotters. This type of artillery fire is dangerous, but not as dangerous as direct fire, when the gun crews can see their target and zero in on it. This, they were sure, the Viet Minh would not be able to do, for it would mean laboriously hauling the guns over the mountains and down the forward slopes facing the French positions.

But this is exactly what the Viet Minh did, without the French even seeing them, for each gun was put in place under heavy camouflage, dug into caves in the mountains so that only the barrel of the gun was sticking out. This meant that it could not swivel to fire but, because of the Viet Minh's preponderance of artillery, this did not matter—each gun was assigned a small area to cover and would fire to set coordinates. By contrast, the French artillery, fewer in number, was placed in the open, because they needed to be able to fire in all directions.

THE DESTRUCTION OF BEATRICE
On Saturday, March 13, the attack on Dien Bien Phu began in earnest. The strongpoint of Beatrice, bristling with guns and barbed wire, was central to the French defenses, as its artillery was supposed to keep Communist fire away from the all-important main airstrip, for the only way Dien Bien Phu could be supplied was by airlift. But late that afternoon, the Viet Minh opened up with everything they had on Beatrice, simply pounding it with repeated artillery fire. One French soldier remembered: "Shells rained down on us without stopping like a hailstorm on a fall evening.

Bunker after bunker, trench after trench, collapsed, burying under them men and weapons."

By eight o'clock, the command bunker in Beatrice had been destroyed by a direct hit. The Viet Minh infantry now attacked the weakened fortress, where the French soldiers fought on into the long night. The last radio message requested artillery fire directly on the only bunker that remained to the French. Then there was silence. A few scattered survivors hid in the jungle and in the morning made it back to French lines, but Beatrice was now in Viet Minh hands.

To make matters worse, the French saw to their horror that previously unrevealed 75 mm enemy howitzers were now in place on the forward side of two nearby hills and could aim directly at the French airplanes scrambling to take off from the airstrip. Everywhere on the night of March 13–14, Viet Minh artillery pounded the French with accuracy and ferocity; French counterbattery fire was mainly ineffectual in silencing the enemy guns, so much so that the French artillery commander killed himself that night with a hand grenade, after muttering: "I am responsible. I am responsible."

De Castries kept this suicide a secret, but in the ensuing days it became clear that he was in deep trouble. On March 15–16, Strongpoint Gabrielle fell to a determined Viet Minh artillery barrage and attack. Just how determined the Viet Minh were—determined and ruthless—can be seen by this anecdote. As the French survivors of Gabrielle were being led away as prisoners by the Viet Minh, they came across a severely wounded guerilla hanging on the barbed wire of the stronghold, his intestines dangling, but still alive. The Viet Minh officer in charge of the prisoners told them: "You can step on him. He has done his duty for the People's Army."

"EVERYTHING RIDES ON US HERE" After the stunning losses of these two strongholds, French morale was down. On the afternoon of March 16, De Castries sent a radio message to his troops that was also heard—as it was intended to be—by enemy units listening in. De Castries began by saying that the French troops were "undertaking ... a battle in which the fate of the whole Indochina War will be decided." He admitted that the French had taken "some pretty hard blows," but claimed that reinforcements were on the way and that, when the sky cleared, bomber missions would pulverize the Viet Minh. He closed by adding: "Everything rides on us here. A few more days and we shall have won and the sacrifices made by our comrades shall not be in vain."

Yet in person de Castries was nowhere near this confident. He knew that even surviving, let alone destroying the Viet Minh, depended on re-supply of troops and materiel by air, and that this was becoming increasingly difficult as spring monsoon weather set in—as were the bombing missions he hoped to bring to bear against the vexing Viet Minh artillery. Another firebase fell—Anne-Marie—and the Viet Minh were able to put anti-aircraft fire right down the throats of the planes landing on the French airstrip—so much fire that the veteran French and American combat pilots flying these missions said it was comparable to what they experienced over Germany in World War II.

All of this was beginning to have an effect on the French command staff at Dien Bien Phu. De Castries's chief of staff, Lieutenant Colonel Keller, broke under the strain, and was found sitting in the most secure part of the command post, wearing a steel helmet. He would not communicate or move, and was finally airlifted back to Hanoi. With one of his senior officers dead by his own hand, another the victim of combat fatigue, de Castries also began to crack. He became—as he had in the past when confronted with casualties—withdrawn, and rarely left his command post. An extraordinary event took place that, according to Bernard Fall, author of the classic history of the Dien Bien Phu battle, *Hell in a Very Small Place*, was known to a fairly wide circle of French officers but was not publicly discussed by the French during or after the battle.

Feeling that de Castries had become ineffective, Lieutenant Colonel Pierre Langlais entered his bunker on March 24 and told him that henceforth he and the other senior officers would control the battle; de Castries would simply send messages to Hanoi and act as if he were in charge. This was, in a sense, a mutiny, but de Castries did not protest. In fact, he and Langlais remained friends who played bridge together during the siege, deep in the bunker at night.

This odd situation has since been debated by historians. De Castries's passivity may have been the result of the brave man's retreat in the face of overwhelming

BERNARD FALL

Bernard Fall was the author of two evocatively titled books on Vietnam that have become classics. One is called *Hell in a Very Small Place*, considered the definitive book about the siege of Dien Bien Phu, and the other is *Street without Joy*, which details the inability of the French to respond to the Viet Minh in the First Vietnam War and also attempts to draw object lessons for the Americans, who were fighting the Second Vietnam War at the time the book was published in 1965.

Fall led a truly adventurous life. Born in Vienna in 1926, he grew up in France, where both of his parents were killed by the Nazis in World War II. Young Fall joined the Resistance and fought an underground battle against the Nazis until the Allies invaded southern France; after that, he joined a Moroccan regiment and was wounded twice while fighting the retreating German forces.

After the war, Fall worked as a research analyst for the Nuremberg War Crimes Tribunal and then, in 1951, moved to the United States on a Fulbright Scholarship and received a PhD in political science at Syracuse University. However, Fall was not destined for a typical academic life. Seeking research for his doctoral dissertation, he accompanied French forces fighting in Indochina and saw first-hand the horrors of the First Vietnam War. Sympathetic to the Communist point of view but admiring the bravery of the French troops, Fall also understood how badly the French had botched the actual fighting of the war, relying far too heavily on mechanization and air power in a country with few roads and plenty of jungle to obscure enemy movement.

On February 21, 1967, the forty-year-old Fall was accompanying a group of United States Marines as they patrolled along Highway I, seeking their elusive Viet Cong enemy. Highway I was, in fact, the famous "*la rue sans joie,*" the street without joy, as the French paratroopers called it, since they so often shed their blood on it. Sensing danger, Fall spoke into his tape recorder. "It smells bad—meaning it's a little bit suspicious," he said. "Could be an amb——" At that point, his jeep ran over a mine and blew up, killing him and ending a life devoted to seeking the truth behind the wars of Vietnam.

BELOW American marines patrol the streets of Hue in February 1968 during the Second Vietnam War. Bernard Fall was accompanying a group of U.S. marines when he was killed on Highway I.

carnage, but his attitude to the situation was also extremely defensive, and he wanted to conserve French forces and supplies and await reinforcements. Langlais felt that reinforcements would not come in time and wanted to act more aggressively, making sorties against the enemy and attempting to take back strongpoints.

"WE'RE BLOWING UP EVERYTHING"

It is probably true that neither approach would have worked, because of the French high command's miscalculations and the brilliance of General Giap. Navarre and his fellow officers were wrong on nearly every count. The French presence at Dien Bien Phu did not induce the Viet Minh to attack in waves—instead, preceded by concentrated artillery fire, the guerillas attacked through previously dug trenches and mined deep underneath the French positions to blow up bunkers with massive explosions, a tactic straight out of World War I. The French could not be re-supplied by air because of the monsoon; totally cut off, outnumbered four to one, they were bait in a trap, part of what Bernard Fall called "a momentous gamble ... that backfired badly." The French troops—and these consisted of regular French army, Foreign Legion battalions, Arabs from Morocco, Senegalese from West Africa, and five thousand Vietnamese—fought bravely on, but to little purpose.

Giap's men continued to destroy strongpoints and shell the airstrips, and to set off mines before launching attacks that gradually narrowed the French perimeter to the size of a baseball stadium. By May 7, 1954, it was clear, even to the senior officers listening in on the radio net in Hanoi, that de Castries and his men were in a hopeless position. Very few of their guns were firing, few supplies had got through, and most of the men were living on instant coffee and cigarettes. There were five thousand seriously wounded French troops and two thousand dead, resting uneasily in a cemetery that was constantly being blown apart by artillery shells. A breakout was considered all but impossible, although a few men in the strongpoint closest to the Laos border did try it.

In a last radio conversation with René Cogny in Hanoi, a devastated de Castries indicated that he wanted to surrender. Cogny replied:

"*Mon vieux*, of course you want to finish the whole thing now. But what you have done until now is surely magnificent. Don't spoil it by hoisting the white flag."

"All right, *mon general*. I only wanted to preserve the wounded."

"Yes, I know. Well, do the best you can ... [But] what you have done is too magnificent to [raise a white flag]. You understand, *mon vieux*?"

De Castries replied with his last words from Dien Bien Phu: "*Bien, mon general*."

A more prosaic transmission was heard shortly after this, the very last from Dien Bien Phu. A radio operator, using his code name, came on the net and said: "This is Yankee Metro. We're blowing up everything around here. *Au revoir*."

A DECISIVE BATTLE While de Castries did not raise the white flag, he and roughly ten thousand French troops were captured. Most were forced to march three hundred miles east to Viet Minh prison camps. About thirty-two hundred of these were later repatriated to France, but at least three thousand died on the march or in prison camps, of starvation, disease, and mistreatment. About seventy French troops managed to escape into Laos. De Castries—promoted now to brigadier general for his role in the battle—was in the custody of the Viet Minh for four months as well, while in Geneva negotiations were underway on a settlement that divided Vietnam into a Communist controlled north and a Western-backed south.

Then, at last, the fifty-two-year-old was released to return to France, where he received a hero's welcome, although privately those in the military continued to raise questions about his lack of aggressiveness at Dien Bien Phu. Whether de Castries, a brave man placed in an impossible situation, had completely broken down will never be known. He lived on to the age of eighty-eight, dying in 1991.

General Vo Nguyen Giap is still alive at the time of writing. He led the North Vietnamese to their victory over the Americans in the Second Vietnam War and is one of the greatest heroes Vietnam has ever known. In various interviews he has given, he is well aware that he beat de Castries and the French at their own game at Dien Bien Phu, outgunning them with artillery the French thought he did not possess and did not really know how to use.

"They wanted a decisive battle and that's exactly what they got at Dien Bien Phu," Giap told an interviewer in 2000. "Except that it was decisive for the Vietnamese and not for the French."

JOHN F. KENNEDY

VERSUS RICHARD M. NIXON

JOHN F. KENNEDY AND RICHARD M. NIXON: RIVALS FOR PRESIDENTIAL POWER

AMERICA REMEMBERS THESE TWO PRESIDENTS as polar opposites—Jack Kennedy, smooth-talking, glamorous, immensely wealthy, handsome as a movie star, and Dick Nixon, often bumbling in speech, a poor boy from California who glowered more than he smiled. These two men, who began as friends and freshman congressmen together, would turn into bitter rivals as they vied for the highest office in the land in one of the dirtiest elections in American history. One was to end up martyred, the other in disgrace.

Yet Kennedy and Nixon were perhaps more alike than we might think. The American television commentator Eric Sevareid, during the contentious election of 1960, said that both Kennedy and Nixon were: "Cool cats ... tidy, buttoned down men ... sharp, opportunistic, devoid of strong conviction and deep passions, with no commitment except to personal advancement." Perhaps more bluntly, future Supreme Court Justice Abe Fortas, then an aide to Kennedy vice presidential candidate, Lyndon Johnson, wrote: "They're both hardworking, both intelligent, and I think neither has a core."

"THE HAVES AND HAVE NOTS" Richard Nixon was born in 1913 in Yorba Linda, California, the second of five sons of Francis Nixon and his wife, Hannah. The family moved to nearby Whittier when Nixon was in his early teens. Francis was only moderately successful in life—he ran a corner grocery store after trying his hand at lemon farming—and Nixon was raised in a home where sticking to a budget mattered considerably. His mother's family were Quakers and this is the religion in which Nixon was raised, eschewing drinking, dancing, swearing, and smoking. Nixon, although shy and almost painfully straight-laced, was smart. He graduated second in his class from Whittier High School and was granted a scholarship to Harvard University—one that he unfortunately had to decline because he lacked the funds for room and board.

Instead, he went to nearby Whittier College, where he excelled in debating, theater, and student politics (he became class president). There is one telling anecdote from these days: at Whittier the elite social club was called the Franklins, and it rejected Nixon for membership. Nixon did not take this lightly. He developed his own social club, dubbed the Orthogonians, who prided themselves on their plebeian roots, eating hot dogs while the Franklins dined on steak. It was the first, but not the last, time that Richard Nixon would be rejected by those who styled themselves his social betters—and the idea that they scorned him would burn within him. "They were the haves and we were the have-nots, see?" Nixon told a journalist years later, referring to the social clubs at Whittier.

By 1936, Nixon had gone to Duke University on a full scholarship, graduated third in his class—an admiring classmate nicknamed him "Iron Butt" for his ability to study all night if need be—and upon graduating returned home to California and worked at the law practice of a family friend in Whittier. It was not terribly satisfying employment, but he needed it to support his family, since he married Thelma "Pat" Ryan in 1940. When the war began, Nixon enlisted and became a supply officer in the navy, eventually ending up in the South Pacific. He did not see combat, but did manage to amass about ten thousand dollars in poker winnings—almost no one was a better poker player than Dick Nixon—which he would put to good use when he returned to the United States in 1945.

"MOST LIKELY TO BE PRESIDENT" If anyone was born one of those "haves" who so bedeviled Richard Nixon it was John Fitzgerald Kennedy. Born in 1917 in Brookline, Massachusetts, he was the son of the legendary Joseph P. Kennedy and Rose Fitzgerald Kennedy, whose father was a prominent Boston politician. Joseph Kennedy was a tough, aggressive and street-smart Boston Irishman who overcame the snobbery of the upper classes who ruled Boston simply by making more money than they could imagine. Working in banking and on Wall Street, he became a multi-millionaire by the time he was thirty-five—his avowed goal—and then turned, during Prohibition, to smuggling bootleg whiskey, which made him even richer. By the time Jack Kennedy was a teenager, his father had gone into the movie business, where he made even more money while pursuing affairs with Gloria Swanson and other actresses of the time. Joe Kennedy's business and personal life may have had a taint of the unsavory, but each of his nine children had a trust fund of at least one million dollars waiting for them when they turned twenty-one.

Young Jack—thin, with tousled brown hair and a bright, flashing smile—went to the elite Choate School in Connecticut, from which he graduated in 1935.

He was well liked there—his yearbook proclaimed him "Most Likely To Be President"—but many noticed that the charming young man had an unusually frail constitution. He had problems with colitis, which caused him to spend a month at the Mayo Clinic, and he suffered from hepatitis and was often jaundiced-looking. And, while he made a lot of friends, there was something standoffish about him. One intimate noticed that he would recoil slightly if someone seemed about to put his hand on his shoulder. "Jack didn't touch and didn't want to be touched," the classmate said.

When Kennedy graduated from Choate in 1935, he sailed to England to study at the prestigious London School of Economics, just as his older brother, Joe, had done—Joe being the golden boy of the Kennedys, the one Joe, Sr., was grooming to become president of the United States—and spent a year there. When he returned, he enrolled in Harvard University. During his time at Harvard, Kennedy visited London again, where his father was now the American ambassador to the Court of St. James; when he got back to Cambridge, he wrote a thesis about the dangers of appeasing Nazi Germany which, upon his graduation in 1940, became a bestselling book called *Why England Slept*. (One reason it was a bestseller, however, was that his father brought up thirty thousand copies.)

In 1941, despite a bad back and various other ailments, Kennedy joined the navy and saw action in the South Pacific as the captain of PT-109, a motor patrol boat that was rammed and sunk by a Japanese destroyer. For Kennedy's actions that night—he towed a wounded crewman to safety on a small island—he was awarded the Navy and Marine Medal, although there were many who felt that any captain who would allow such a small, highly maneuverable craft to be rammed by a destroyer—it was the only time it happened in the war—could not have been a very good leader of his men.

"A CANDIDATE FOR CONGRESS" Both Nixon and Kennedy returned from the war to a changed America. The United States had been triumphant and would soon enter a period of prosperity but, for now, inflation was rampant, consumer goods scarce, and housing hard to find. Plus, with the ascendancy of Russia and Stalin, Americans were becoming fearful that Communists had begun infiltrating the United States—infiltrating labor unions, schools, even the government. It was a time of paranoia, but a time when a crafty politician could get elected playing on such fears.

When Richard Nixon came back from the South Pacific he sat down and considered his options, like so many ex-servicemen. While he was doing so, he got a note from a longtime family friend, a wealthy banker named Herman Perry, which began: "Dear Dick, I am writing you this short note to ask if you would like to be a candidate for Congress on the Republican ticket in 1946." Nixon had dreamed about going into politics and this chance was too good to pass up. Bankrolled mainly by his poker winnings, Nixon campaigned for the seat held by five-term

Democratic Congressman Jerry Voorhis in the Twelfth Congressional District in southern California. Hiring a political consultant who told him he must "define his opponent" immediately, Nixon attacked Voorhis because the congressman was supported by the CIO, the massive labor union that, Nixon claimed, was infiltrated by Communists.

In a debate between the two candidates, Nixon produced a paper that he said showed that Voorhis had Communist support. He then proceeded to walk over to Voorhis, holding the paper dramatically high above his head, and asked him to read it. Voorhis was taken aback by the turn of events, fumbled for an answer, and that was all Nixon needed. The former naval commander beat Voorhis with fifty-six percent of the vote.

When Jack Kennedy returned from the war, his mind was already set on politics. His brother Joe had been killed when his plane was shot down over France in 1944, and Joe, Sr., had picked Jack as the heir apparent. When a congressman from Boston vacated his seat in the House to become mayor of Boston, Kennedy threw his hat into the ring. He had it easy all the way. Kennedy money was thrown at voters all over the district. One Democratic politician remembered: "If you agreed to invite a few friends to your house to meet Jack, they brought in a case of mixed booze, hired a caterer, and gave you a hundred bucks which was supposed to pay for a cleaning woman." In fact, the money was simply a bribe, as was the Kennedy family habit of giving people fifty dollars to "help out" at the polls on election night.

Politically, Kennedy was calling himself "a fighting conservative" and taking shots at "clever and brilliant Moscow propagandists" who were infiltrating the Democratic left wing. This played well in working-class Boston—as did the cash handouts—and Kennedy won with seventy-three percent of the vote.

FRESHMEN TOGETHER However different their runs at Congress were, thirty-three-year-old Nixon and twenty-nine-year-old Kennedy entered the House of Representatives together in the class of 1946. After the incoming congressmen were sworn in, Kennedy attended a press reception and was introduced to Richard Nixon. An aide noticed Kennedy seemed impressed.

"So you're the guy who beat Jerry Voorhis!" he exclaimed to Nixon. "How does it feel?"

"I suppose I'm elated," said Nixon, rather awkwardly, but soon they were chatting away happily. By chance they were put on the same committee—the Education and Labor panel—where, Nixon said, they sat at opposite ends of the table like "a pair of unmatched book ends." Kennedy liked Nixon so much that he would tell people: "Listen to [Nixon]. He's going places." But despite their friendship, they were in different political parties. After only a week in Congress, they took part in their first one-on-one debate, in McKeesport, Pennsylvania, over the Taft-Hartley Labor Bill—which sought to curb the power of organized

THE CHECKERS SPEECH

Nixon had provided much of the nastiness in the 1952 presidential campaign by "red-baiting" the Democrats, going after Adlai Stevenson as an "egghead" and a "lefty." Democrats, therefore, were quite pleased in September, when the *New York Post* revealed that the vice presidential candidate had, as senator, been the beneficiary of a secret slush fund of $18,000 set up by wealthy Californian businessmen.

Both Democrats and Republicans called for Nixon's resignation. Eisenhower, now a complete convert to the power of television, held off firing Nixon to let him make a public appearance on television, to explain it all to the nation.

On Tuesday night, September 23, the Republican National Committee paid $75,000 to have Nixon appear live just after *The Milton Berle Show*—the most popular show in America—thus insuring a huge audience for what would become known as the "Checkers" speech.

Nixon—by turns defiant and wheedling—claimed that the people smearing him were Communist sympathizers trying to "silence" him. However, despite this, he was willing to "bare his soul." He first talked of his wife, Pat, noting fondly that she was so named because she had been born on St. Patrick's Day. (Actually, her real name was Thelma and she was born the day *before* St. Patrick's Day.) He went on to point out that Pat did not have a mink—only a "respectable Republican cloth coat."

Nixon filled viewers' minds with numerous figures—he said that he and Pat owed his parents $3,500 on which they regularly paid interest, that they invested in government savings bonds, that they struggled to pay off a $20,000 mortgage. None of this addressed the slush fund, but it created a brilliant image of the Nixons as a typical American couple trying to make ends meet. Nixon then kicked into high gear with the defiant revelation that a political supporter had given his kids a dog that they had named Checkers: "And you know the kids love the dog and I just want to say right now that regardless of what they say about it, we're gonna keep it."

It was a brilliant, manic, instinctive performance and the American public flooded the Eisenhower campaign with letters and telegrams supporting Nixon. Eisenhower said: "Dick, you're my boy!" but never trusted him again.

One more poignant note comes from Ted Rogers, the producer who gave Nixon his "ten minute," "thirty second," and "cut" symbols during the broadcast. Even after the camera stopped rolling, Rogers said, Nixon would not cease making his appeal. "Even though I saw his head nod on the 'cut' symbol, he did not stop talking." Emotionally overwrought, Nixon kept talking and walking towards the camera, making an imploring gesture with his hands, until he actually hit it with his shoulder. Which seemed to wake him up, and he began weeping copiously.

LEFT Richard Nixon, at that time the vice presidential candidate for the Republican Party, makes a speech on television during the 1952 presidential campaign.

labor. Nixon, by far the more skilled debater, was for it, Kennedy against, but—in a foreshadowing of what was to come—Kennedy won on charisma. A picture published the next day showed him smiling and relaxed, while Nixon, with his ever-present five o'clock shadow, seemed furtive, almost fugitive-like.

Other differences between the two men soon emerged. While Nixon went home each night to his wife and their two young daughters, Kennedy led the life of a playboy bachelor. His conquests were, to put it mildly, legion. His townhouse was known locally as "the Hollywood Hotel."

"He really liked girls," a Democratic politician of the same era noted, girls who were mainly stewardesses and secretaries. "But Kennedy never got emotionally involved. He'd sleep with a girl and then have [an aide] take her to the airport the next day."

Nixon—old "Iron Butt" himself—was known for an incredible work ethic, putting in long hours at the office and often coming home with reams of paperwork. Kennedy, according to a secretary who worked for him for six years, was "rather lackadaisical" and "didn't know the first thing about what he was doing." To be fair, this may have been because of his persistent illnesses. He was diagnosed with Addison's disease, which meant that his adrenal glands would fail unless he took daily doses of steroids; he was terribly thin and yellow-looking from malaria caught in the Pacific; and his back was so bad (he had re-injured it in the PT-109 crash) that he often used crutches to walk. Friends described him as obsessed with the notion that he would die an early death.

"TRICKY DICK" Perhaps predictably, Kennedy had a lackluster career in the House of Representatives, while Nixon rose to great heights, especially because his investigative work while a member of the House Un-American Activities Committee (HUAC) helped convict Alger Hiss, a State Department official, of spying for Soviet Russia. During the televised hearings, Nixon was a constantly visible presence and became well known to the American public. In 1950, he ran for a Senate seat in California, defeating the Democrat Helen Gahagan Douglas in one of the dirtiest senatorial races California had ever seen. Nixon, accusing Douglas of being a Soviet sympathizer, called her "the Pink Lady," and said she was "pink right down to her underwear." As his old campaign advisor had told him, he was "defining the opposition." He beat Douglas handily, but not before she had nicknamed him "Tricky Dick," a tag that would stick with him for the rest of his life.

Two years later, the thirty-nine-year-old Nixon was chosen by Dwight Eisenhower to run as his vice president, an honor that advanced his career well ahead of Jack Kennedy's, but to which Kennedy responded graciously, sending Nixon a note that read: "Dear Dick: I was tremendously pleased that the convention selected you as V.P. I was always convinced that you would move ahead to the top—but I never thought it would come this quickly."

Interestingly enough, Kennedy had just won a prize as "handsomest" congressman—a shallow enough honor, but when you couple it with the fact that he was taking a course from CBS on how to employ television to his best advantage, one understands that he, well before Nixon, intuitively understood the value of this new medium. And he, too, had his electoral successes in 1952, beating Henry Cabot Lodge of Massachusetts to enter the United States Senate. Although Nixon had a rough time as Eisenhower's running mate in the general election, Eisenhower was elected by seven million votes. As chance would have it, Kennedy and Nixon were given offices directly across the hall from each other in the Senate Office Building—Nixon was there in his position as President of the Senate—and their relationship remained cordial. Nixon even wrote a letter recommending Kennedy for membership in the exclusive Burning Tree golf club.

"OH, GOD, DON'T LET HIM DIE" Both men were climbing the American political ladder, but the stresses of their jobs were taking their toll. As vice president, Nixon found that his boss, Dwight Eisenhower, paid little attention to him, while the Democrats, knowing that he would be a future candidate for president, inveighed against him as a "demagogue" and a "liar." Nixon was so distraught that he thought of dropping out of politics; he even took the extreme step, in those days, of visiting a psychoanalyst.

Jack Kennedy's problems were even more serious. After finally deciding on surgery to fix his constant back problems, he nearly died during the operation. It was reported that he was mortally ill. Nixon's Secret Service guard later remembered his boss, with tears running down his cheeks, saying: "Poor brave Jack is going to die. Oh, God, don't let him die." As it happened, Jack recovered and he and his new wife, Jacqueline, thanked Nixon profusely for his support, but the amiable relations between the two men were about to be strained. As the 1956 national election approached, Kennedy maneuvered to be made Democratic candidate Adlai Stevenson's vice presidential running mate. Kennedy had a genuine shot at the job, but in order to gain support from Stevenson's liberal wing of the Democratic party, he had to attack the Eisenhower–Nixon ticket, which he did in a speech on the floor of the Democratic National Convention, saying that the two were "tough candidates, one who takes the high road and one who takes the low road."

These were rough words from the man Nixon had only two years earlier prayed for, with tears running down his face. As it happened, Kennedy was not picked as Stevenson's vice president, and the Eisenhower–Nixon team was once again victorious. But Adlai Stevenson set the tone for what would come in 1960 by spending much of his campaign attacking Dick Nixon: "Our nation stands at a fork in the political road," he said. "In one direction lies a land of slander and scare; the land of the poison pen ... the land of smash and grab and anything to win. This is Nixonland."

"TWO MEN ON THIRD" As the election of 1960 approached, it became harder and harder for Kennedy and Nixon to have offices directly across the hall from each other. As Kennedy's secretary Evelyn Lincoln put it: "they were like two men on third, each continuing to eye home plate while keeping a wary eye on the other." Each, of course, had started running for president well before the nominating conventions. Typically, Kennedy did it through glamour. He appeared on the cover of *Time* magazine, saw a television series made out of his PT-109 escapade, wrote the 1956 bestseller *Profiles in Courage* (or pretended to write it—see sidebar "Profile in deception?" on page 353), which won the Pulitzer Prize, and even carefully spent a day in a photographer's studio picking exactly the right image to be reproduced on posters in the coming election.

Nixon resented Kennedy's effortless access to good press—the "haves" once again having it all—while almost everything he did met with contempt. Even Kennedy admitted "Dick Nixon is the victim of the worst press that ever hit a politician in this country," but he played into it. In 1959, as he went around the country gathering support for his presidential bid from influential groups of Democrats, he had a standard joke he would tell. He had brought Dick Nixon with him, he would say, to taste a local delicacy. If it happened to be poisoned and they both died, said Kennedy, "I feel I shall have performed a great public service by taking the vice president with me."

Nixon, for his part, simply did not take Kennedy seriously as a candidate. Underestimating the power of charisma wedded to modern media, he thought Kennedy was a "lightweight," as one aide said. "We never thought of him as [an] effective guy."

In fact, Kennedy had become quite effective. While Nixon, as Eisenhower's vice president, was virtually assured of the presidential nod from his party, Kennedy had to fight for his against party bosses who thought he was too young and too Catholic—for there had never been a Catholic president in American history—to win. Campaigning mainly against Hubert Humphrey in the primaries before the general election, Kennedy showed them they were wrong. He beat Humphrey in Wisconsin and then, in a pivotal victory, destroyed him in West Virginia, a state where the voters and party bosses were bought with plenty of Kennedy dollars.

Kennedy won the Democratic Party's nomination in 1960 and Nixon became the Republican candidate. Now when they saw each other outside their offices, Kennedy would smile, but Nixon seemed shaken. It appeared to some observers that he may have realized, for the first time, that he might lose to the "lightweight."

THE DEBATE Ironically, in 1960, Richard Nixon decided that for once he was going to take the high road. He would be, he declared, the "New Nixon," above board, open, a politician for the future. For in 1960 people, tired of eight years of Dwight Eisenhower (respectable but boring), were desperate for change. Kennedy knew this as well, and took as his slogan "the New Frontier"—the meaning was

TWENTY-FIVE CENTS

NOVEMBER 7, 1960

TIME

THE WEEKLY NEWSMAGAZINE

CANDIDATE
KENNEDY

$7.00 A YEAR

VOL. LXXVI NO. 19

RIGHT John Kennedy, Democratic candidate for president, on the cover of *Time* magazine, November 7, 1960. His handsome, confident appearance was a decided vote-winner.

vague but it sounded forward-looking. The 1960 campaign was fast moving and hard hitting, with the candidates now traveling almost exclusively by plane and Richard Nixon vowing to visit all fifty states—and keeping his vow.

The Democrats were not about to let Nixon create a "new" persona. Former President Harry Truman told voters that if they voted for Nixon "they might go to hell." A famous poster showing a glowering and unshaven Nixon appeared, with the line "Would you buy a used car from this man?" Even Nixon's own boss, President Eisenhower, got into the act. When an interviewer asked him if Nixon had participated in any major decisions during his administration, he said: "If you give me a week, I might think of one."

Kennedy joined in the chorus against Nixon and it must have seemed to the vice president that they had never been friendly. Nixon had made the mistake of comparing himself to Thomas Jefferson, third president of the United States, when visiting Jefferson's home state of Virginia. When Kennedy went to Virginia he reminded people that Jefferson could plot eclipses, play the violin, survey fields, and dance the minuet. "Now what has *he* got in common with Mr. Nixon?"

Privately, he seems to have worked himself up into a frenzy against his opponent, telling one friend that Nixon was "a filthy, lying son-of-a-bitch, and a very dangerous man."

Late in August, when Nixon injured his knee by banging it against a car door, Kennedy sent him a get well telegram and Nixon responded in kind, but it was only for show now. The two men were about to meet in one of the most famous presidential candidate debates in American history and the first ever on television. Four debates were arranged, but it was the first, on September 26, in Chicago, Illinois, that was the one that counted. How the candidates prepared for it provides a perfect microcosm of who they were.

On the eve of the debate, the two men were running neck and neck in the race. Jack Kennedy arrived in Chicago a day and a half before the debate, and the first thing he asked his aides when getting off the plane was, "Any girls lined up?" He and his men took the top two floors of the Palmer House hotel, where Kennedy had the run of the place and could have privacy to tan himself on the roof. He prepared by studying 3 x 5 inch cards with his aides while lying on the bed in his bathrobe

"A POLITICAL BUGGING"

When Richard Nixon was elected in a landslide victory in 1972 for his second term as president, it looked like he had reached the high point of his political life, ascending higher than the murdered Jack Kennedy had ever done.

Unfortunately, there was the little matter of Watergate. During the 1972 campaign, Nixon's Committee to Re-Elect the President (CREEP) had sent ex-CIA agents into the Watergate Office Complex in Washington, D.C., in order to bug the headquarters of the Democratic National Committee. They were caught and, as the conspiracy unraveled before the American public, it was learned that Richard Nixon had, at least tacitly, sanctioned the break-in and then ordered the CIA to obstruct the FBI's probe of the event. There were other revelations—many of them captured in Nixon's own words, from tape recorders running in the Oval Office (a common practice of presidents from Roosevelt through Nixon)—and Nixon was finally forced to resign his office.

"I could not muster much moral outrage over a political bugging," Nixon said later, and although mistrust of Nixon was so high after Watergate that most people thought he was being disingenuous, the former president was just being honest.

and listening to Peggy Lee albums. An hour and a half before the beginning of the debate, he visited a call girl in one of the rooms in the hotel and emerged fifteen minutes later with "a big grin on his face," according to one friend. He then headed for the television studio.

Nixon, on the other hand, arrived in Chicago only the night before the debate, tired from barnstorming through eleven states and plagued by a fever from his still-infected knee. He refused to see people the next day and spent six hours cramming for the debate by studying policy reports. When he finally did get to the studio, he once again banged his knee getting out of the car, leaving him in great pain.

When Kennedy came in, said one observer, the two men shook hands "like prizefighters."

"How're you doing?" Kennedy said, casually.

"You have a big crowd in Cleveland," Nixon replied.

Kennedy then proceeded to ignore Nixon and those watching felt that it was here that Nixon began to feel intimidated, leading to a crucial error on his part. When Kennedy was asked if he wanted makeup, he said no—he was so suntanned, in any event, that he looked "like a young Adonis," according to a writer present. Probably because Kennedy had refused it, Nixon did, too. But Nixon did not look like a Greek god. He was pale, in pain, and his always heavy beard cast a dark shadow across his face. He finally did agree to put on a product called Lazy Shave, a kind of roll-on powder meant to disguise five o'clock shadows, but it merely gave him an even ghostlier pallor.

To further erode Nixon's confidence, Kennedy left the room and waited until three minutes before airtime to come walking confidently out onto the set. When the debate began—before a television audience of sixty million people—Nixon was already defeated. Even so, he gave a good enough performance that those listening on the radio thought he had won. But those watching on television—those who saw the handsome, confident Kennedy and the pale, sweating Nixon—knew he had lost. Nixon's own running mate, Henry Cabot Lodge, later said: "That son of a bitch had just lost the election."

Television, it turned out, was where it counted. Of those watching the debate, forty-three percent said Kennedy had won, twenty-nine percent thought it had been a tie, and twenty-three percent responded that Nixon had won. And a poll taken soon afterward saw Kennedy ahead now, forty-nine to forty-six percent.

"NO ONE STEALS THE PRESIDENCY" In the end, Nixon did lose—although not by very much. When all the votes had been totaled in November 1960, Kennedy had won by 119,450, less than one-tenth of one percent. Nixon won among working-class Republicans, among those who distrusted the glittering Kennedy, and among those who felt that Nixon's foreign policy experience counted for something.

In fact, it is quite possible that Richard Nixon won the presidency in 1960 but had it stolen by his former hallmate in the Senate Office Building. There were serious reports of voting irregularities in Texas, home of Kennedy's vice presidential running mate, Lyndon Johnson, where dead men voted, where phony registrations abounded, and where as many as ten thousand votes may have been manufactured for Kennedy. The reports coming from the pivotal state of Illinois were even worse. There, Nixon had taken 93 out of the state's 102 counties but somehow fallen short in Cook County, the state's most populous district, run by Kennedy-controlled political boss Richard Daley—and losing Cook County meant losing Illinois.

The Kennedys nervously expected Richard Nixon to demand a recount and so Jack, now all charm, called him up the Saturday after the election and asked to meet with him. Nixon said nothing about contesting the results of the election, and neither did Kennedy. What he got was a photo opportunity, Nixon shaking his hand and smiling, a photo that told the country all was well between the two men. Later, an investigative reporter for the New York *Herald Tribune*, Earl Mazo, would write a series of articles detailing the Democratic theft of votes from Nixon, articles that would seem to say that Nixon had the election stolen from him. One day, Mazo got a call from Nixon, who was still in his office in the Senate Office Building, waiting out his term as vice president. He asked Mazo to stop publishing the articles, in the interests of national unity.

"No one steals the presidency of the United States," he told the reporter.

Mazo agreed and John Fitzgerald Kennedy was inaugurated in January of 1961, with Richard Nixon looking on. While the two men would meet again in the three years before Kennedy was assassinated, they would never again be friends. Kennedy, insiders said, was stunned by how close the election was—he had underestimated Nixon's appeal to voters who thought he would keep them more secure from foreign threats.

As for Nixon? While he spoke bravely about national unity, deep inside he felt the election had been stolen from him. In 1972, he sent the CIA into the Watergate office complex to try to steal secrets from the Democrats. It was not something he really needed to do—in fact, it cost him his presidency—but one gets the feeling that he did it because, even after a decade and more, with Kennedy dead and gone, he hungered for some kind of revenge.

PROFILE IN DECEPTION?

Did John F. Kennedy really write *Profiles in Courage*, the bestselling book that won him the Pulitzer Prize in 1957 and helped cement his reputation as a literary man and intellectual?

Kennedy came up with the idea for the study of eight United States senators who had the courage to stick by their convictions to do unpopular things that turned out to be right. Recuperating from his latest back operation, he fleshed out the book in his mind and then called his friend and speechwriter Theodore Sorenson to research the book for him. All well and good—most historians use researchers. But it appears that Sorenson—along with others, who included Georgetown University Professor Jules Davids and the respected scholar and Kennedy family friend Arthur Schlesinger, Jr.— actually drafted the chapters. Kennedy, while he may have written some portions of the book, simply told his thoughts and ideas to Sorenson and Davids and they wrote the book for him. According to historian Herbert Parmet, who has made a definitive study of the issue, it appears that Kennedy "served principally as an overseer, or, more charitably, as a sponsor and editor."

BIBLIOGRAPHY

Barber, Richard. *Henry Plantagenet*. New York: Roy Publishers, 1964.

Beevor, Anthony. *Stalingrad: The Fateful Siege: 1942–1943*. New York: Viking Press, 1998.

Bleuel, Hans Peter. *Sex and Society in Nazi Germany*. Philadelphia and New York: J. P. Lippincott Company, 1973.

Bobrick, Benson. *Angel in the Whirlwind: The Triumph of the American Revolution*. New York: Simon & Schuster, 1997.

Bradford, Sarah. *Disraeli*. New York: Stein & Day, 1983.

Brookhiser, Richard. *Alexander Hamilton: American*. New York: The Free Press, 1999.

Brundage, James A. *Richard Lion Heart: A Biography*. New York: Charles Scribner's Sons, 1974.

Cooper, Leonard. *The Age of Wellington: The Life and Times of the Duke of Wellington, 1769–1852*. New York: Dodd, Mead & Co, 1963.

Craig, William. *Enemy at the Gates: The Battle for Stalingrad*. New York: E. P. Dutton, 1973.

Descola, Jean. *The Conquistadors*. New York: The Viking Press, 1957.

Dunn, Jane. *Elizabeth and Mary: Cousins, Rivals, Queens*. New York: Alfred A. Knopf, 2004.

Erickson, Carolly. *The First Elizabeth*. New York: Summit Books, 1983.

Fall, Bernard. *Hell in a Very Small Place: The Siege of Dien Bien Phu*. New York: De Capo Press, 1966.

Farago, Ladislas. *Patton: Ordeal and Triumph*. New York: Ivan Obolensky, Inc., 1964.

Fleming, Thomas. *Duel: Alexander Hamilton, Aaron Burr and the Future of America*. New York: Basic Book, 1999.

Gallo, Max. *The Night of the Long Knives*. New York: Harper & Row, 1972.

Gelb, Norman. *Ike and Monty: Generals at War*. New York: William Morrow & Co., 1994.

Goldsworthy, Adrian. *The Punic Wars*. London: Cassell & Co., 2000.

Green, Peter. *The Greco-Persian Wars*. Berkeley and Los Angeles: University of California Press, 1998.

Isenberg, Nancy. *Fallen Founder: The Life of Aaron Burr*. New York: Viking Press, 2007.

Karnow, Stanley. *Vietnam: A History*. New York: Viking Press, 1991.

Kershaw, Ian. *Hitler: 1889–1936: Hubris*. New York: W. W. Norton & Co., 1998.

Knowles, David. *Thomas Becket*. Stanford, California: Stanford University Press, 1970.

LaQueur, Walter. *Stalin: The Glasnost Revelations*. New York: Charles Scribner's Sons, 1990.

McBain, Richard P. *Lives of the Popes: The Pontiffs from St. Peter to Pope John Paul II*. San Francisco: HarperSanFrancisco, 1997.

McCullough, David. *Truman*. New York: Simon & Schuster, 1992.

McLynn, Frank. *Villa and Zapata: A History of the Mexican Revolution*. New York: Carroll & Graf, 2000.

Massie, Robert K. *Peter the Great: His Life and World*. New York: Alfred A. Knopf, 1980.

Matthews, Christopher. *Kennedy and Nixon: The Rivalry That Shaped Postwar America*. New York: Simon & Schuster, 1996.

Parenti, Michael. *The Assassination of Julius Caesar: A People's History of Ancient Rome*. New York: The New Press, 2003.

Perret, Geoffrey. *Old Soldiers Never Die: The Life of Douglas MacArthur*. New York: Random House, 1996.

Randall, William Sterne. *Benedict Arnold: Patriot and Traitor*. New York: William Morrow & Co., 1990.

Reeves, Thomas C. *A Question of Character: A Life of John F. Kennedy*. New York: The Free Press, 1991.

Schom, Alan. *One Hundred Days: Napoleon's Road to Waterloo*. New York: Atheneum, 1992.

Slocombe, George. *William the Conqueror*. New York: G. P. Putnam's Sons, 1959.

Smith, Anthony. *Explorers of the Amazon*. New York: Viking Penguin, 1990.

Strayer, Joseph & Munro, Dana C. *The Middle Ages: 395–1500*. New York: Meredith Corporation, 1970.

Thomson, George Malcolm. *The Crime of Mary Stuart*. New York: E. P. Dutton & Co., 1967.

Tierney, Brian. *The Crisis of Church and State 1050–1300*. Englewood Cliffs, New Jersey: Prentice-Hall, Inc., 1964.

Trotsky, Leon. *Stalin*. New York: Stein & Day, 1967.

Volkogonov, Dmitri. *Trotsky: The Eternal Revolutionary*. New York: The Free Press, 1996.

Warren, W.L. *King John*. New York: W. W. Norton & Co., 1961.

Weir, Alison. *Eleanor of Aquitaine: A Life*. New York: Ballantine Books, 1999.

Wicker, Tom. *One of Us: Richard Nixon and the American Dream*. New York: Random House, 1991.

Winston, Richard. *Thomas Becket*. New York: Alfred A. Knopf, 1967.

Woodham-Smith, Cecil. *The Reason Why*. New York: McGraw-Hill, Inc., 1954.

ACKNOWLEDGMENTS

Diana Hill, Murdoch editor par excellence, has been wonderfully smart and patient as I worked to get *Rivals* to where it should be. Thanks to Emma Hutchinson, who has ably guided the manuscript through editing and helped bring the characters to life with brilliant photos. Christine Eslick copyedits were incisive and helped sharpen the final manuscript, while Peter Long and Jackie Richard's design has really enhanced these important stories. Thanks also to Amanda McKittrick for organising the artwork, and finally to Will Kiester, whose brainchild *Rivals* originally was.

PHOTOGRAPHY CREDITS

Bridgeman Art Library / Photolibrary: cover images, pp.18-19, p.22, p.24, p.25, pp.34-35, p.46, p.55, pp.58-59, p.73, p.81, p.84, p.88, p.89, p.93, p.99, p.100, p.101, p.105, p.106, pp.110-111, p.114, p.115, pp.120-121, p.124, p.130, p.131, pp.138-139, p.144, p.146, p.157, p.159, p.160, p.161, p.169, p.174, p.175, pp.184-185, p.189, p.200, p.202, p.204, p.205, p.213, p.214, p.224, p.235, p.251, p.271

Corbis: p.172, p.229, p.325

Getty images: p.2, p.10, p.11, p.32, p.36, p.37, p.43, p.48, p.49, p.62, p.63, p.68, p.76, p.77, p.94, p.97, p.129, p.143, p.147, p.165, p.181, p.187, p.188, p.216, p.217, p.223, p.228, p.232, p.236, pp.240-241, p.242, p.244, p.245, p.252, p.255, p.256, p.258, p.259, p.267, p.268, p.274, p.277, p.281, p.282, p.284, pp.286-287, p.291, p.292, p.294, p.295, p.301, p.303, pp.306-307, p.310, p.316, p.319, p.320, p.324, p.329, p.330, p.333, p.335, p.336, p.338, p.339, pp.344-345, p.349, pp.350-351

Library of Congress: p.151, p.154, p.196, p.311

INDEX

Page numbers in *italic* refer to illustrations